HISTORIC PHOTOS OF
PITTSBURGH

TEXT AND CAPTIONS BY MIRIAM MEISLIK

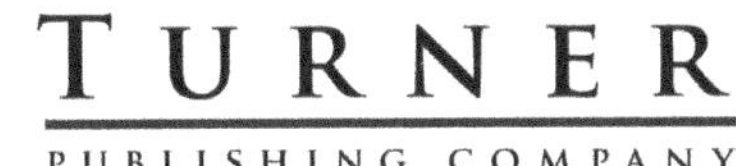

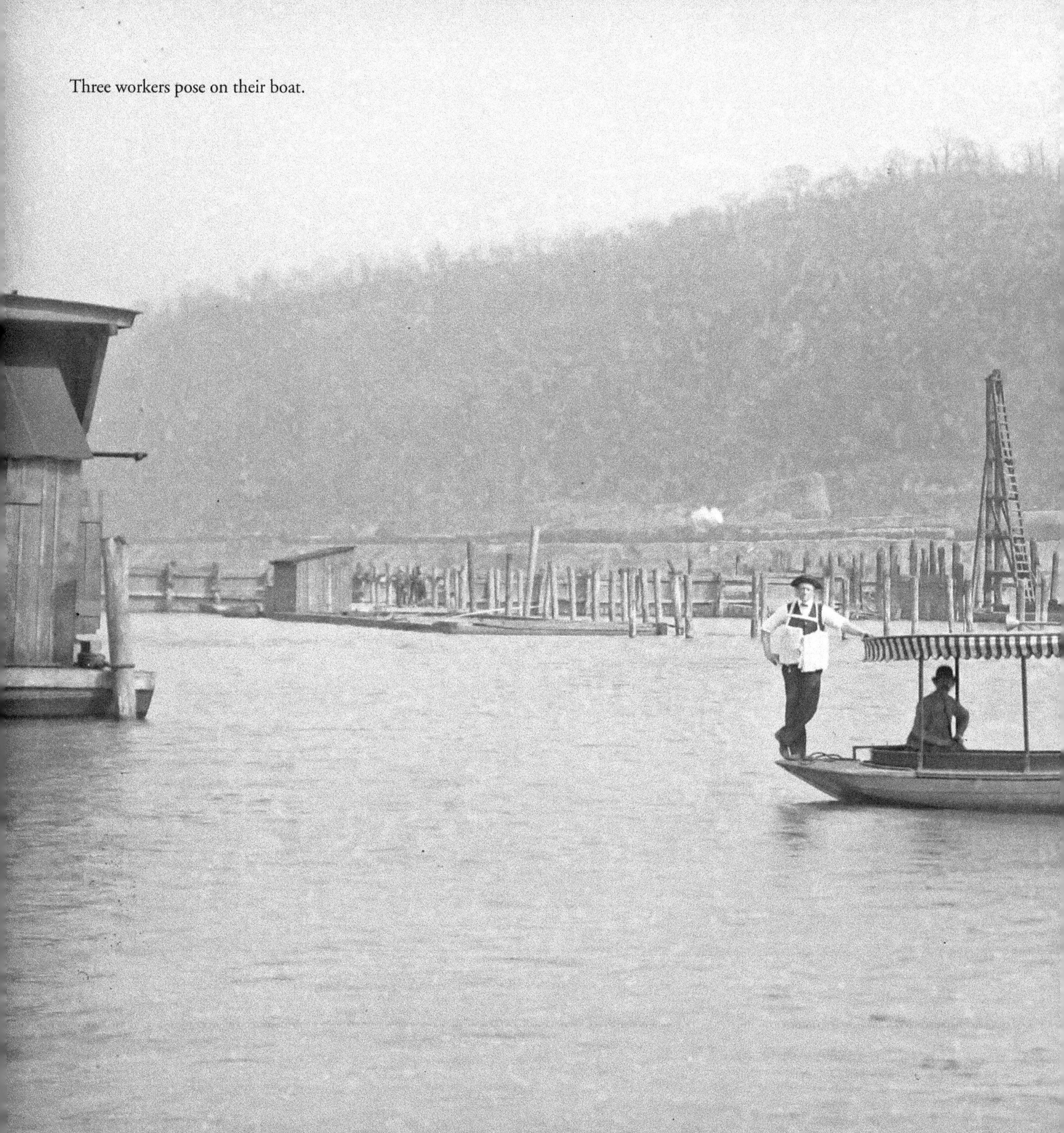

Three workers pose on their boat.

HISTORIC PHOTOS OF
PITTSBURGH

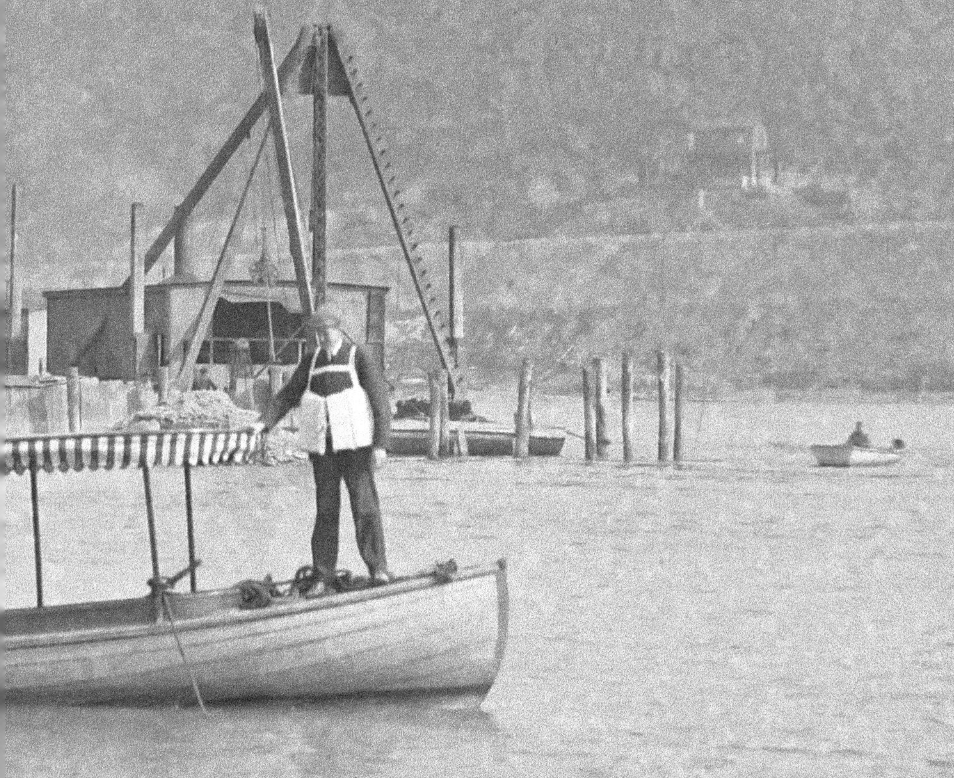

Turner Publishing Company
www.turnerpublishing.com

Historic Photos of Pittsburgh

Library of Congress Control Number: 2006937088

ISBN: 978-1-59652-330-2

Printed in the United States of America

ISBN 978-1-68336-944-8 (hc)

Contents

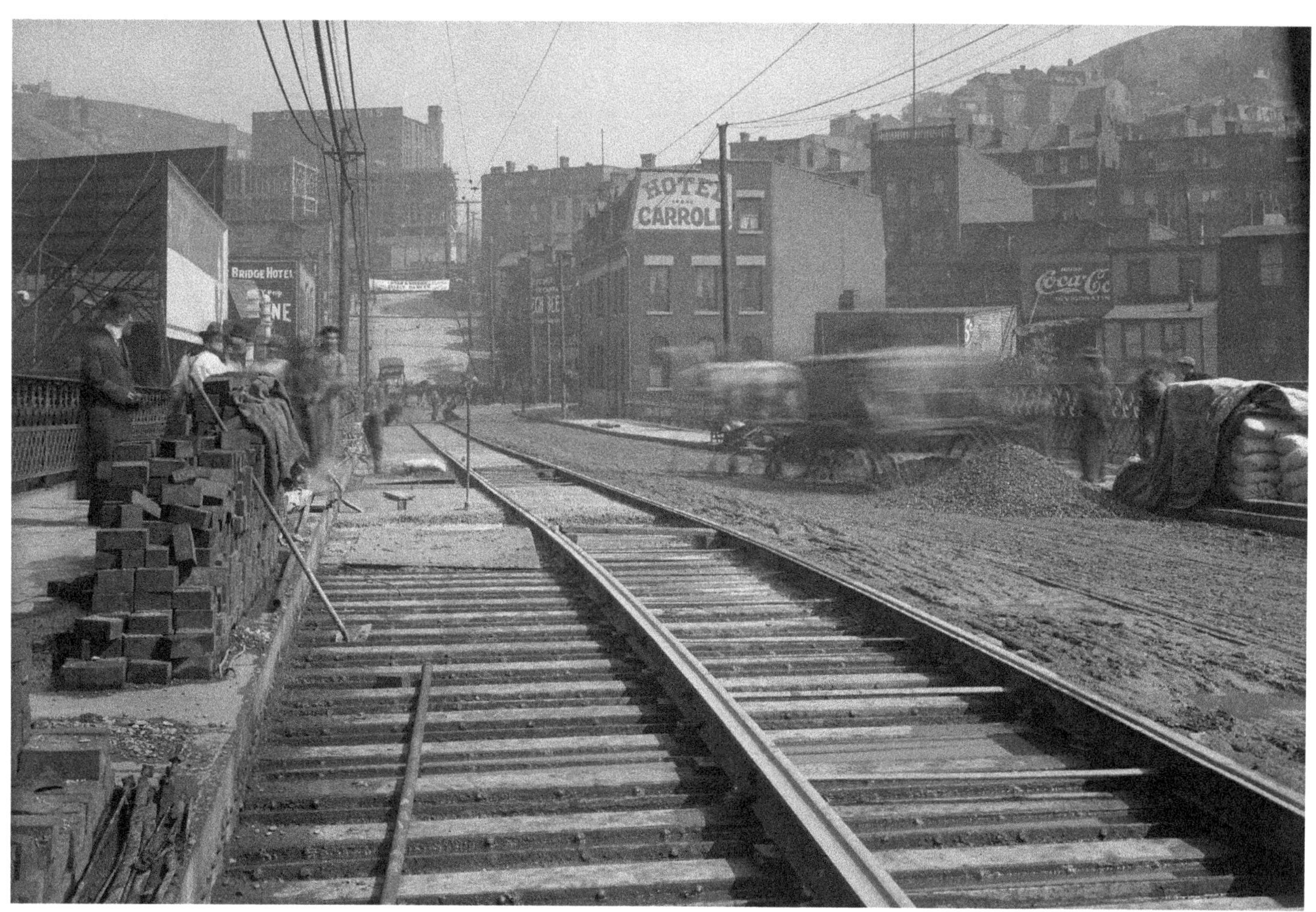

Rails are being repaired at the end of the South 22nd Street Bridge approach in 1910.

Acknowledgments

This volume, *Historic Photos of Pittsburgh,* is the result of the support of many individuals and departments at the University of Pittsburgh. It is with great appreciation that we acknowledge their valuable contributions and their generous support:

Rush G. Miller, Hillman University Librarian and Director, University Library System, University of Pittsburgh
Michael J. Dabrishus, Assistant University Librarian for Archives and Special Collections
Digital Research Library (DRL), University of Pittsburgh

We would also like to thank the following individuals for their valuable contributions and assistance in making this work possible:

Ronald Baraff, Rivers of Steel
Kate Colligan, Archives Service Center, University of Pittsburgh
Donald Doherty
David Grinnell, Historical Society of Western Pennsylvania
Michael Lee
Ted Tarka, Digital Research Library (DRL), University of Pittsburgh

Preface

As I began reviewing photographs to be included in this book, something struck me. No matter what era I was trying to represent, they all seemed to have the same theme. Pittsburgh may be a city of bridges, may be remembered as steel capital of the world, but it is also a city that continues to reinvent itself. These photographs represent a lively, growing city that doesn't fear change.

Nowhere does change really become more apparent than in downtown Pittsburgh. Residents may have started at the Point, but they quickly spread out along George Wood's original street plan and beyond. Even the precursor to the University of Pittsburgh couldn't stay in one place, moving from its original home near the current location of Smithfield Street to Fifth Avenue and Grant Street, across the river to Allegheny City for a brief time, then back to Pittsburgh, and finally settling in Oakland.

Landmark buildings helped the city grow. With the help of prominent architects, H. H. Richardson, Henry Hornbostel, and Frederick Osterling, among others, Pittsburgh acquired the Allegheny County Courthouse and Jail, the City-County Building, and the Henry Clay Frick–financed Union Arcade. Frick also financed the construction of the Frick Building and the William Penn Hotel. By the 1950s, the city was transformed with the clearing of the Point for Point State Park and the Gateway Center office complexes. New buildings weren't limited to downtown. Oakland would see the rise of the Cathedral of Learning, the Mellon Institute, and Heinz Chapel. The North Side would become home to the Allegheny Center Mall consisting of shopping, offices, and residential space.

Of course, nothing makes Pittsburgh what it is more than the people who live here. The images collected here attempt to show the character of the people and their neighborhoods.

This project represents countless hours of research and review. I am most grateful to those mentioned in the acknowledgments of this work, without whom this project could not have been completed. Inspiration was also found in the works of Walter Kidney. He is deeply missed.

—Miriam Meislik

With the exception of cropping images where needed and touching up imperfections that have accrued over time, no other changes have been made. The caliber and clarity of many photographs are limited by the technology of the day and the ability of the photographer at the time they were made.

Images in this volume have been arranged chronologically into six sections of time. In each of these sections we have made an effort to capture various aspects of life through our selection of photographs. People, commerce, industry, recreation, transportation, infrastructure, and religious and educational institutions have been included to provide a broad perspective.

We encourage readers to reflect as they drive or walk the streets of Pittsburgh, enjoy the rivers and parks, and experience the amenities of this bustling metropolitan area. It is the publisher's hope that in utilizing this work, longtime residents will learn something new and that new residents will gain a perspective on where the region has been, so that each can contribute effectively to its future.

—Todd Bottorff, Publisher

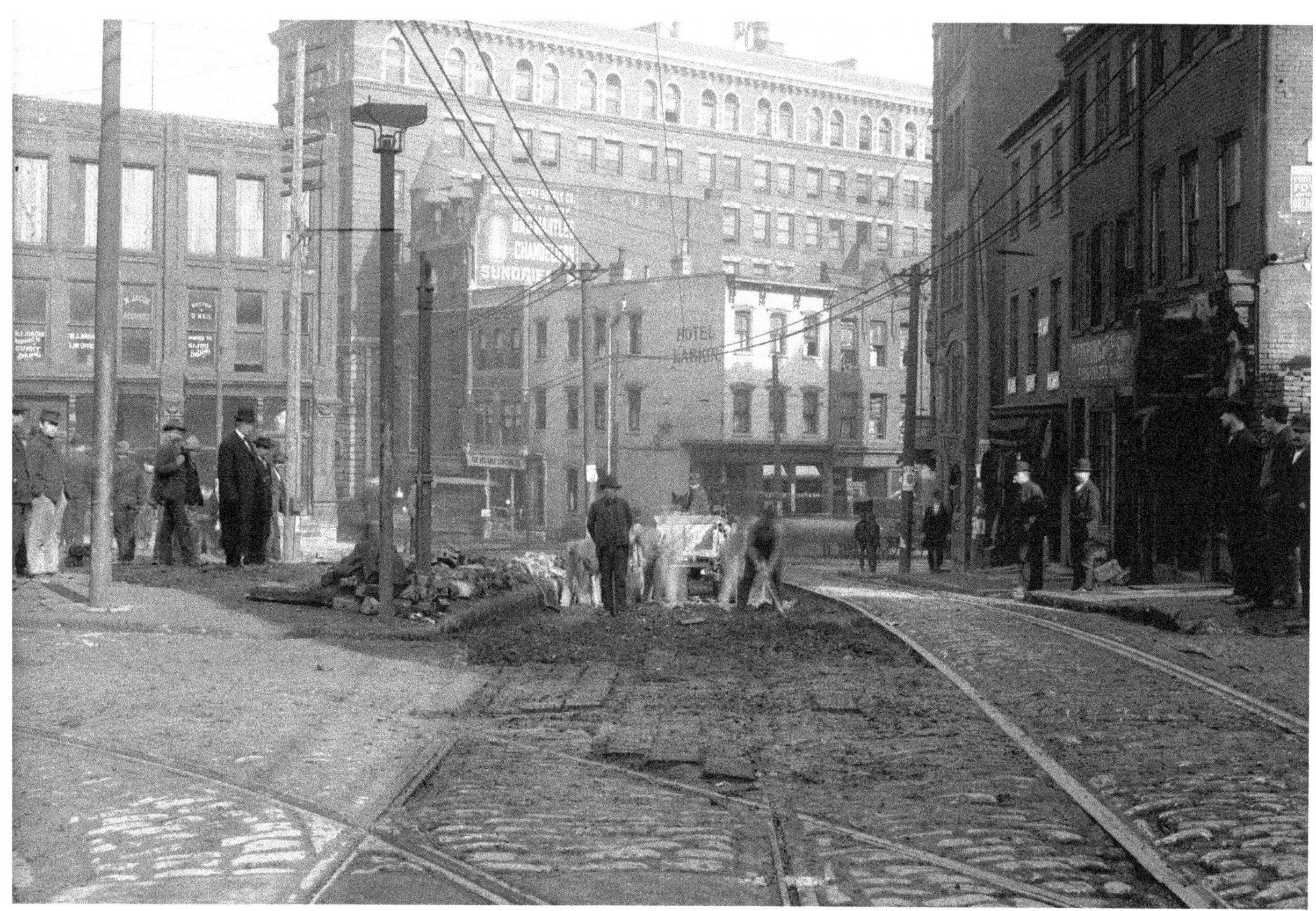

Sixth Avenue and Webster Avenue facing Grant Street and the Hotel Larkin downtown. Other businesses of interest include the Pittsburg Hotel Supply Fish & Oyster House, the Reliable Lighting Co., the Incandescent Supply Co., and a portent of things to come—window signs indicating that businesses have "removed" to new locations.

A Growing City

(1800s–1899)

Pittsburgh of the 1800s was trying to maintain itself as the "Gateway to the West," 100 years after George Wood had determined the layout of its streets. But the city had grown dramatically from its days as Fort Pitt and was growing beyond its origins at the Point. It started the 1800s with nearly 1,600 residents; it would close the century with a population of more than 230,000. Pittsburgh was reinventing itself as an industrial center with shipbuilding, glass manufacturing, railroads, and, of course, iron works, foundries, and steel at the center of this change.

Education played an equally important role. The Pittsburgh Academy, later known as the University of Pittsburgh, had been established in 1787 in the downtown area and was a significant factor in the city's development throughout the 1800s.

Transportation options also improved greatly during this time. While river transportation was still a vital part of the economy, inland transportation such as railroads for commercial and personal ventures and trolley lines would grow in number and popularity.

The Pittsburgh of this time still seemed rural in some respects. Although several large homes existed in Shadyside, Aspinwall, Castle Shannon, Oakland, and other areas, great expanses of open land remained undeveloped.

Professional and amateur photographers beautifully captured this era. The Pittsburgh Amateur Photographers' Society, including prominent members Edith Darlington Ammon and her brother O'Hara Darlington, was one such hobbyist group that recorded images of Pittsburgh at this time. Life in Shadyside was captured by Charles Hart Spencer. The work of photographers like these preserved this dramatic period in Pittsburgh's life for contemporary people and the future to enjoy.

As an important shipping port, a leader in coal, coke, and steel production, home to a leading university, and with a continually growing population, Pittsburgh stood well poised to enter the twentieth century.

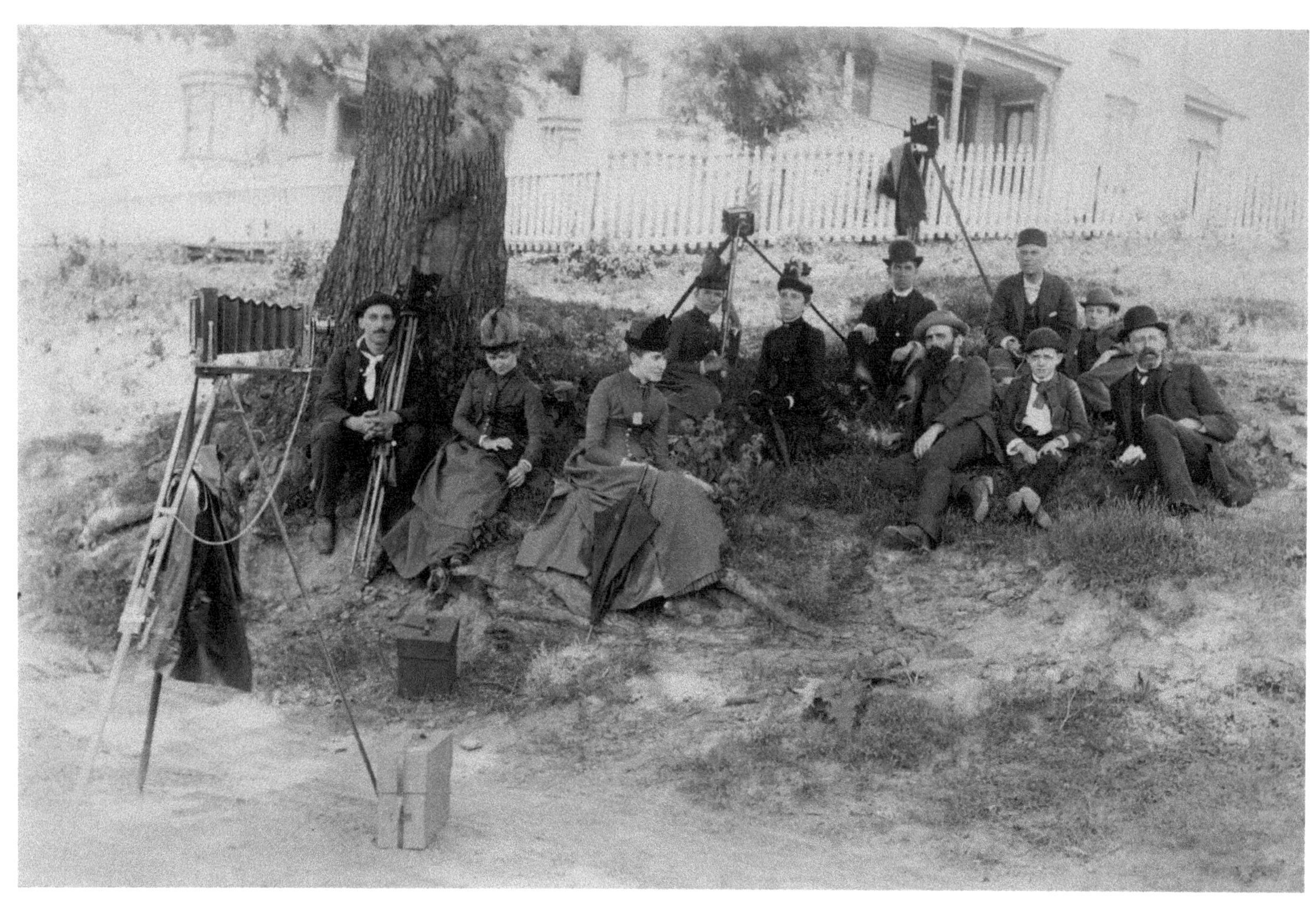

Members of the Pittsburgh Amateur Photographers' Society around 1887 gathered for a group portrait. Among its members were Edith Darlington and O'Hara Darlington, as well as prominent Pittsburghers such as Lucien and Marvin Scaife, and Industrialist C. C. Mellor. The youngest member, Charlie Davis, was a mere 12 years old.

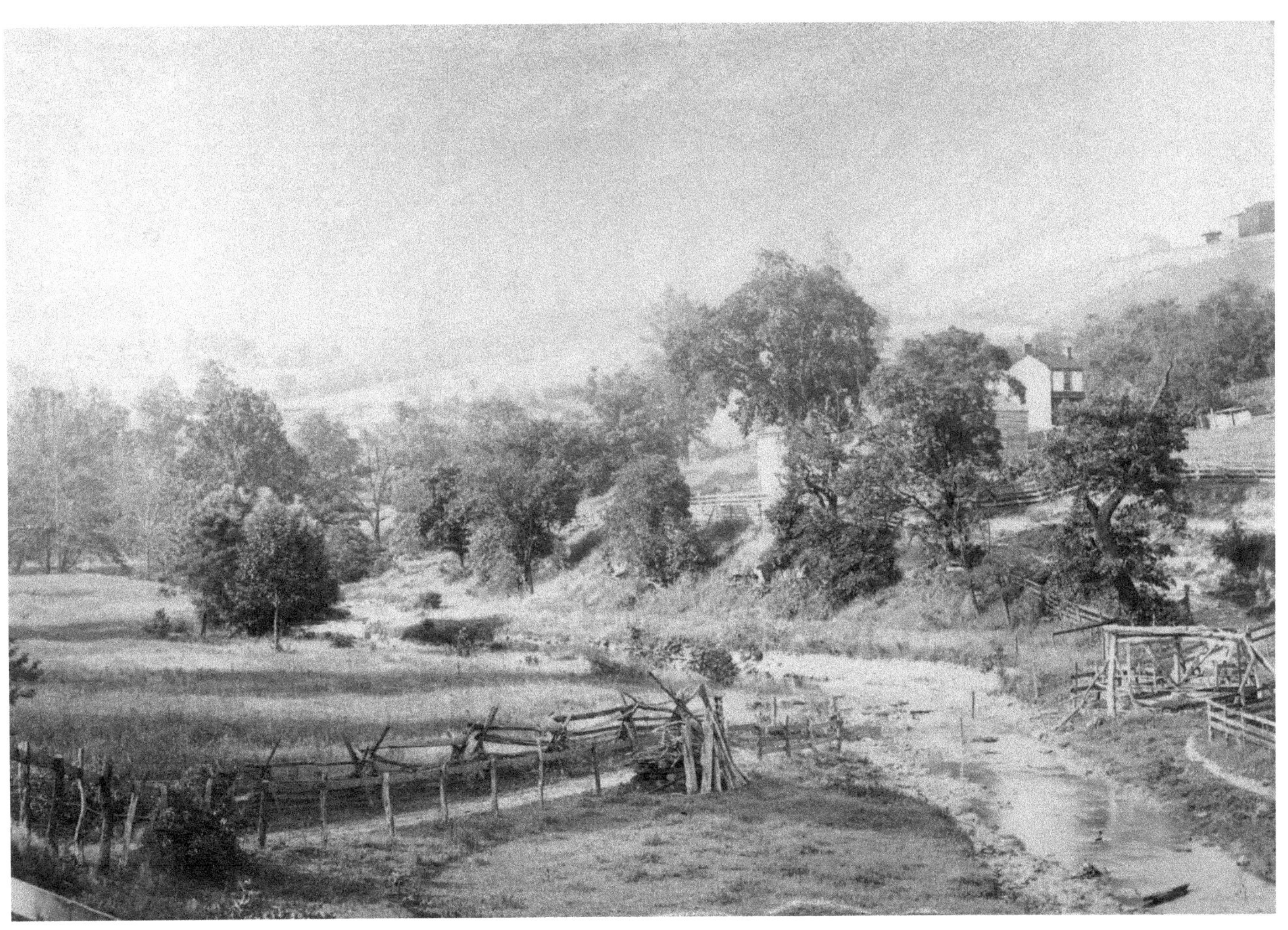

Landscape near the Castle Shannon Railroad near Fair Haven, photographed by A. S. Murray around 1886. The Pittsburgh and Castle Shannon Railroad was a narrow-gauge railroad built in 1871 to connect Pittsburgh and Castle Shannon. In 1905, it was leased by Pittsburgh Railways for use by its streetcars.

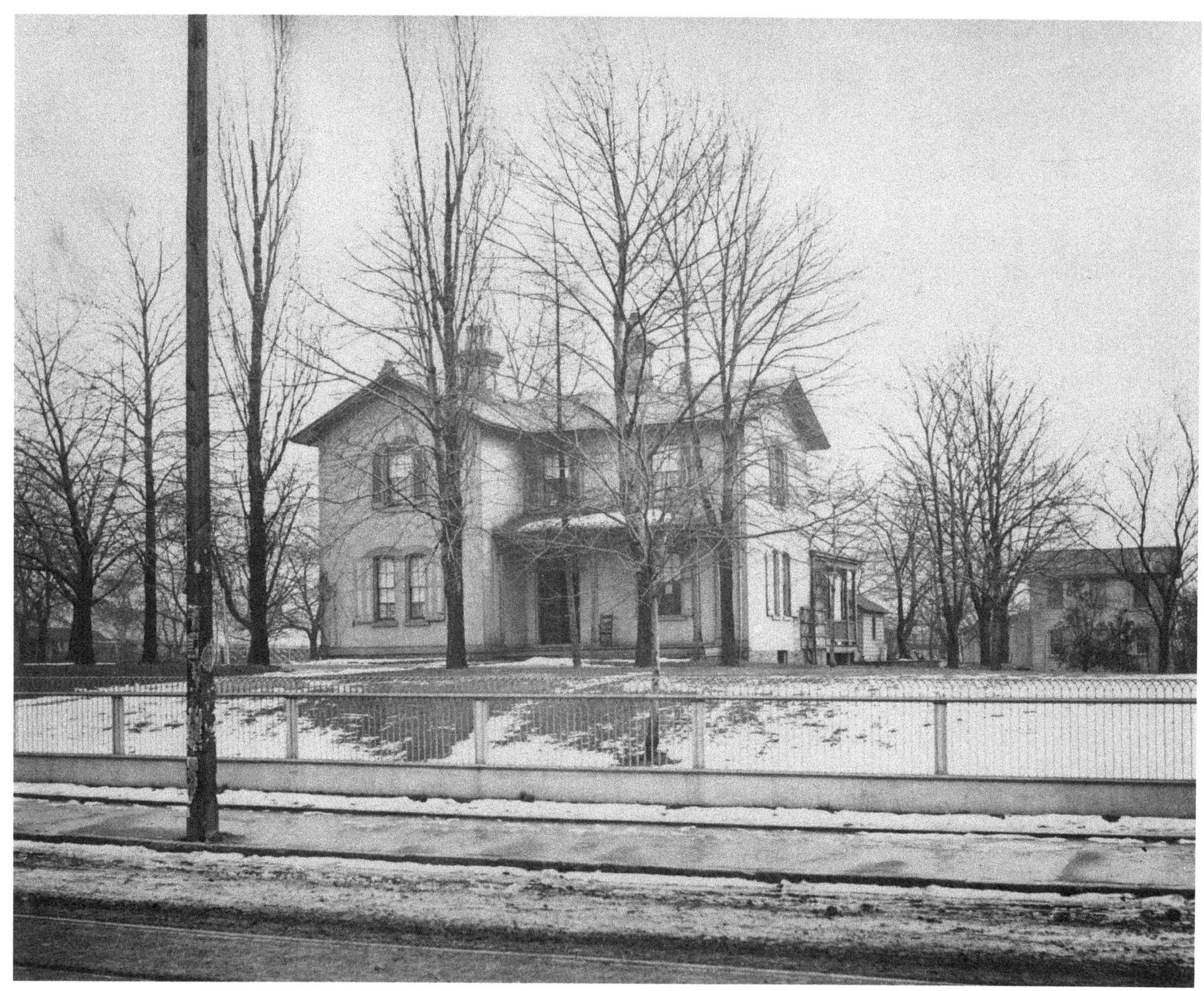

The Browne House, as it appeared on February 11, 1880. The house was located at 4208 Fifth Avenue near Grant Boulevard, now Bigelow Boulevard, in the Oakland neighborhood on property that was referred to as Frick Acres and owned by Henry Clay Frick. By 1926, construction for the 42-story, Gothic-revival Cathedral of Learning on the University of Pittsburgh campus was under way on the Browne House site.

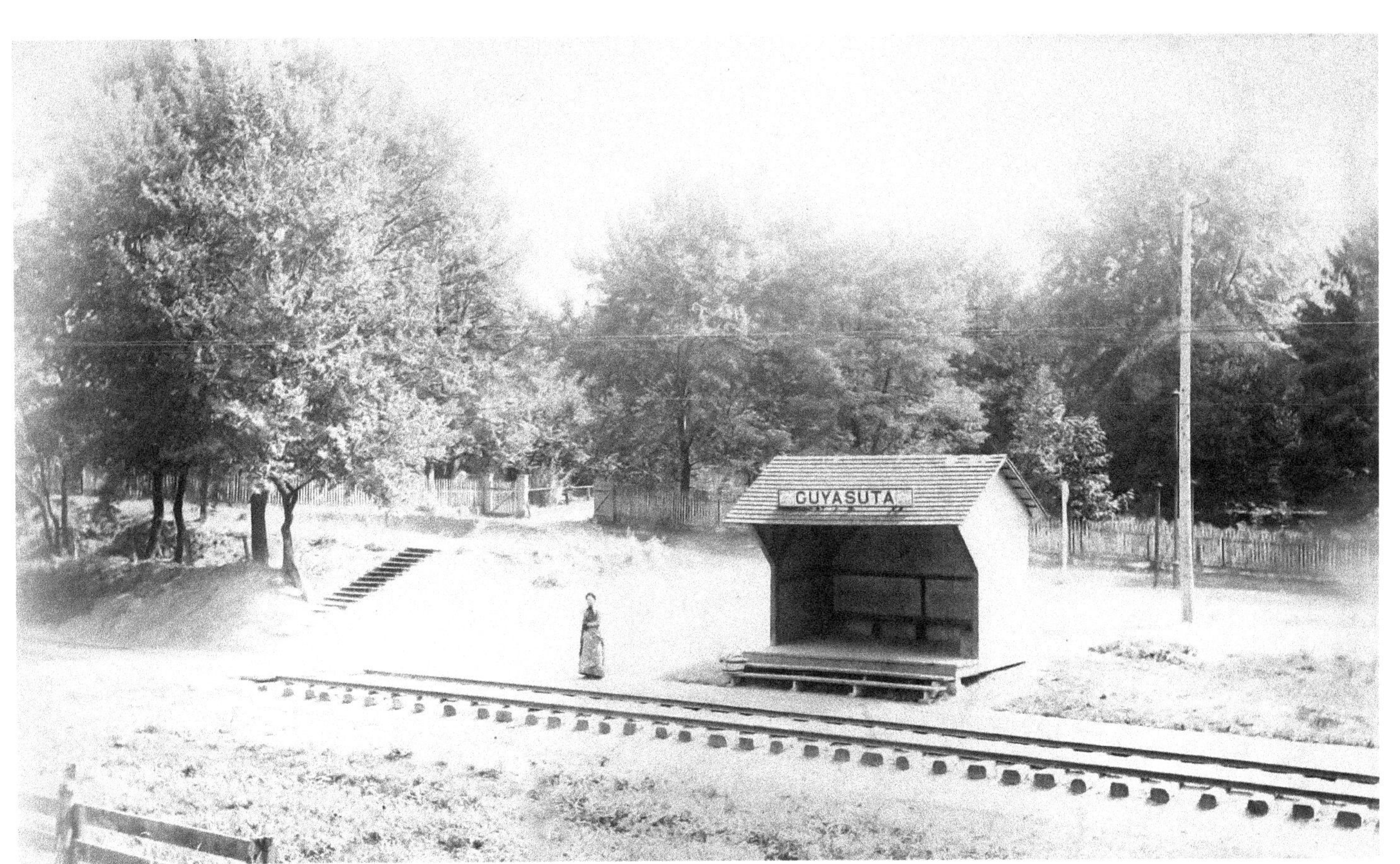

A Guyasuta train platform, May 30, 1887, as photographed by Edith Dennison Darlington Ammon.

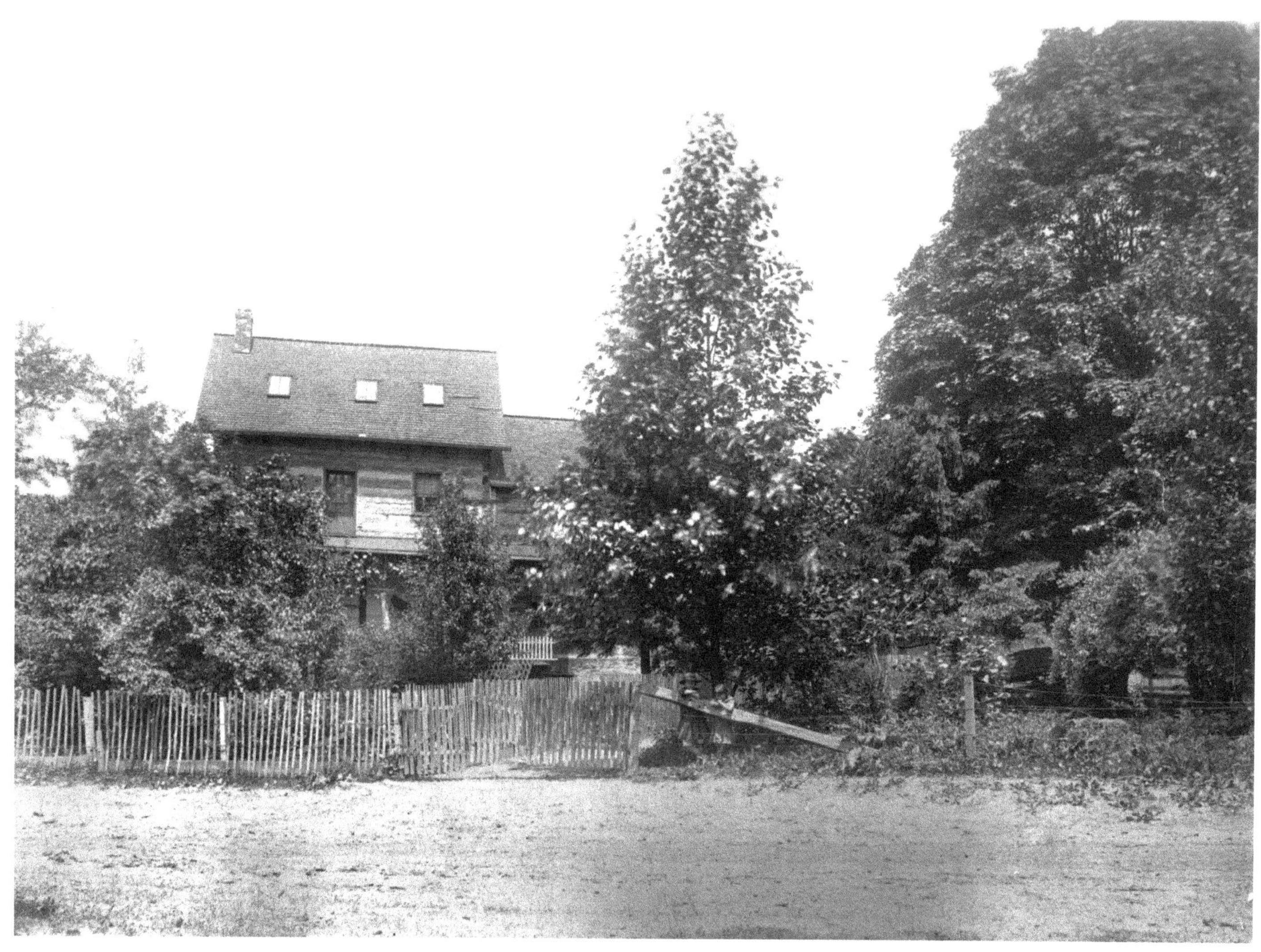

The Swisshelm House, around 1885–1888, as photographed by L. S. Clarke. Though she didn't live here at the time the photograph was taken, Jane Grey Swisshelm once owned this home located in Swissvale near Nine Mile Run. Jane had careers as a journalist, nurse, activist, artist, abolitionist, and mother. She was also responsible for much of the street layout of Swissvale.

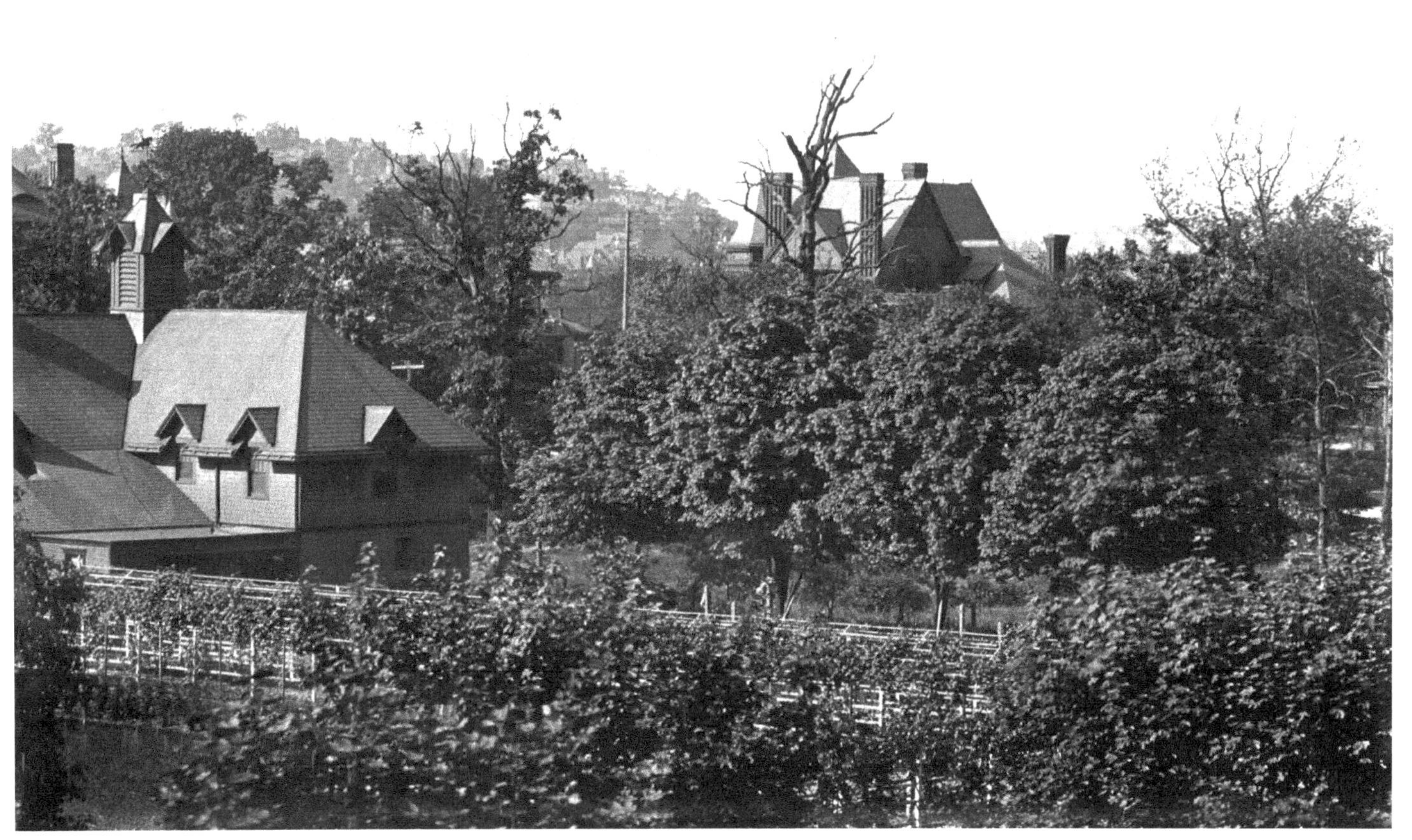

Rooftops and gardens of Shadyside taken in 1898 by Charles Hart Spencer.

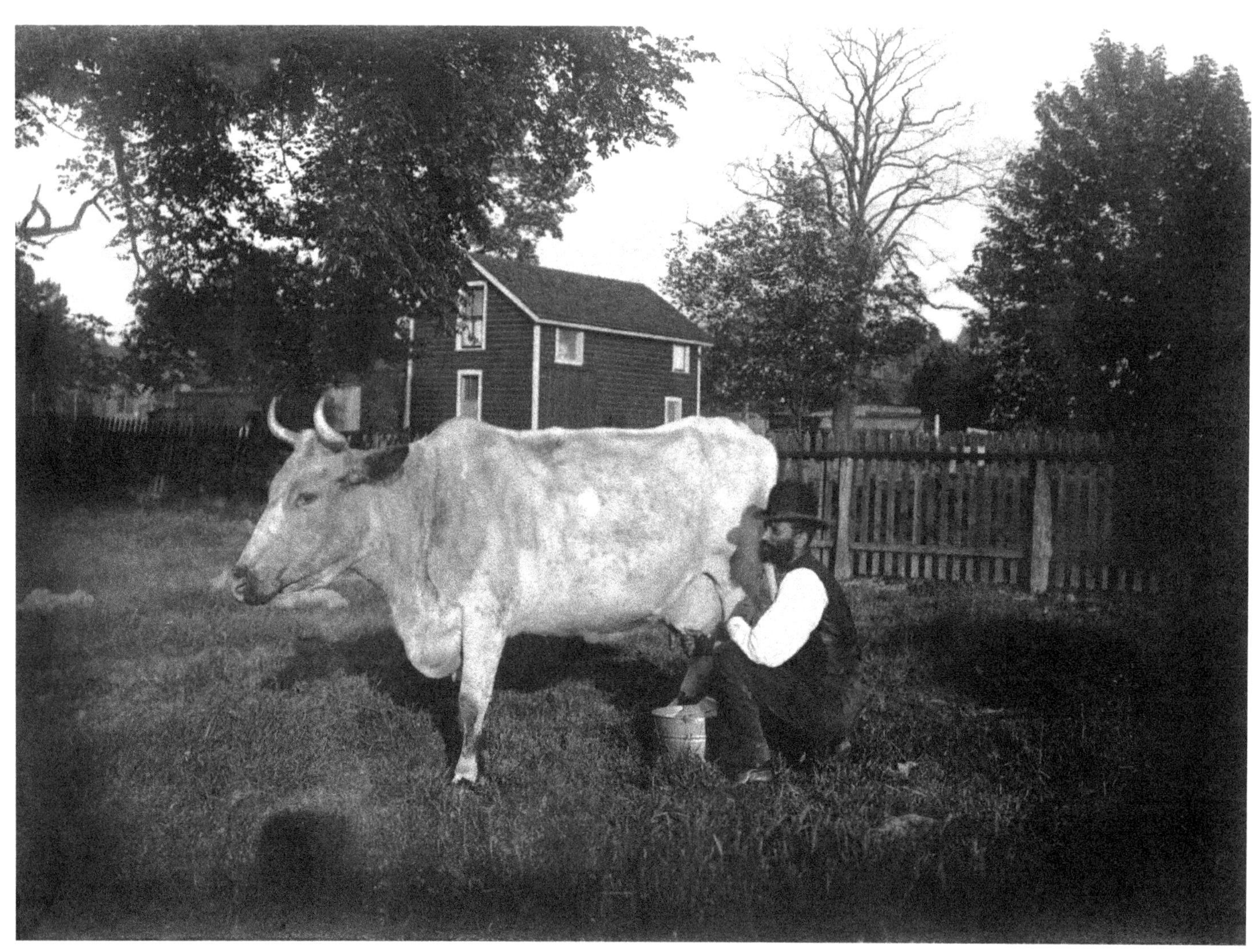

Mr. John Organ milks a cow on the Spencer family property in Shadyside.

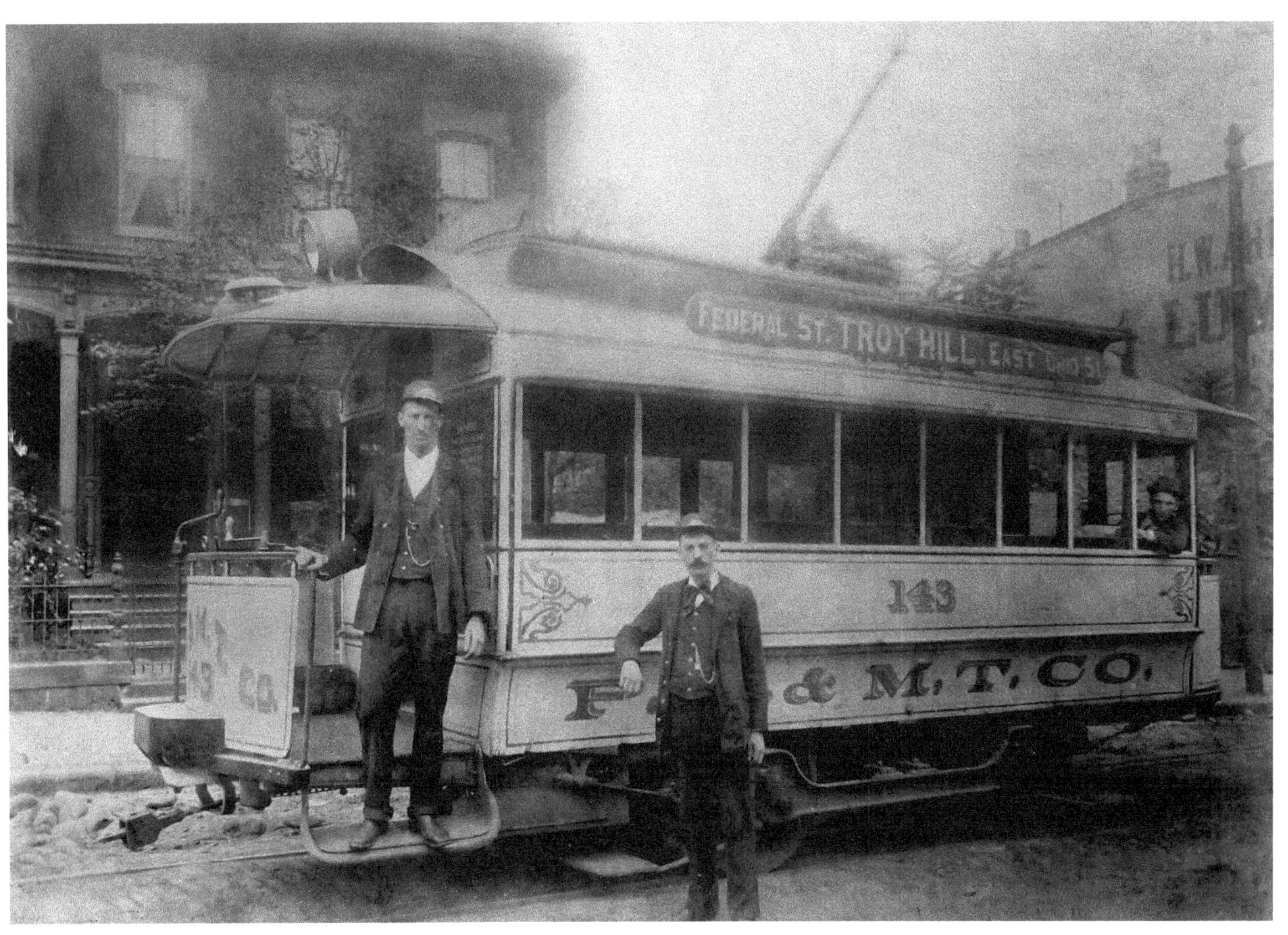

A Pittsburgh, Allegheny and Manchester Traction Company electric streetcar around 1889.

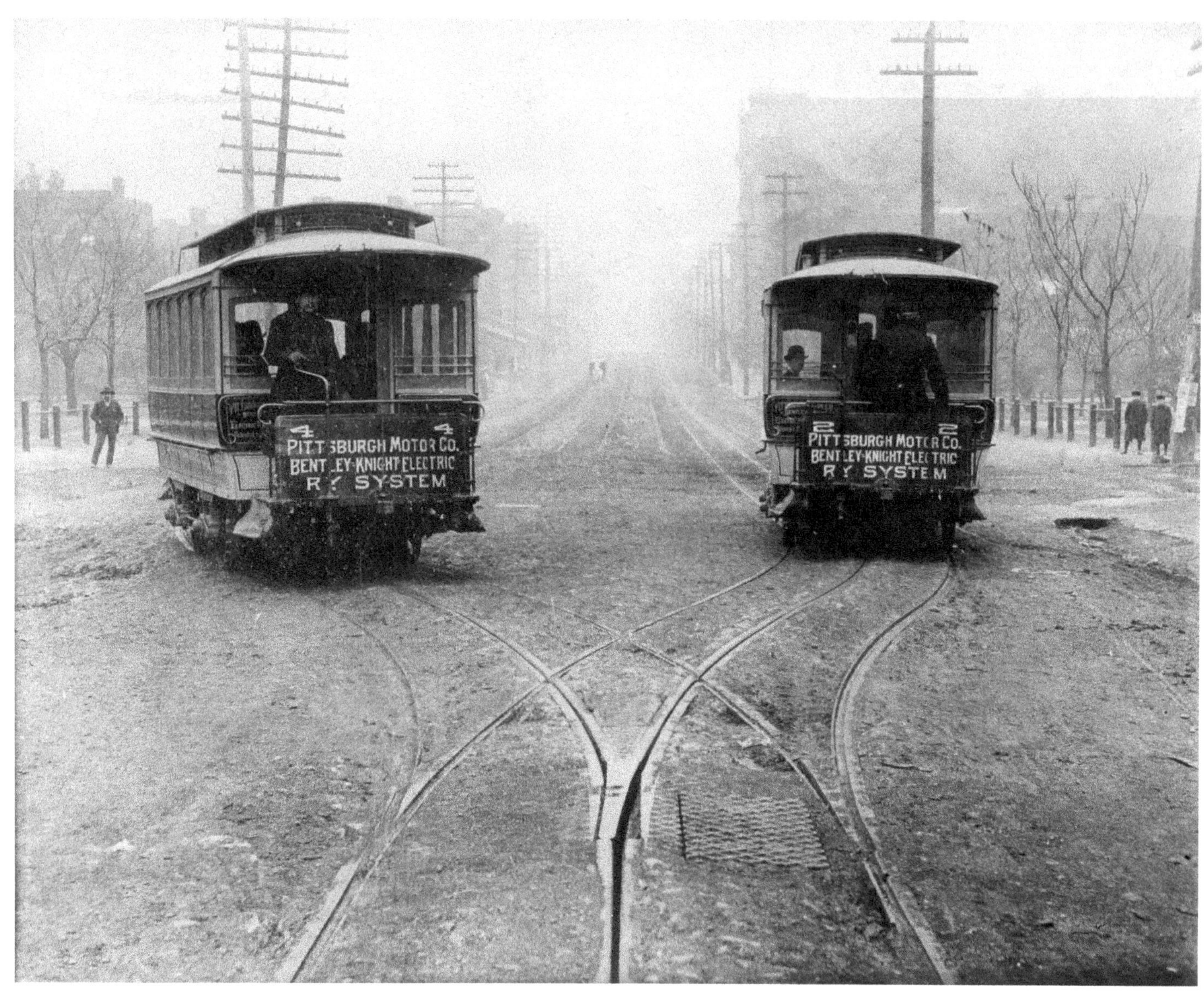

Early Bentley-Knight Centre Conduit System electric cars nos. 2 and 4 of the Federal Street line on Federal Street in Allegheny City. These experimental electric cars were introduced in Pittsburgh beginning in 1888.

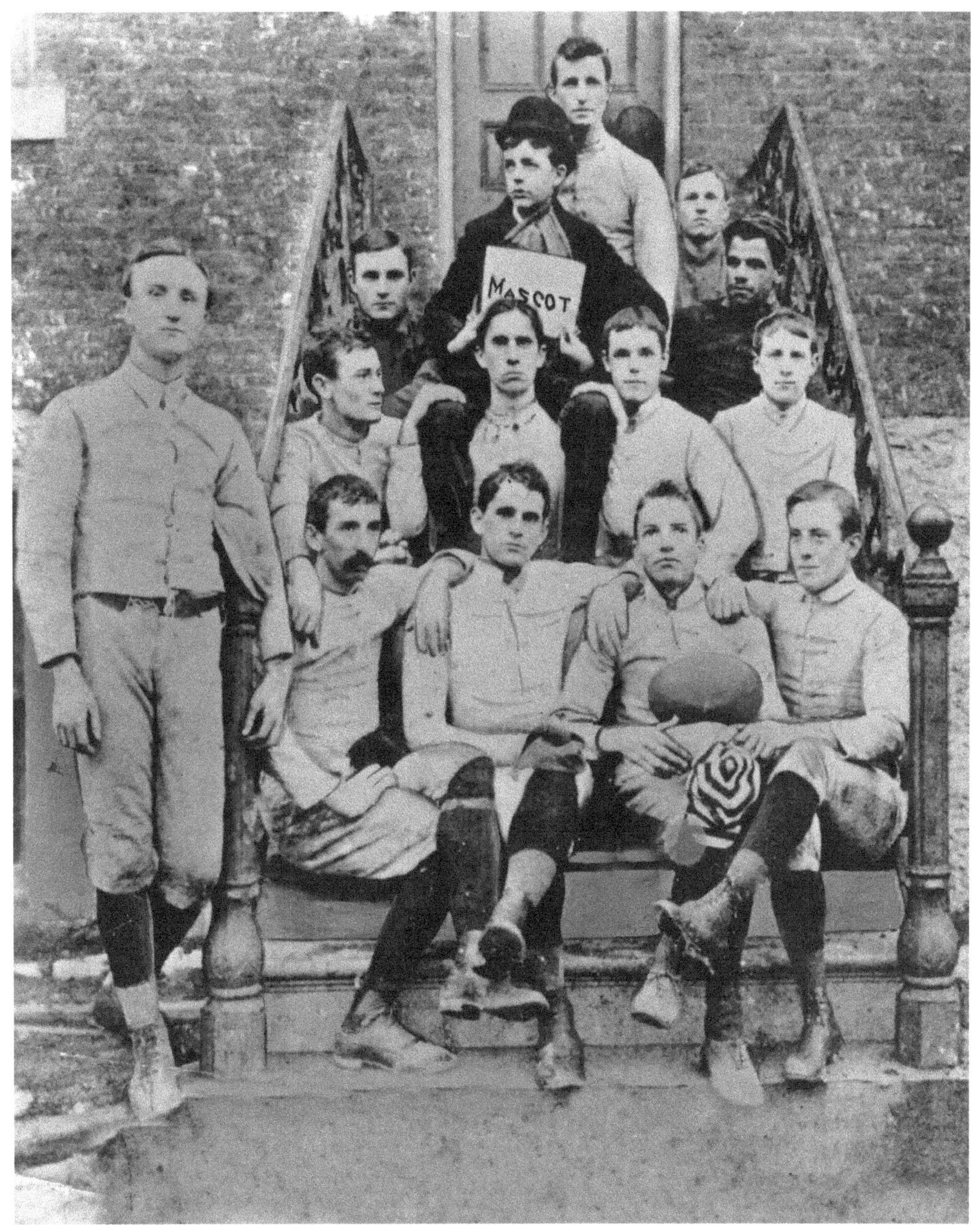

The Western University of Pennsylvania football team poses for a group portrait during its founding year, 1889. The team record that year was 0-1. It wouldn't post a winning season until 1892. Not a bad showing—the team didn't have a coach until 1893.

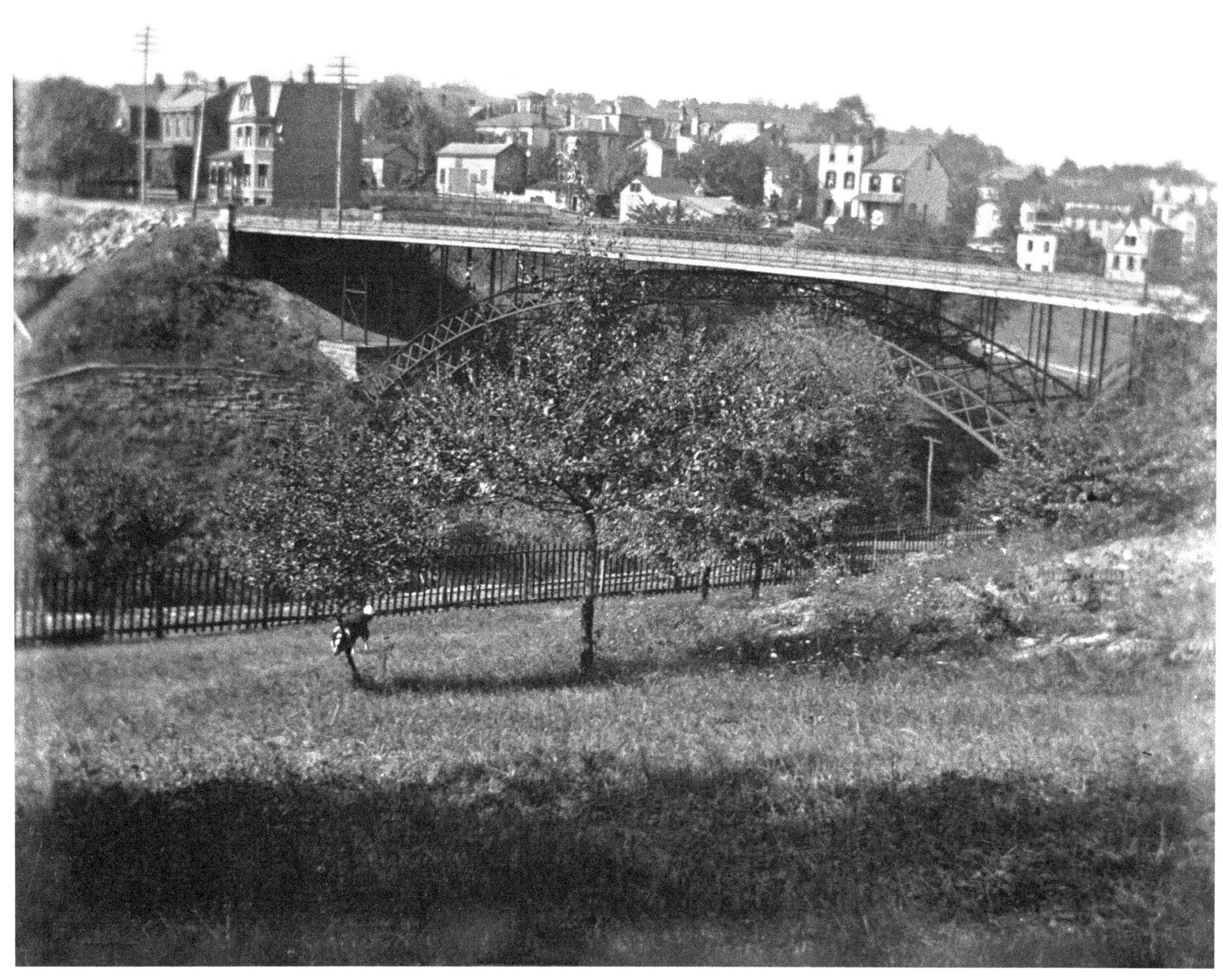

The Junction Hollow Bridge in 1889 as seen from Springbank, the family property of Judge Christopher Magee. According to the 1886 *Atlas of the Vicinity of the Cities Pittsburgh and Allegheny,* the property was located in Oakland near Forbes Street and Neville Street just above the Pittsburgh Junction Railroad. This northward-facing view was taken by Walter P. Magee, son of Christopher.

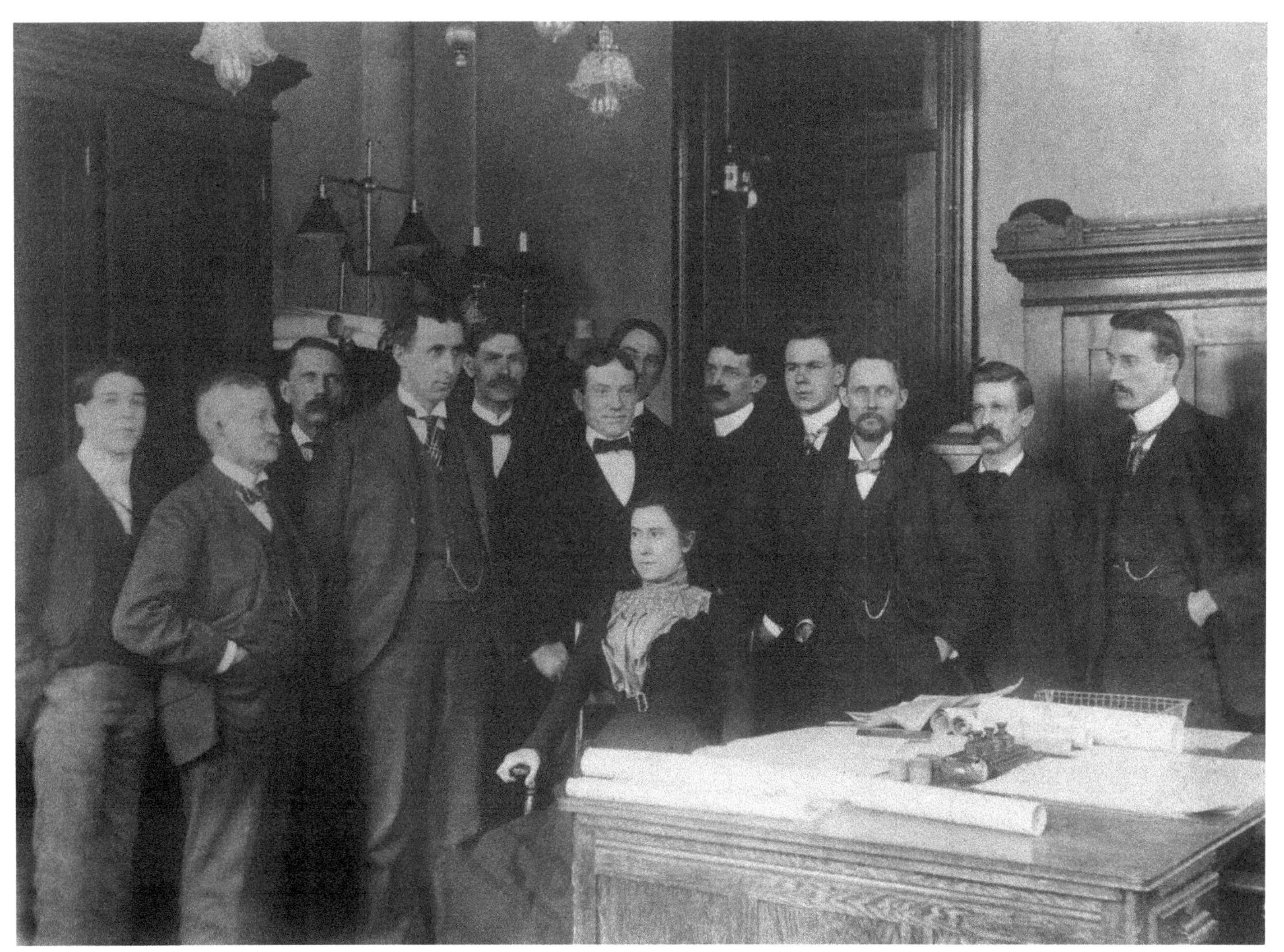

Office staff of the Chief Engineer of the Pittsburgh and Lake Erie Railroad pose for a photograph in 1892.

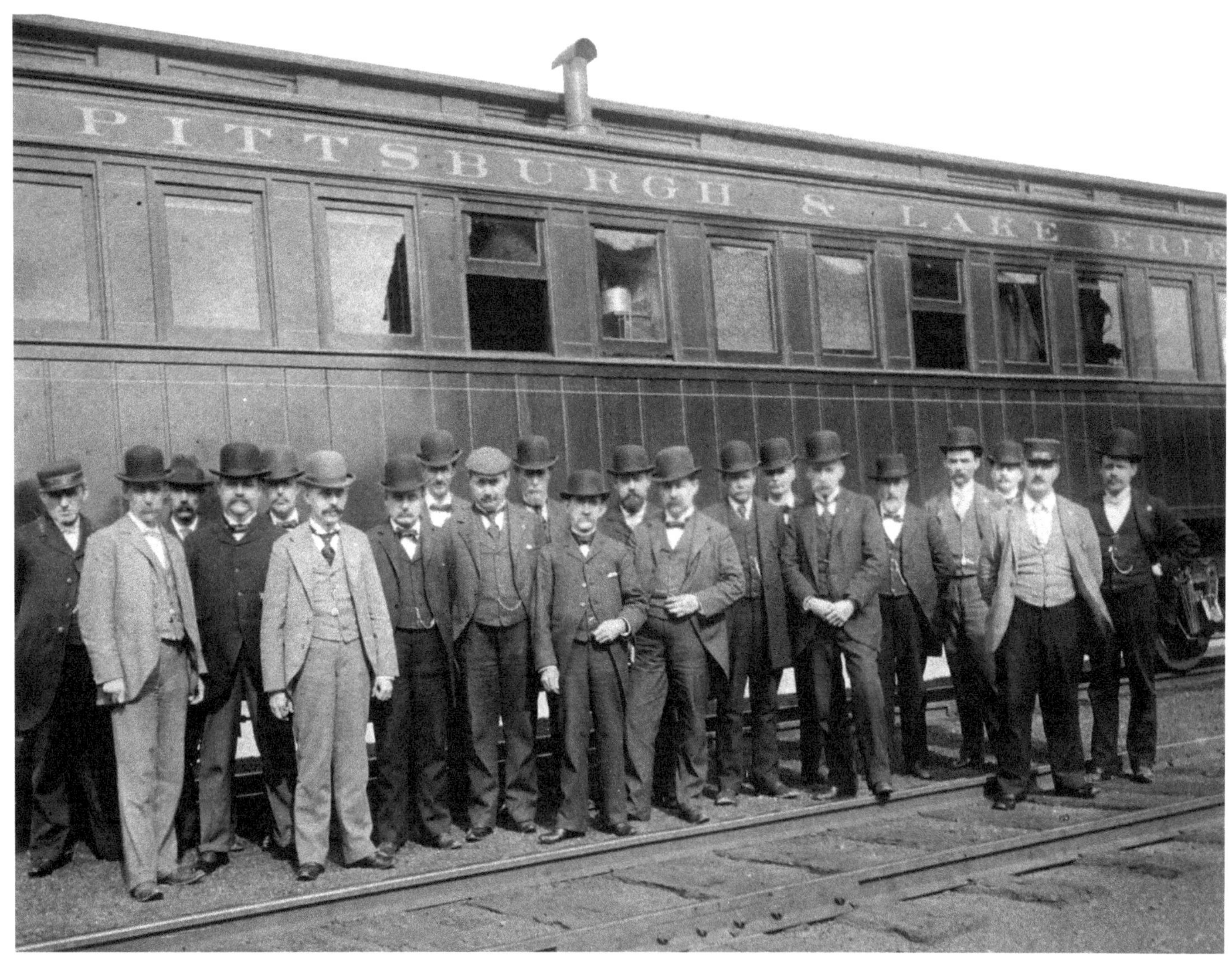

Railroad employees near the Pittsburgh and Lake Erie Railroad pay car, around 1886–1896.

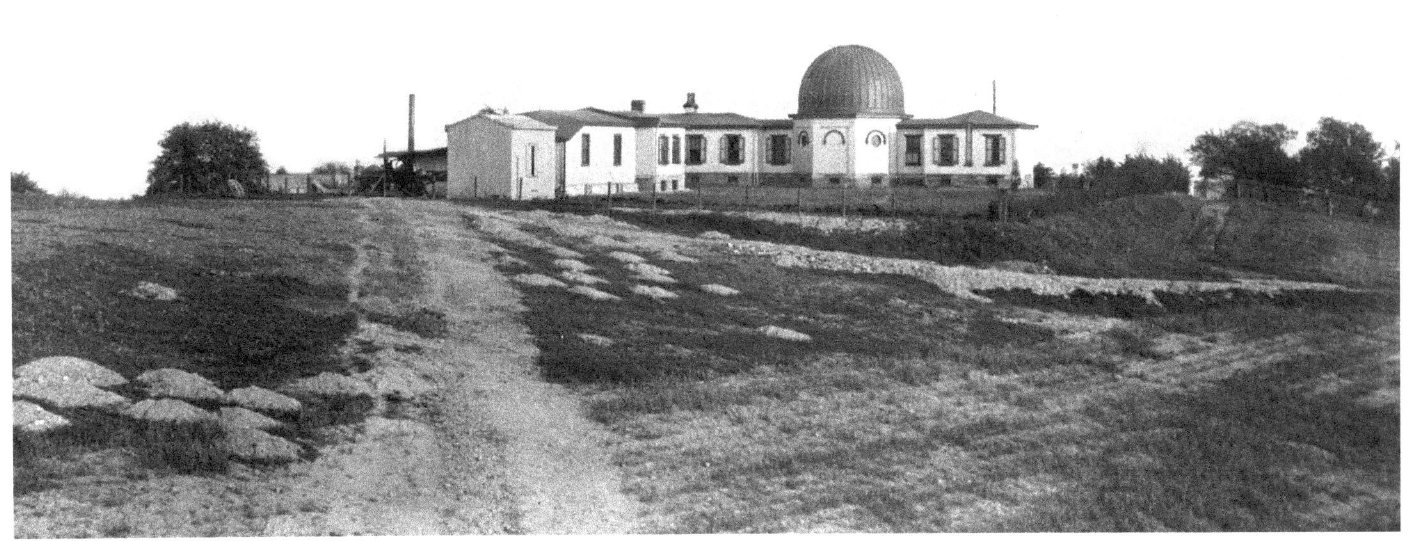

Allegheny Observatory as it existed in 1886 in Allegheny City, now part of Riverview Park located on Pittsburgh's North Side.

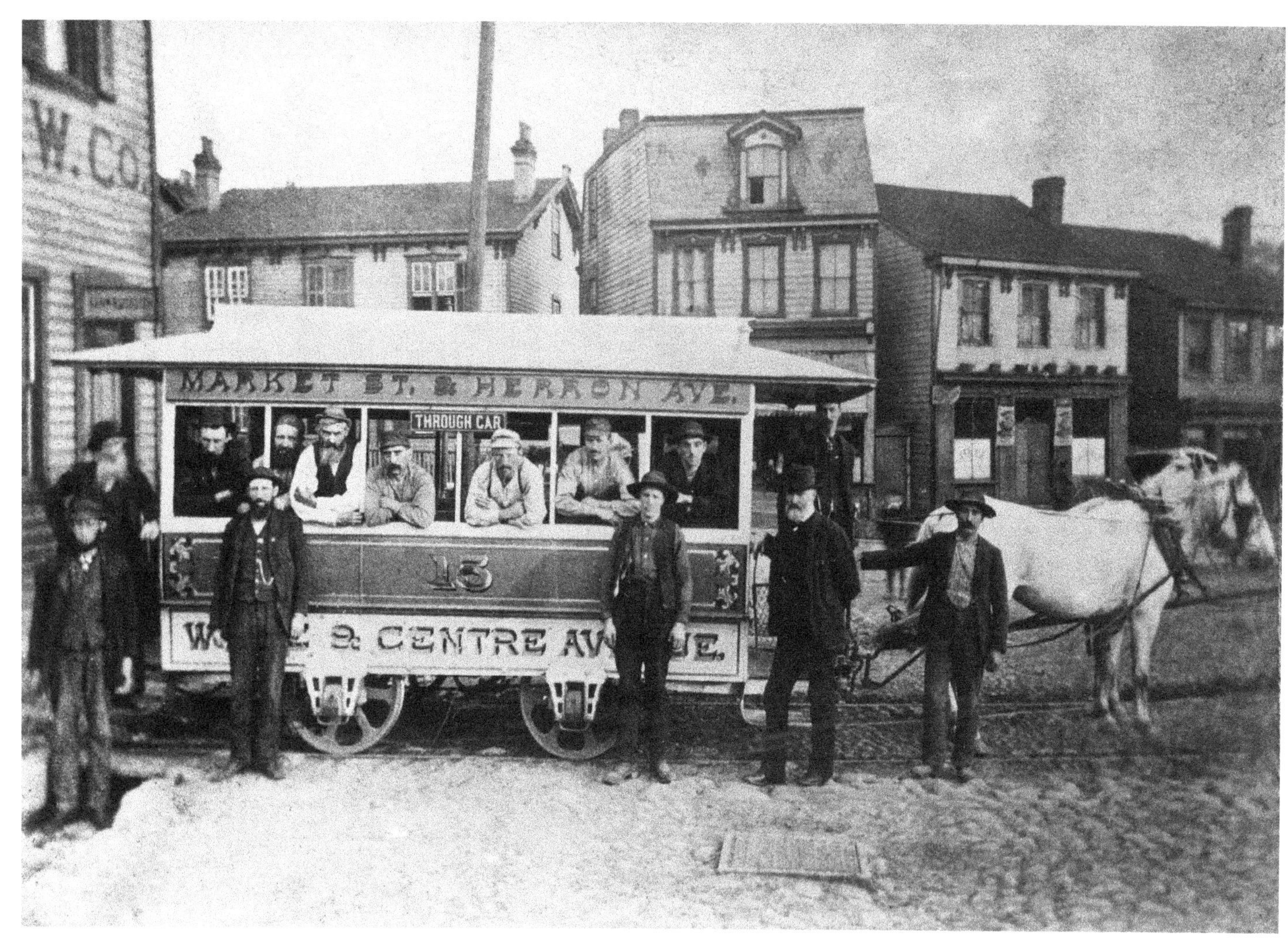

A Central Passenger Railway Company horse-drawn trolley car providing transportation to the Hill District. This view was recorded at Herron Avenue and Bryn Mawr Street sometime after 1888.

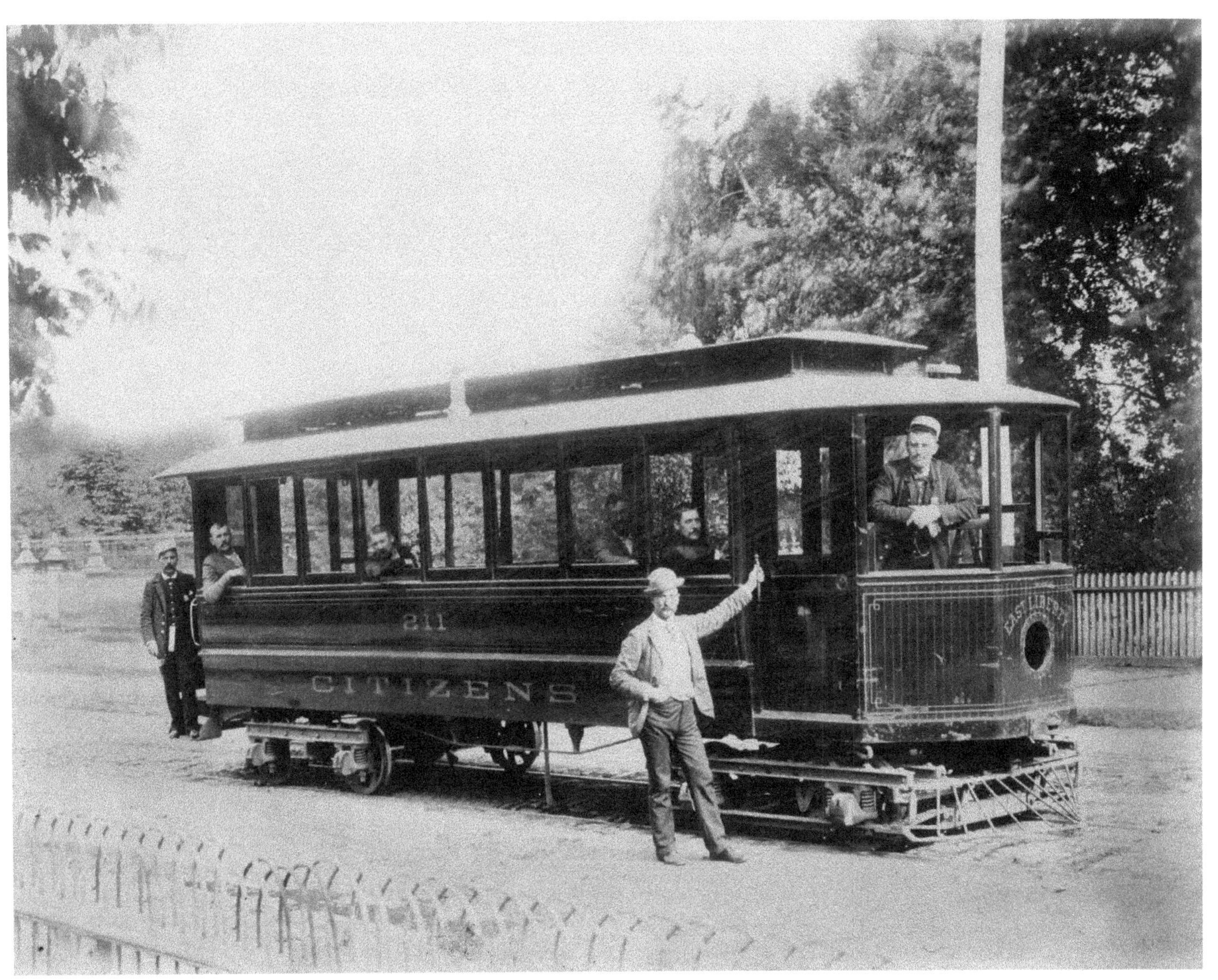

Citizens Passenger Rail car no. 211 on July 23, 1889. This was one of three cable car companies to operate in Pittsburgh. This line ran from downtown along Penn Avenue to East Liberty.

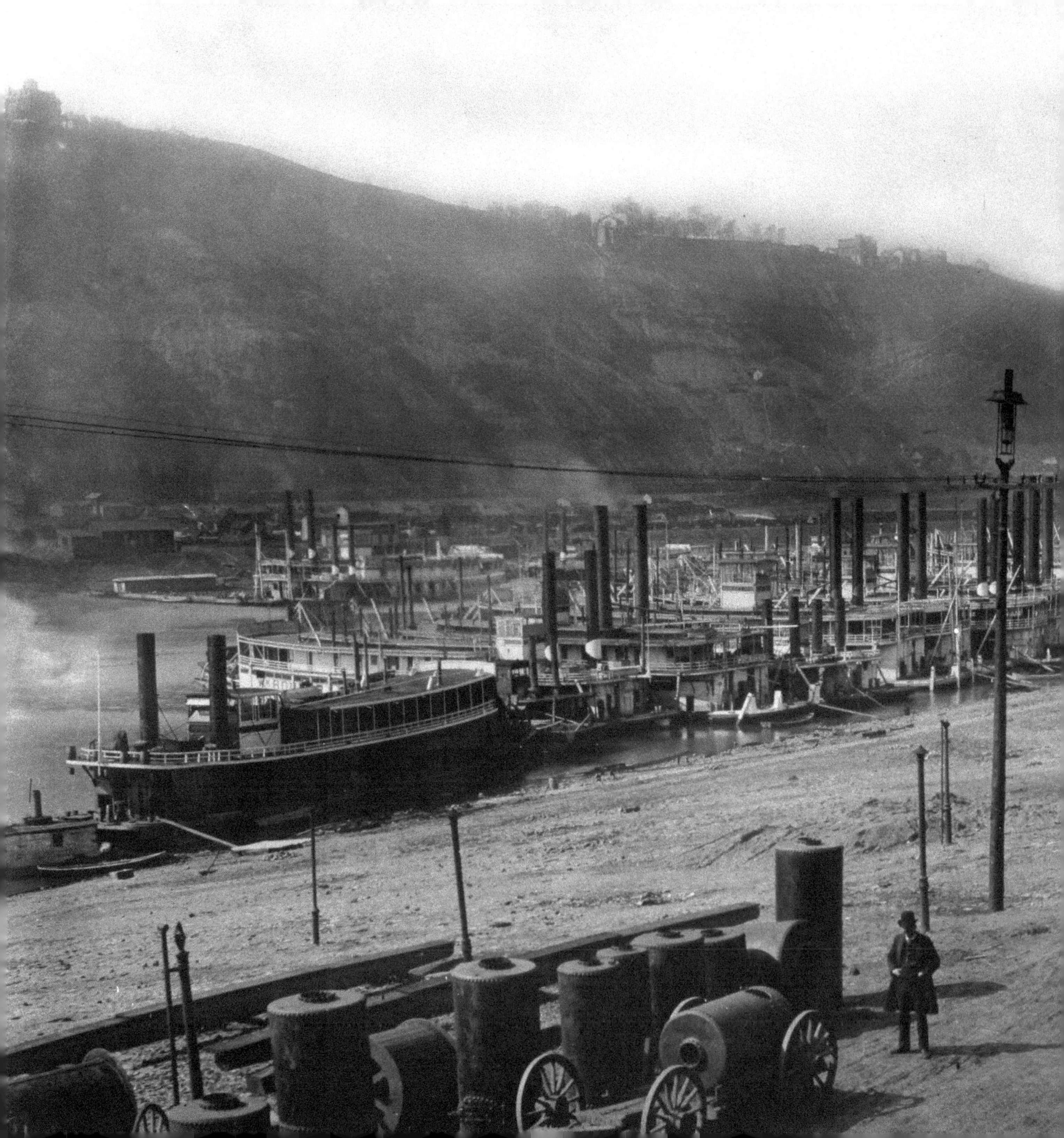

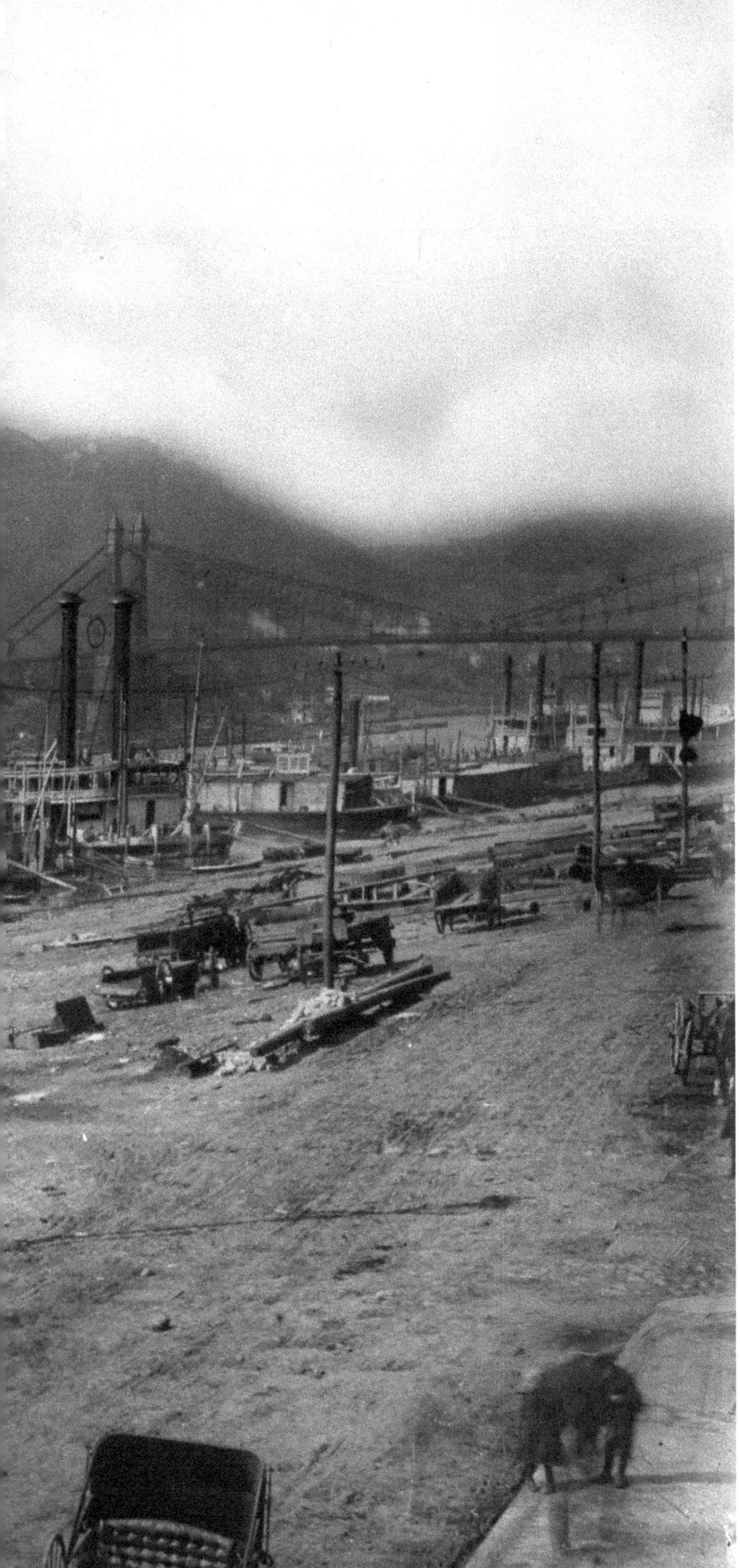

The Monongahela River and wharf, around 1886. In the 1800s, this area was an important center of commerce and a travel gateway for Pittsburgh. It was constantly lined with steamers, packet ships, and cargo, and was a point of departure for travelers. These boats appear to be waiting for the river to rise.

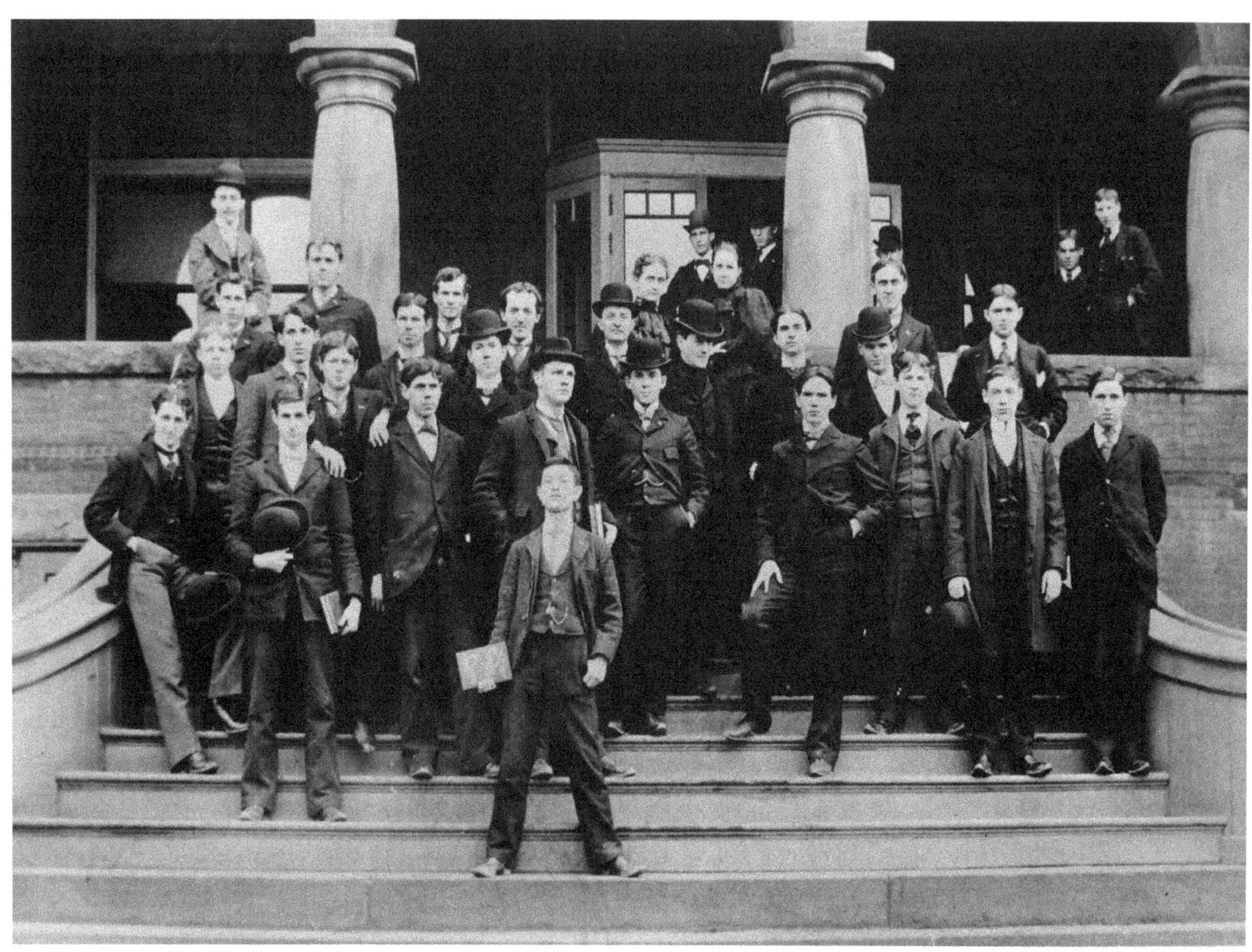

This Western University of Pennsylvania class photo around 1896 features Stella and Margaret Stein, the first women admitted to study at the university. They graduated in 1898, with Margaret continuing her studies, becoming the first woman to obtain a master's degree from Western University, in 1901.

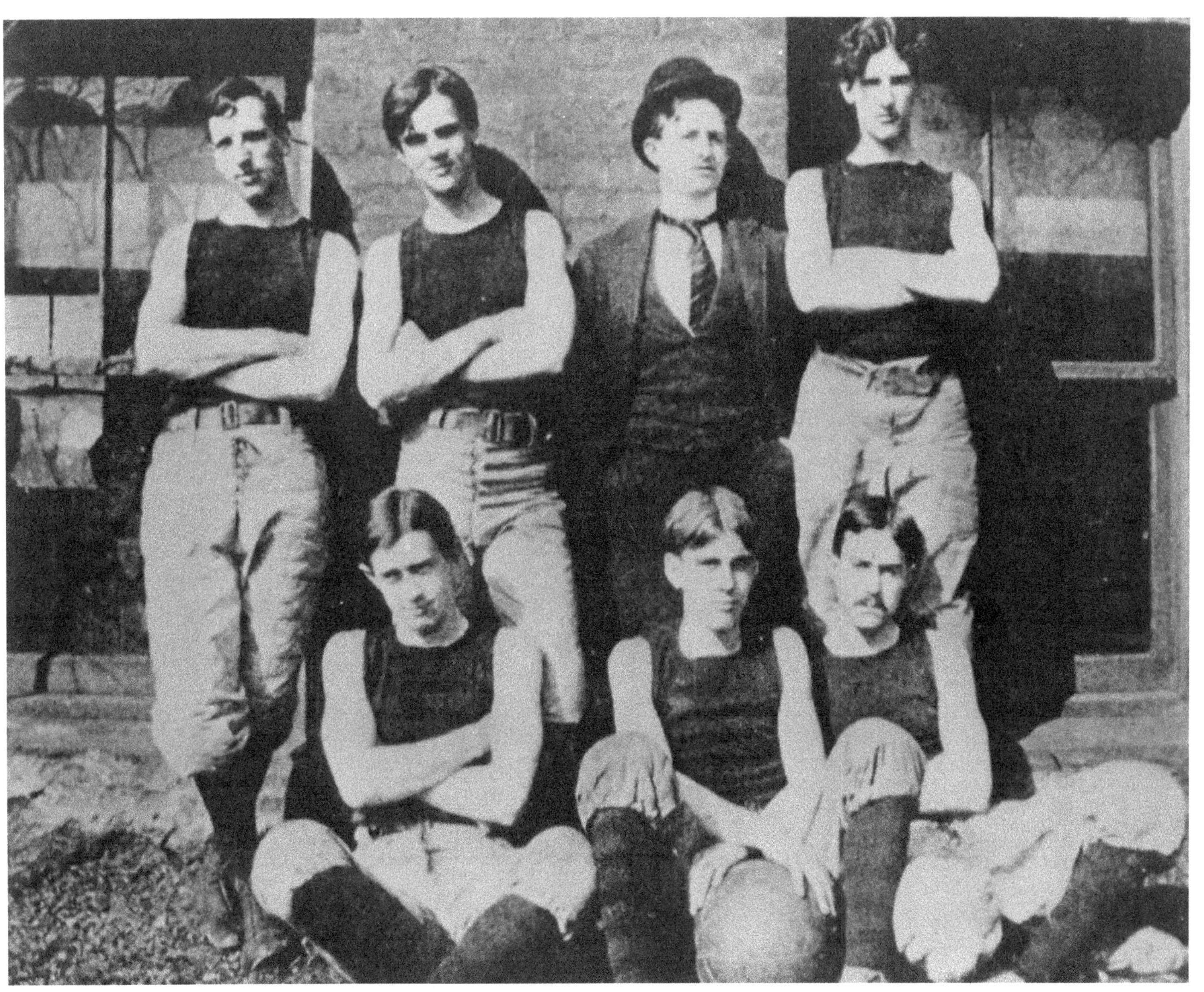

The Western University of Pennsylvania basketball team in 1897. Sitting left to right are S. K. Hunter, Frank M. Roessing, and Guy D. Wallace. Standing left to right are H. R. Hammer, C. S. Lambie, C. F. O'Hagan, and H. G. Hammer.

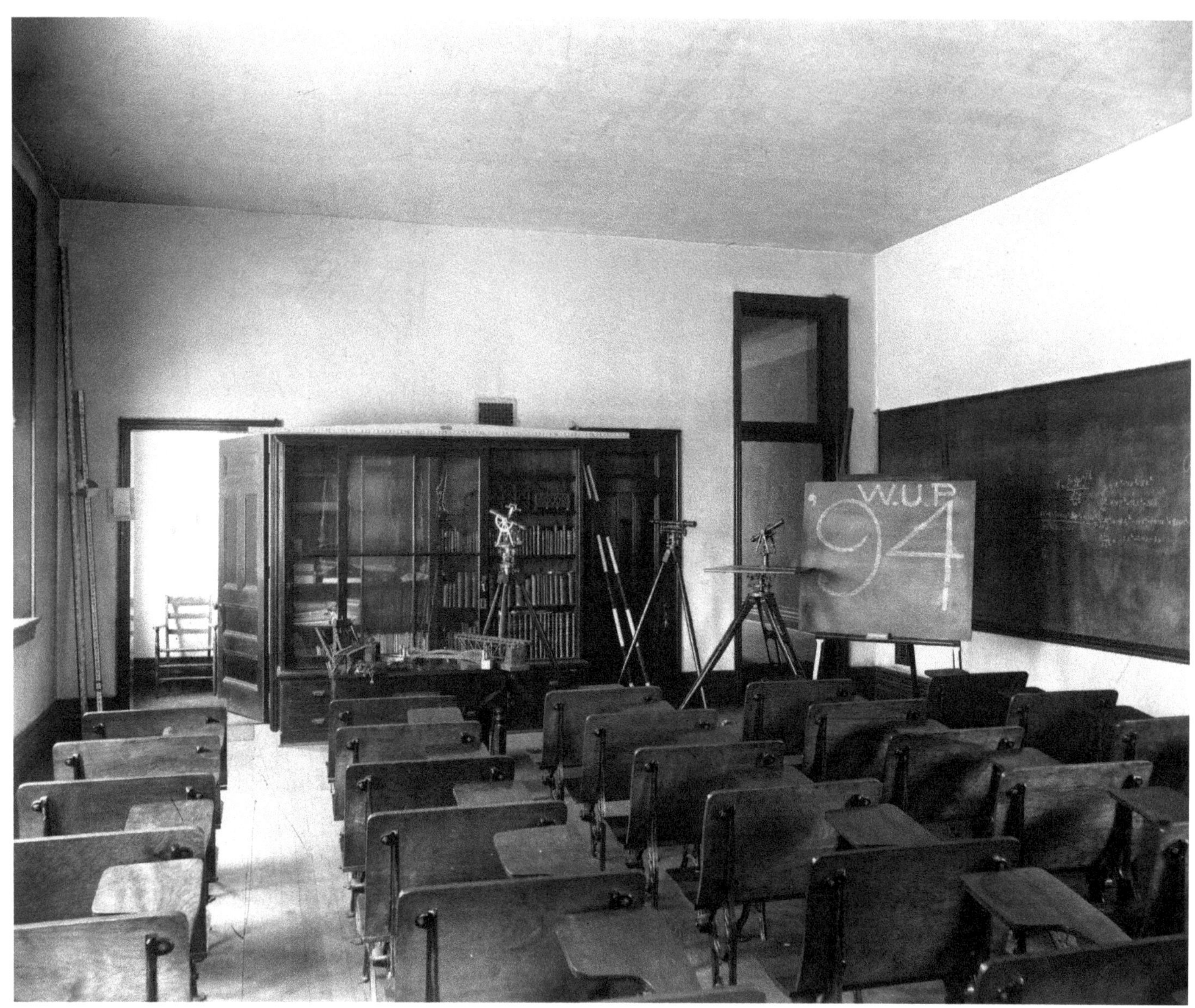

A Western University of Pennsylvania engineering classroom, in 1894. Formerly known as the Pittsburgh Academy and later the University of Pittsburgh, the university had several locations downtown, before moving to Allegheny City. The university had moved to its permanent home in Oakland by 1909.

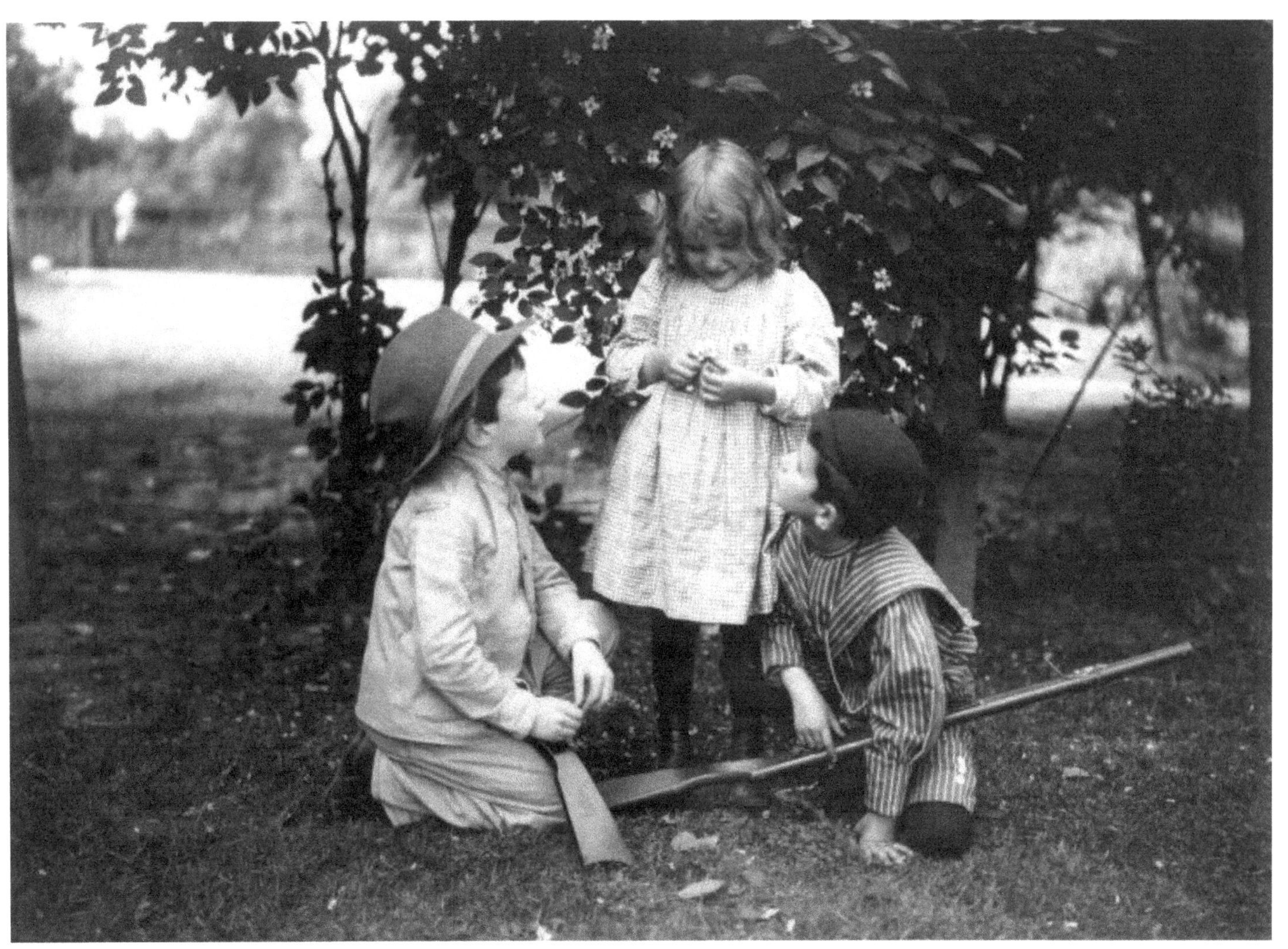

The Spencer children Mary and Mark in their Shadyside yard with their friend George Macbeth, in June 1899. Their father, Charles Hart Spencer, was the photographer.

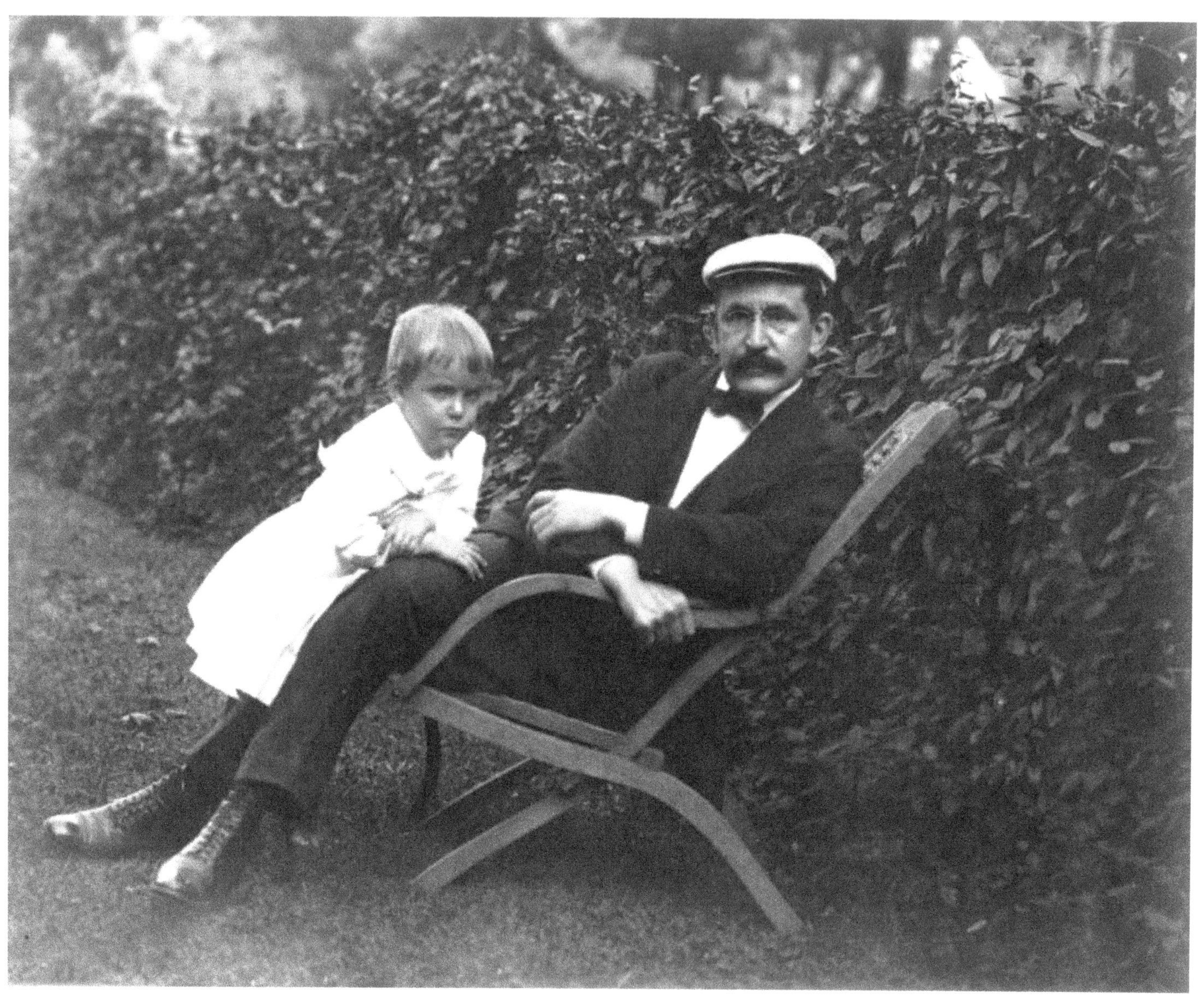

Charles Hart Spencer and Elizabeth Blue Spencer in their Shadyside yard, in September 1899. Spencer was an avid photographer who seemed to prefer being behind the lens—most of his photographs show the children, his wife, friends, household staff, family pets, and environs.

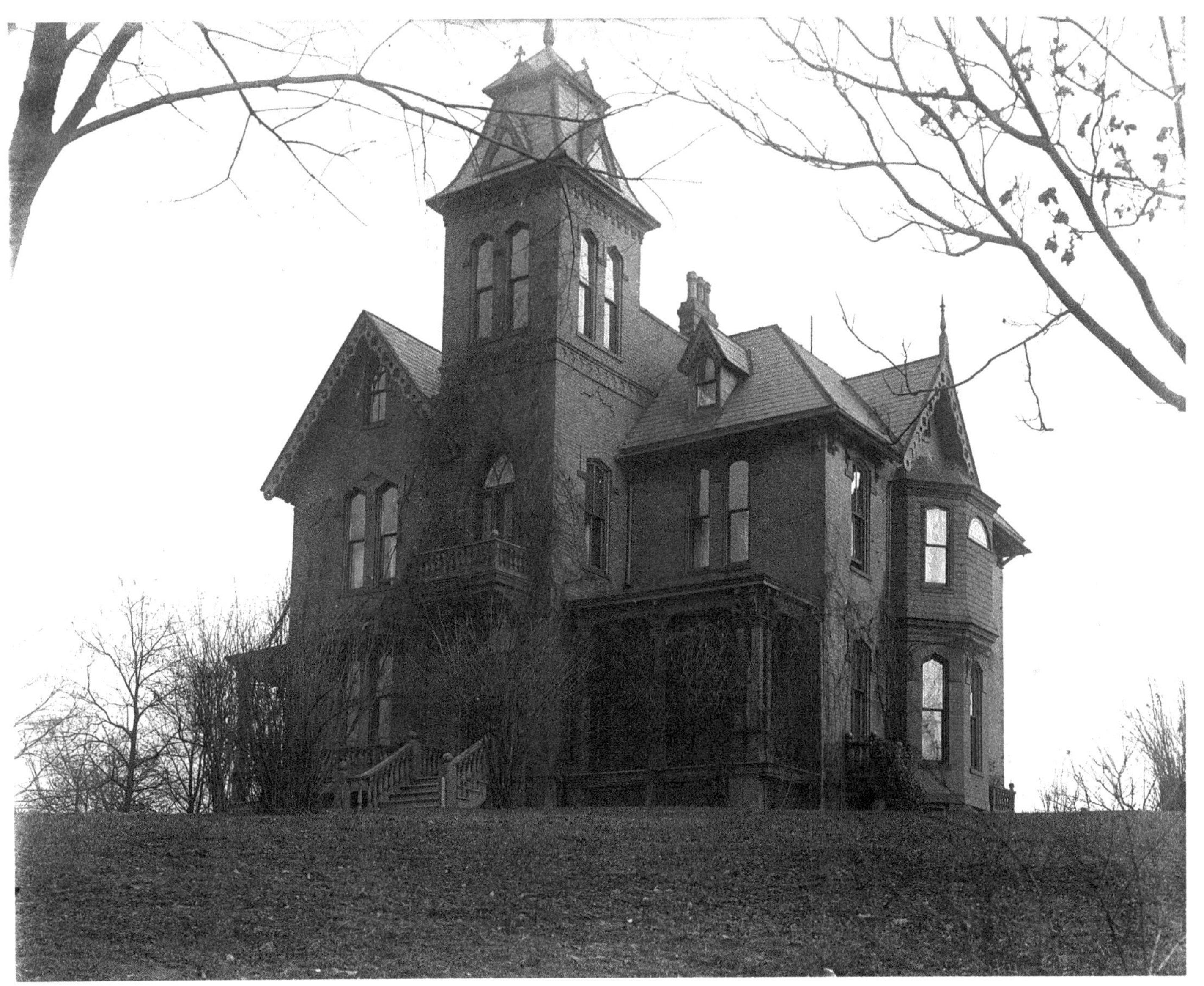

This is Springbank from the hillside, photographed by Walter P. Magee. The home was located near Forbes and Neville streets just above the Pittsburgh Junction Railroad.

Workers at Carnegie Steel Company's Homestead Steel Works.

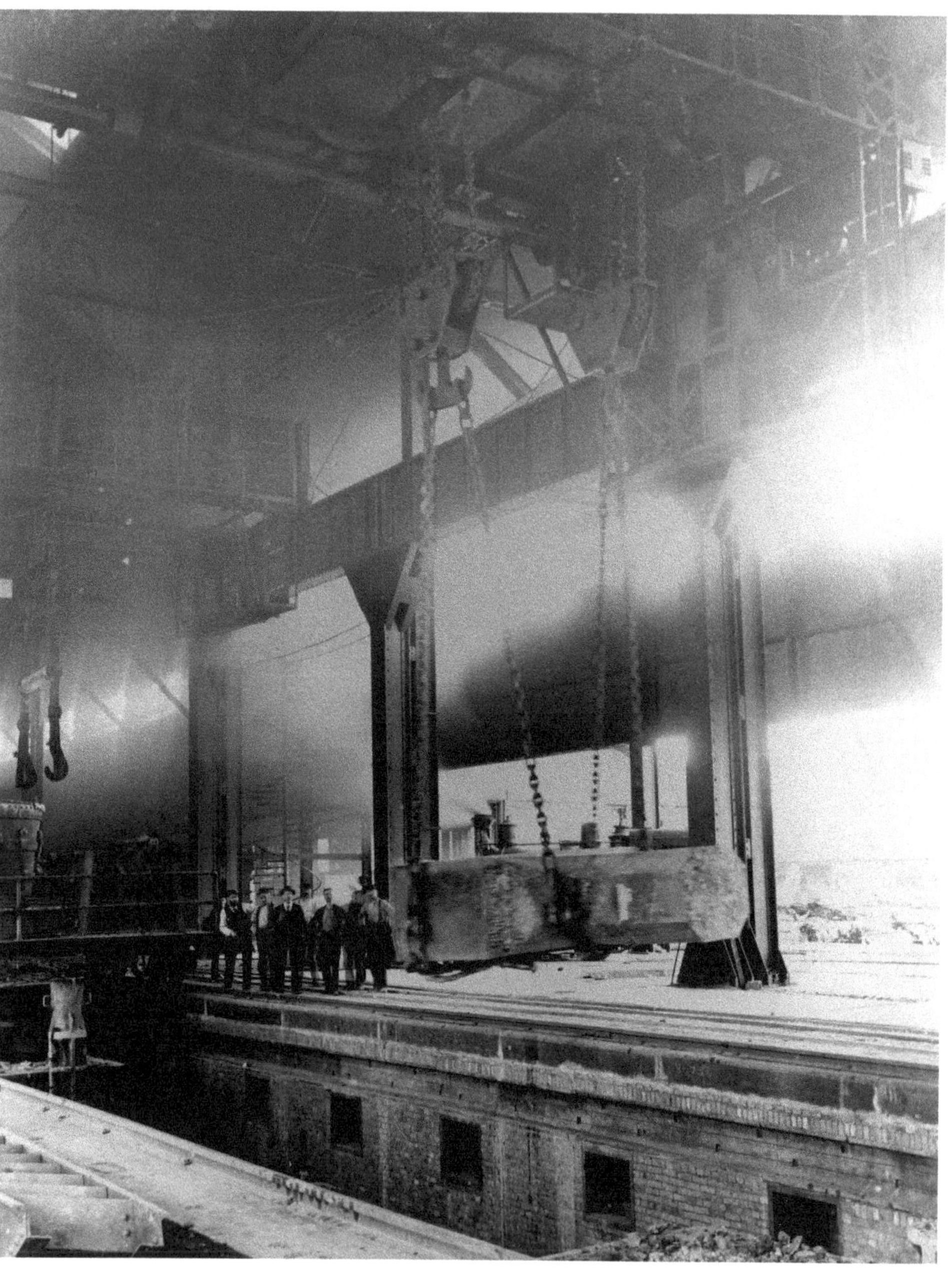

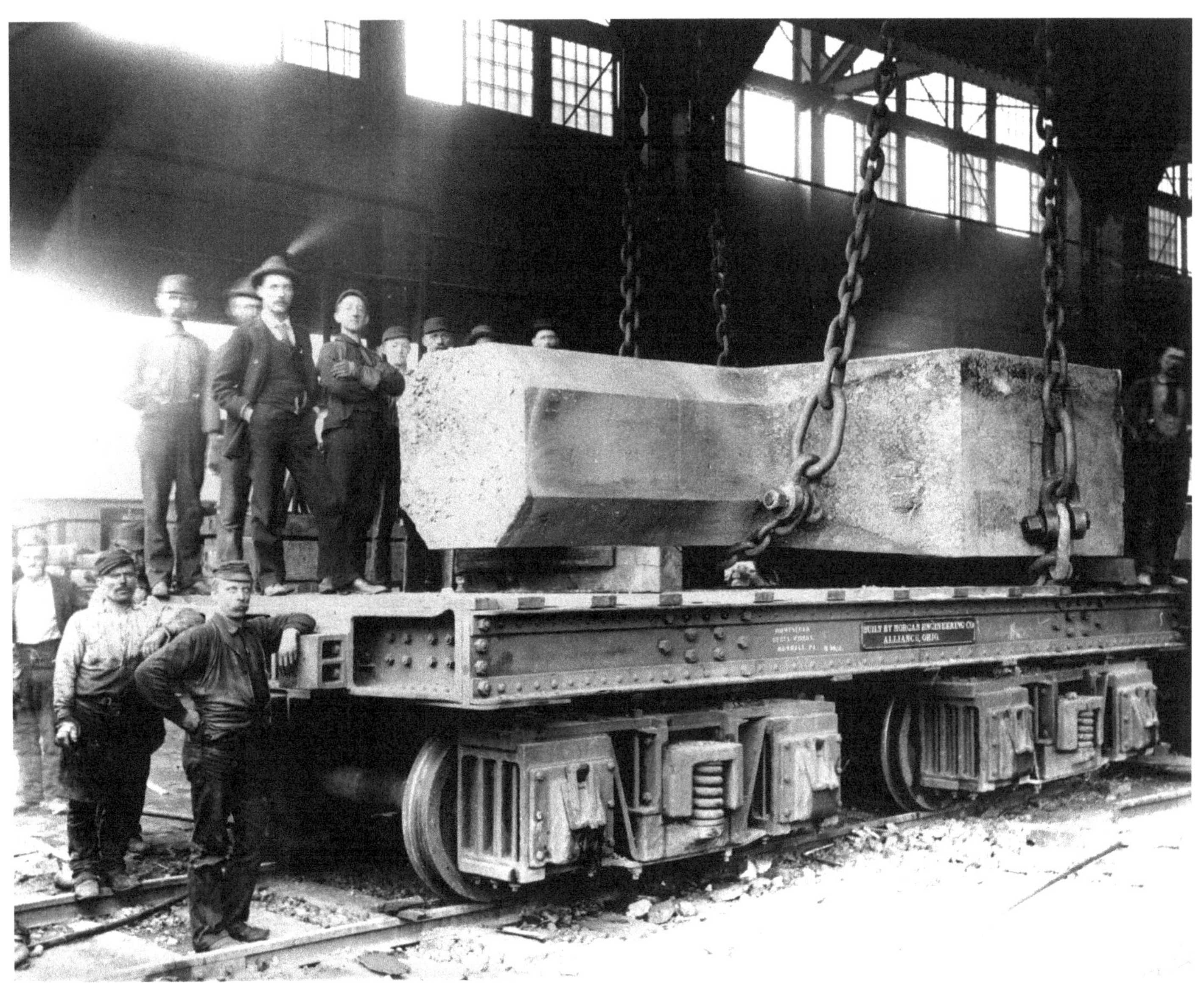

Workers at the Homestead Steel Works pose with a 90-ton ingot, loaded and ready for shipment to the Armor Plate Division, around 1892–1895.

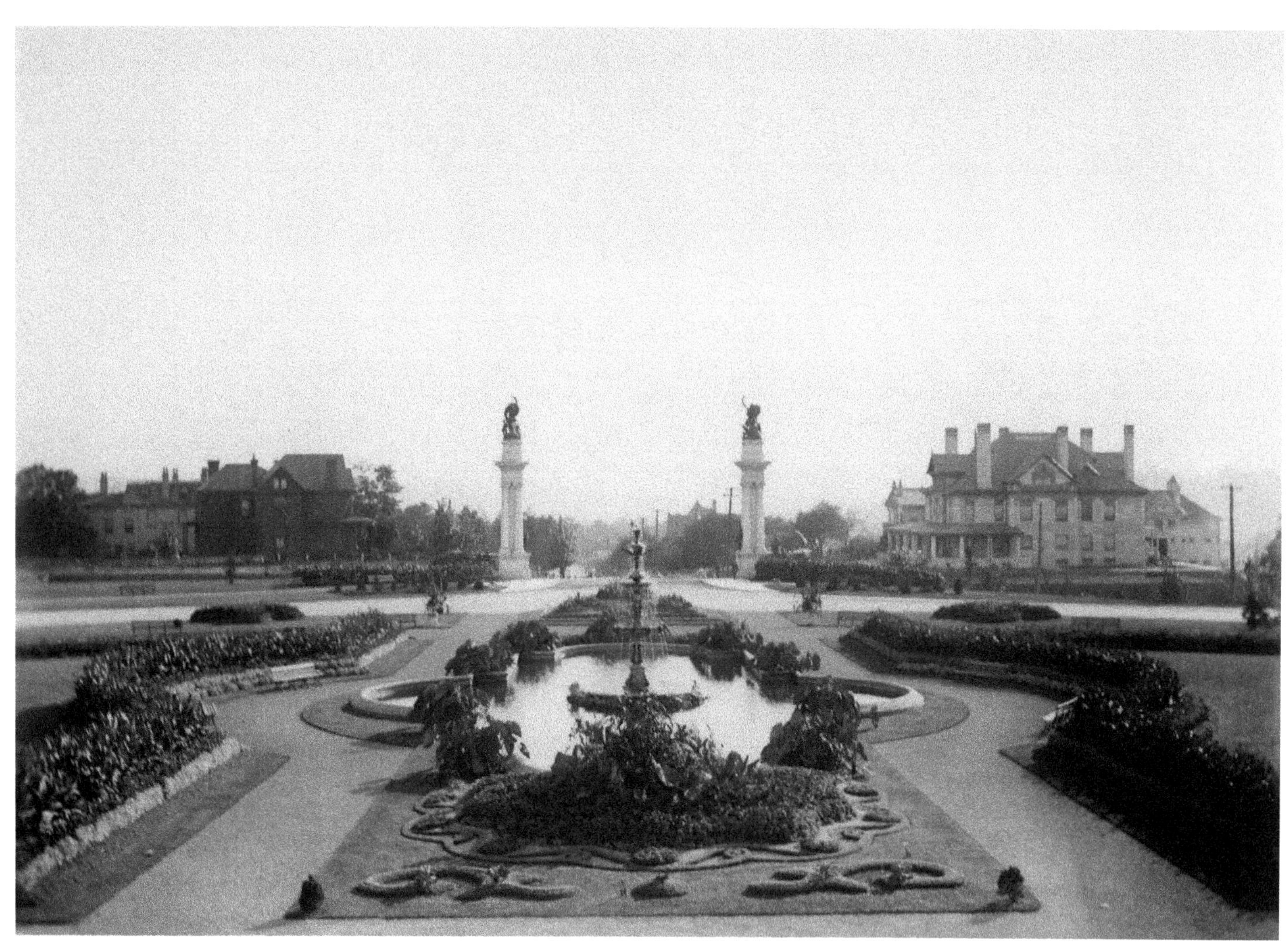

The grand entrance to Highland Park around 1900, featuring bronze statues designed by Giuseppe Moretti perched atop columns, was created for the sum of $45,000. The park originally opened in 1893 on 46 acres. It would grow to encompass 366 acres.

Hills Come Down, Buildings Go Up

(1900–1919)

Between 1900 and 1919, Pittsburgh was in a constant state of change. Advances in the city's infrastructure improved the quality of life, encouraged building, and forever altered the city's landscape.

Road improvements were made to streets such as Fifth Avenue, Butler Street, Forbes Avenue, and Federal Street. The sewer system was enhanced throughout the city, and water treatment facilities were constructed in Aspinwall. New tracks for the trolley system were part of the street improvements.

Beautiful bridges cross Pittsburgh's three rivers, but the "City of Bridges" has plenty of spans inland as well. The 22nd Street and Sheraden bridges were among several that were improved during this period of progress.

Perhaps the biggest change to the city's landscape came in 1912 when, after two years of planning, work to change the grade of Grant's Hill began, a project that dramatically affected the entire downtown area. Frederick Law Olmsted, Jr., wrote of this plan in his report *Pittsburgh: Main Thoroughfares and the Down Town District,* adopted by the Committee on City Planning in 1910. He detailed required changes in grade, ranging from 8 to 14.5 feet. To improve transportation, roads such as Sixth Avenue, Diamond Street, and Fifth Avenue were significantly cut, while others such as Webster and Oliver avenues were widened.

While hills were coming down, buildings were going up. The downtown skyline gained the Union Arcade (Union Trust Building) and the William Penn Hotel, both financed by industrialist Henry Clay Frick, who had his own building at the corner of Diamond (Forbes) and Grant streets. In Oakland, Forbes Field was born, replacing the frequently flooded home of the Pittsburgh Pirates, Exposition Park on the North Side.

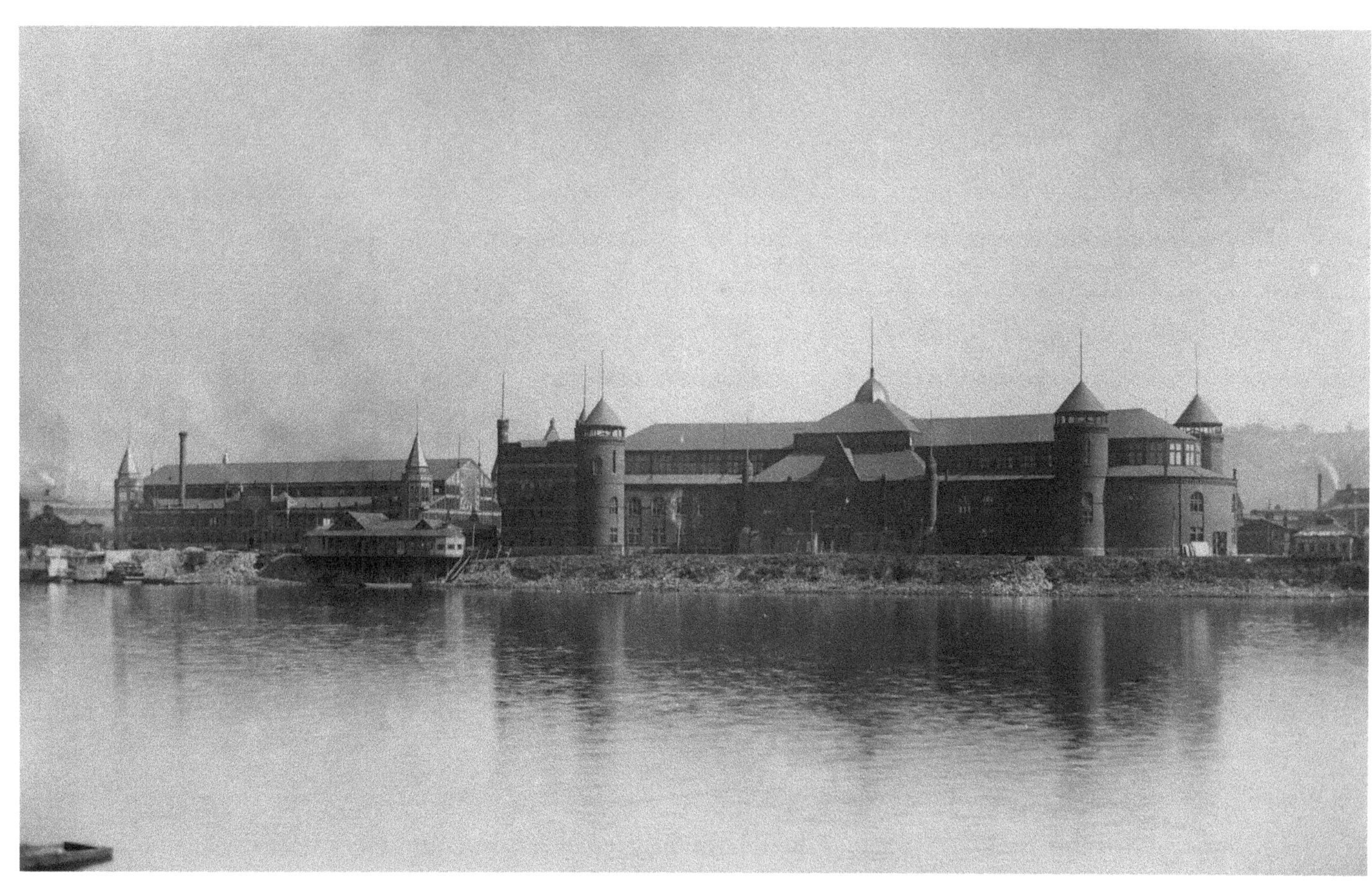

The Western Pennsylvania Exposition buildings, seen here around 1900, were designed in 1889 by Joseph Stillburg. They were built at a cost of $350,000, with the Marshall Foundry & Construction Company responsible for construction of the iron-and-glass Machinery Hall, visible on the left, and Murphy & Hamilton responsible for the main hall, on the right. A fire in 1901 burned part of the main hall, which required rebuilding. The Exposition buildings were torn down in the early 1950s after years of neglect.

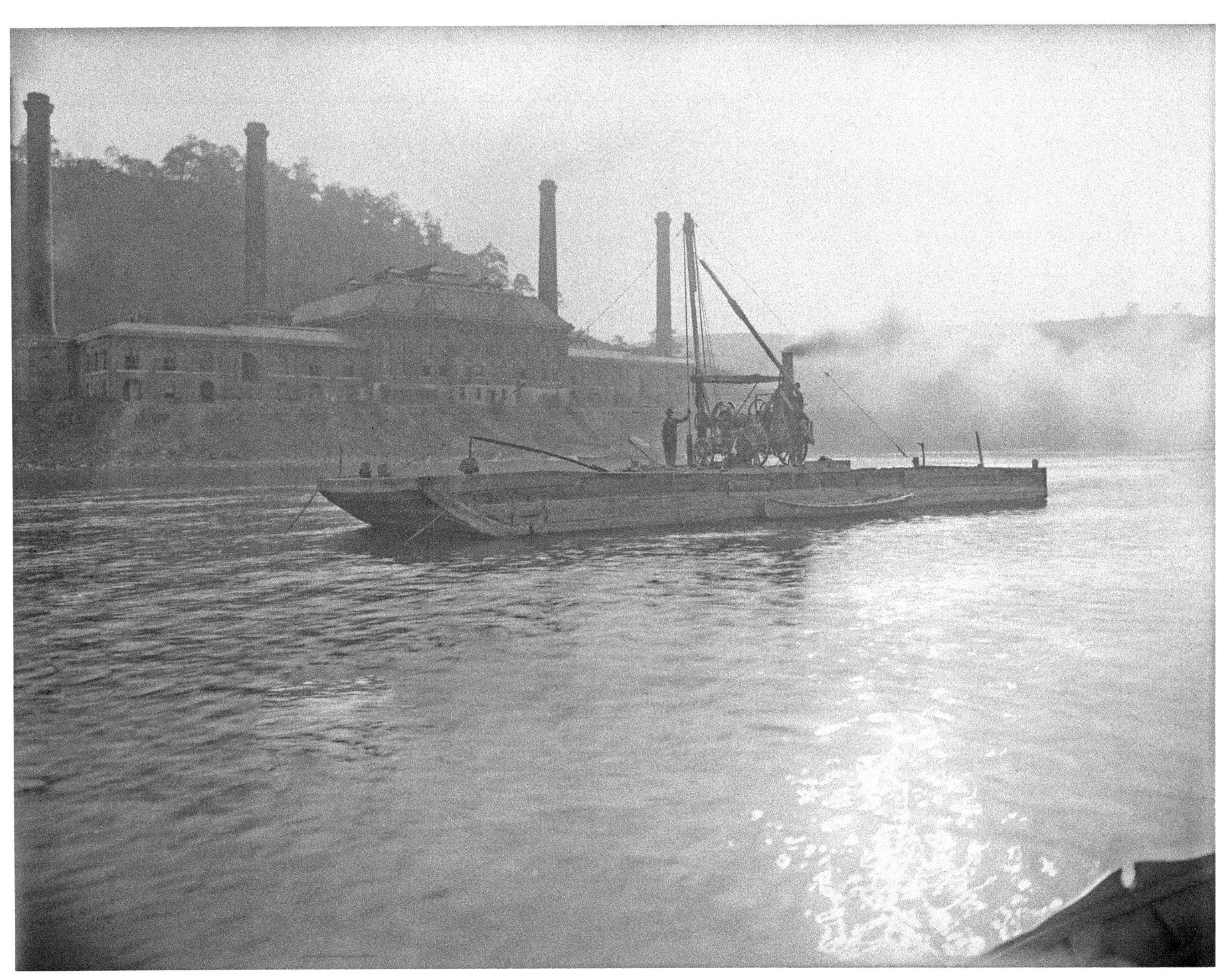

A river barge, loaded with a steam engine, lies at anchor on the Allegheny River.

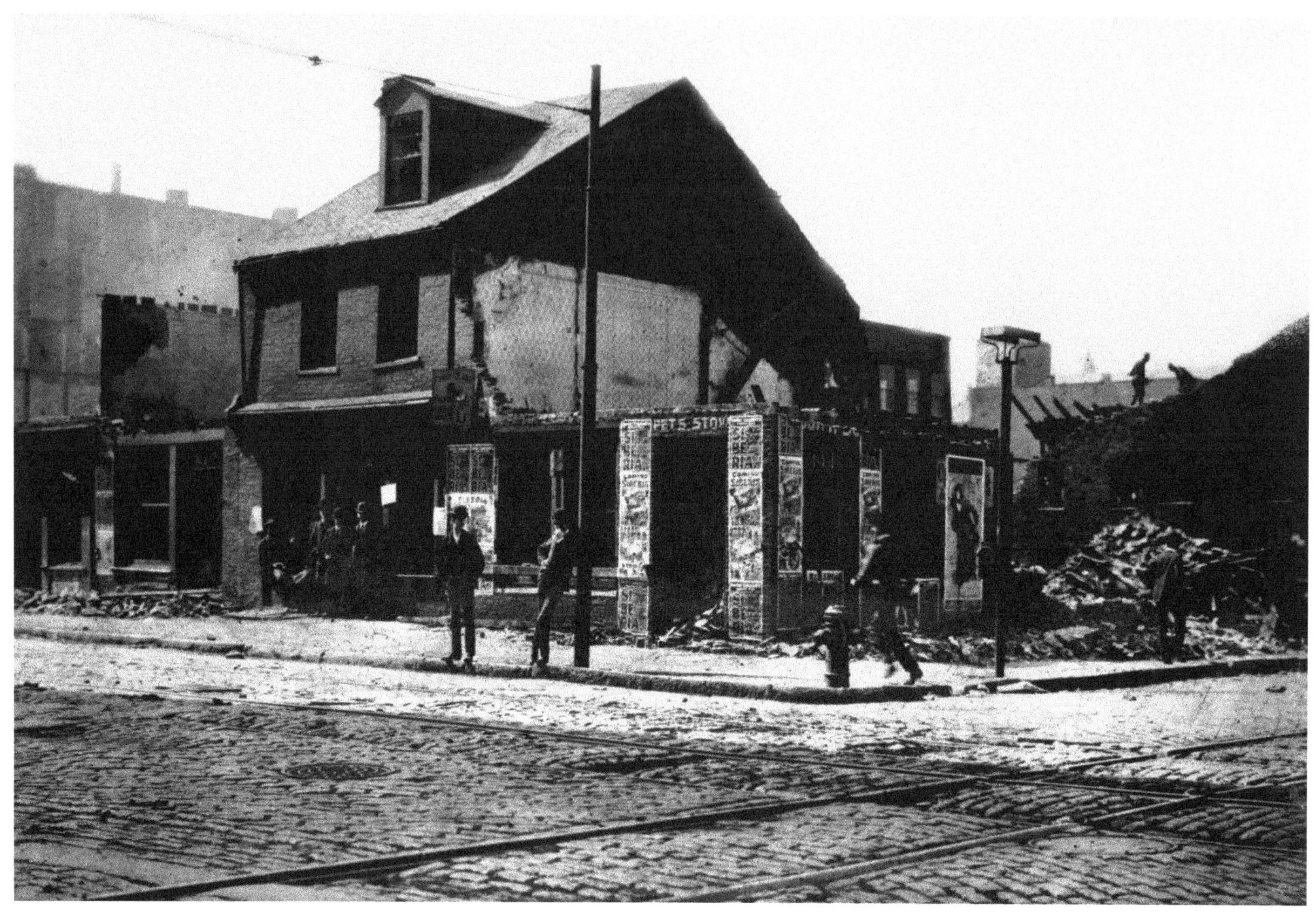

The northwest corner of Penn Avenue and Barbeau Street at the Point, around 1900.

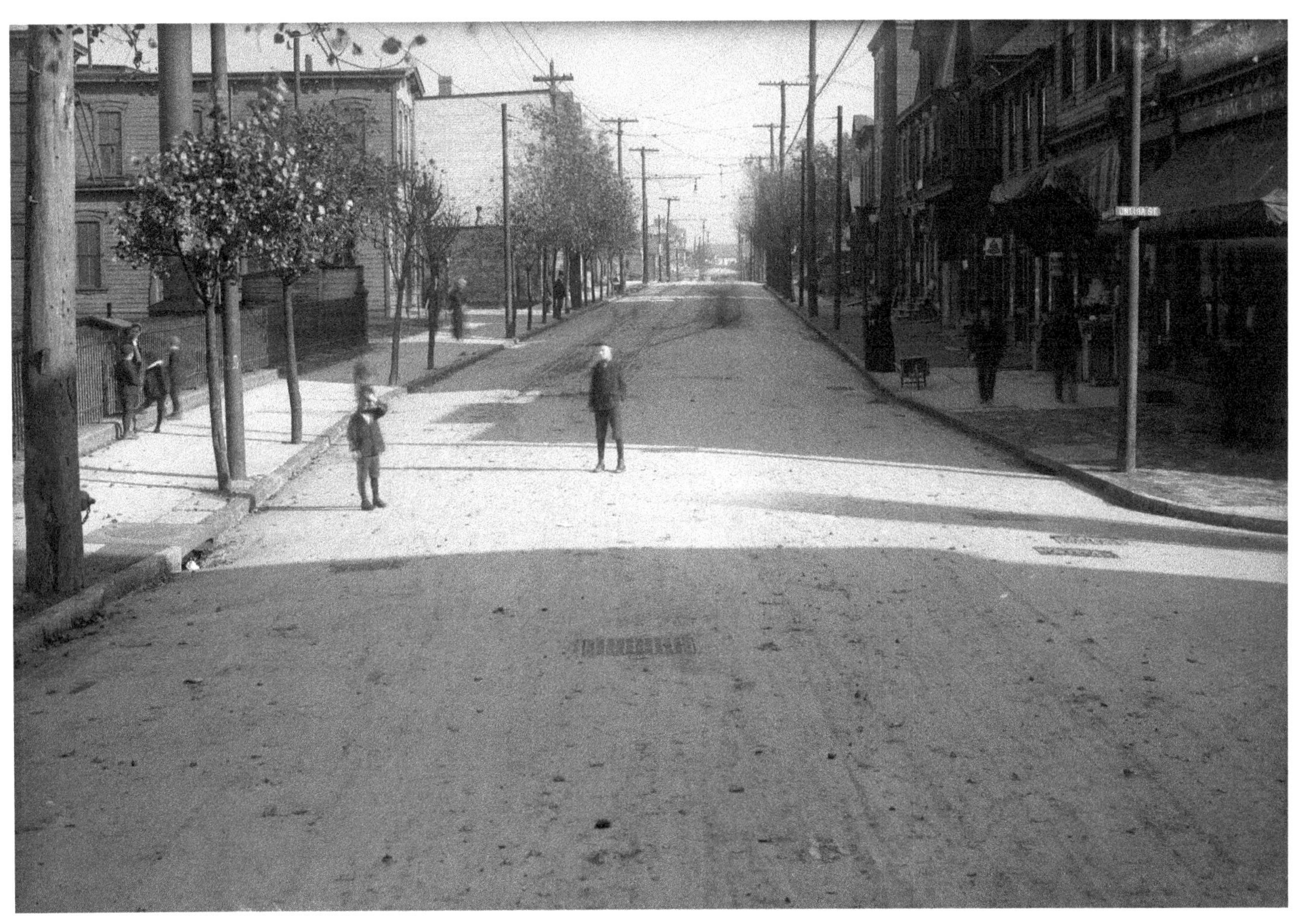

Curious youngsters gather on Grandview Avenue at Oneida Street on Mount Washington in 1907. This view faces east.

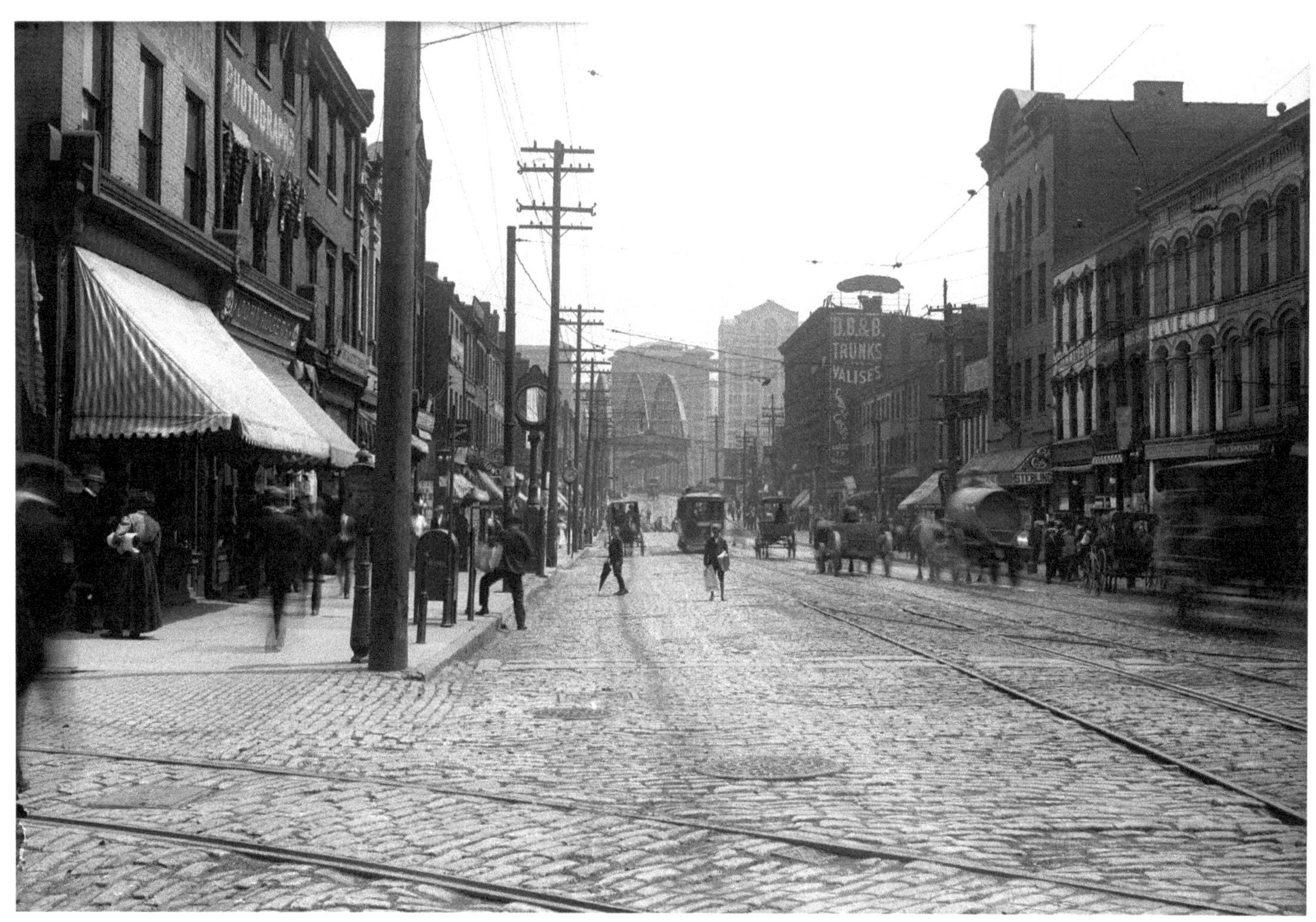

This view of Federal Street at Lacock Street on Pittsburgh's North Side facing the Sixth Street Bridge (formerly the Federal Street Bridge) and downtown was recorded two years after Pittsburgh moved to annex Allegheny City, June 12, 1906. This area is now home to the Pittsburgh Pirates and PNC Park.

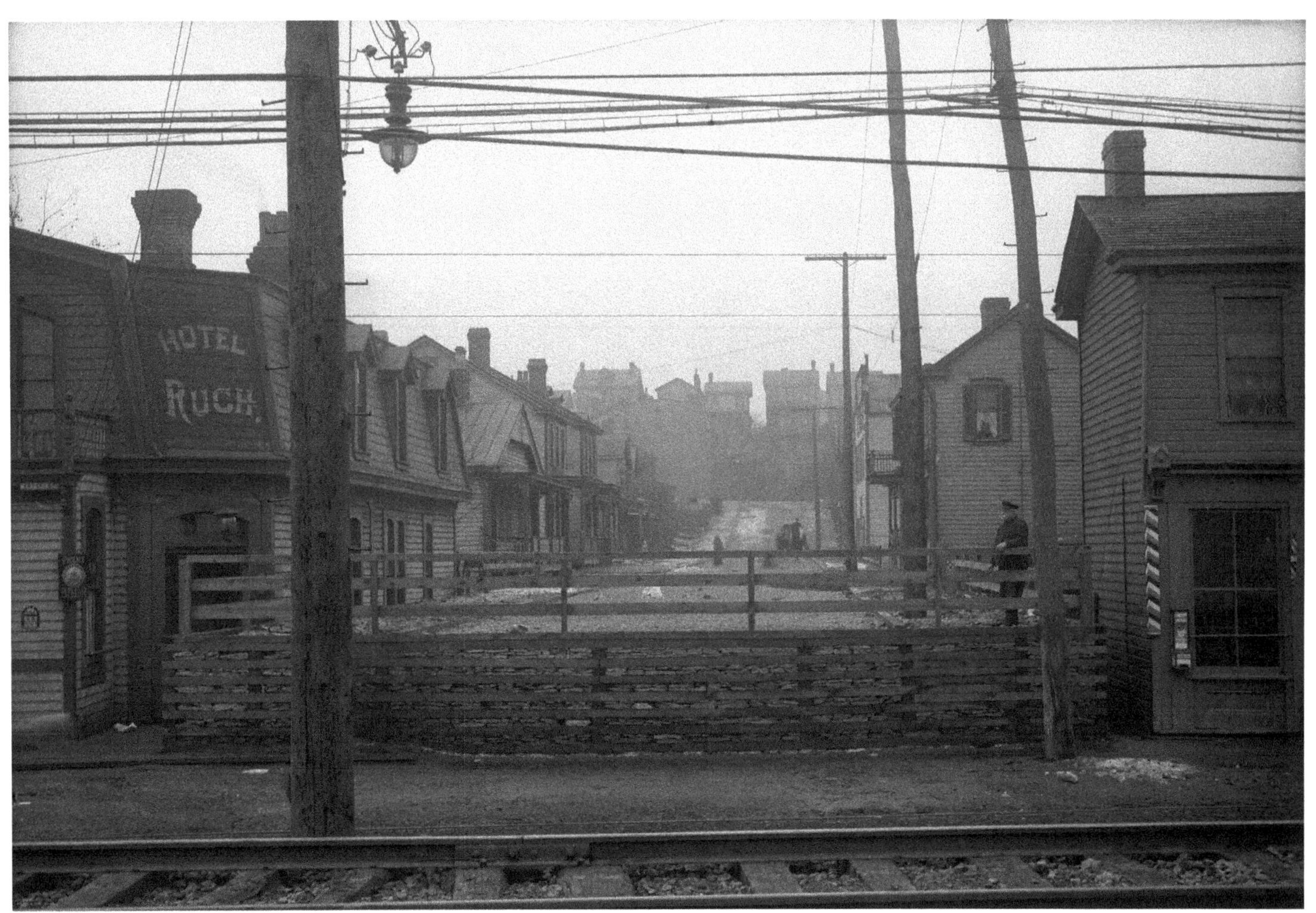

An elevated Sagamore Street at West Carson Street as seen from the GP&C Railroad tracks, around 1910.

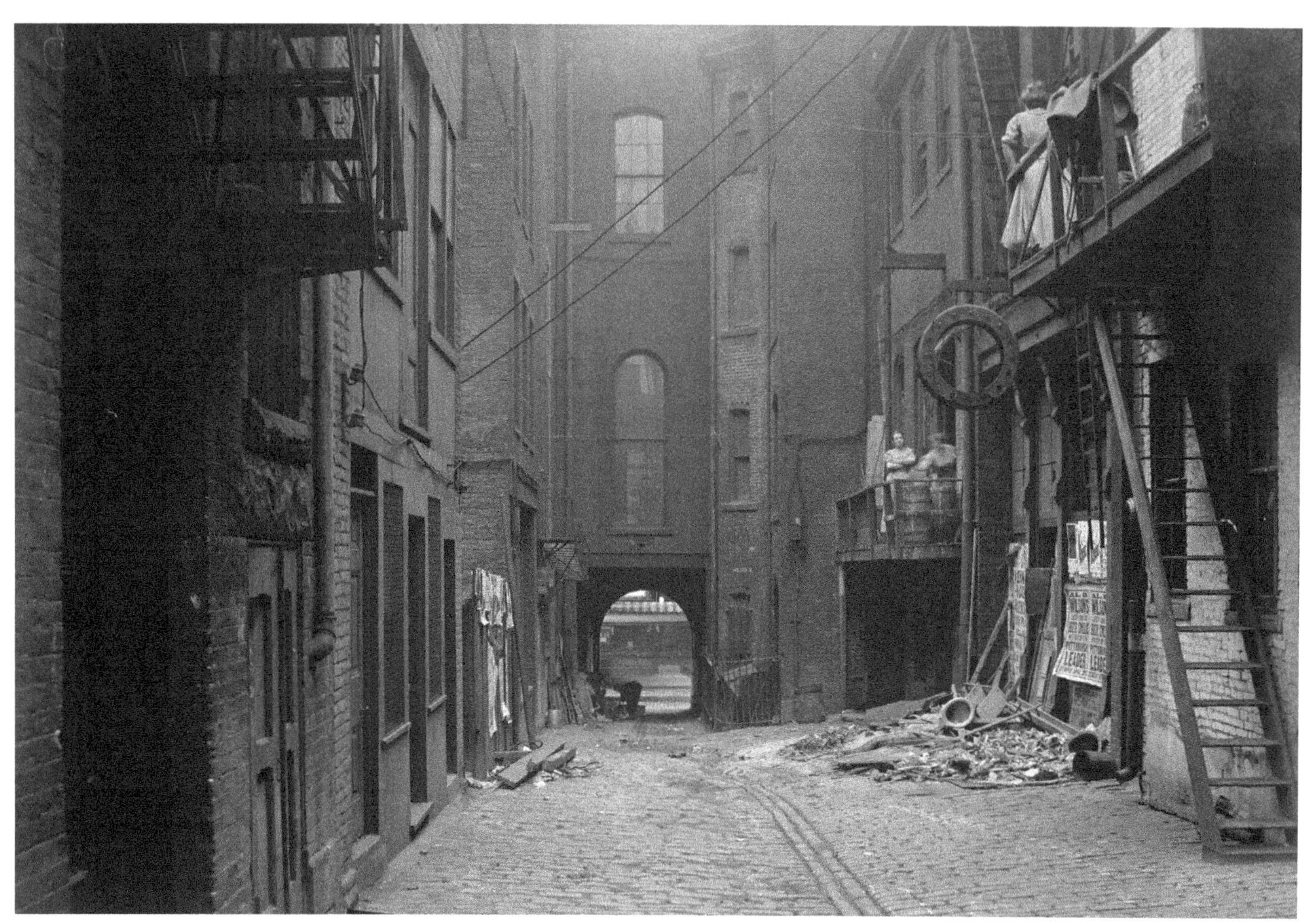

Lemon Alley, facing Smithfield Street downtown, in 1911.

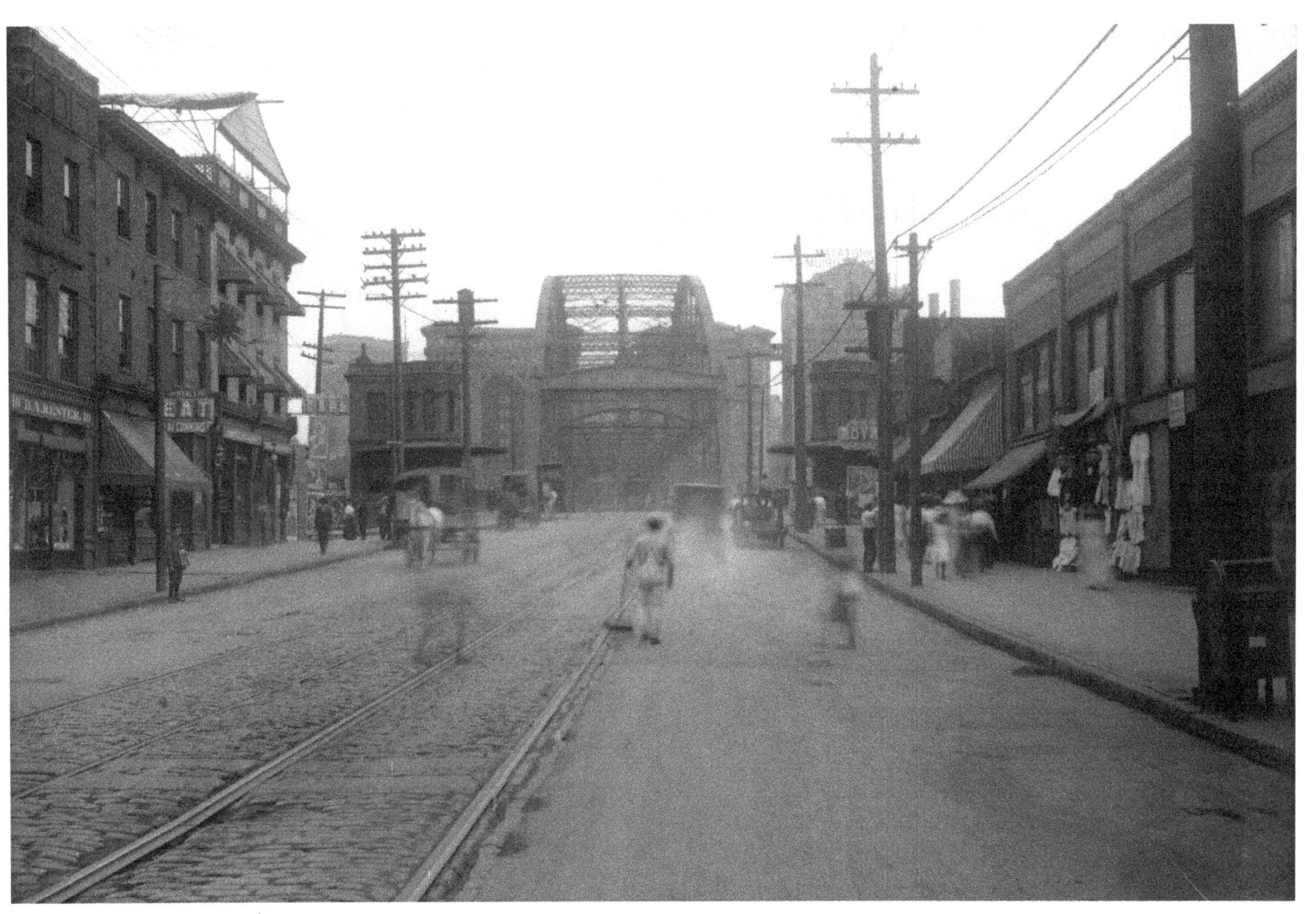

Federal and Isabella streets facing the Sixth Street Bridge, in 1911. This area is now home to the Pittsburgh Pirates and PNC Park.

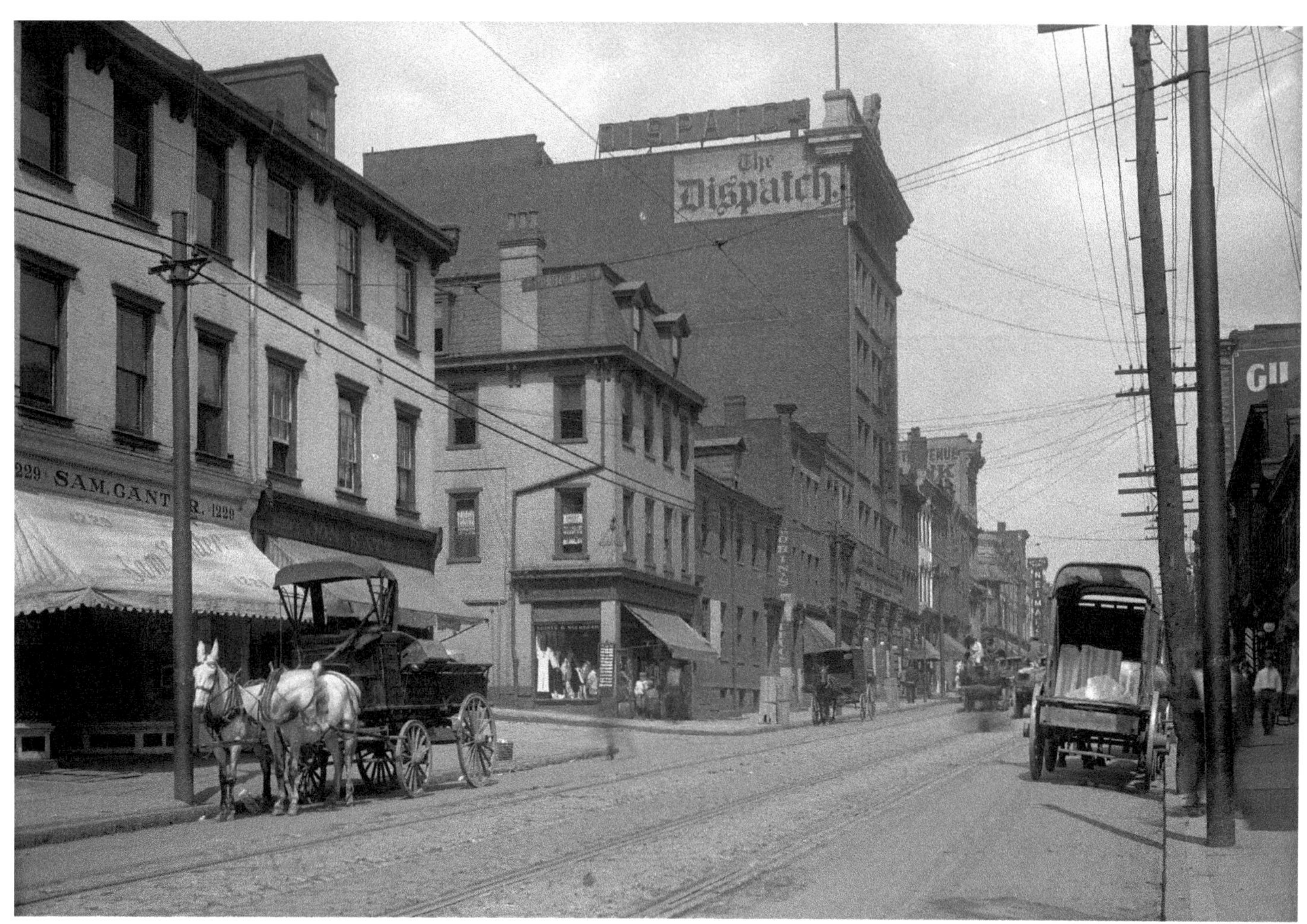

The Pittsburgh Dispatch building and the Fifth Avenue business district, as they appeared in 1911.

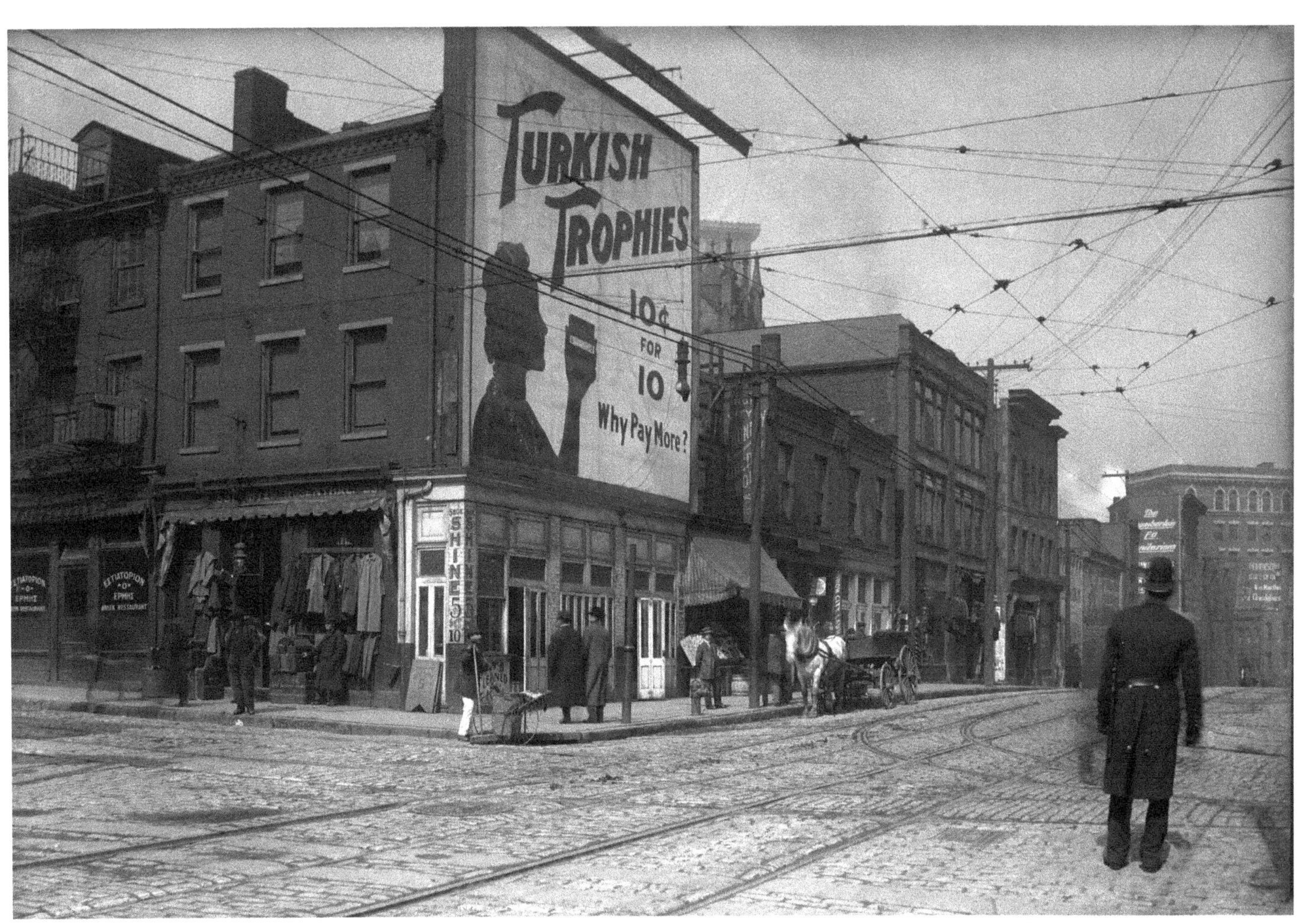

The intersection of Sixth Street and Wylie Avenue, downtown, around 1912 with views of local businesses including a Greek restaurant, a shoeshine shop, and the Iron City Laundry.

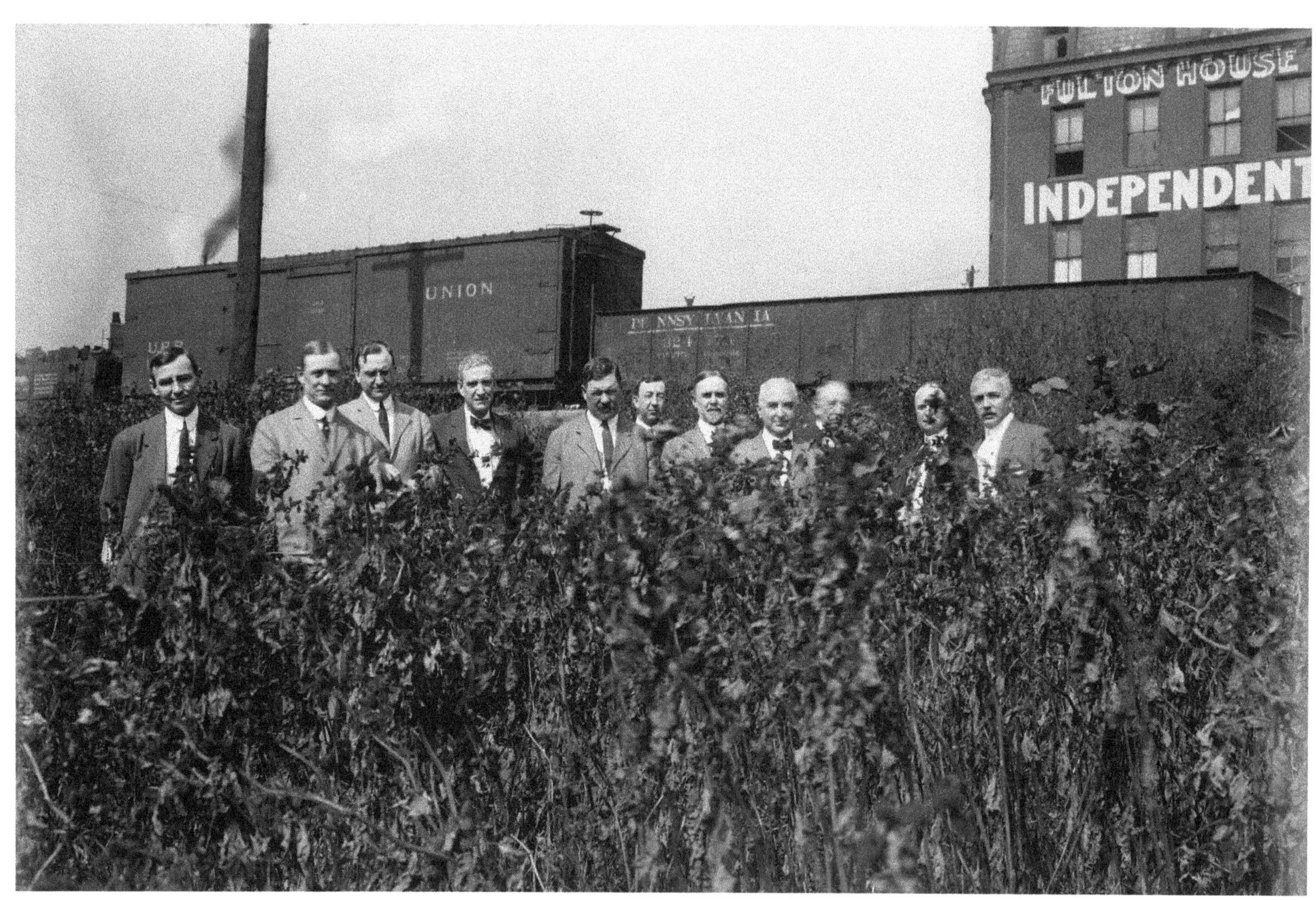

Mayor William A. Magee and members of the Pittsburgh City Council pose on the Monongahela Wharf in 1912.

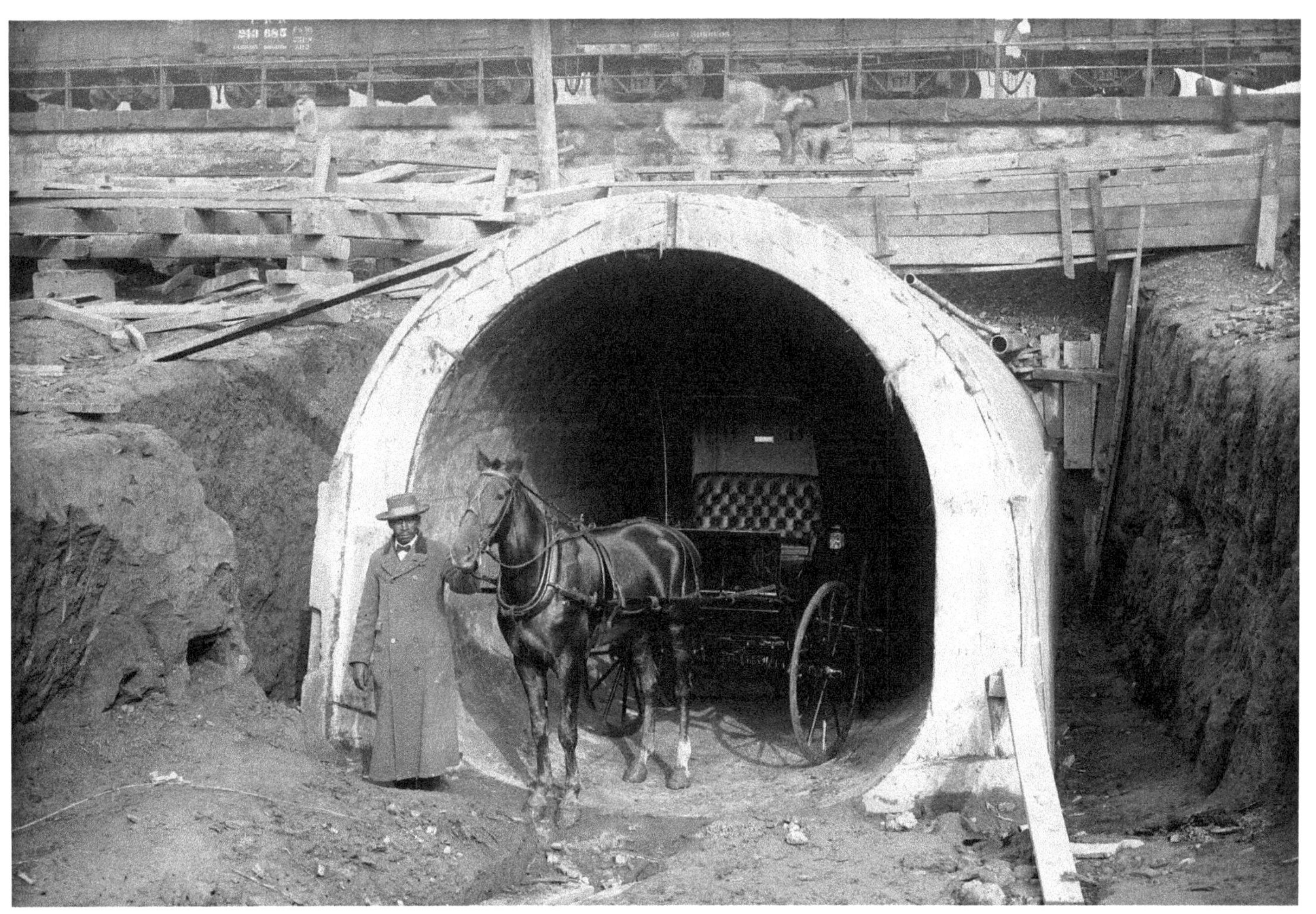

Man and carriage appear from a conduit beneath the Pennsylvania Railroad tracks.

Construction of the Sheraden Bridge crossing the Pittsburgh, Cincinnati, Chicago, and St. Louis Railway is under way in this view facing east. The Sheraden passenger station is to the left. At one time, "Sheraden" carried various spellings. This western neighborhood was named for William Sheradan, a large landowner and property developer with the Sheraden Land & Improvement Company. It can trace its origins to 1872, when it was known as Sheridanville.

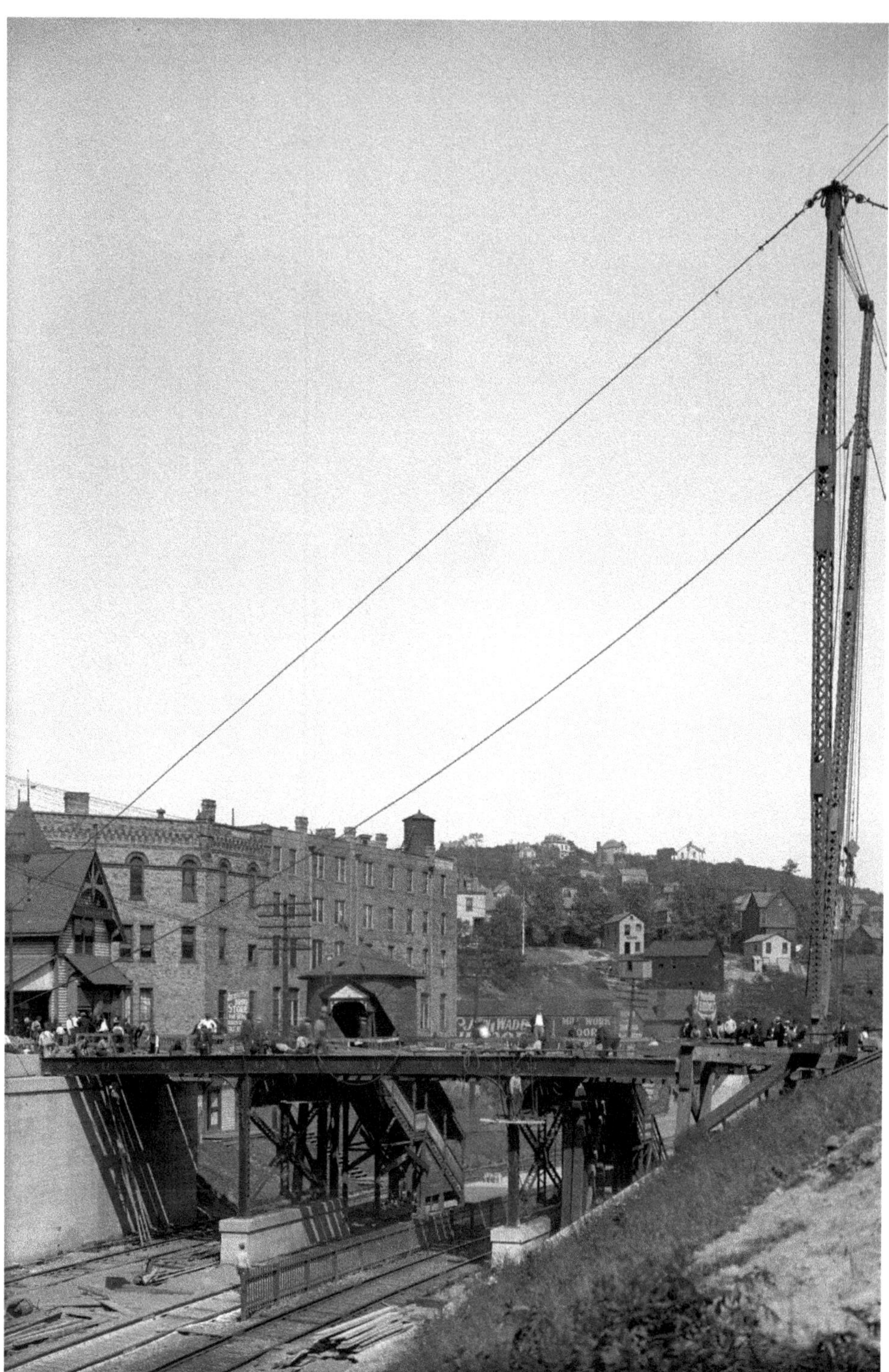

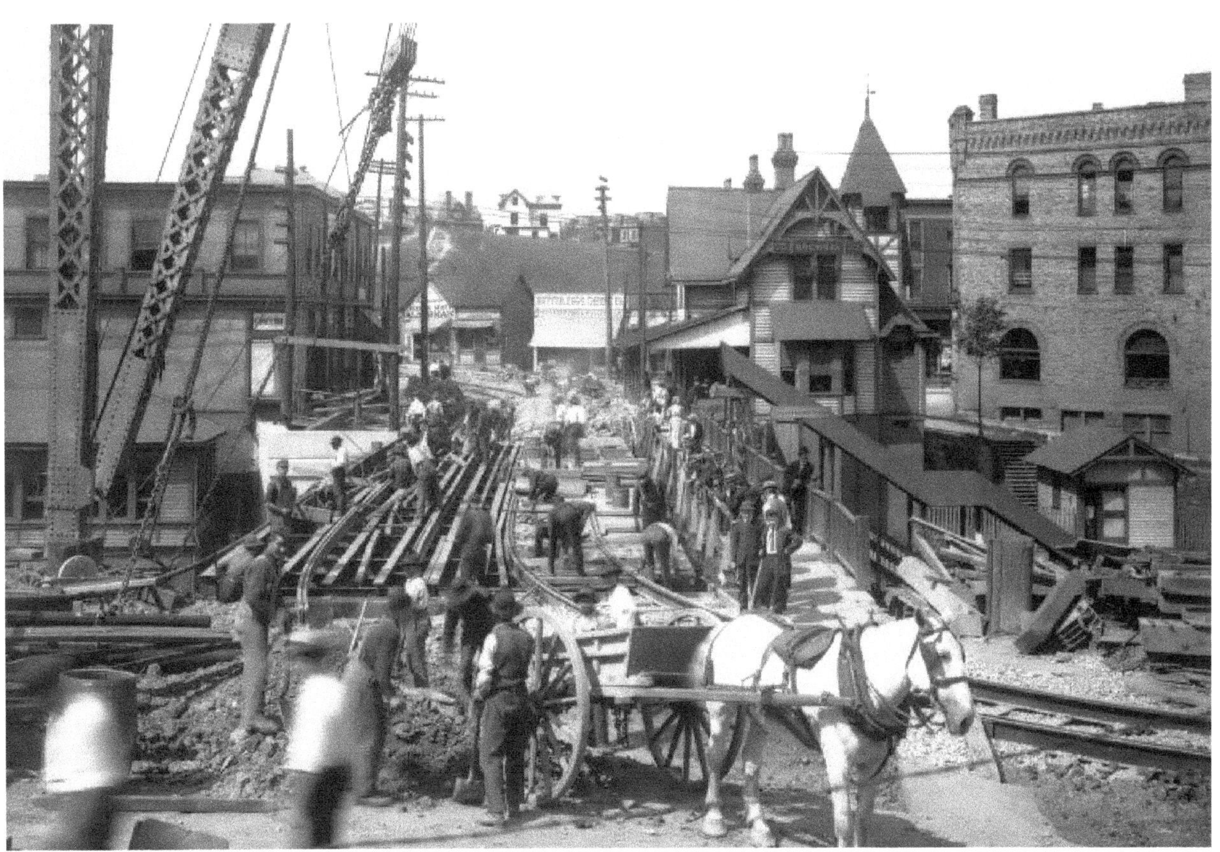

A view of Sheraden Bridge under construction, facing north across the bridge. The Sheraden train station stands to the right of the bridge.

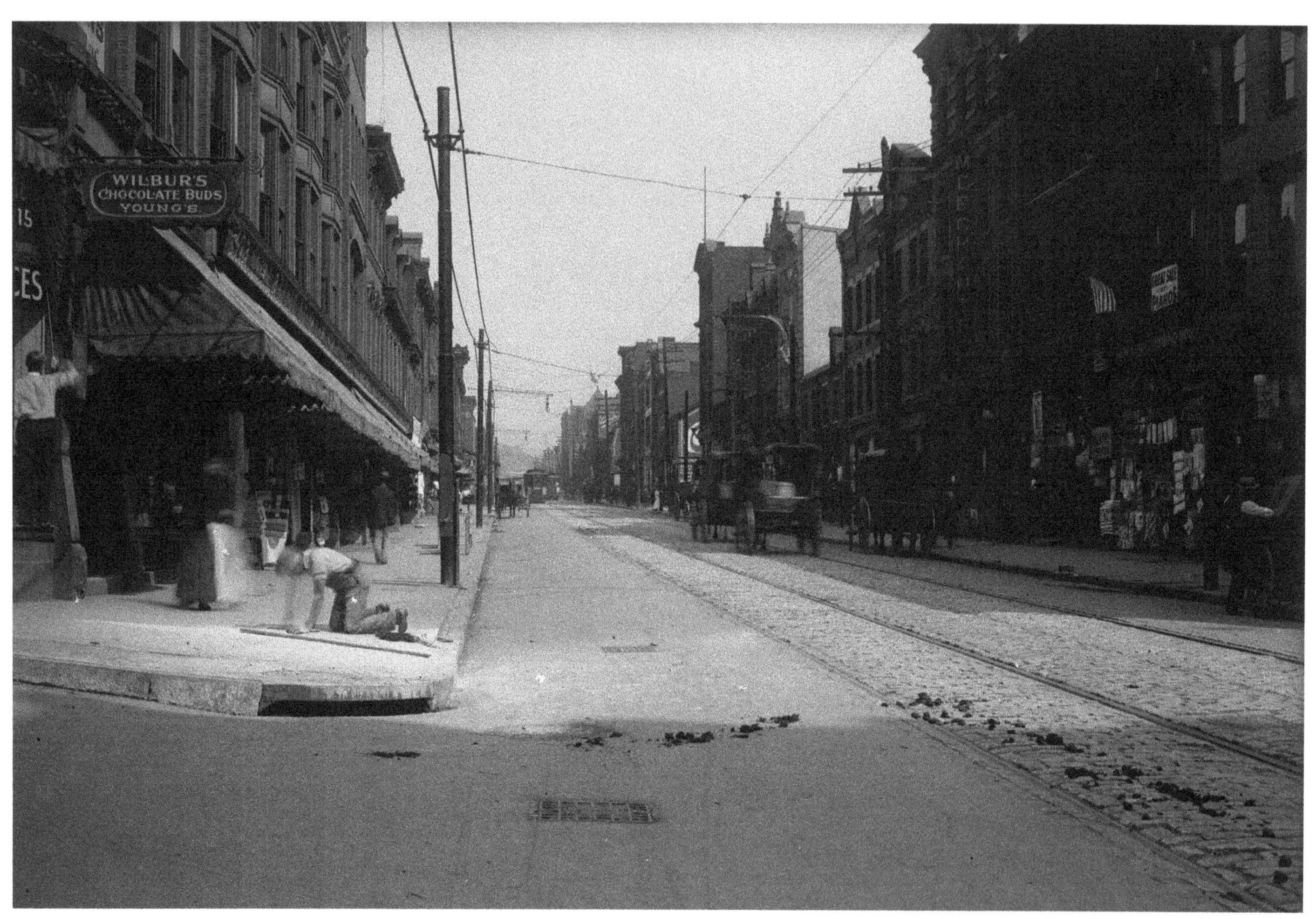

Pianos and other merchandise are for sale in the business district in the 1400 block of Fifth Avenue at Stephenson, Uptown.

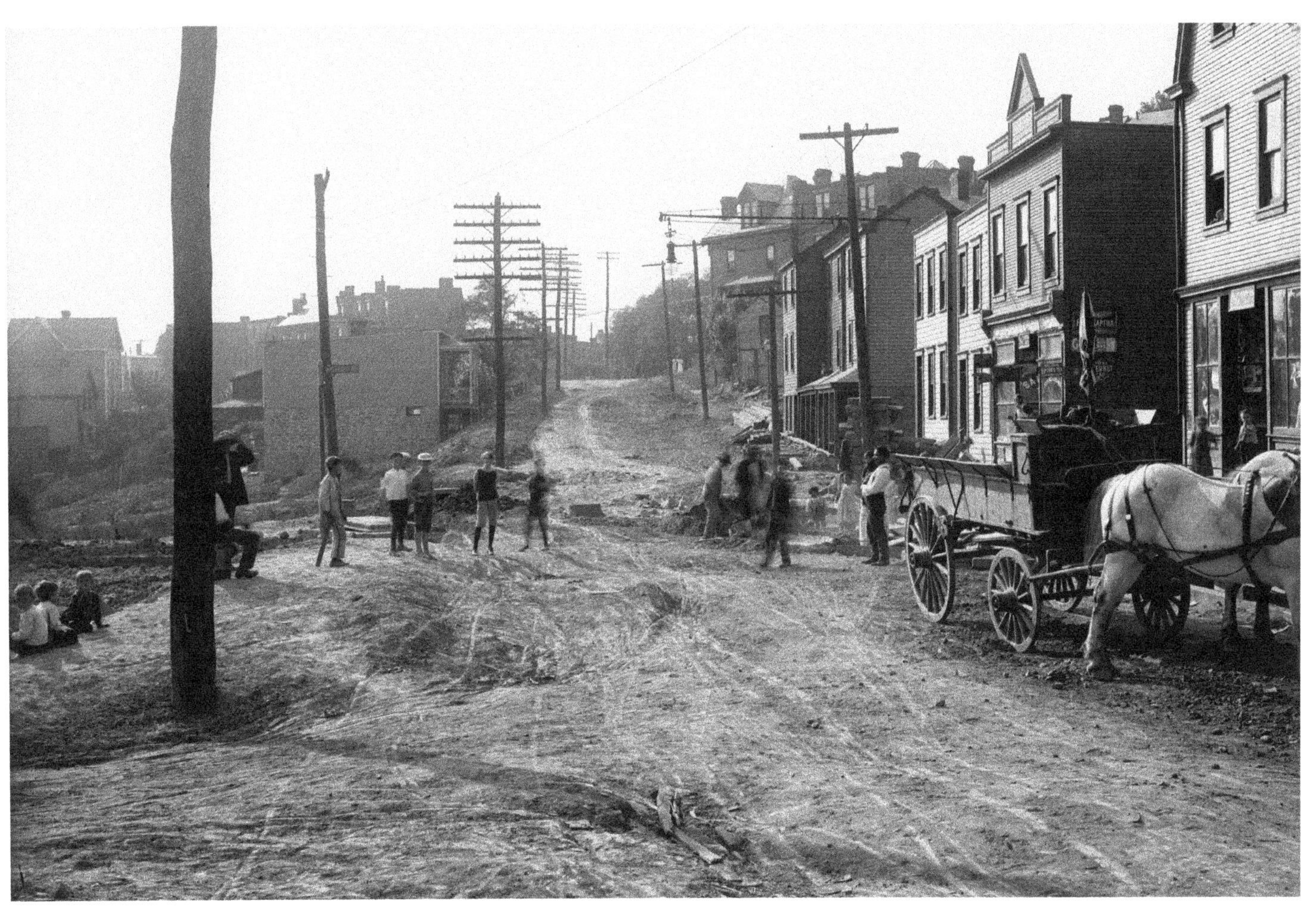

Road construction at the intersection of Chaucer Street and Murtland Avenue facing Lincoln Avenue in the Homewood.

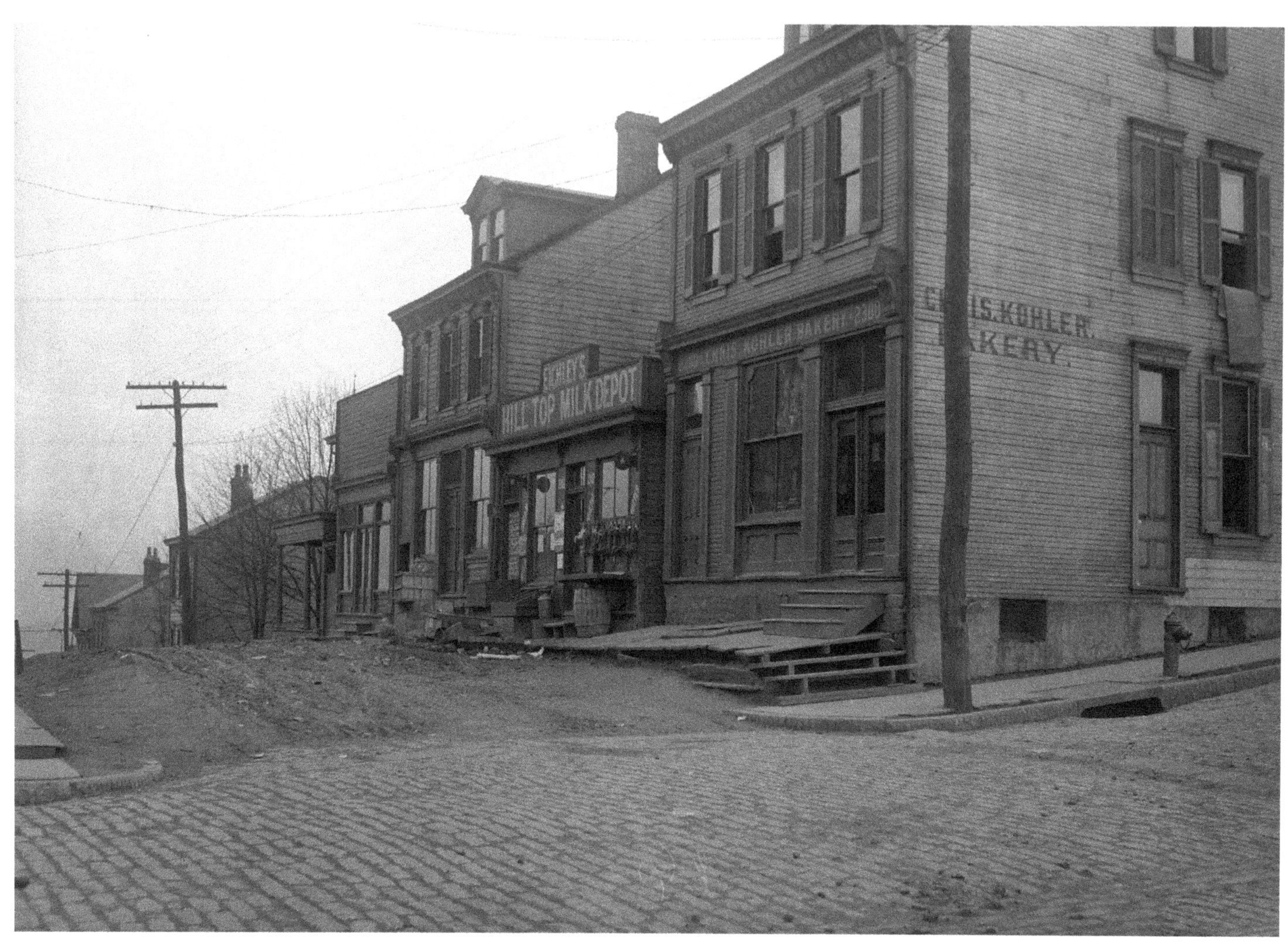

Eichley's Hill Top Milk Depot is open for business on Salisbury Street, in this view from Sterling.

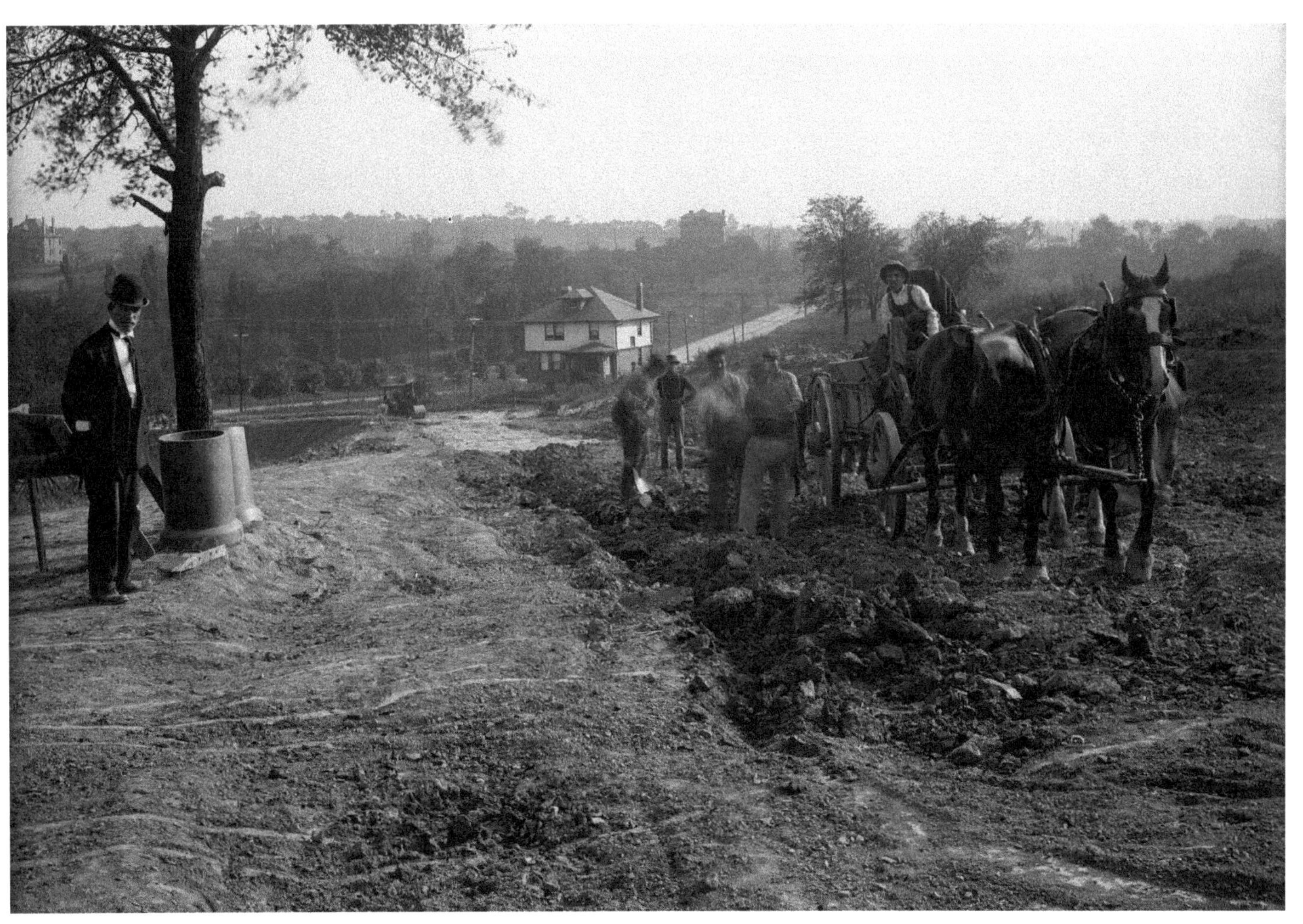

Pittock Street at Nicholson Street facing Shady Avenue in Squirrel Hill, with a view of construction in progress.

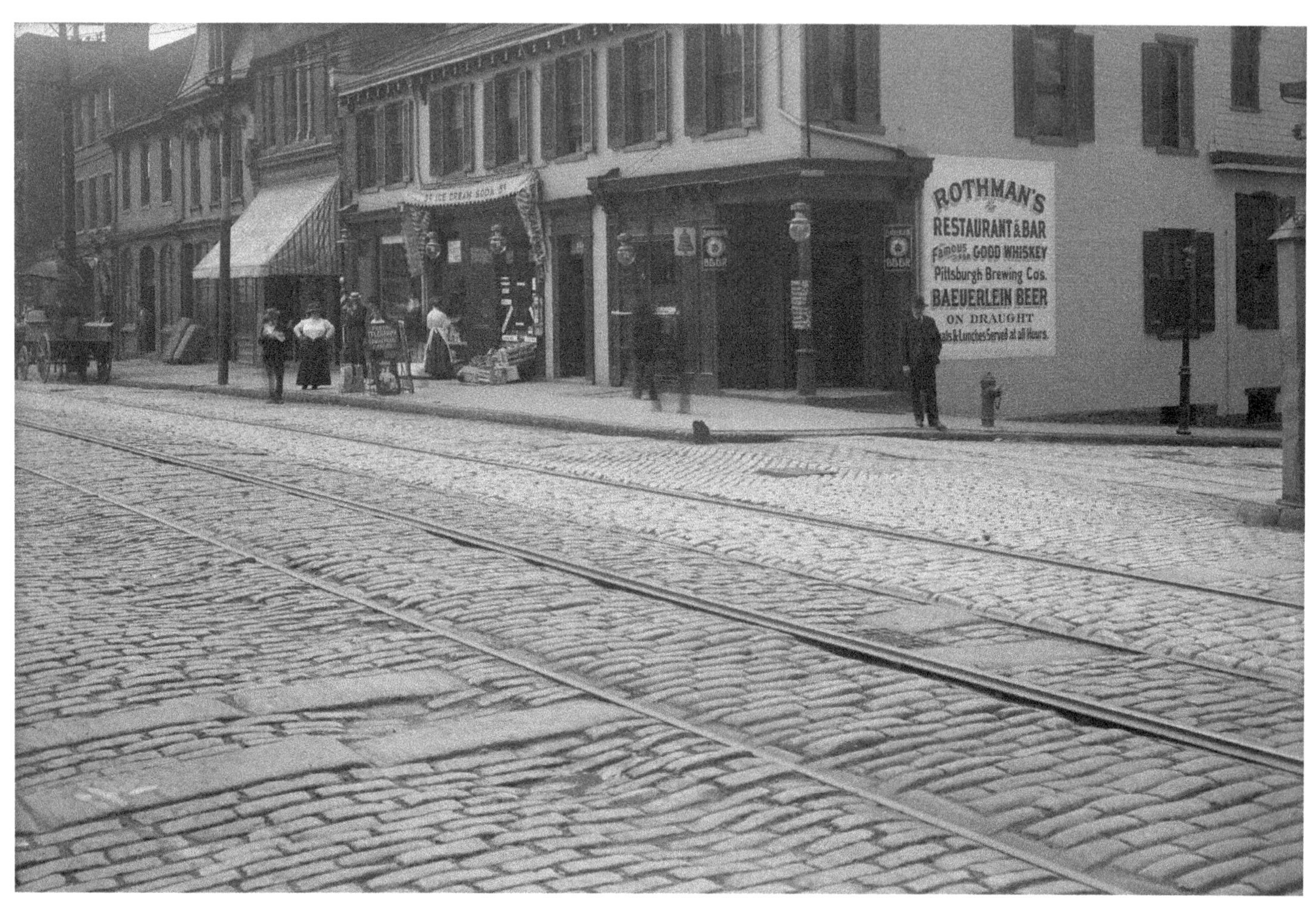

The cobblestone paving is clean swept in front of Rothman's Restaurant and Bar at the corner of Butler and 39th streets in Lawrenceville.

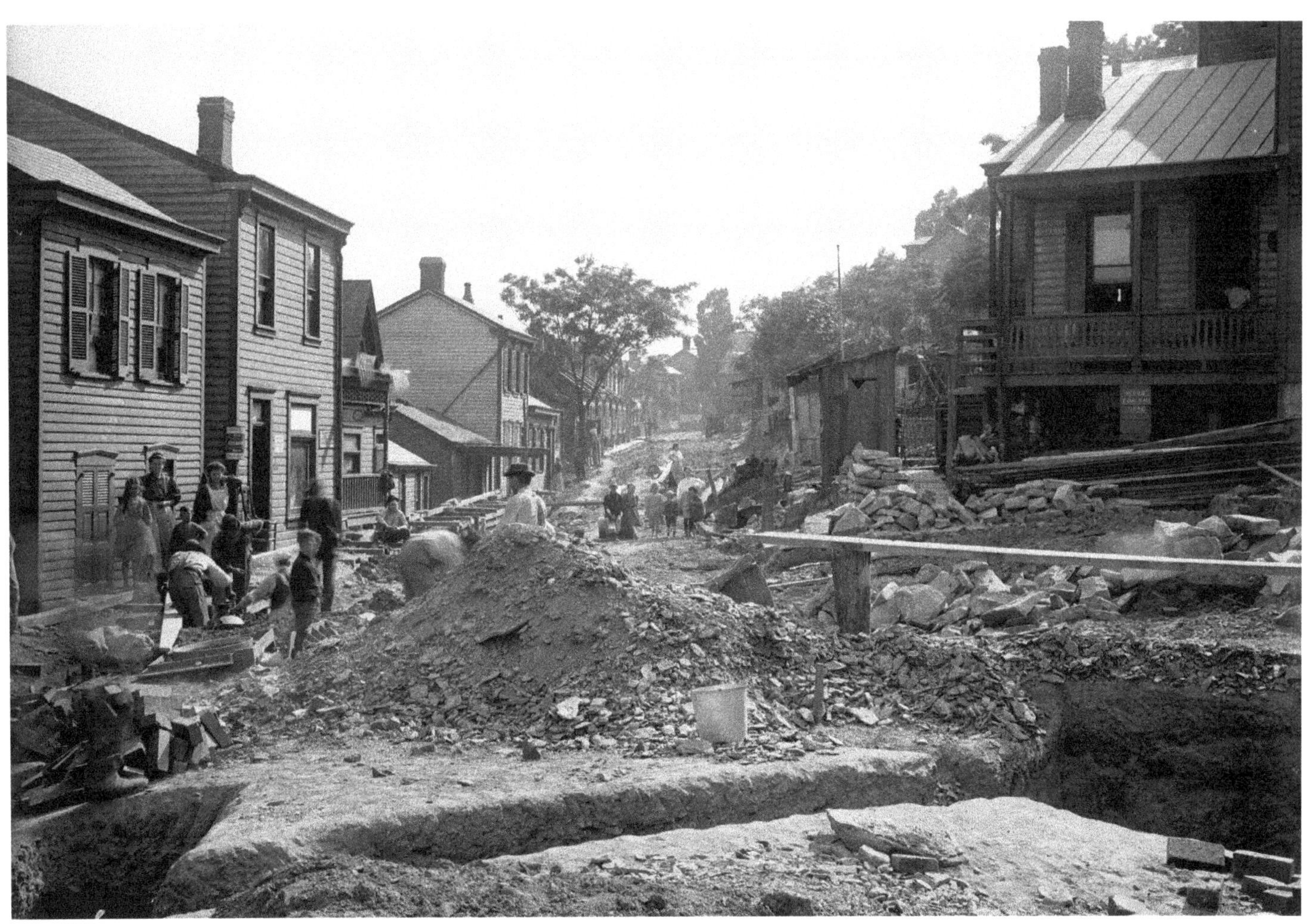

The neighborhood experiences an upheaval as road, sidewalk, and sewer construction progresses near the intersection of Excelsior and Eureka streets facing Emerald Street, where a group of children watch the proceedings.

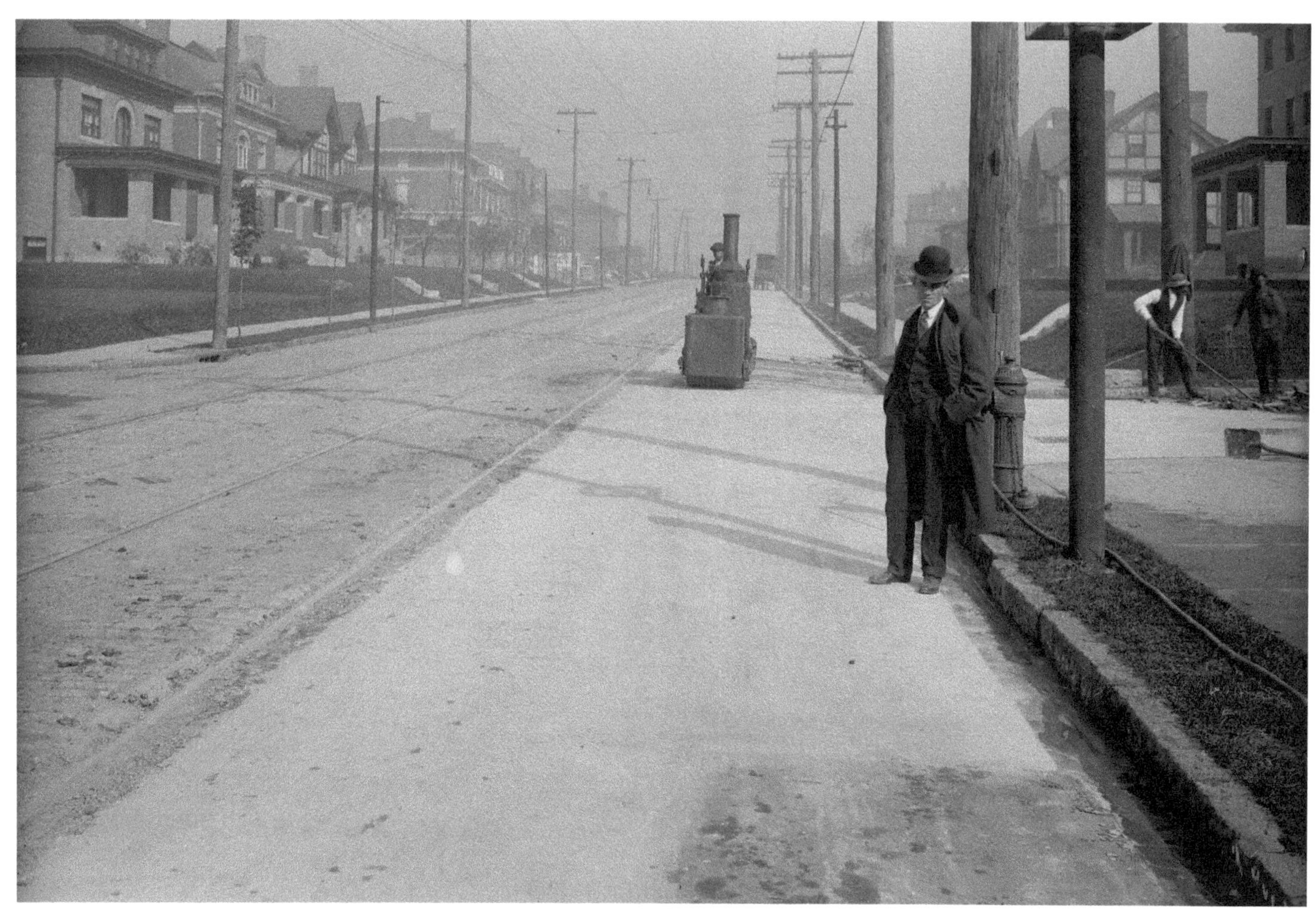

A steam-powered steamroller works on the road at the intersection of Negley Avenue and Hampton Street, facing north.

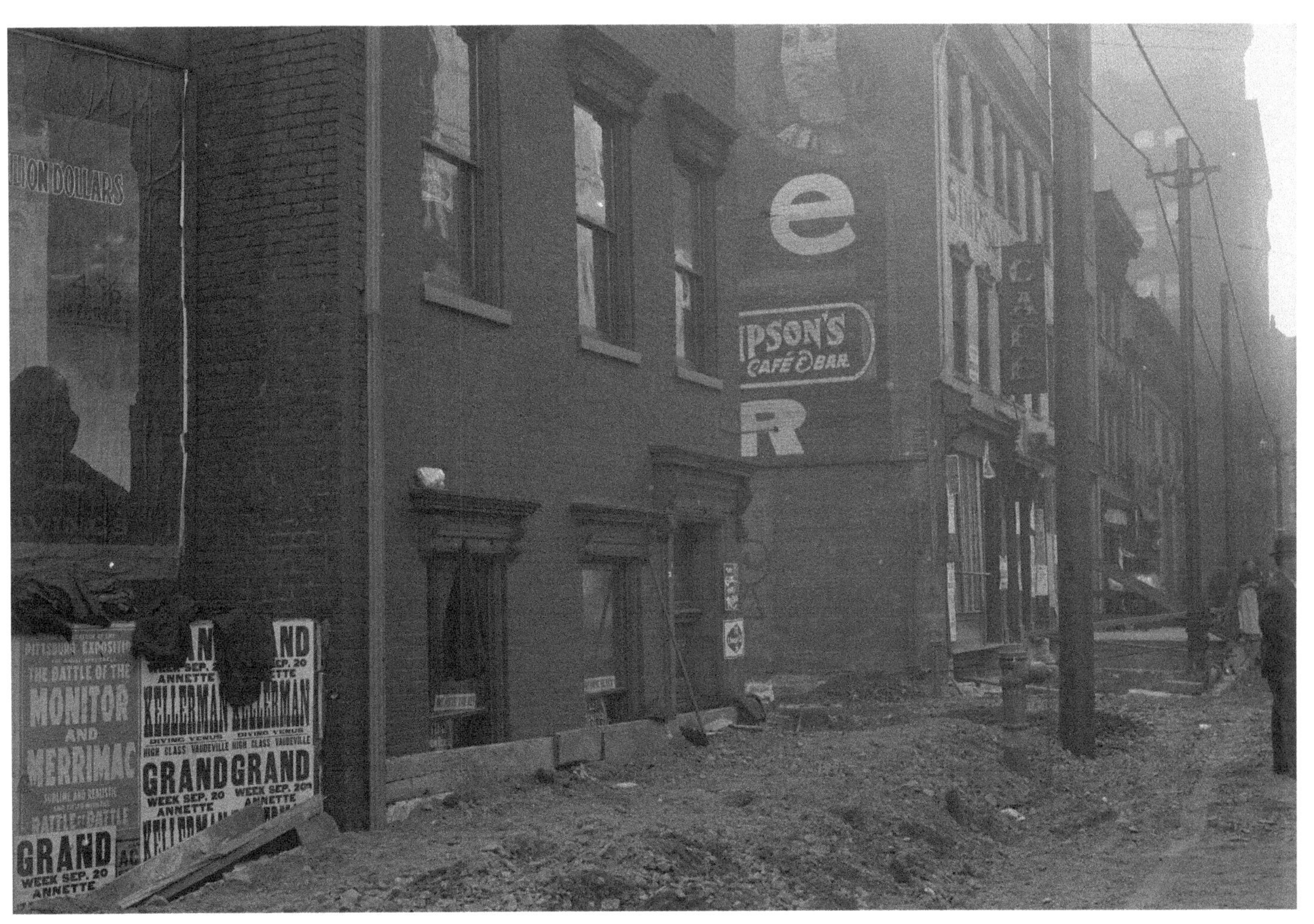

Goings-on at 129 9th Street downtown, below Penn Avenue. The cafe was known as Simpson's.

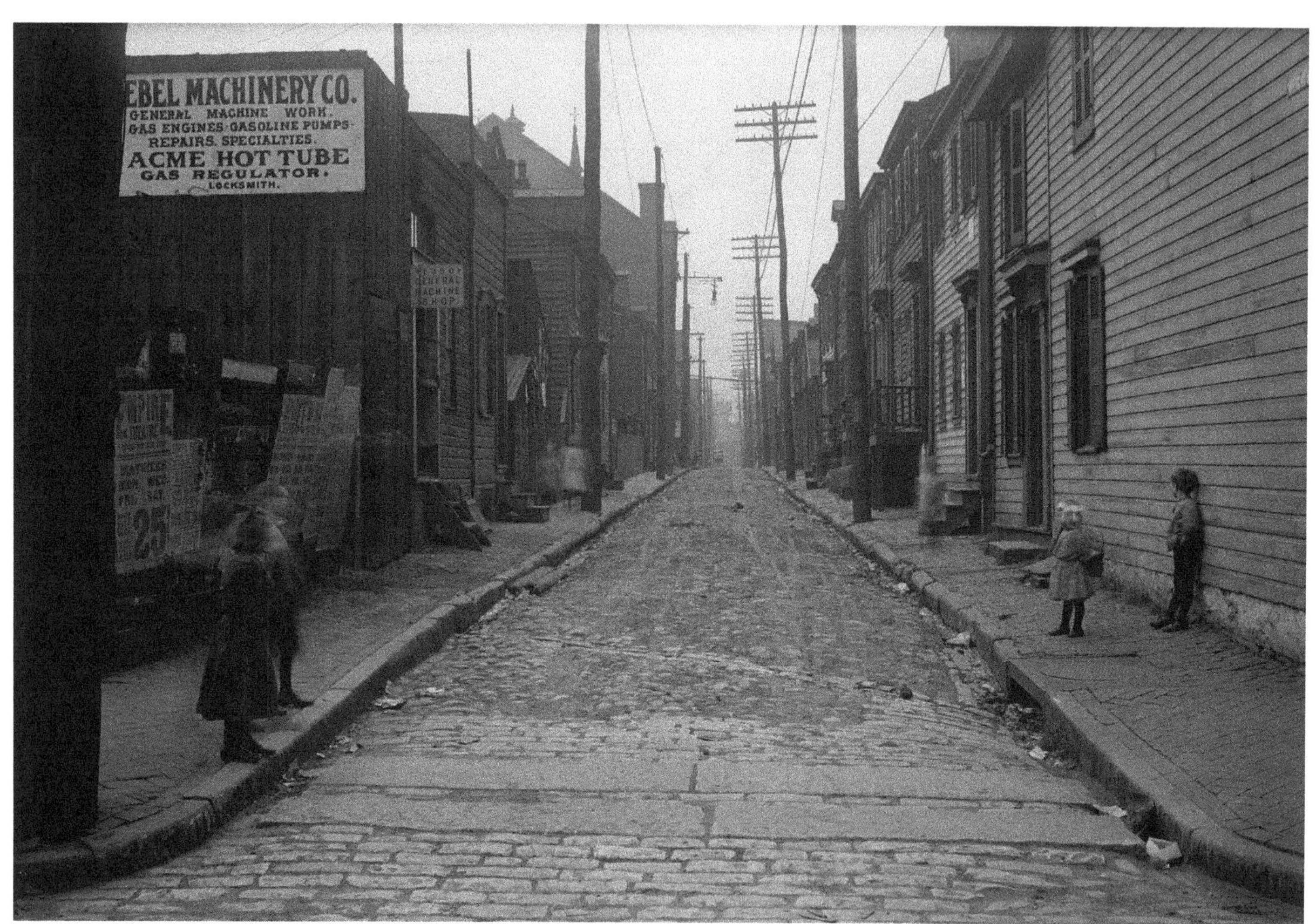

Wright's Alley homes and businesses near South 20th Street facing 19th Street.

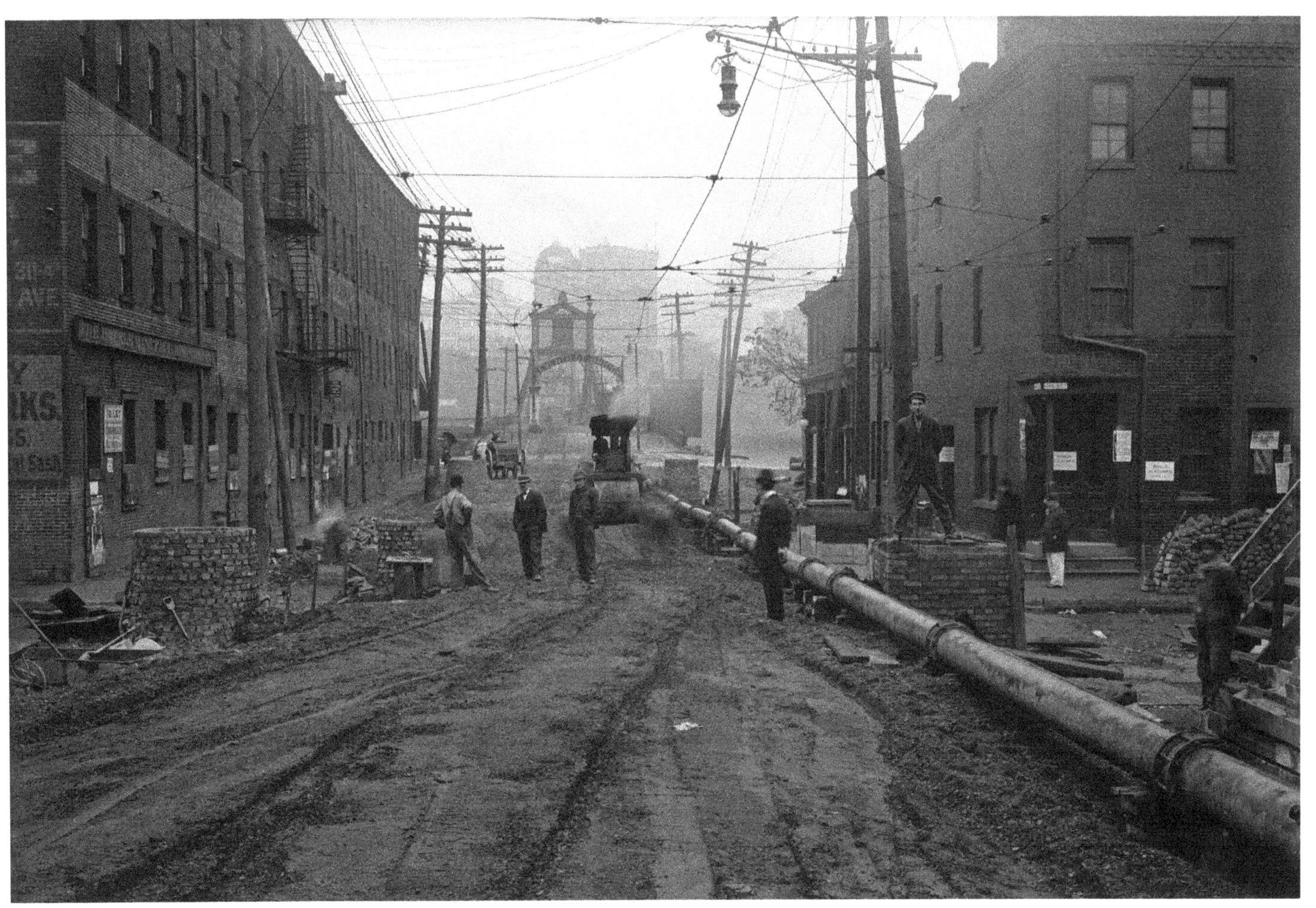

Sandusky and General Robinson Street facing the Seventh Street Bridge, with downtown Pittsburgh just visible through the haze. The bridge was designed by Gustav Lindenthal, who also designed the Smithfield Street Bridge. The Seventh Street Bridge was erected in 1884 and survived until 1925, when it was replaced. The Andy Warhol Museum now sits on this corner.

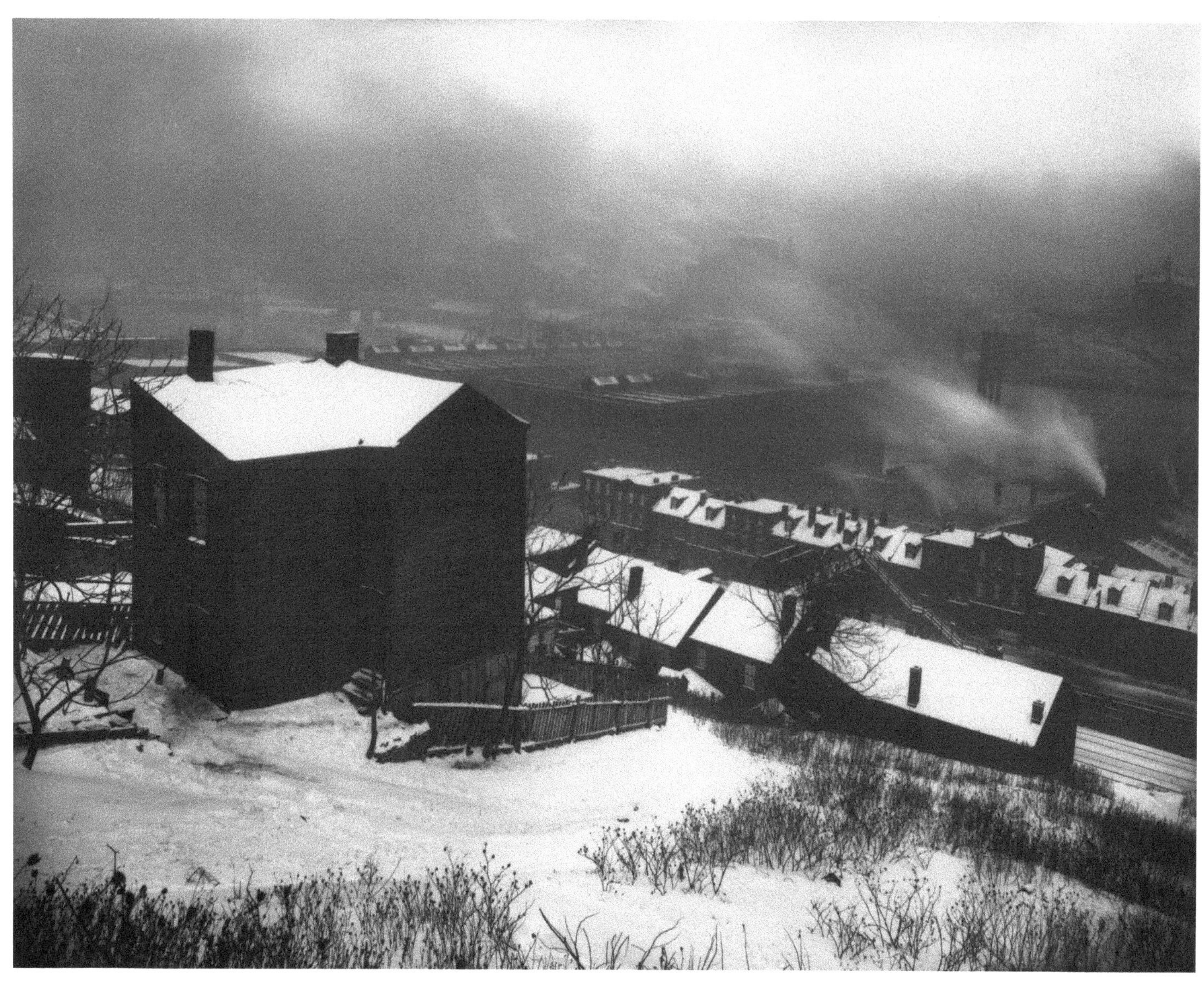

A wintry view of the South Side from Brownsville Avenue looking toward the Monongahela River and downtown Pittsburgh. Closer looks reveal the Pittsburgh Terminal Warehouse and Transfer Company.

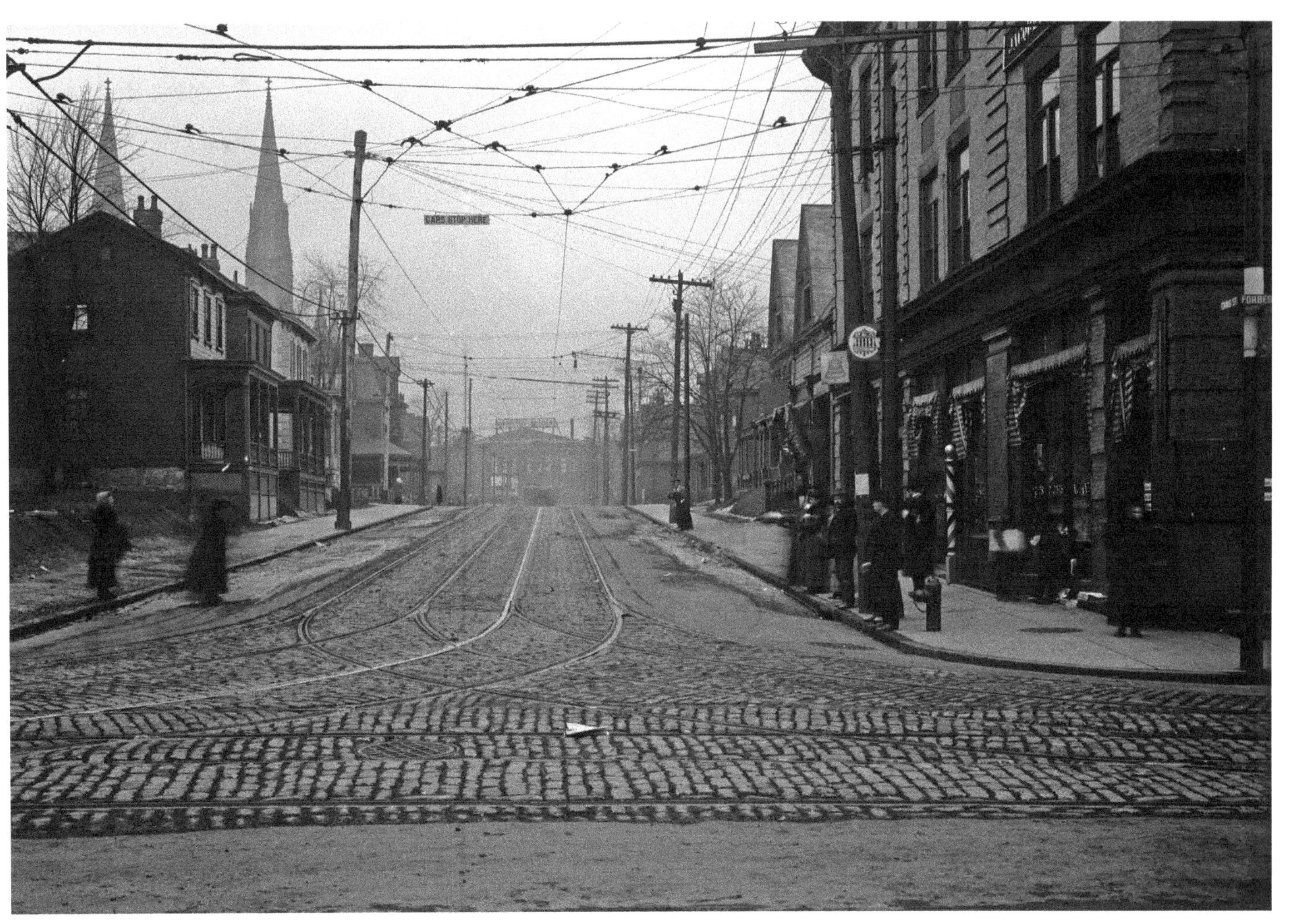

Craig Street as seen from the south end of the street at Forbes Avenue, facing north toward the Duquesne Garden and the spires of St. Paul's Cathedral in Oakland. On the sign at right, ice cream cones are advertised at five cents apiece.

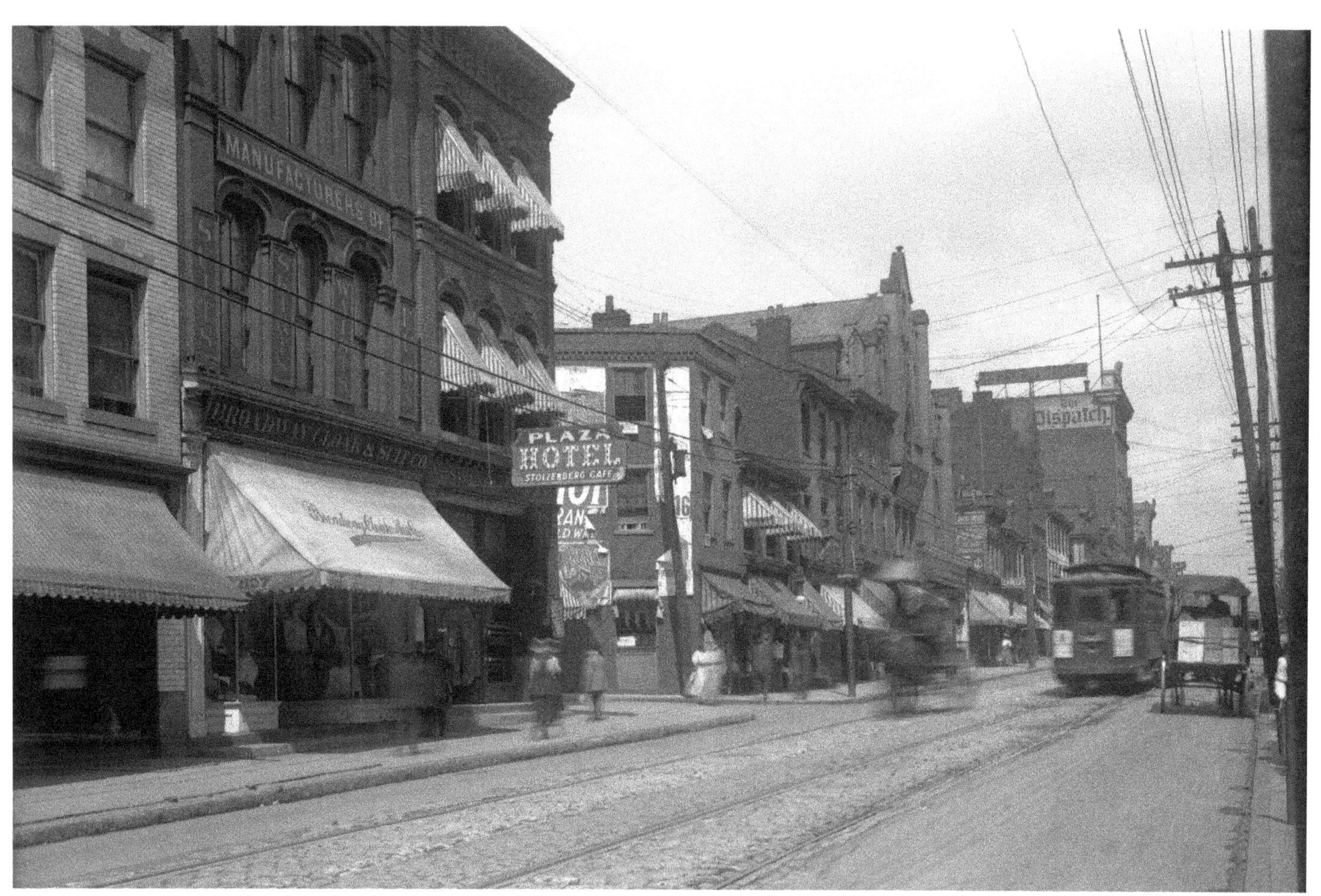

The 1100–1200 block of Fifth Avenue in the Uptown neighborhood between Logan Street and Elm Street.

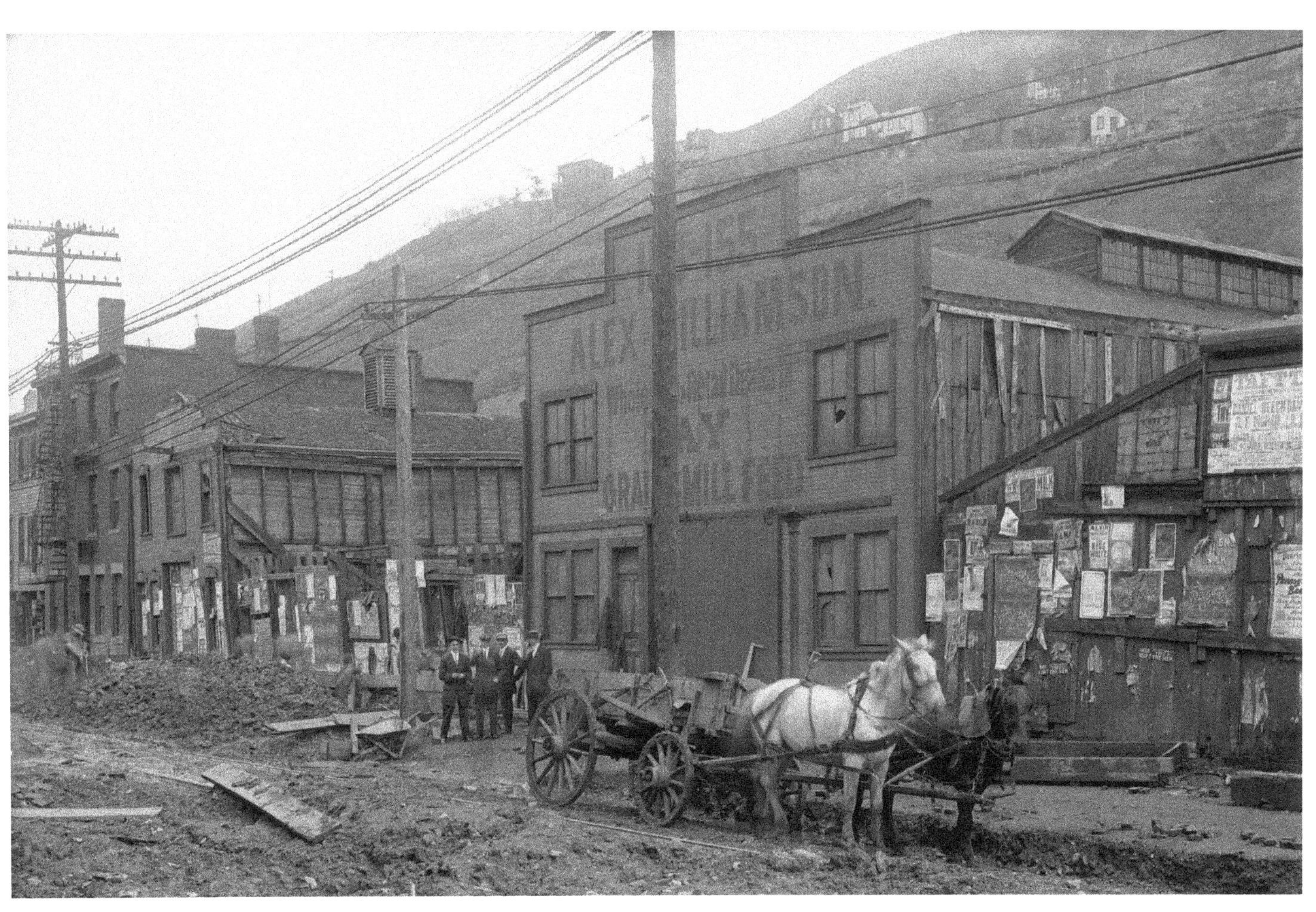

Alex Williamson was a dealer in wholesale and retail hay and feed at 153-155 South Main Street between Mill and Saw Mill Run.

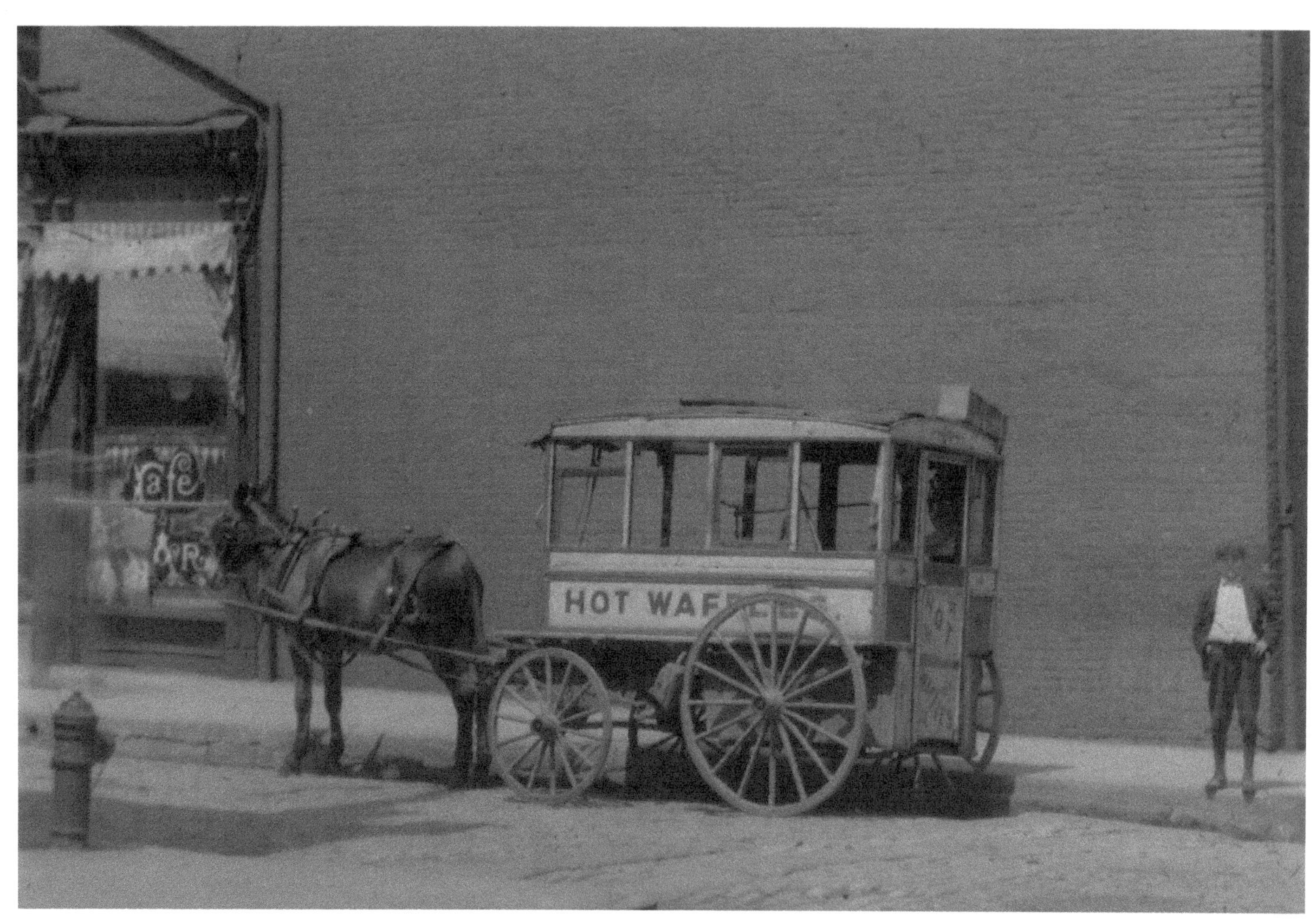

A street vendor sells "Hot Waffles" in 1912.

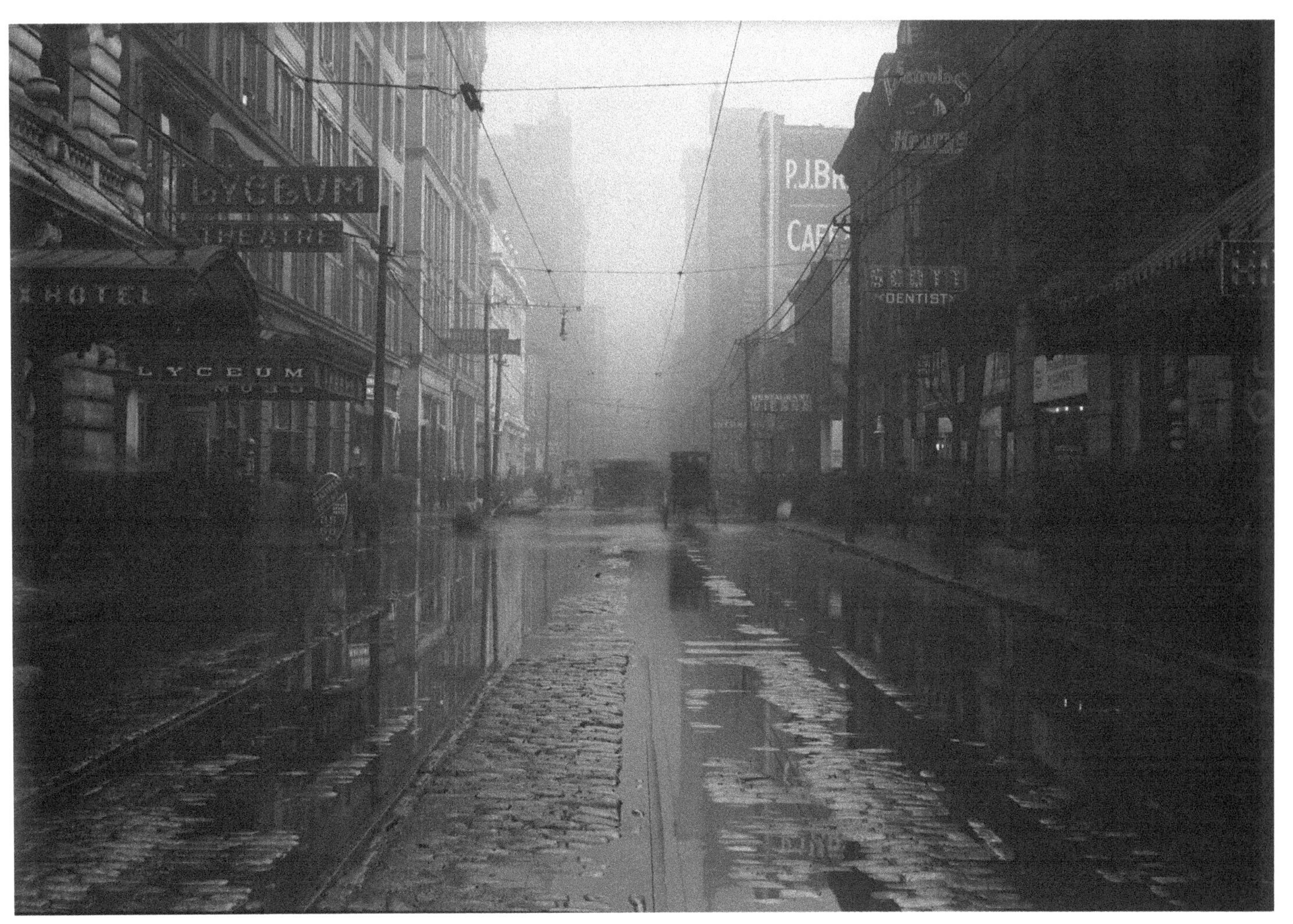

The Lyceum Theatre on Penn Avenue during the flood of January 9, 1913.

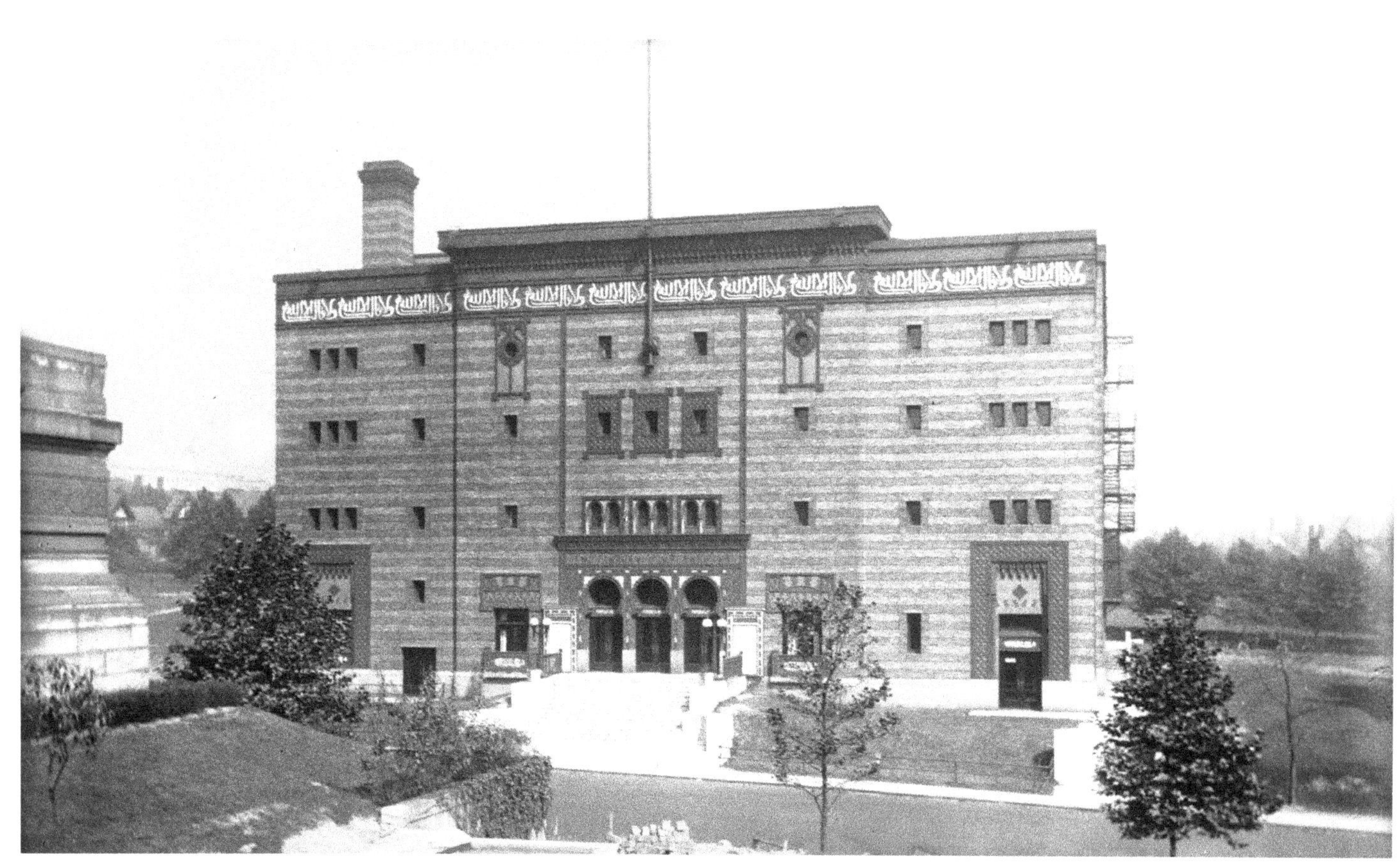

Syria Mosque, as it appeared sometime after 1913, was located near the Soldiers and Sailors Memorial Hall on Bigelow Boulevard.

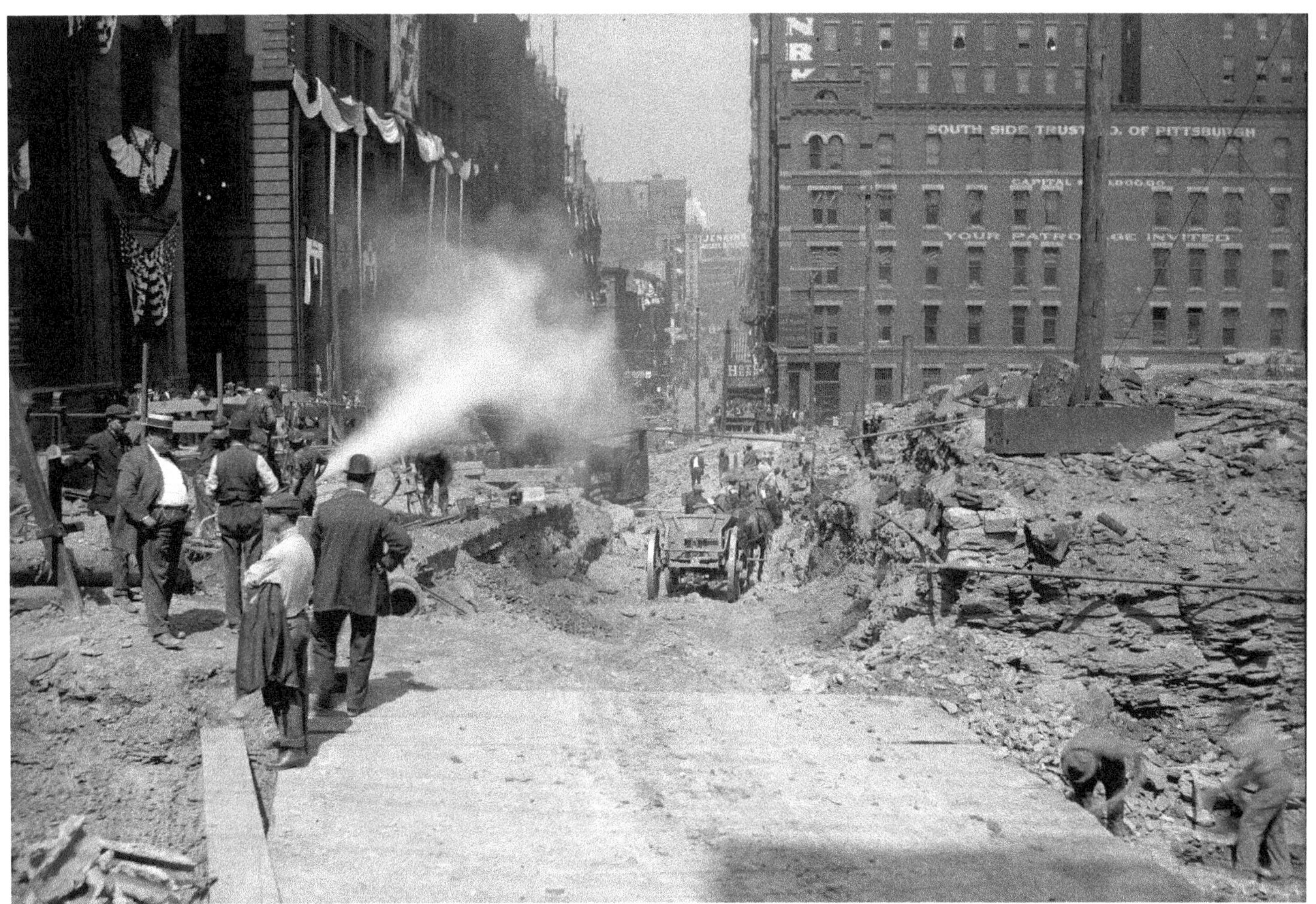

The "hump" at Grant's Hill, between the Hill District and downtown, is lowered in 1912. This view shows the work in progress at the intersection of Fifth Avenue and Grant Street. Planning for the project began in 1909 and work was completed in 1913. The project improved the gradient of Grant and Diamond streets, and Oliver, Fifth, Sixth, Webster, and Wylie avenues.

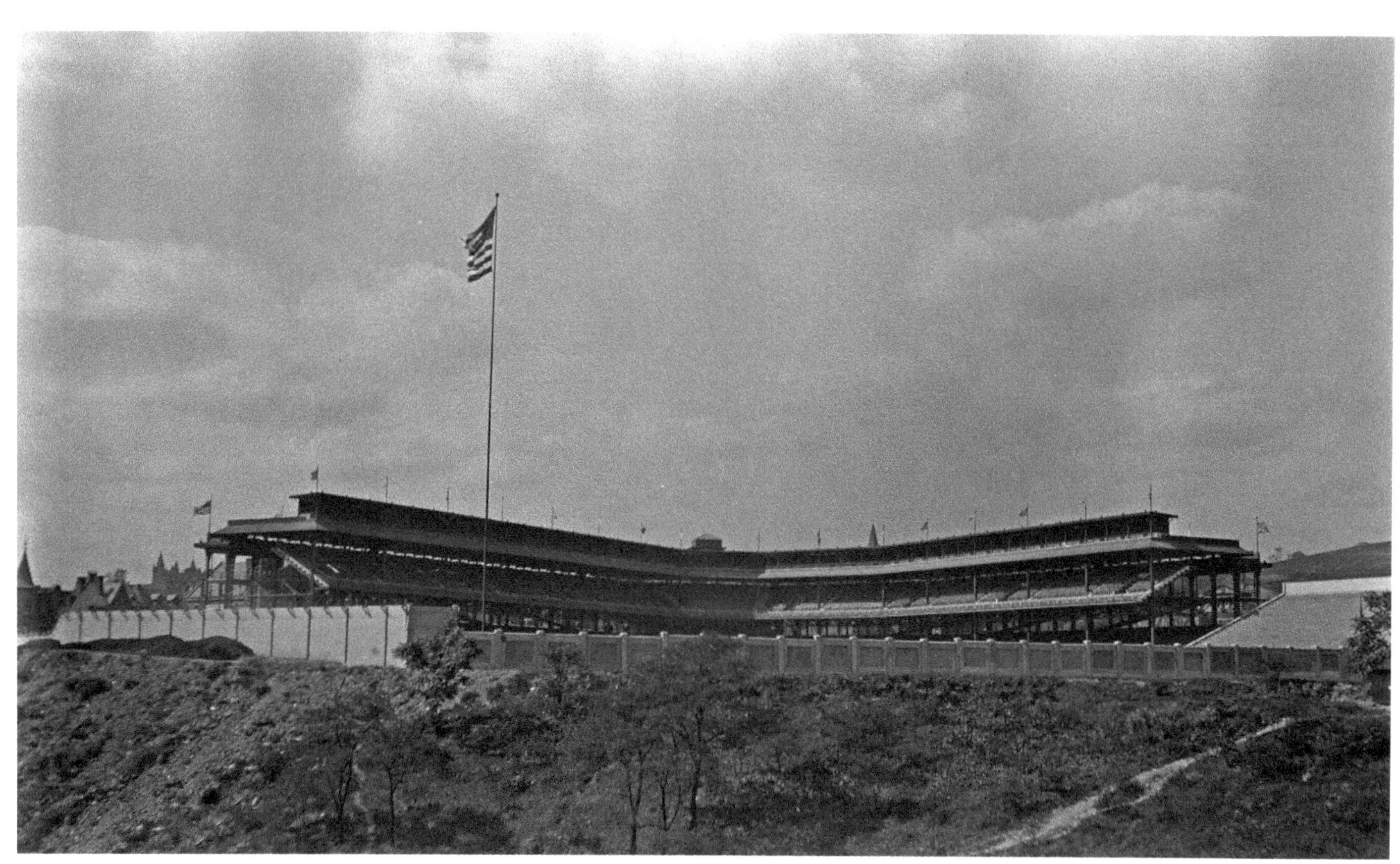

Forbes Field as seen from St. Pierre Ravine sometime between 1907 and 1913, when the ravine was filled with debris from the Hump District project.

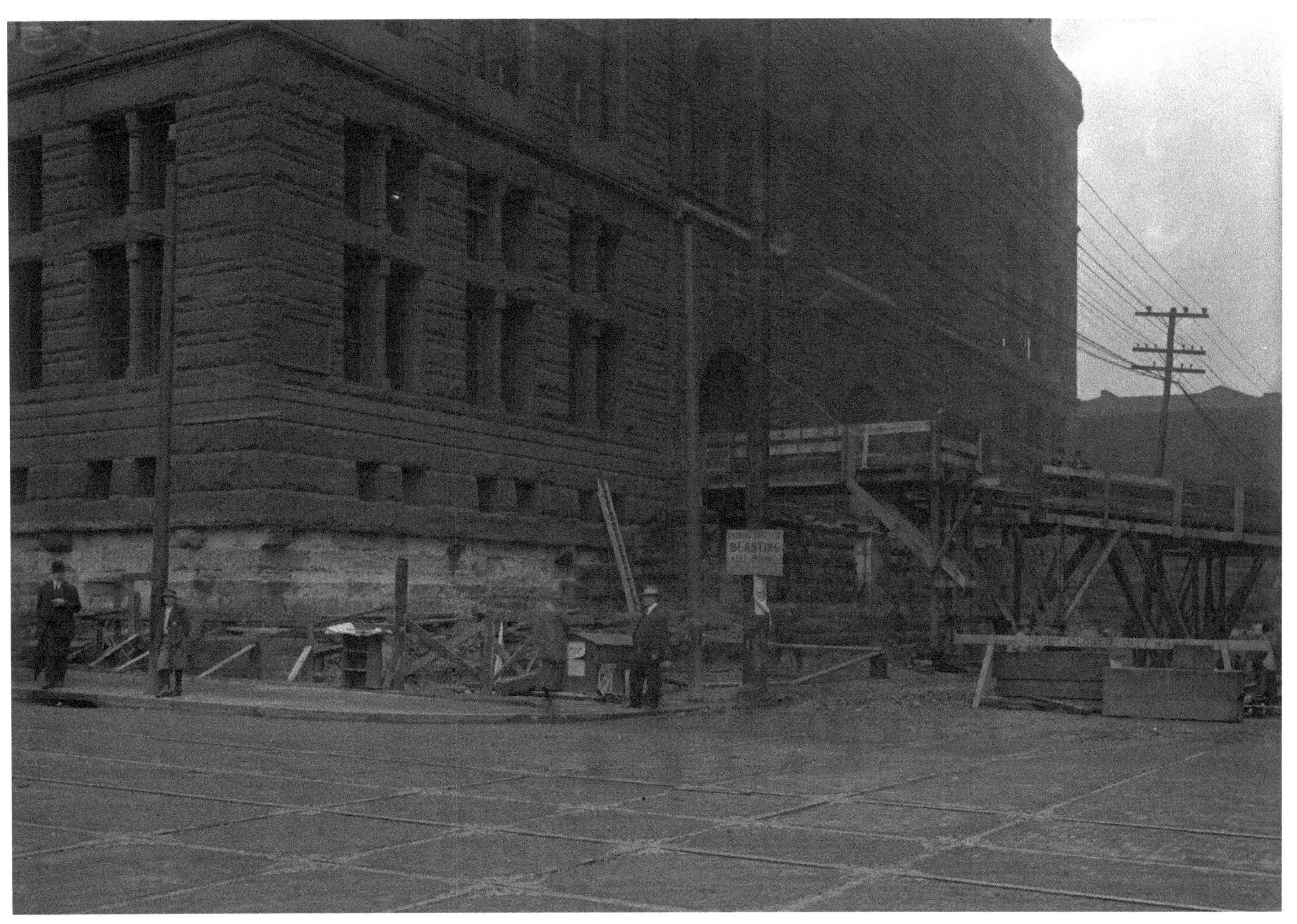

Allegheny County Courthouse at Grant Street from the corner of Fifth Avenue, March 26, 1913, photographed during the "Hump" project.

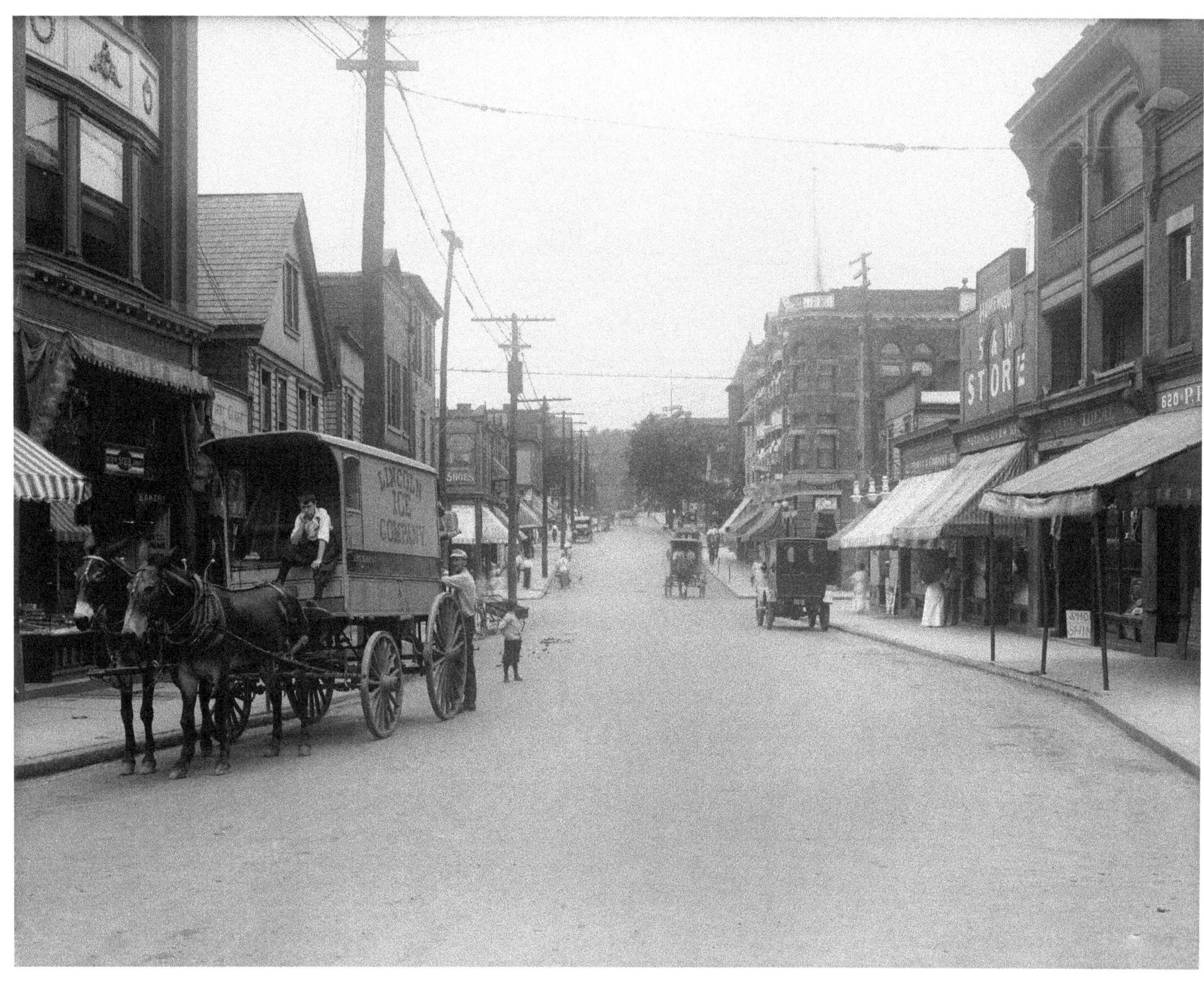

A Lincoln Ice Company delivery wagon pulls up in front of the Nicholas Bakery at 619 Homewood Avenue in 1914. Across the street, nothing costs more than ten cents at the Homewood 5 & 10.

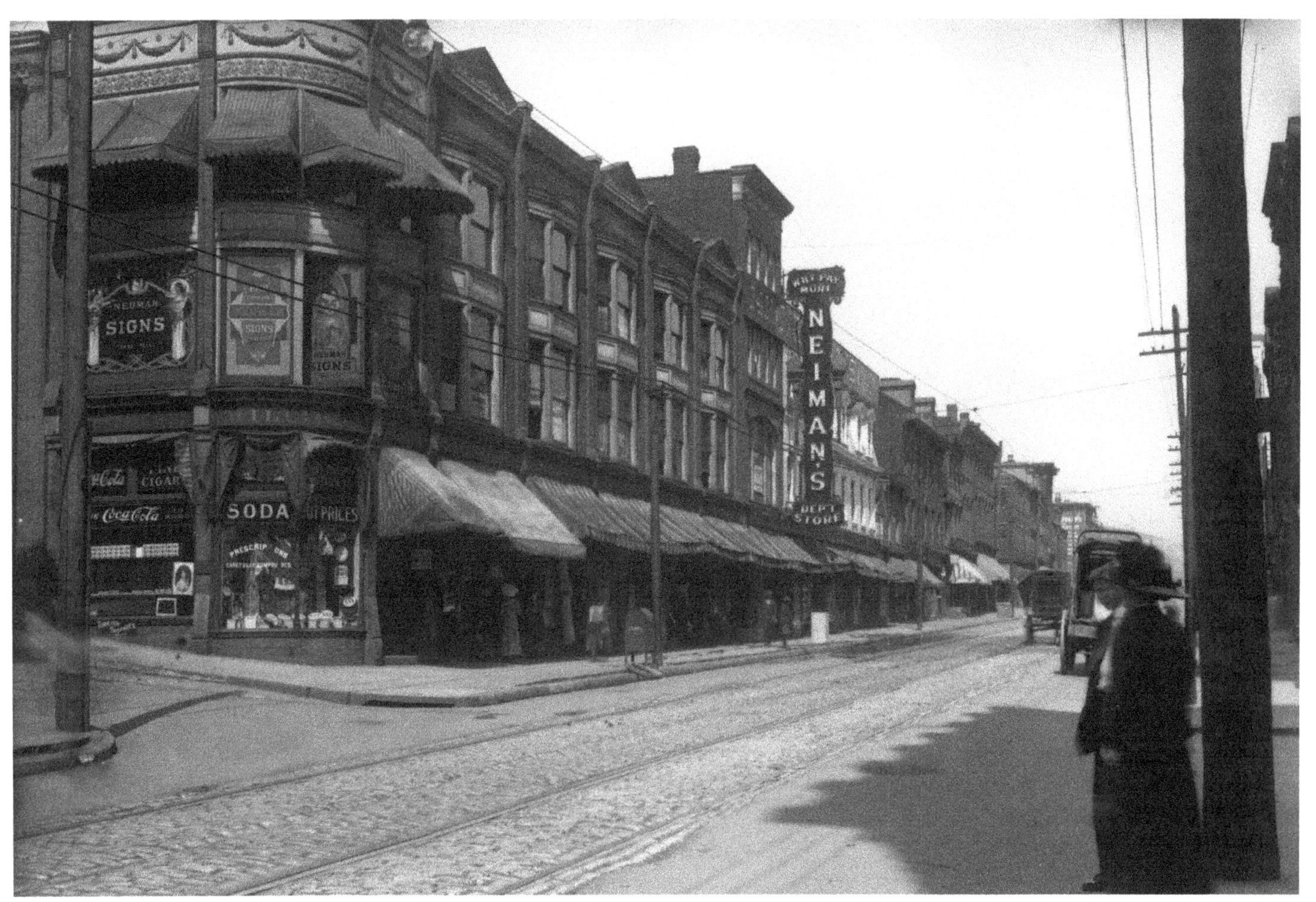

Neiman's Department Store is open for business on Fifth Avenue between Stephenson and Pride streets. Long before the advent of computer-generated signage, businesses like Neuman Signs employed skilled craftsmen to hand-letter signs of all kinds. The skill required a steady hand, a sharp eye, and long hours of practice, yet those with enough pluck to master it, when lacking recourse to trade schools, were self-taught.

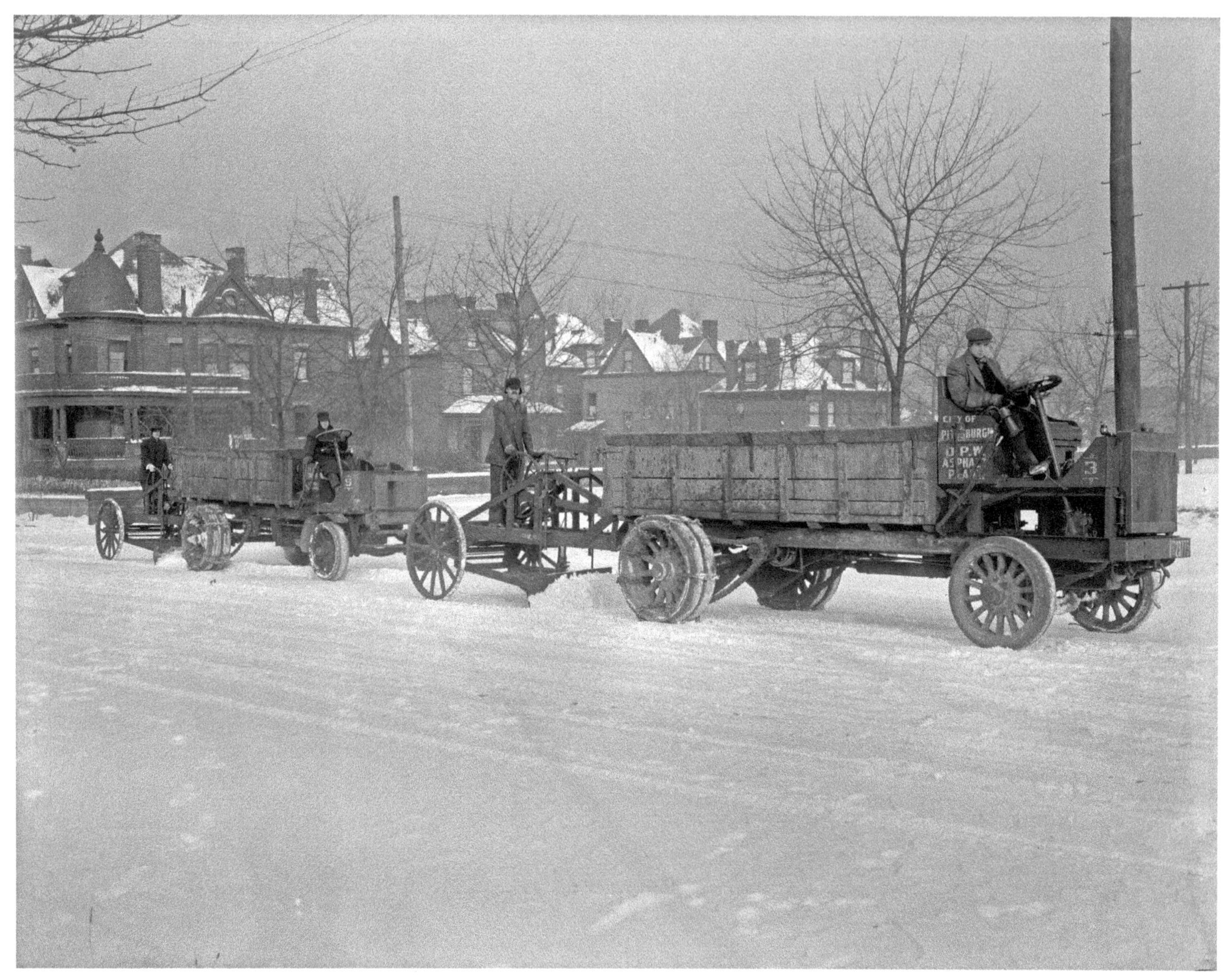

The Pittsburgh Department of Public Works demonstrates snowplowing in 1914.

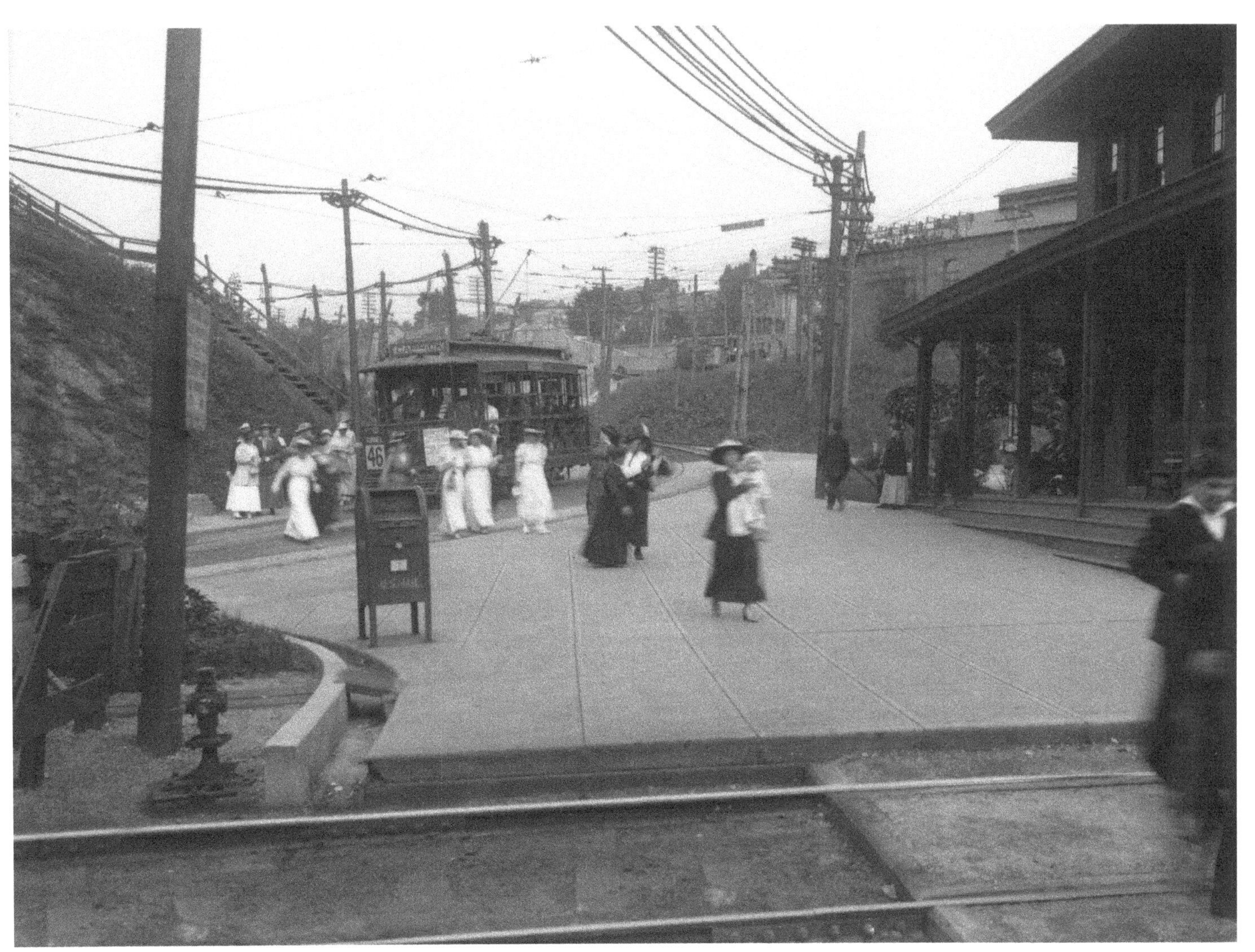

Passengers debark the Carrick Street streetcar in 1916.

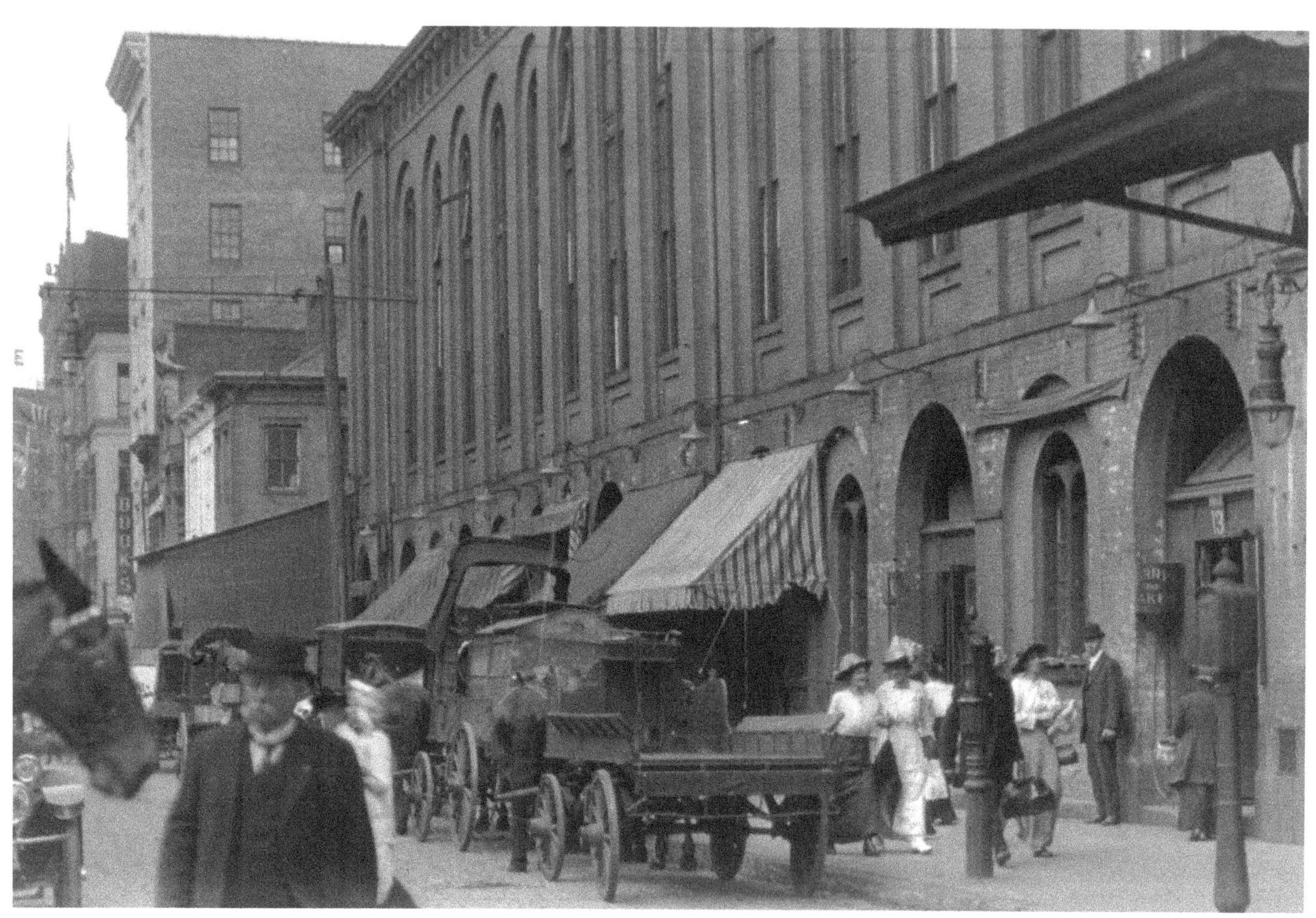

The Diamond Market, downtown, in 1914.

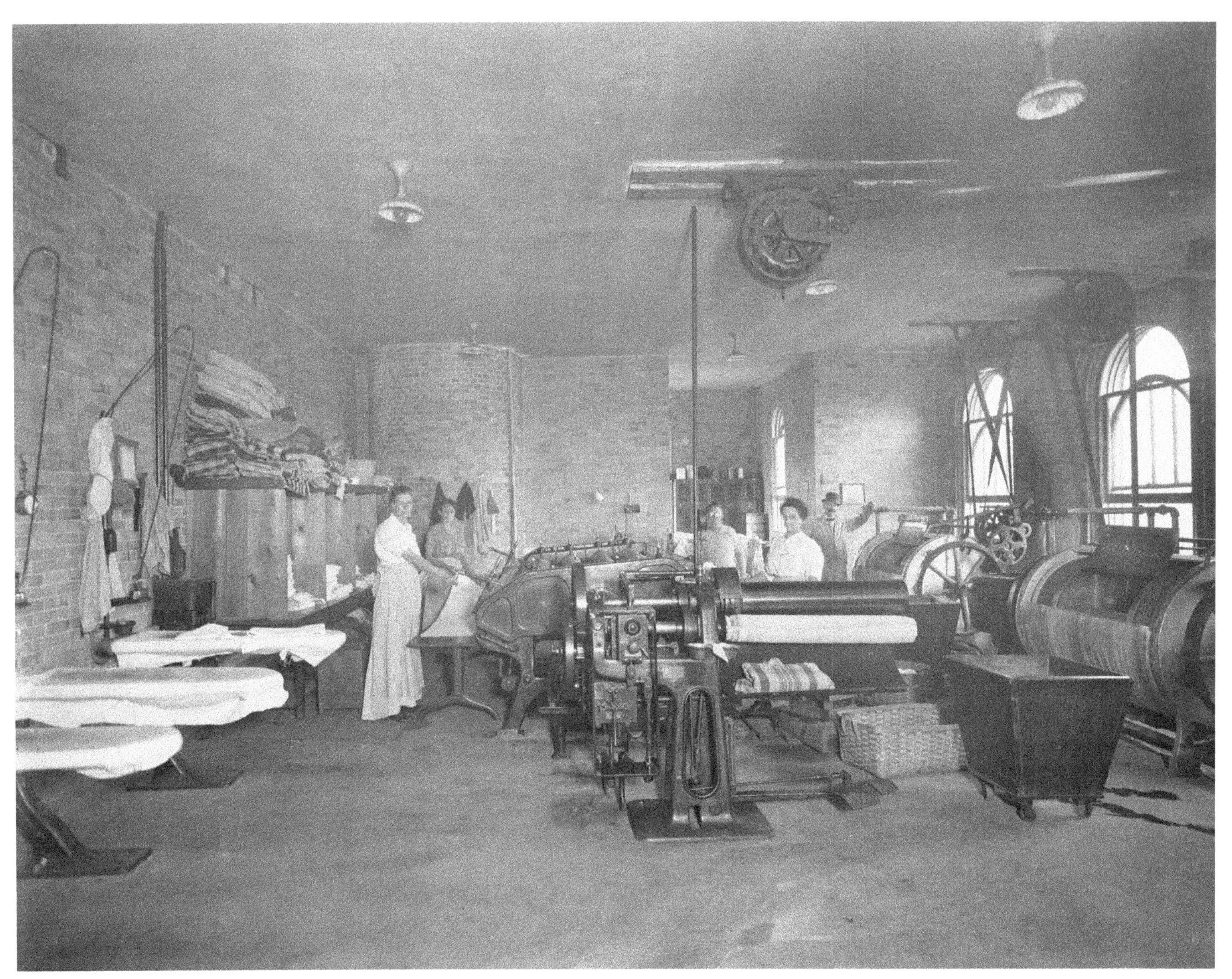

Laundry facilities of the Municipal Hospital in 1914.

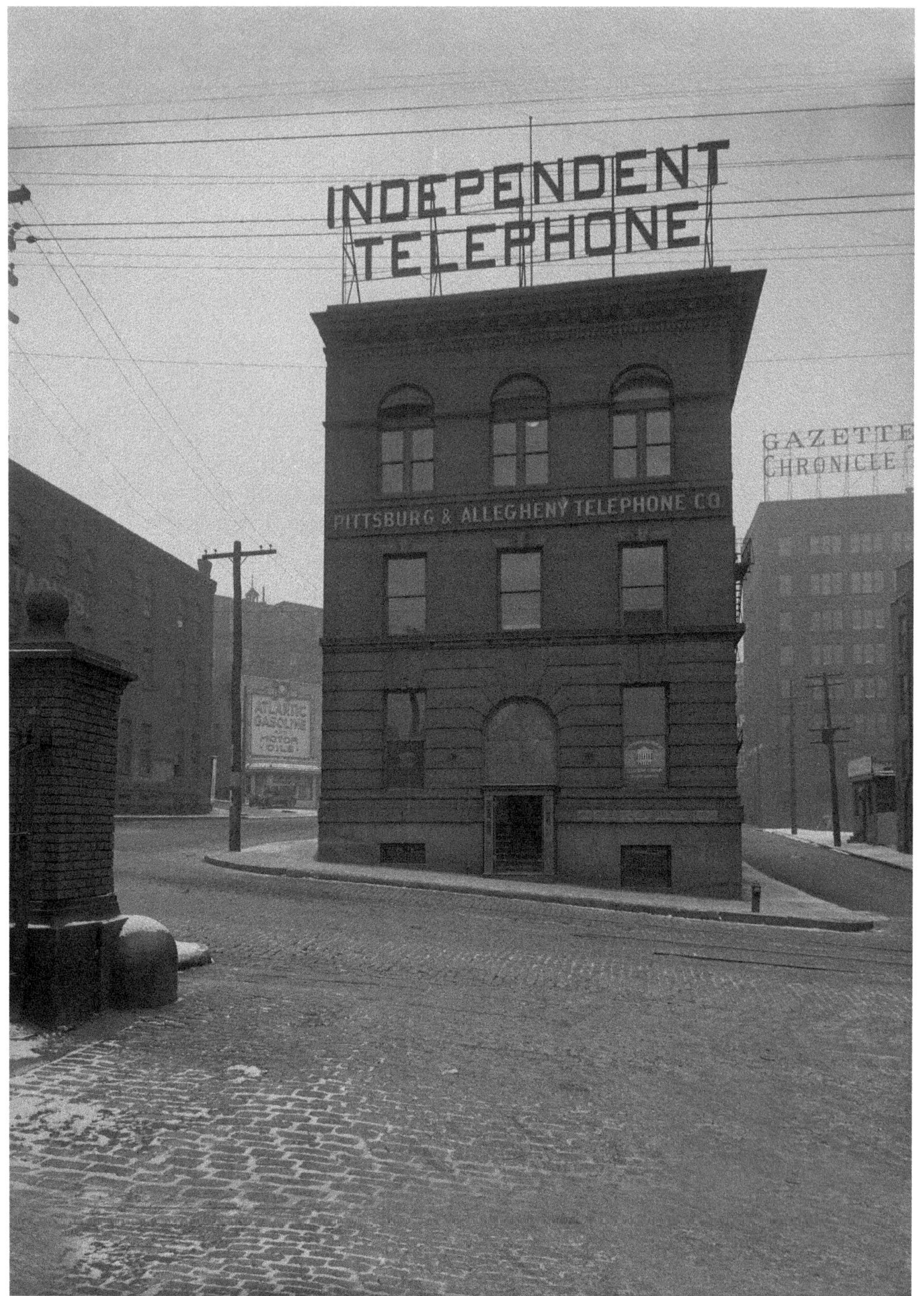

The Pittsburgh and Allegheny Telephone Company Building at Seventh Avenue and Grant Boulevard. The Gazette-Times and Chronicle Telegraph newspaper building is visible in the background.

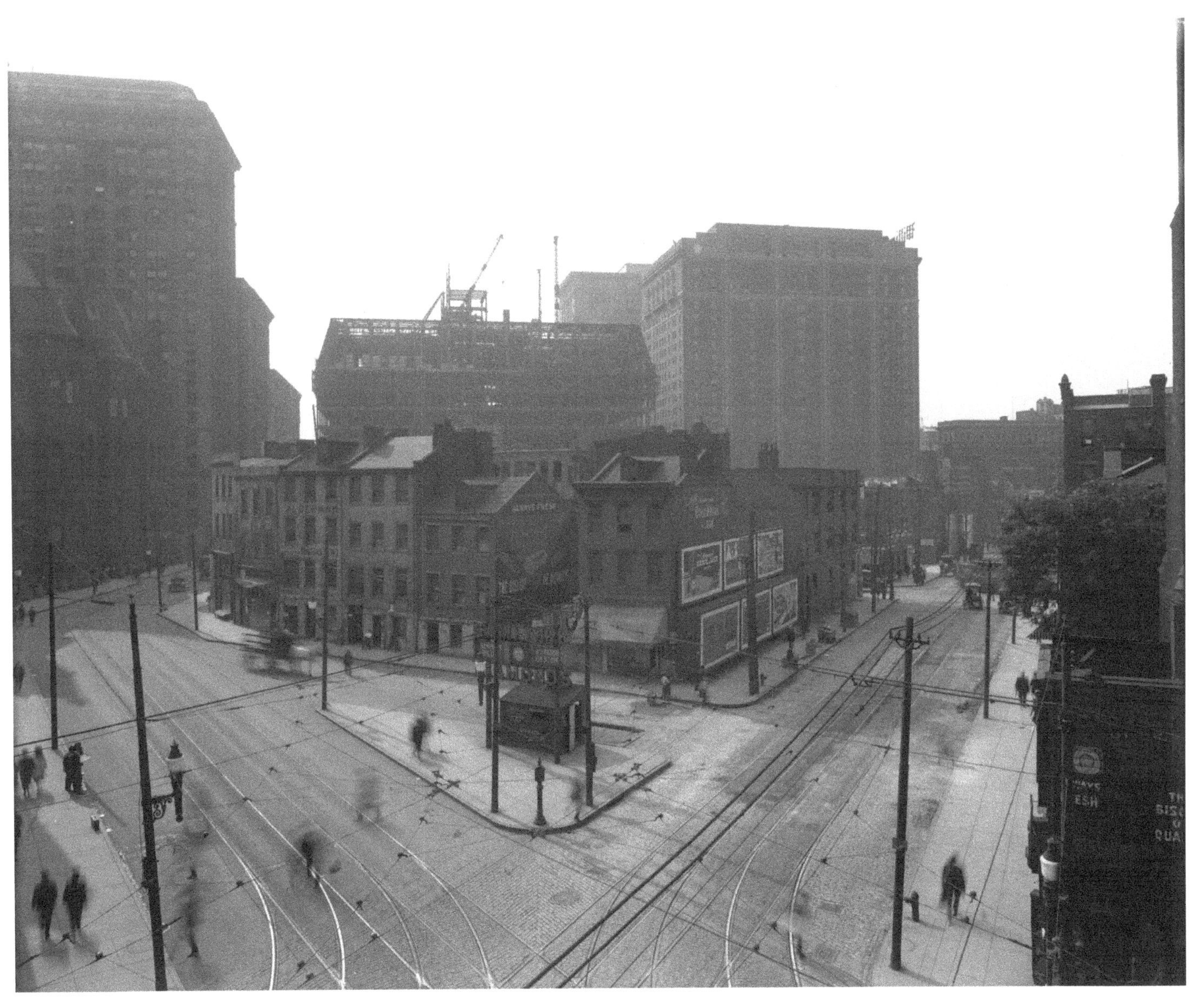

A view of Fifth and Sixth avenues facing west, showing the construction of the Union Arcade.

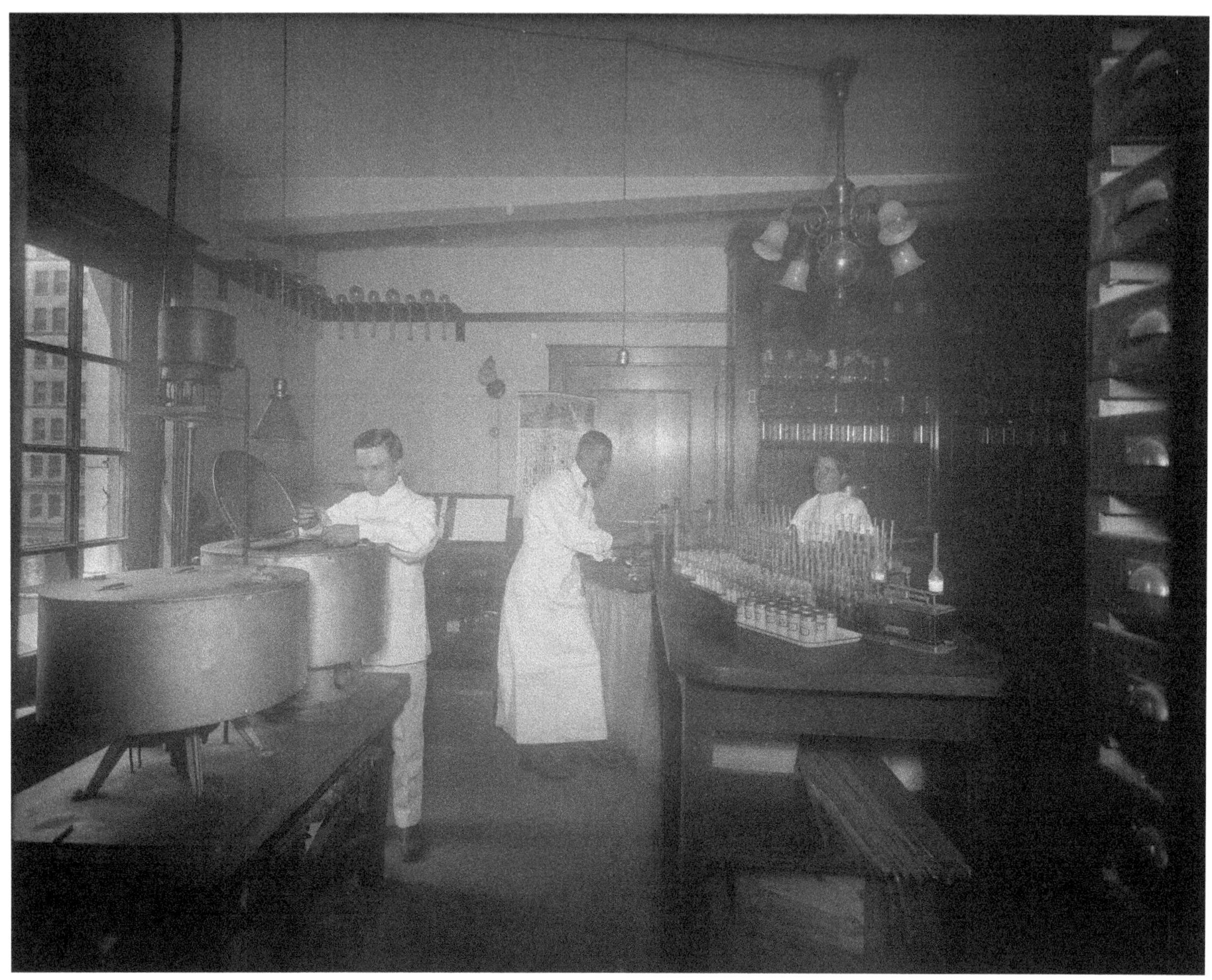

Testing milk at the Pittsburgh Food Division in August 1914.

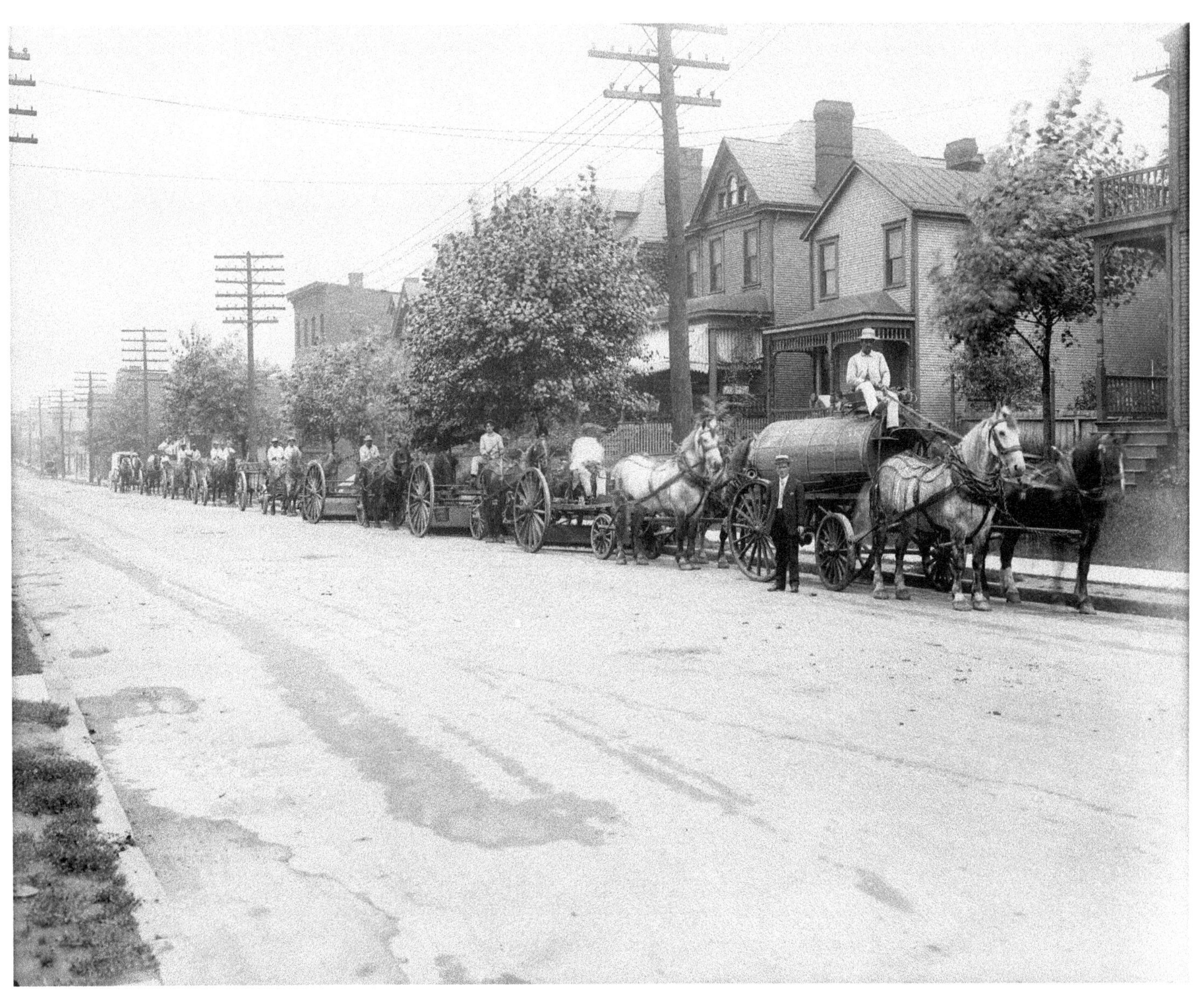

A Department of Public Works street-cleaning crew.

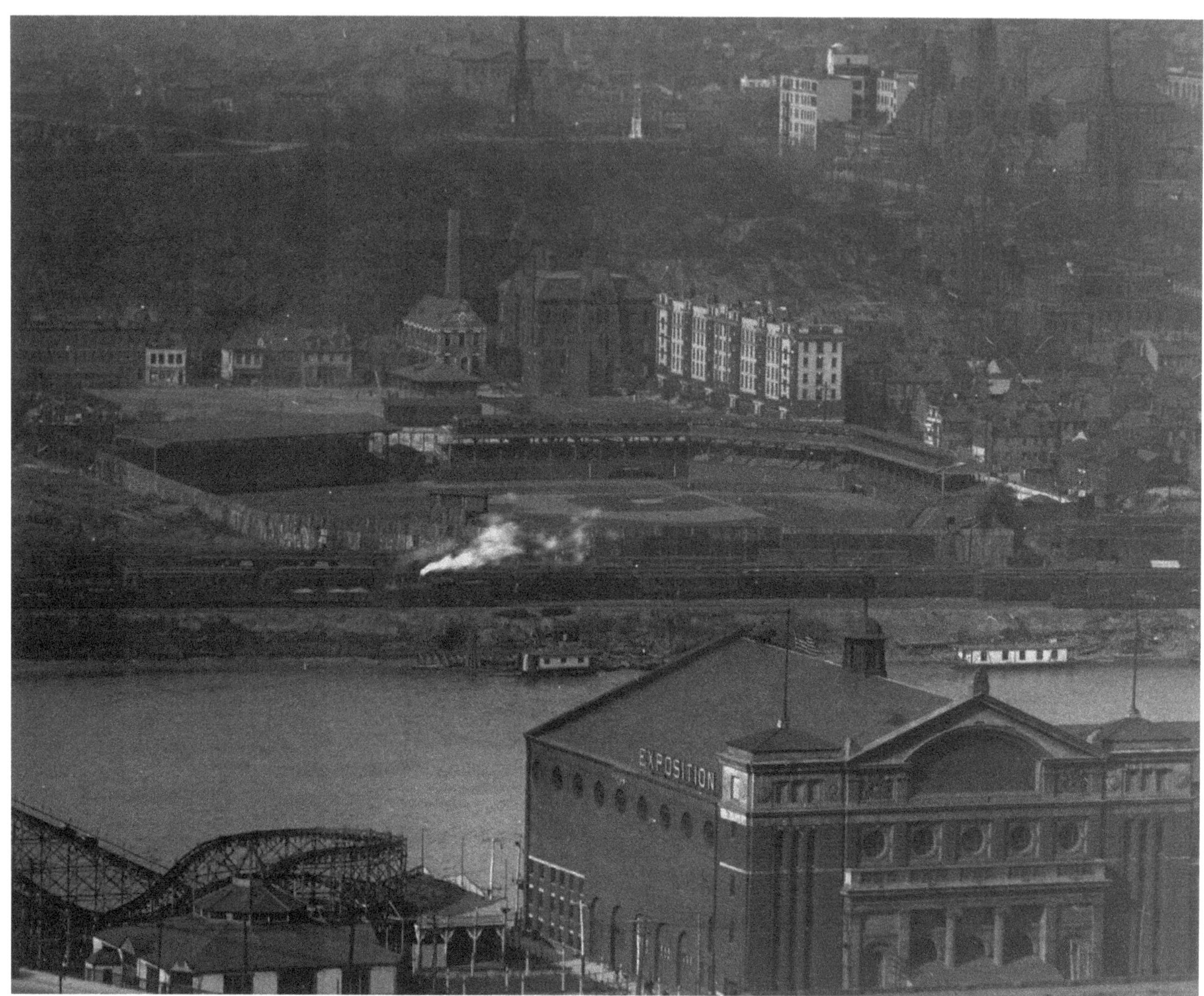

The Western Pennsylvania Exposition buildings, complete with roller coaster and merry-go-round near the Point, facing across the Allegheny River to the North Side and Exposition Park, former home to the Pittsburgh Pirates. The Exposition buildings were designed in 1889 by Joseph Stillburg and were the site of expositions and activities until the early 1950s. The Pirates left Exposition Park in 1909 for Forbes Field only to return to this area to play at Three Rivers Stadium and then PNC Park.

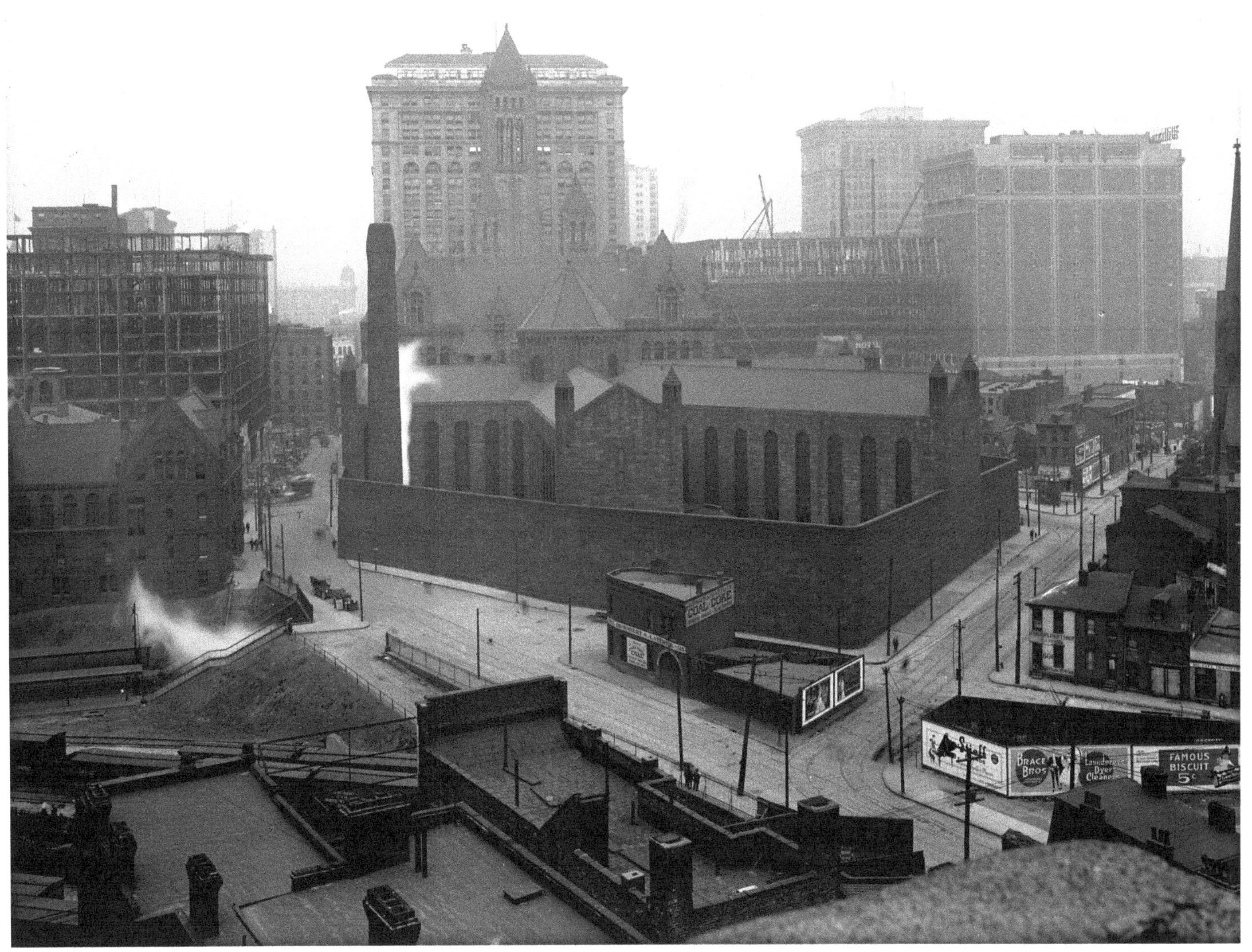

In this view of downtown, the Allegheny County Courthouse and Jail, designed by Henry Hobson Richardson, appears in the foreground. Beyond that are the City-County and the Union Trust (Union Arcade) buildings, under construction. Also in the foreground is another Richardsonian building, the Allegheny County Mortuary. This building was moved back one block in 1929 to make way for the County Office Building.

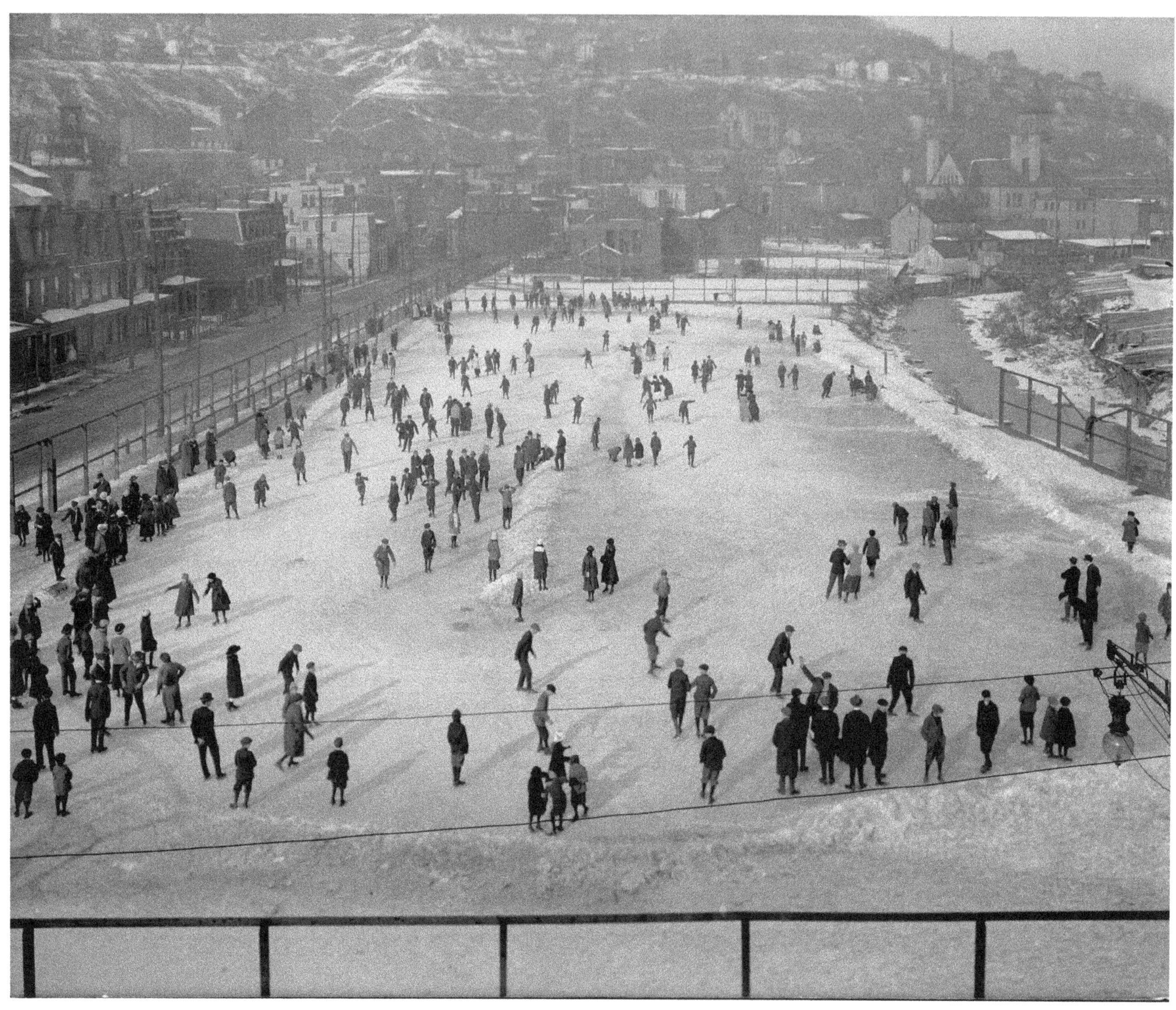

Ice-skaters enjoy a winter day in the West End.

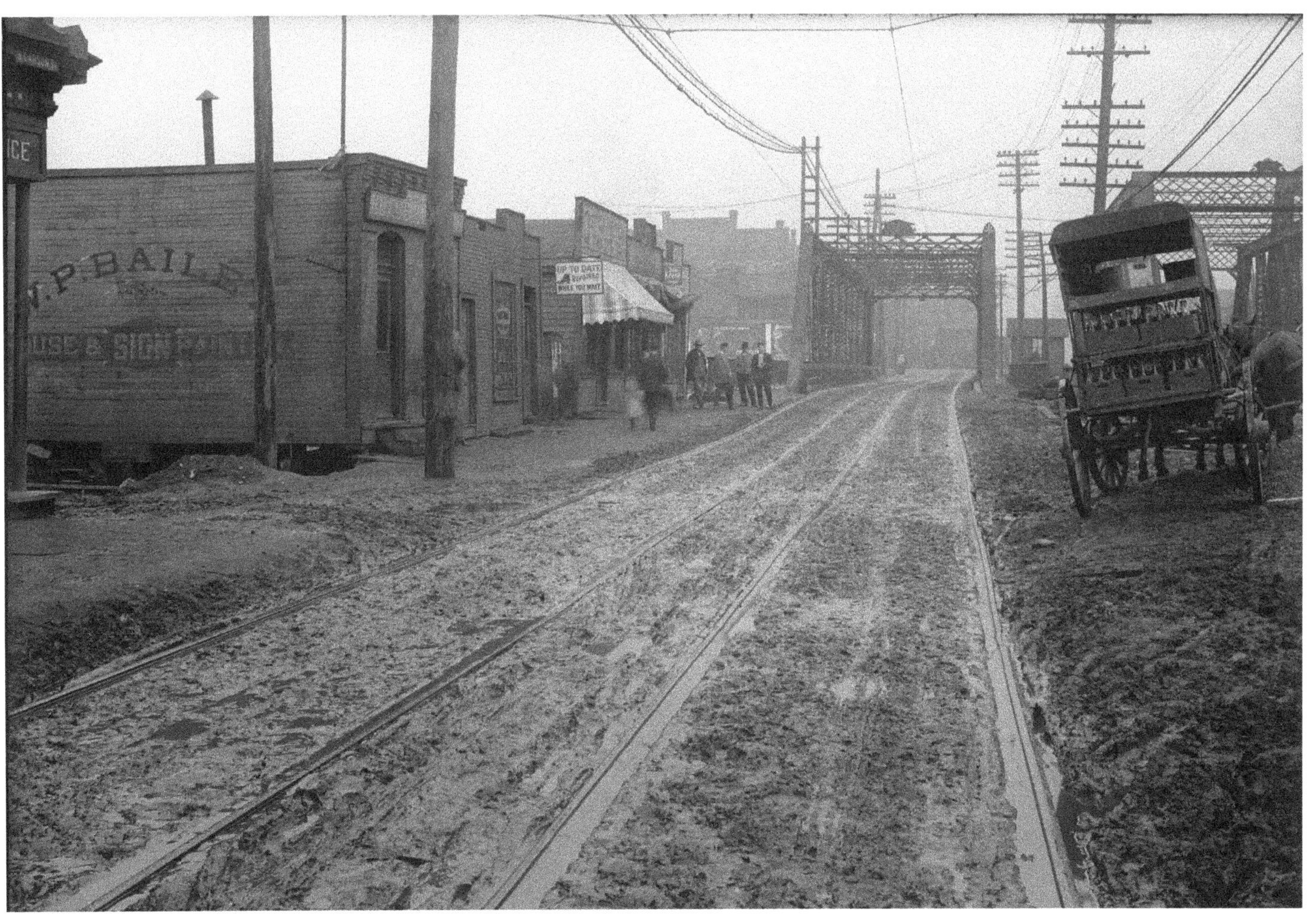

The city photographer identified this location as West Carson Street facing west at Fernwood Street, which the street sign at upper-left appears to confirm. Conflicting street signs mounted on the building housing W. P. Bailey, wallpaper hanger and painter, suggest the view is actually of River Avenue at First Street, but there is no additional evidence to support that notion.

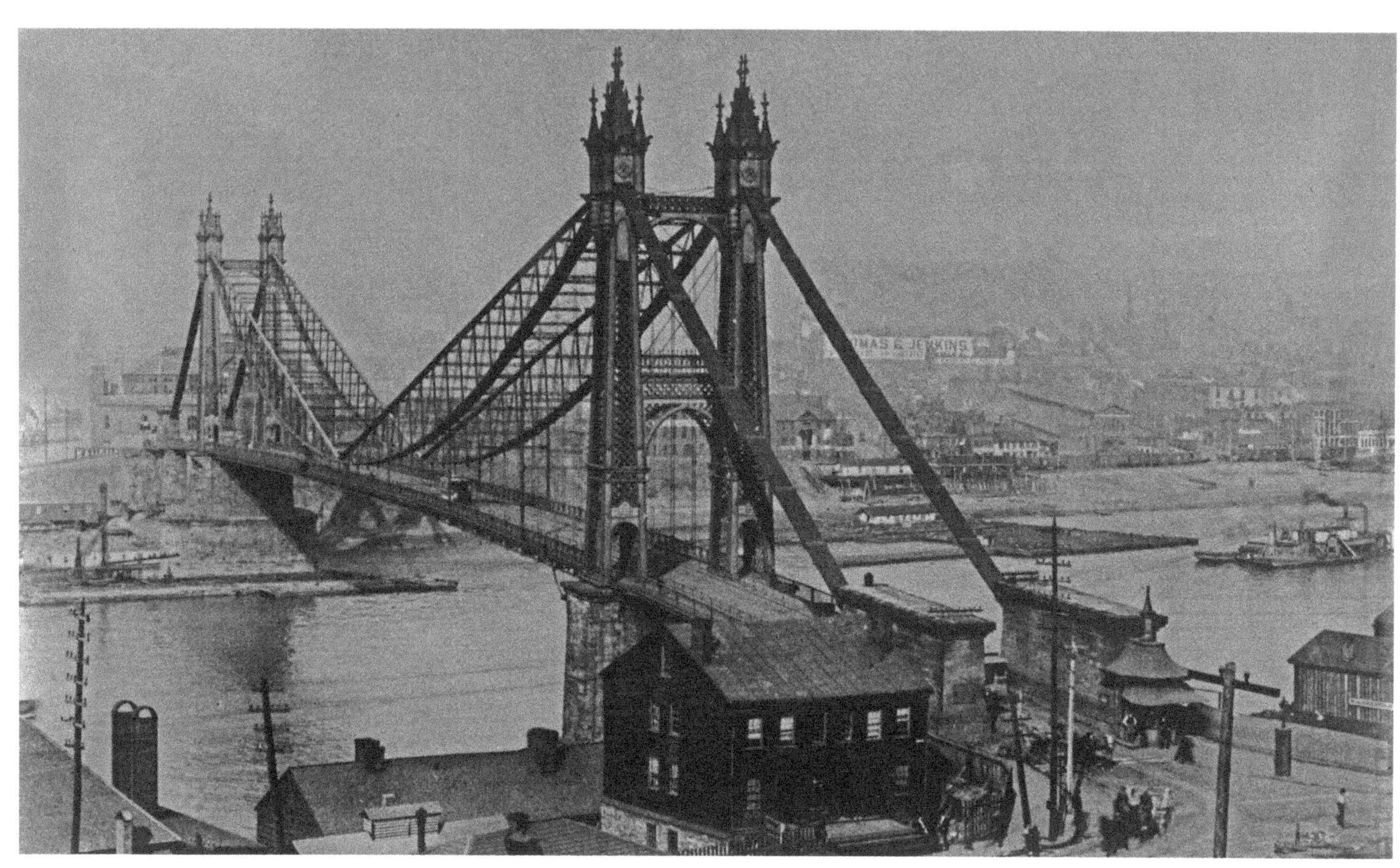

The first bridge at the point connecting Pittsburgh to the South Side was designed by Edward Hemberl of American Bridge Company. Constructed around 1876, it stood until 1927 when it was replaced.

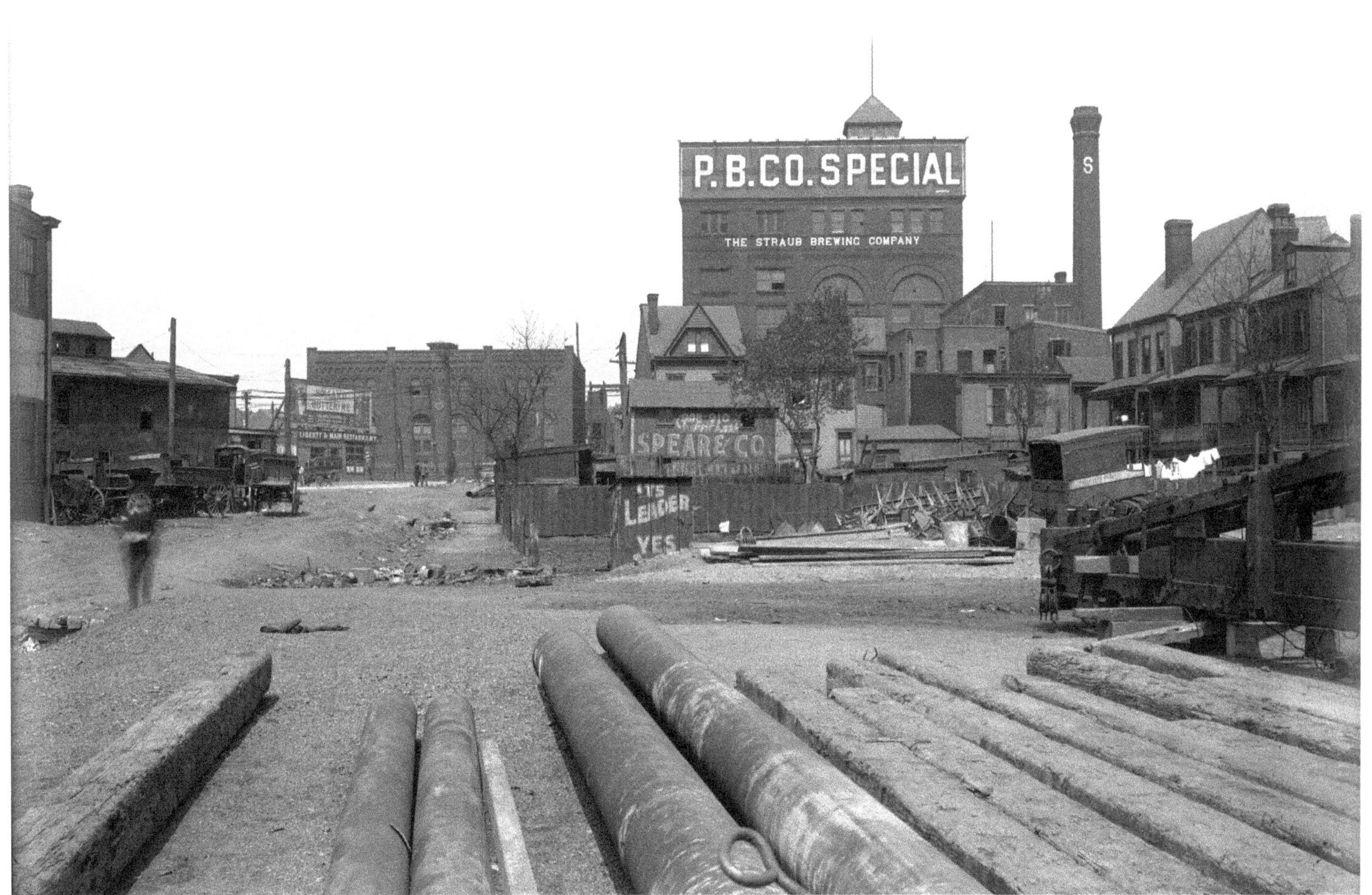

The Straub Brewing Company, Bloomfield, photographed from the area near the Bloomfield Bridge.

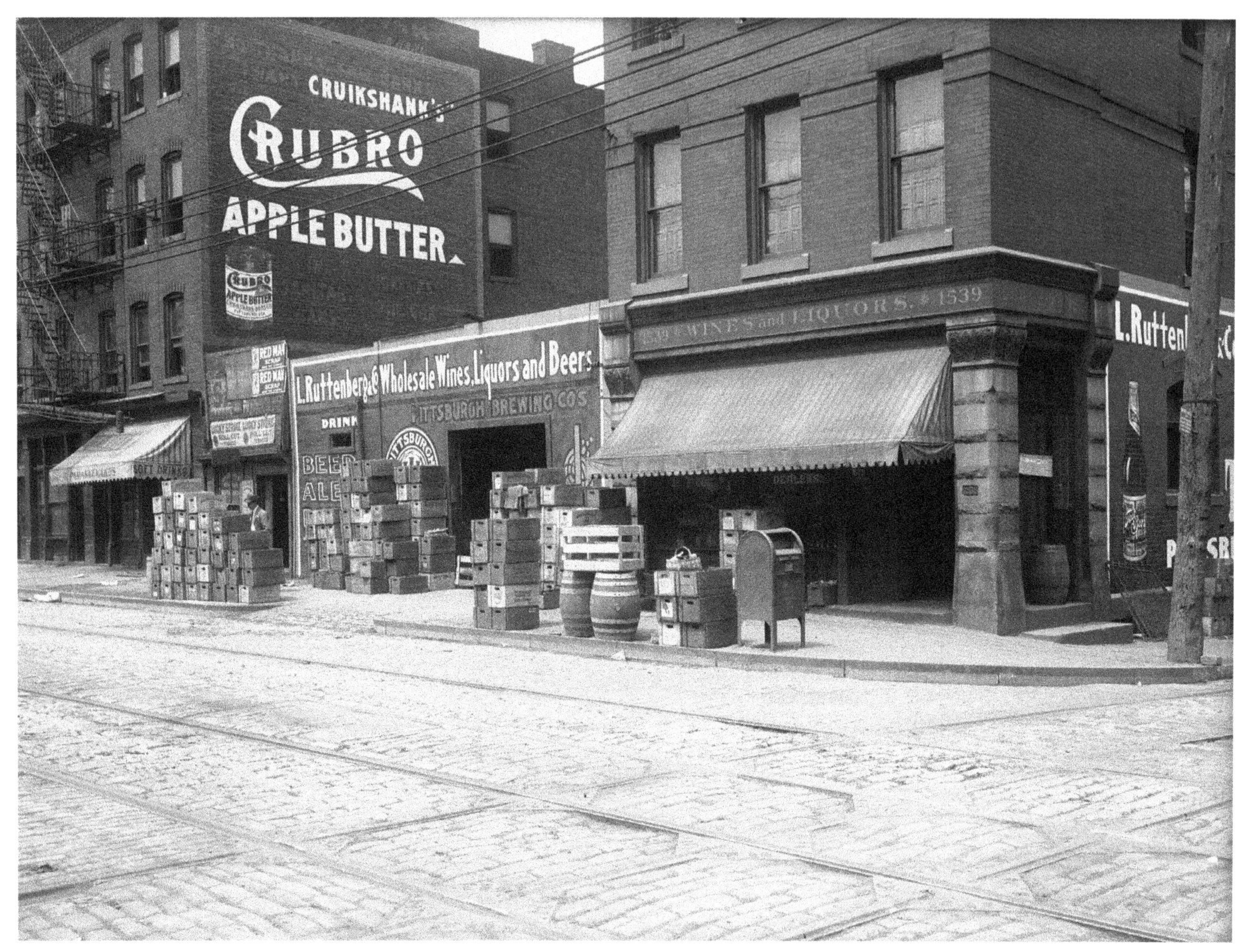

The Strip District.

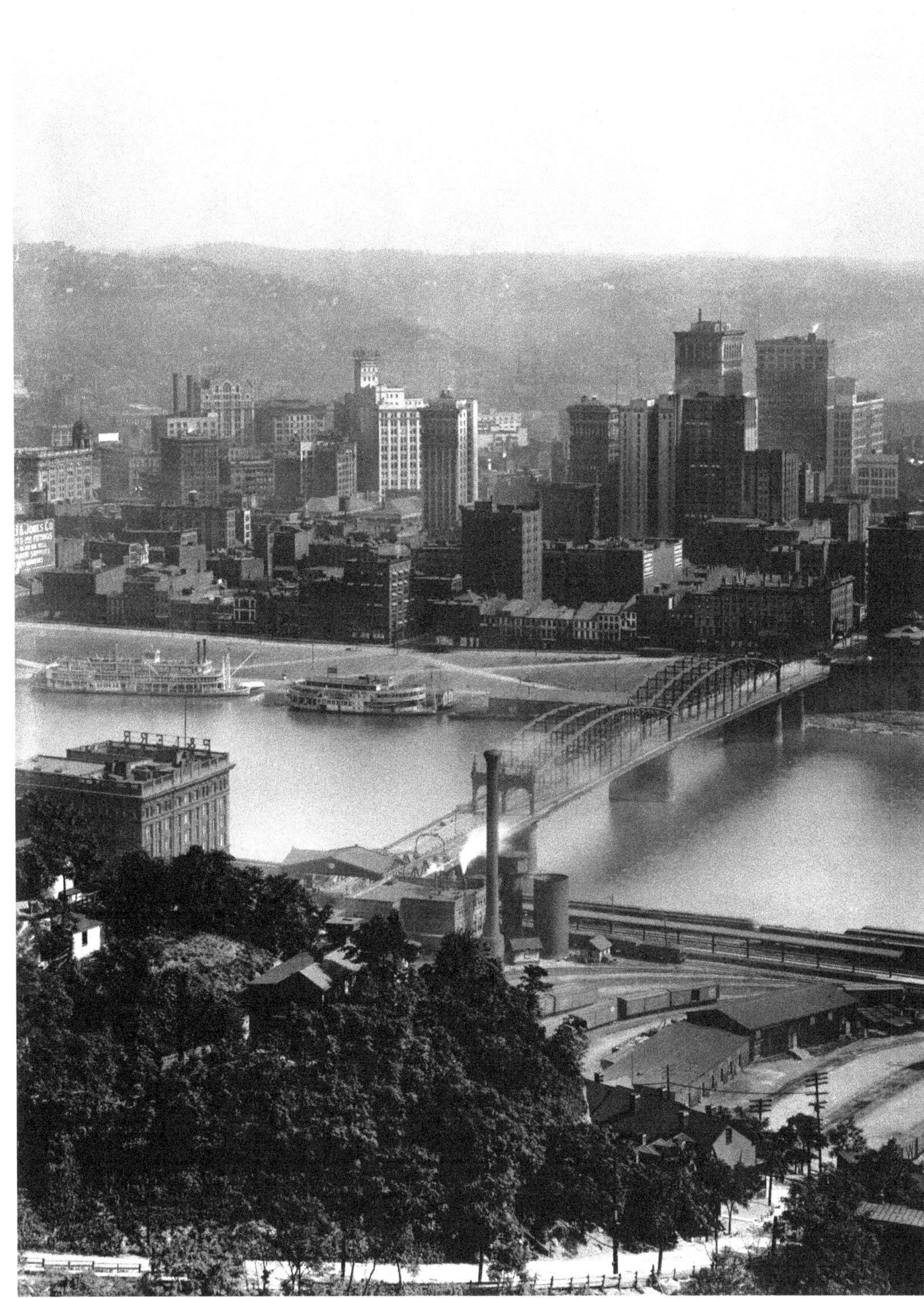

View of the South Side, downtown, and Monongahela River from the Mount Washington hillside recorded between 1910 and 1914. A close look reveals the Smithfield Street Bridge, the Pittsburgh and Lake Erie Railroad Station, and yards on the south side of the river. The north side of the river features the Monongahela Wharf and the Monongahela House at the end of the Smithfield Street Bridge.

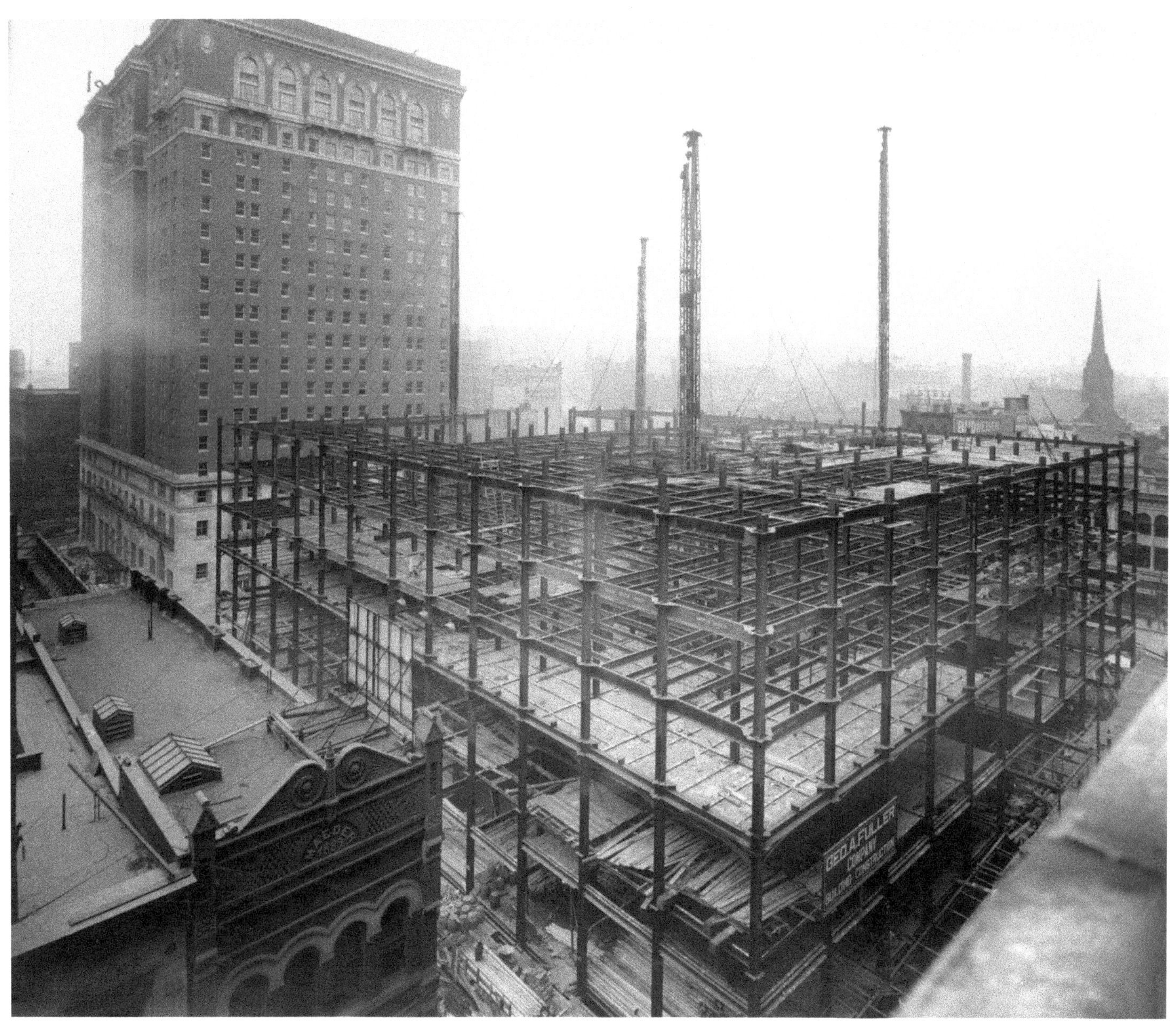

The Union Arcade rises in the shadow of the recently completed William Penn Hotel. The Flemish-Gothic-style Union Arcade, financed by industrialist Henry Clay Frick, was built between 1915 and 1916 and designed by Frederick Osterling. Rumor had it that Frick financed the construction of the Union Arcade, the William Penn, and the Frick buildings so that he could overshadow Andrew Carnegie's building on Fifth Avenue. The Union Trust Company purchased the building in 1923, changing the name to the Union Trust Building.

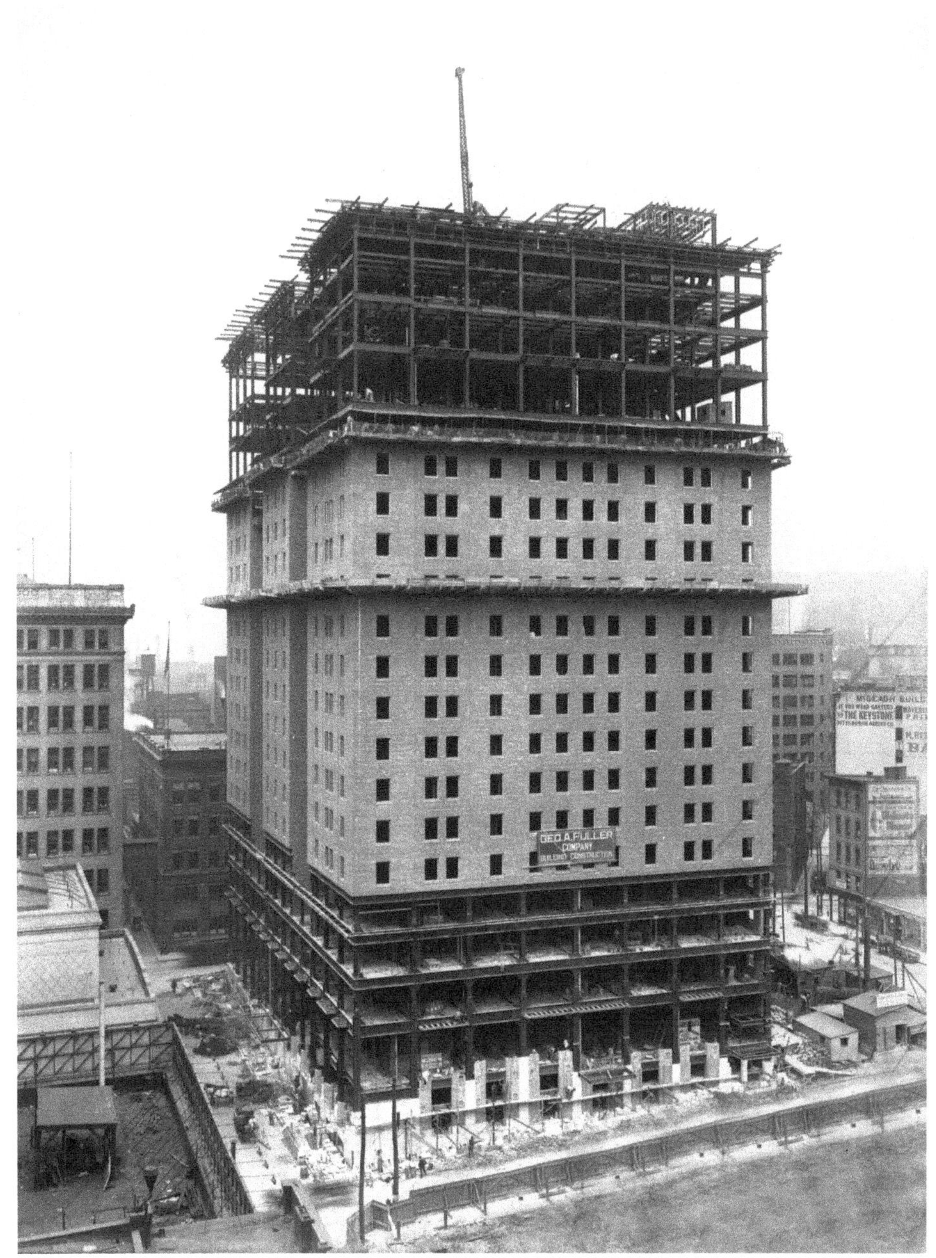

The William Penn Hotel under construction in 1915. The William Penn, built between 1914 and 1916, was designed by Benno Jansen & Franklin Abbot as a 23-floor structure. Surrounded by Grant Street and Sixth and Oliver avenues, it opened in March 1916.

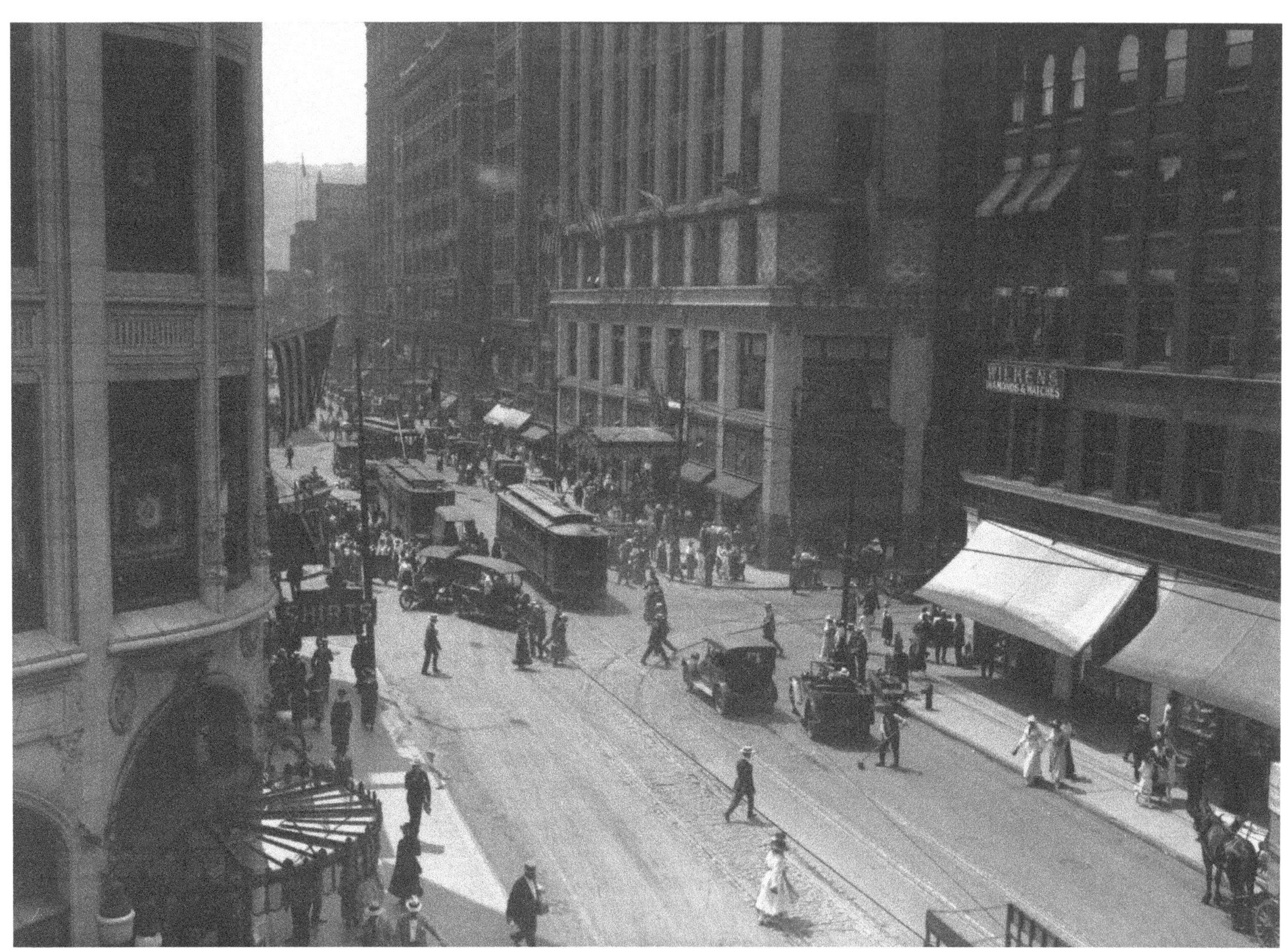

The Rosenbaum Company and the F. W. Woolworth Company 5 & 10 line a bustling Liberty Avenue in 1917.

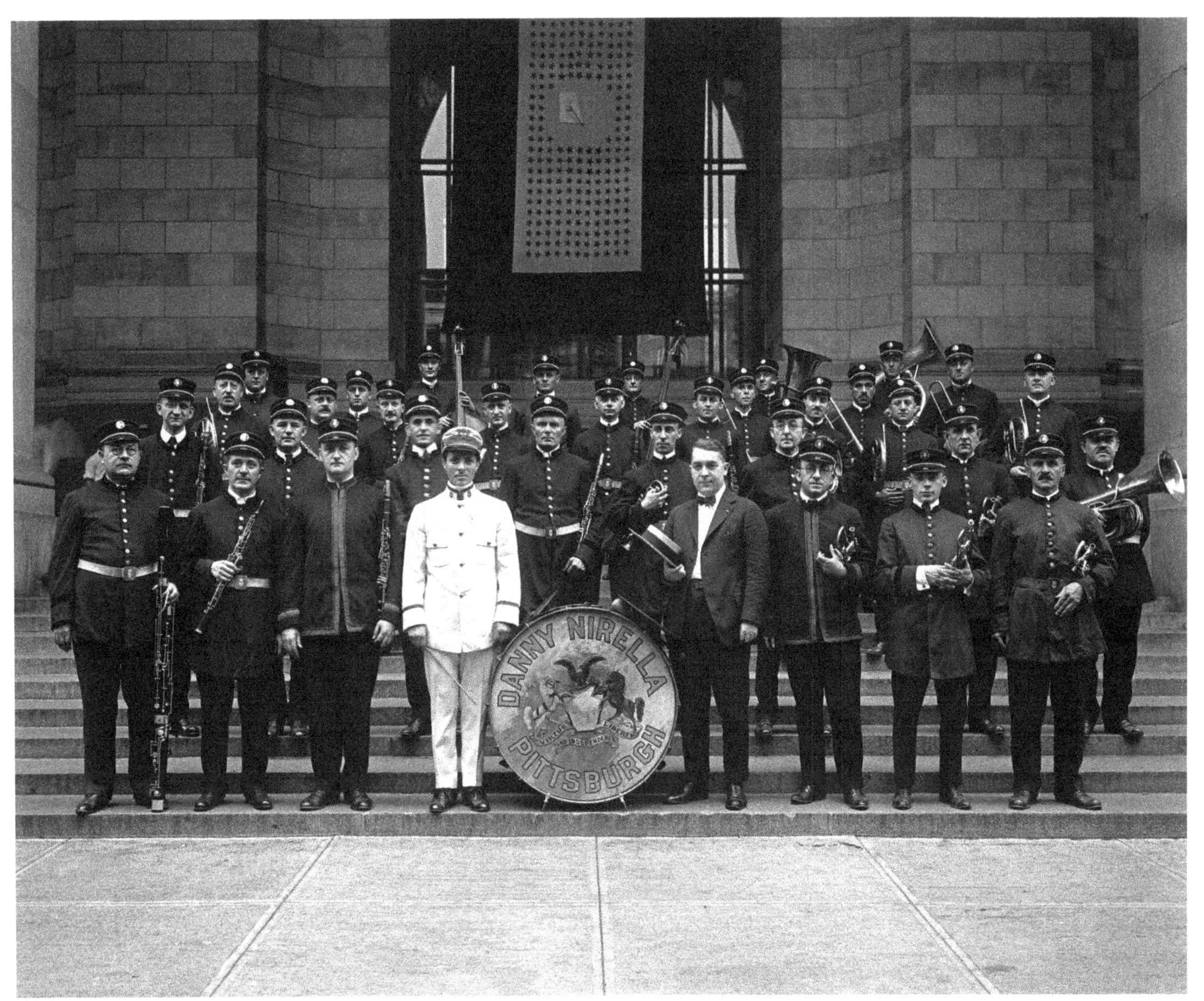

The Municipal Band, featuring Danny Nirella, in 1918.

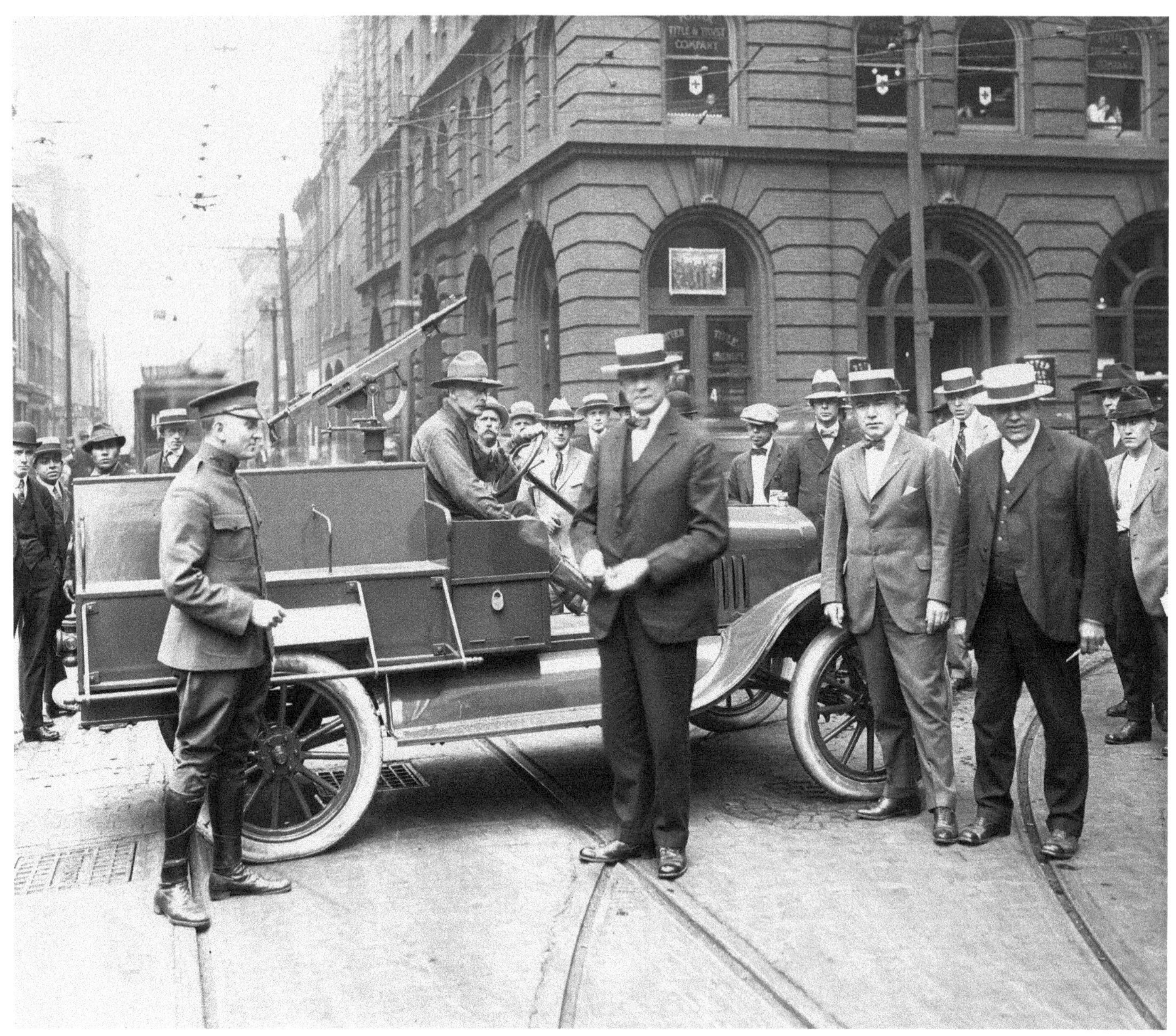

The Pennsylvania Reserve Militia with a machine gun in 1918. World War I was in progress and Pittsburghers were getting involved.

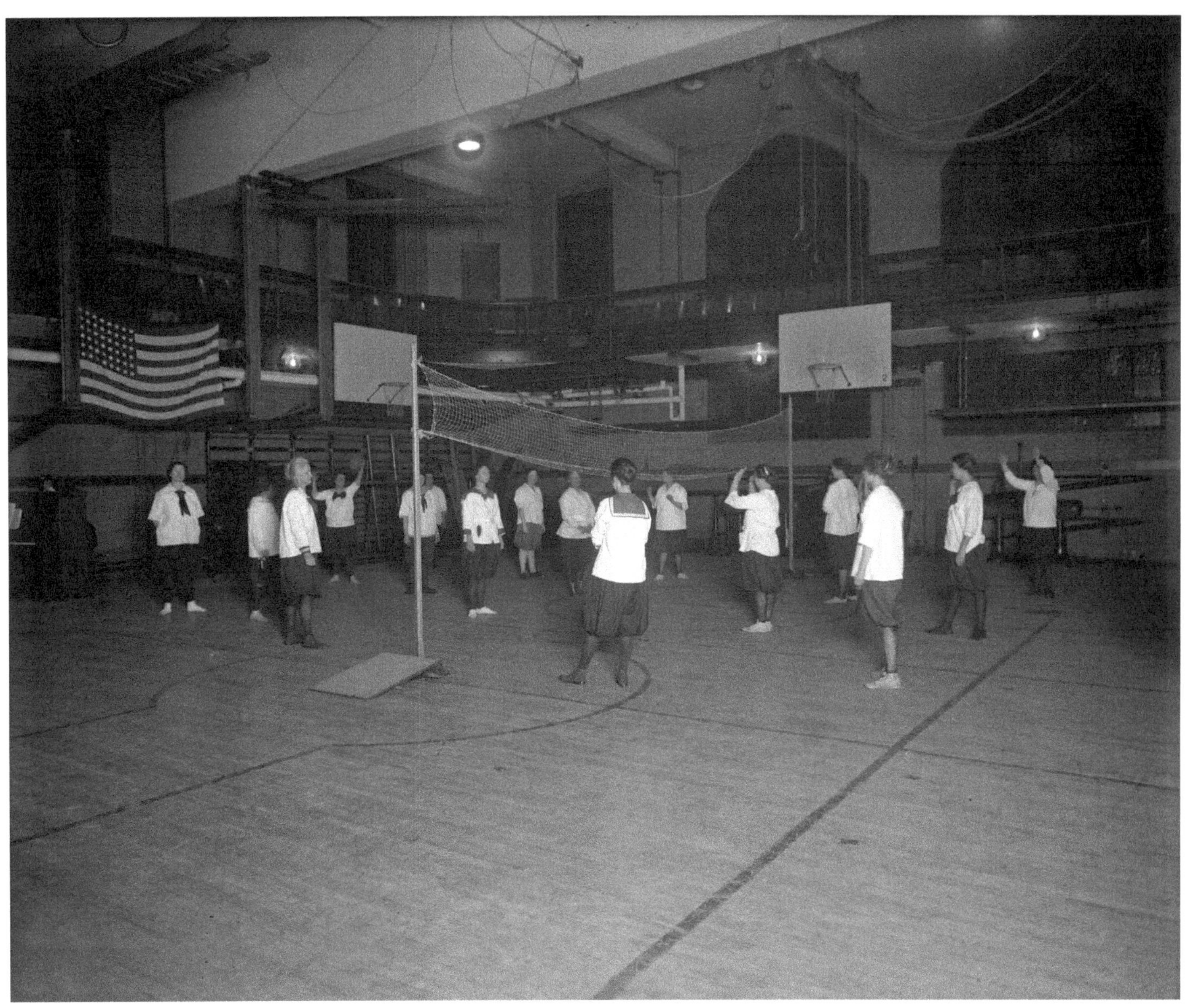

A game of intramural volleyball is under way at South Hills High School in 1918.

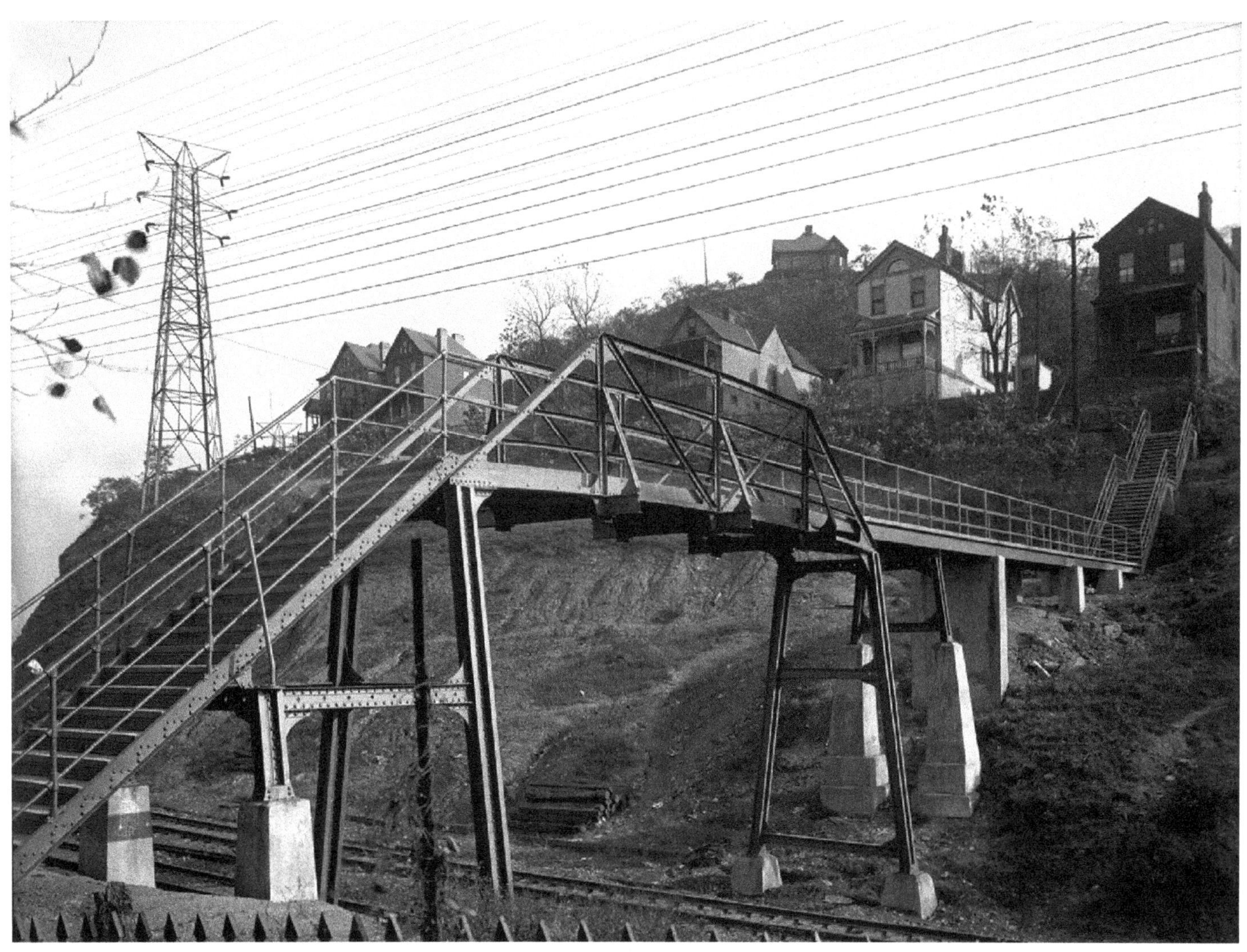
Oregon Street footbridge, 1919.

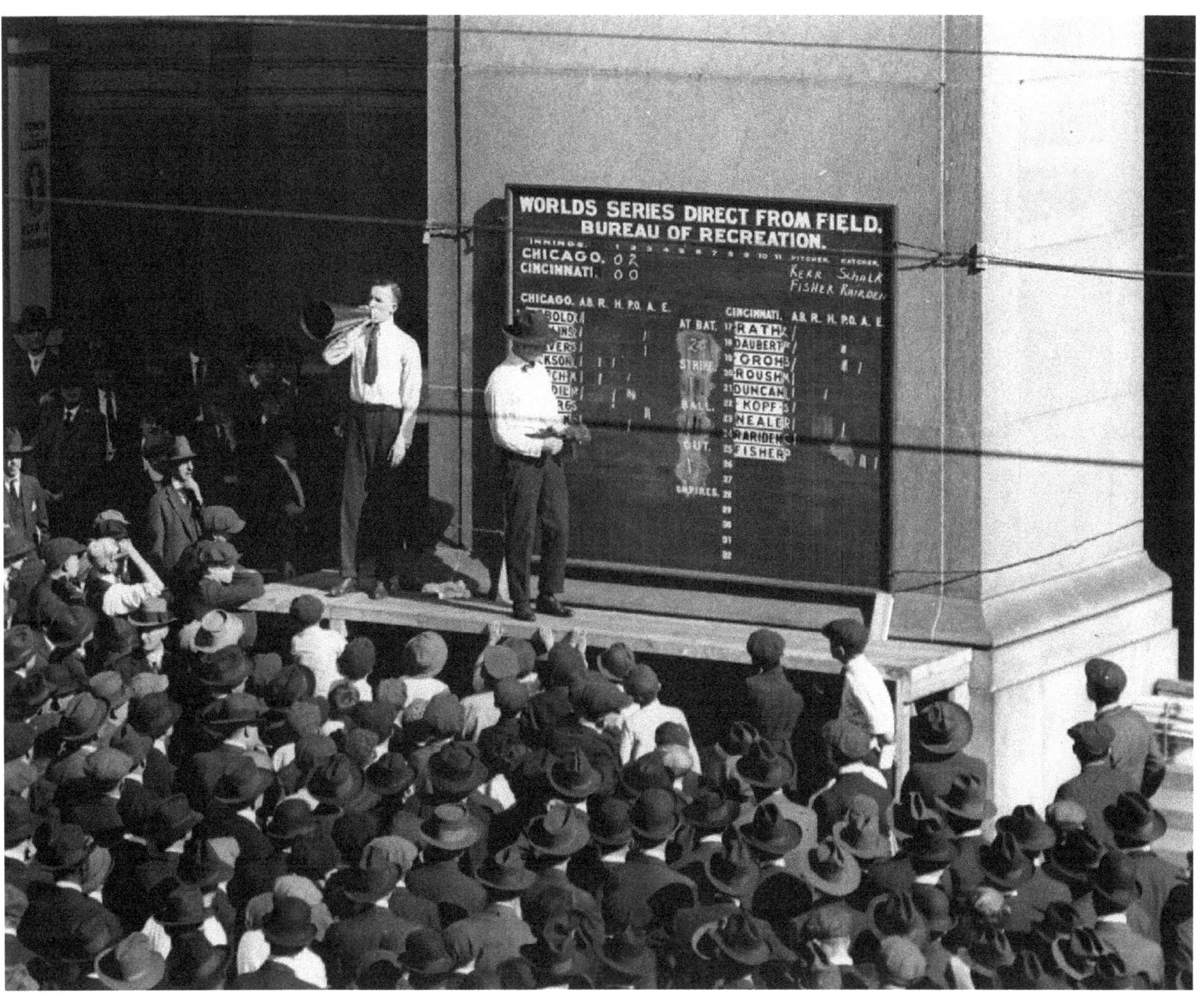

People gather outside the City-County Building to hear game three of the 1919 World Series at Comiskey Park, between the Chicago White Sox and the Cincinnati Reds. Although the Sox would win this round, the Reds would win the series, 5-3. Afterward, eight White Sox players would be accused of having thrown the 1919 World Series and would be banned from professional baseball.

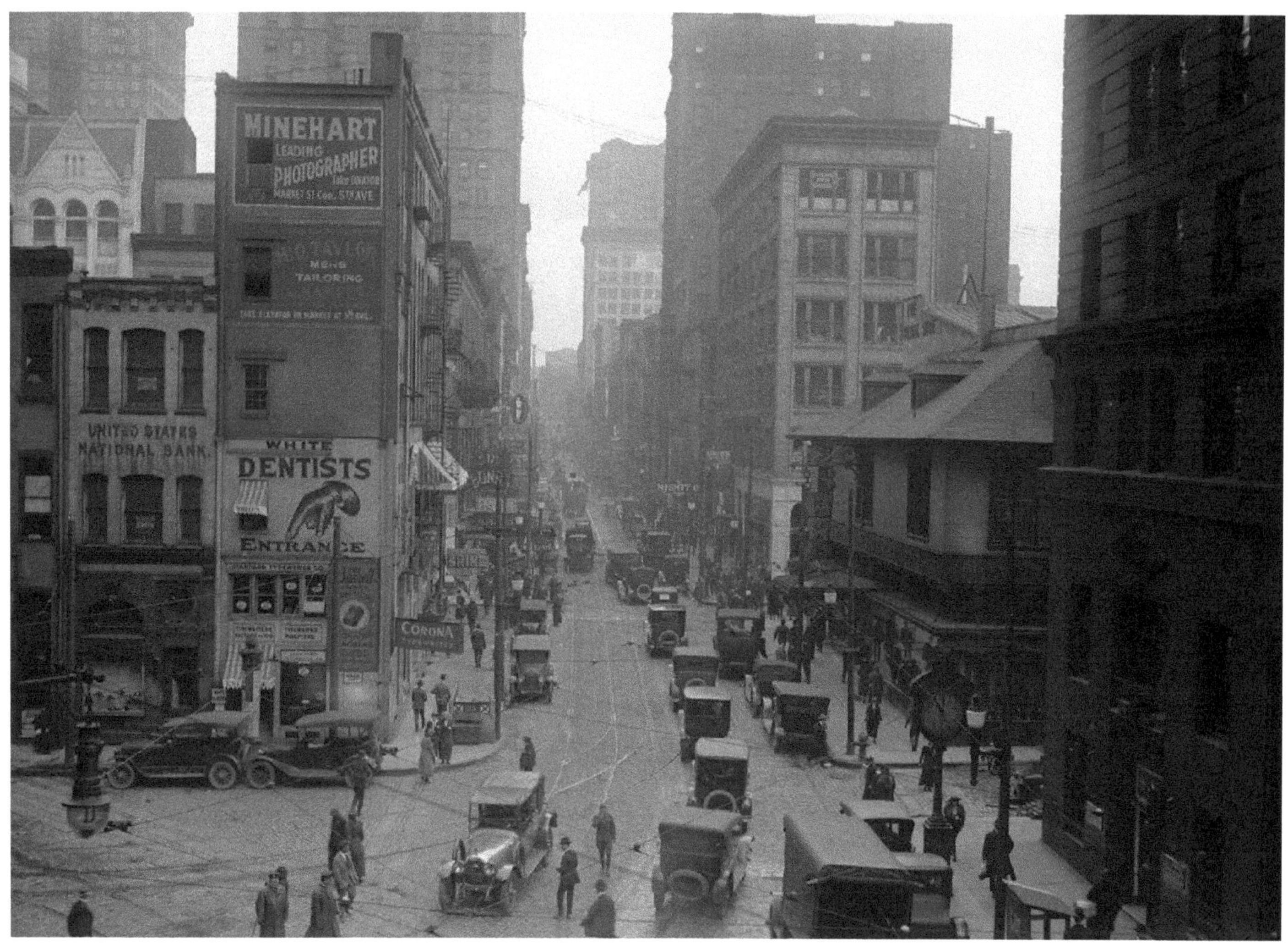

Fifth Avenue and Graeme Street are bustling at 11:00 A.M. This eastward-looking view shows area businesses, including the Regal Shoe Company, White Dentists, and Standard Typewriters, featuring the Barret portable adding, listing, and computing machine.

Moving Forward

(1920–1929)

Pittsburgh in the 1920s was an exciting place. Where else could a multitude of employment opportunities and bountiful shopping be found? Modes of transportation had multiplied. Called the most expensive road in the world at $1,600,000, the Boulevard of the Allies opened to traffic in 1923. Other travel options included trolleys, trains, and inclines. Care for a little recreation? Options included car camping in Schenley Park or a visit to the 380-acre Frick Park, dedicated in 1927. There were playgrounds located in every neighborhood and pools for a good swim.

The city was improving itself with public works projects involving roads, water and sewage, new parks, and new bridges. Dilapidated buildings were removed and new structures erected. In the field of health care, the Tuberculosis Hospital on the former Leech Farm and Municipal Hospital in Oakland were built.

With the return of the University of Pittsburgh a little more than a decade before, high-quality education was available. Pitt Stadium, the Cathedral of Learning, and the Falk Clinic were all built during this time.

The Bettis Airfield was dedicated in 1926, followed by a visit from Charles Lindbergh in 1927 as he made a stop on his 92-city, 48-state flight across the United States. It took him two and a half hours to fly from Cleveland to the airfield. He was greeted with all the pomp befitting a hero with a parade and ceremony at the University of Pittsburgh's Pitt Stadium.

The Equitable Gas tank explosion of November 15, 1927, leveled many homes and buildings within a 20-mile radius. Workmen using acetylene torches were repairing a 5-million-cubic-foot tank when it exploded, touching off explosions in the two neighboring tanks. Twenty-six people died and more than $4 million in damages ($47 million in today's currency) occurred.

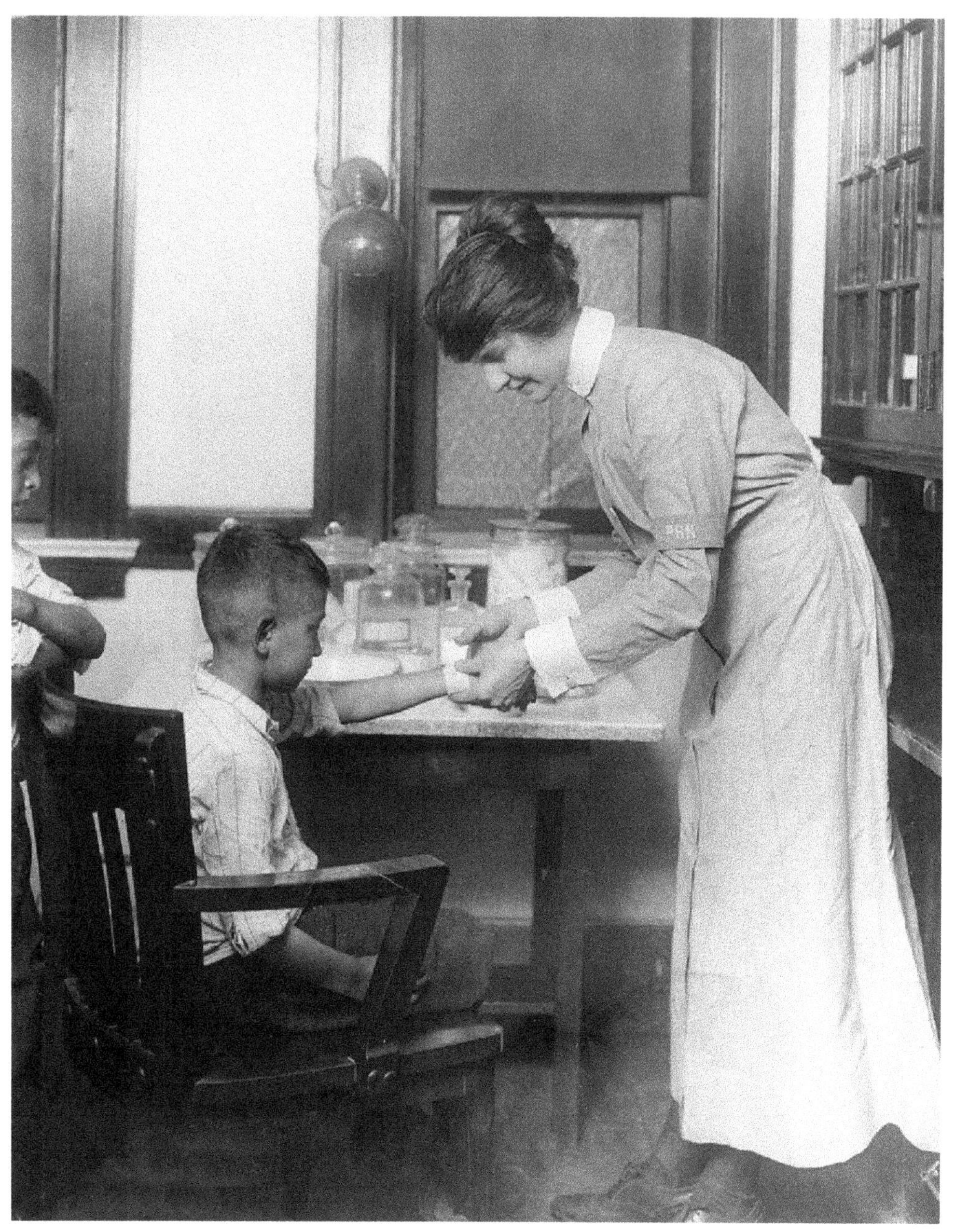

A Public Health Nurse from the Irene Kaufmann Settlement Nursing Service attends a young patient around 1920.

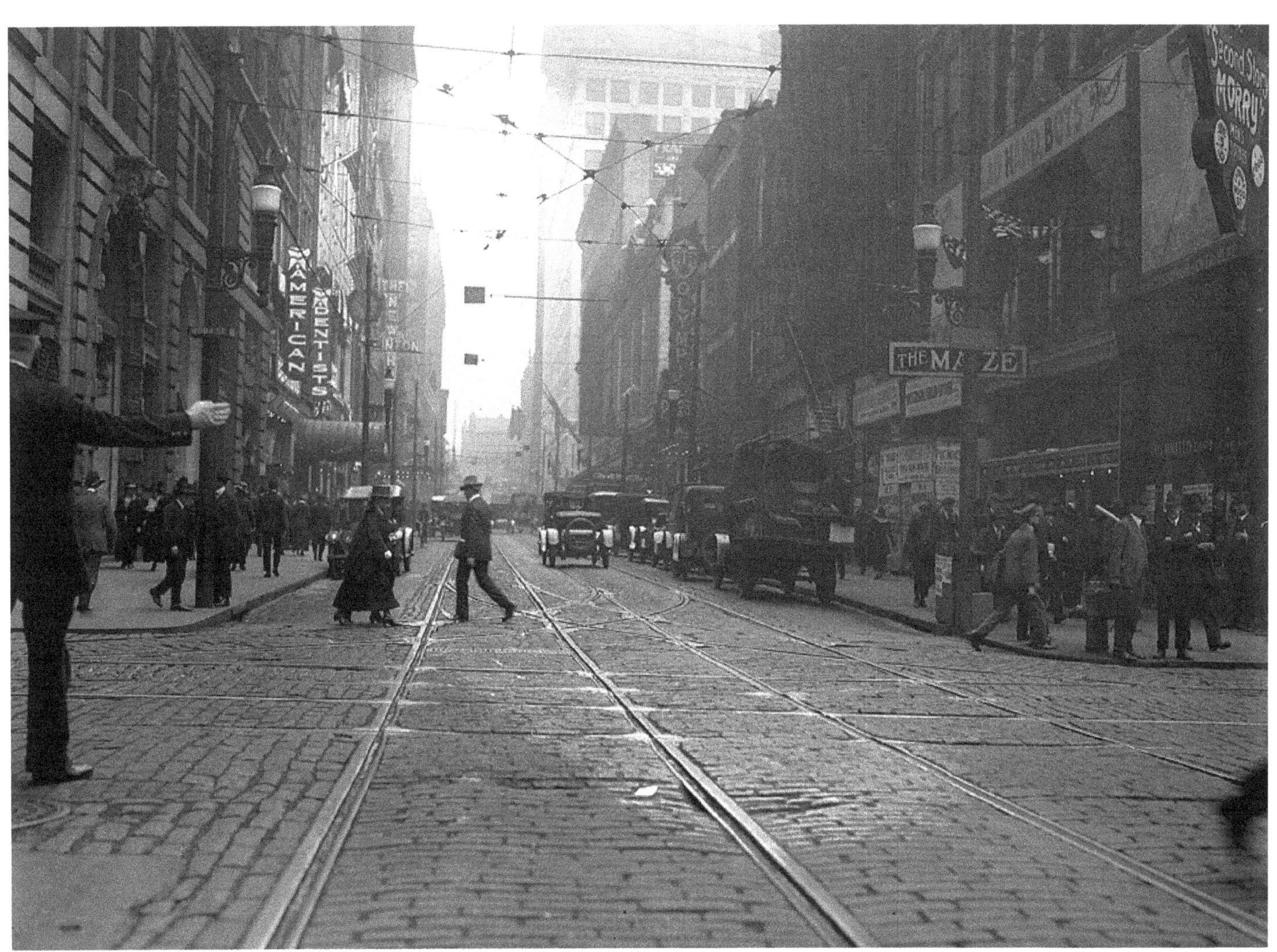

Fifth Avenue at Wood Street facing east toward Smithfield.

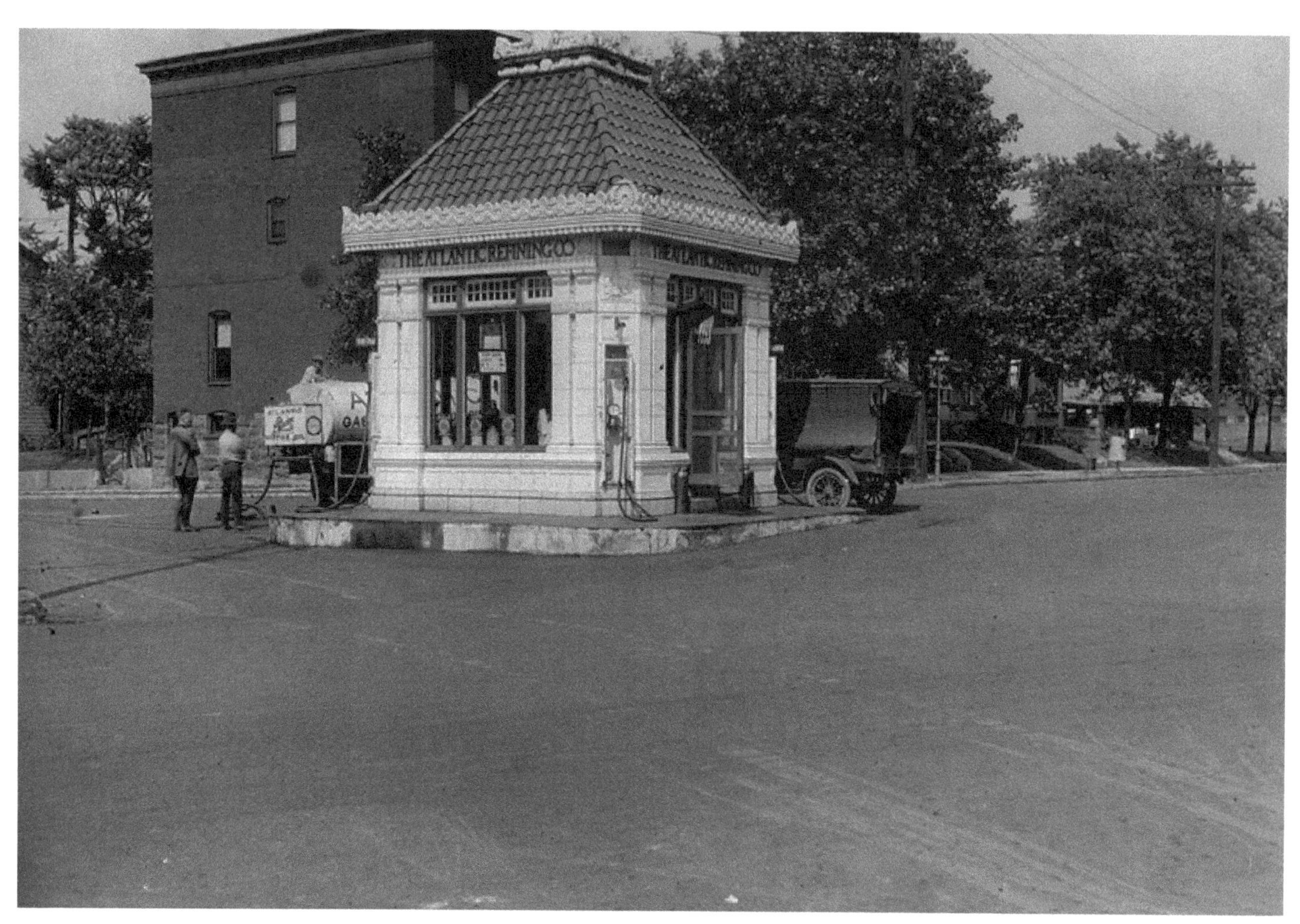

An Atlantic Refining Company station, 1921.

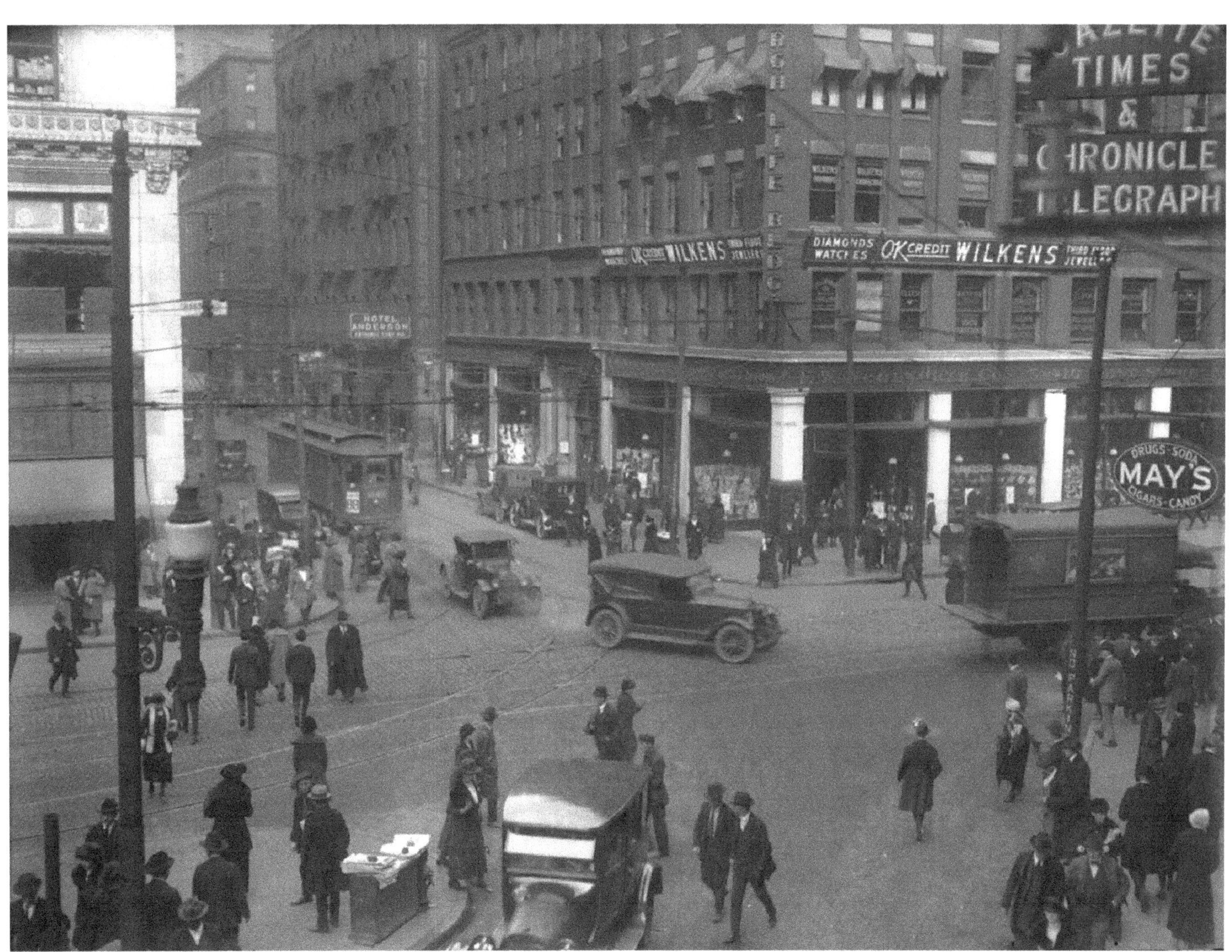

The Pittsburgh *Gazette-Times & Chronicle Telegraph* prints all the news at Liberty Avenue and Sixth Street. The Pittsburgh Life Building, which houses the F. W. Woolworth Co. and Wilkens Jewelers, and the Hotel Anderson are also in view.

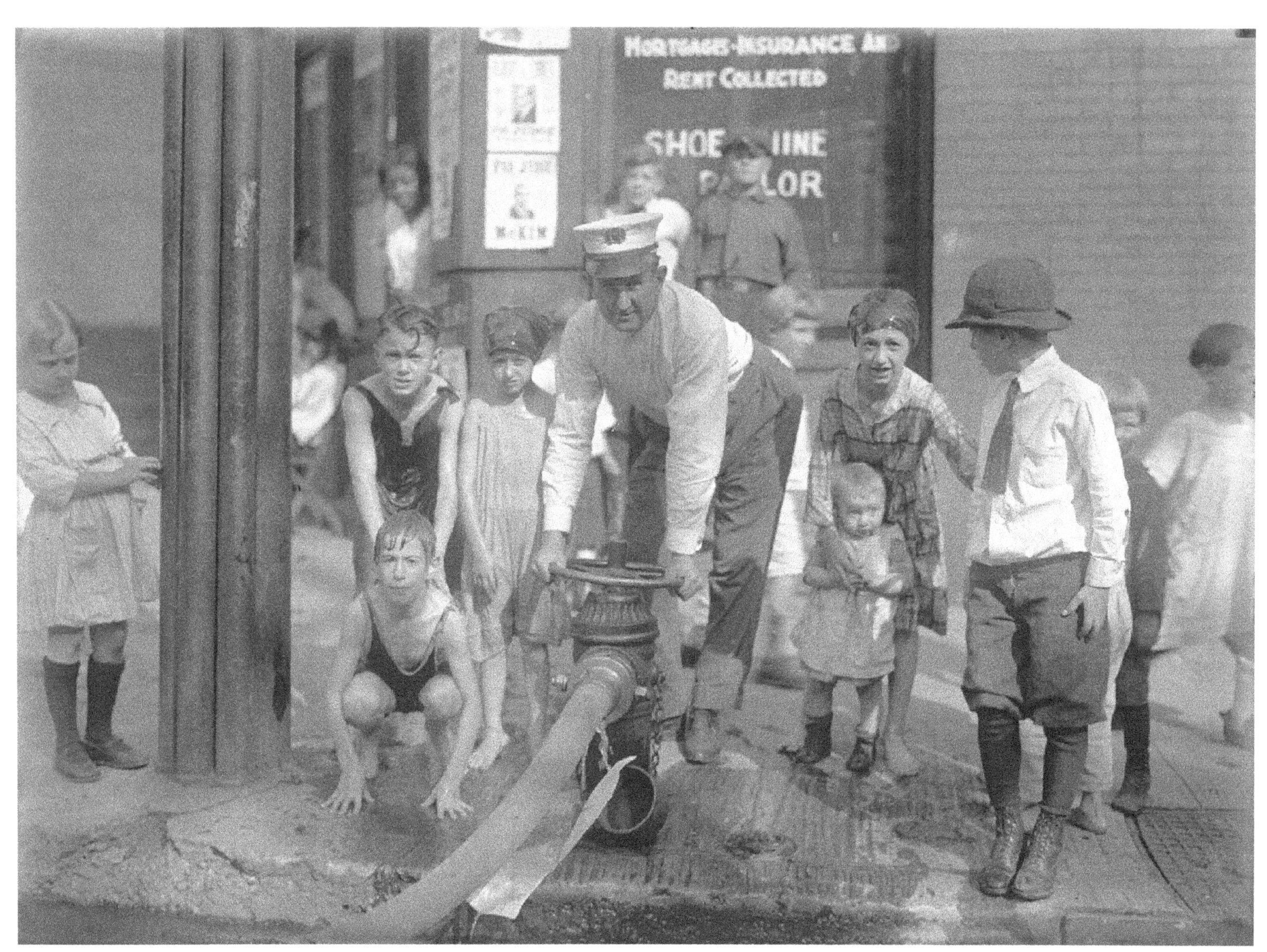

Cooling down on a warm 1921 summer afternoon.

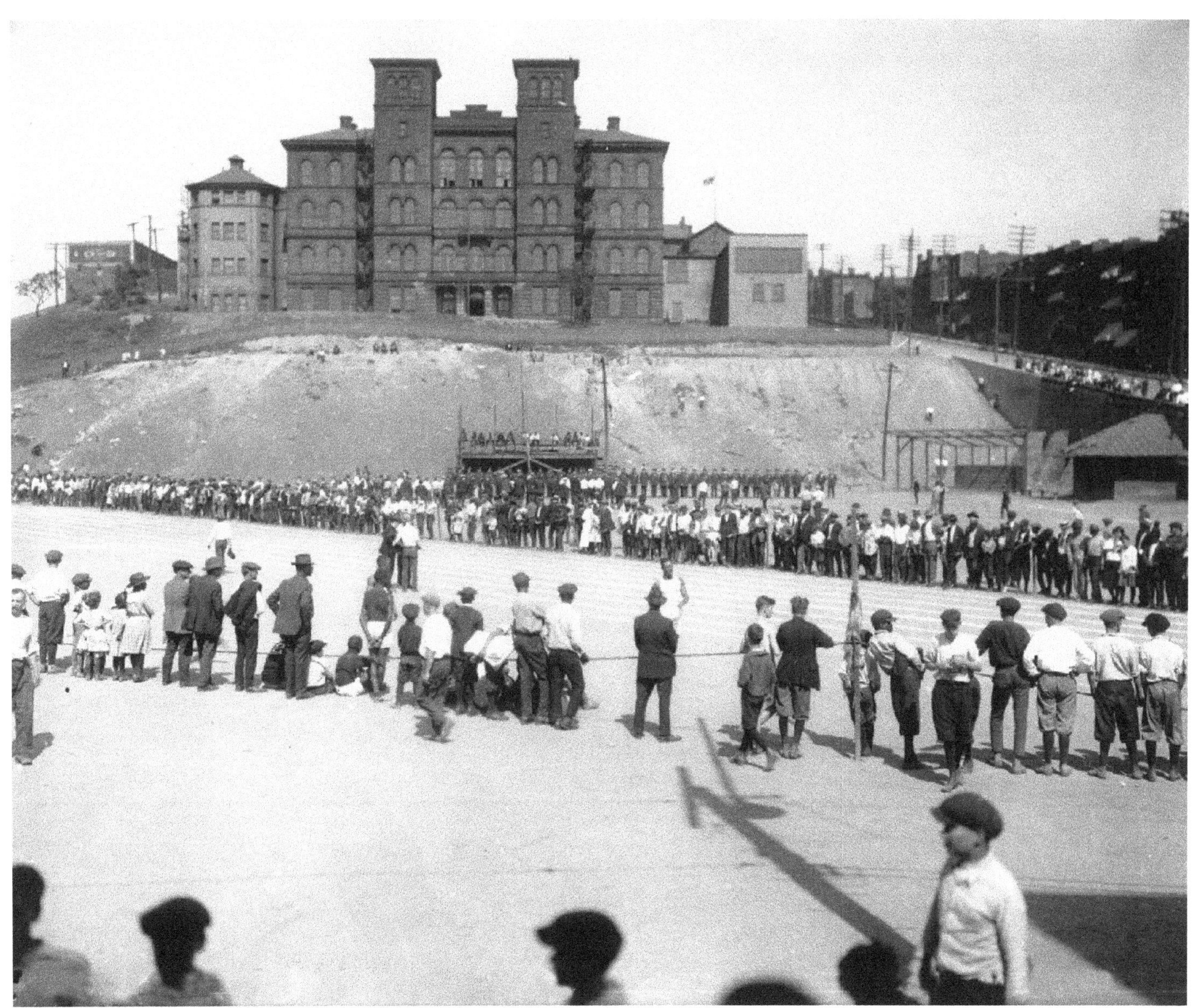

A Washington Park track and field meet in 1921.

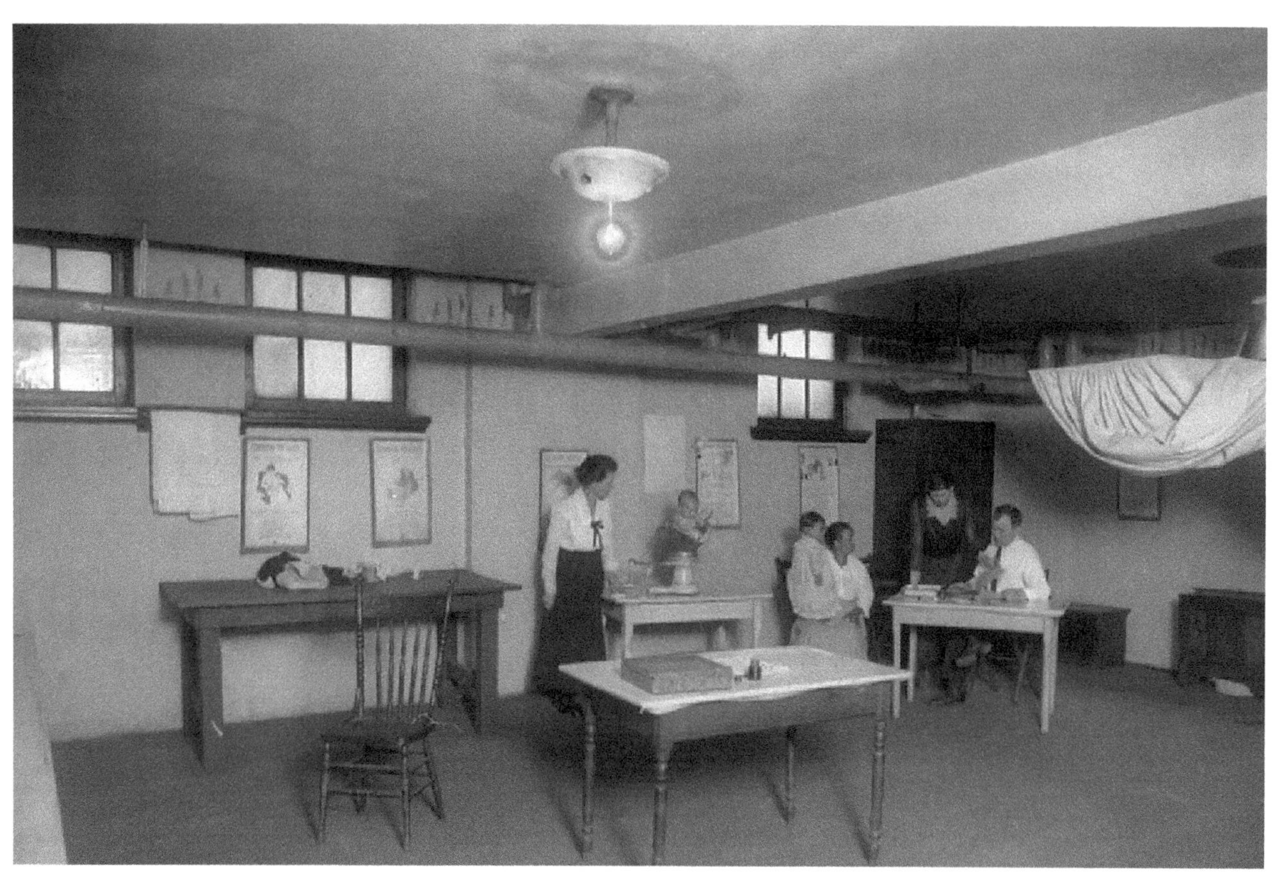

Toddlers get good marks during a check-up in 1922.

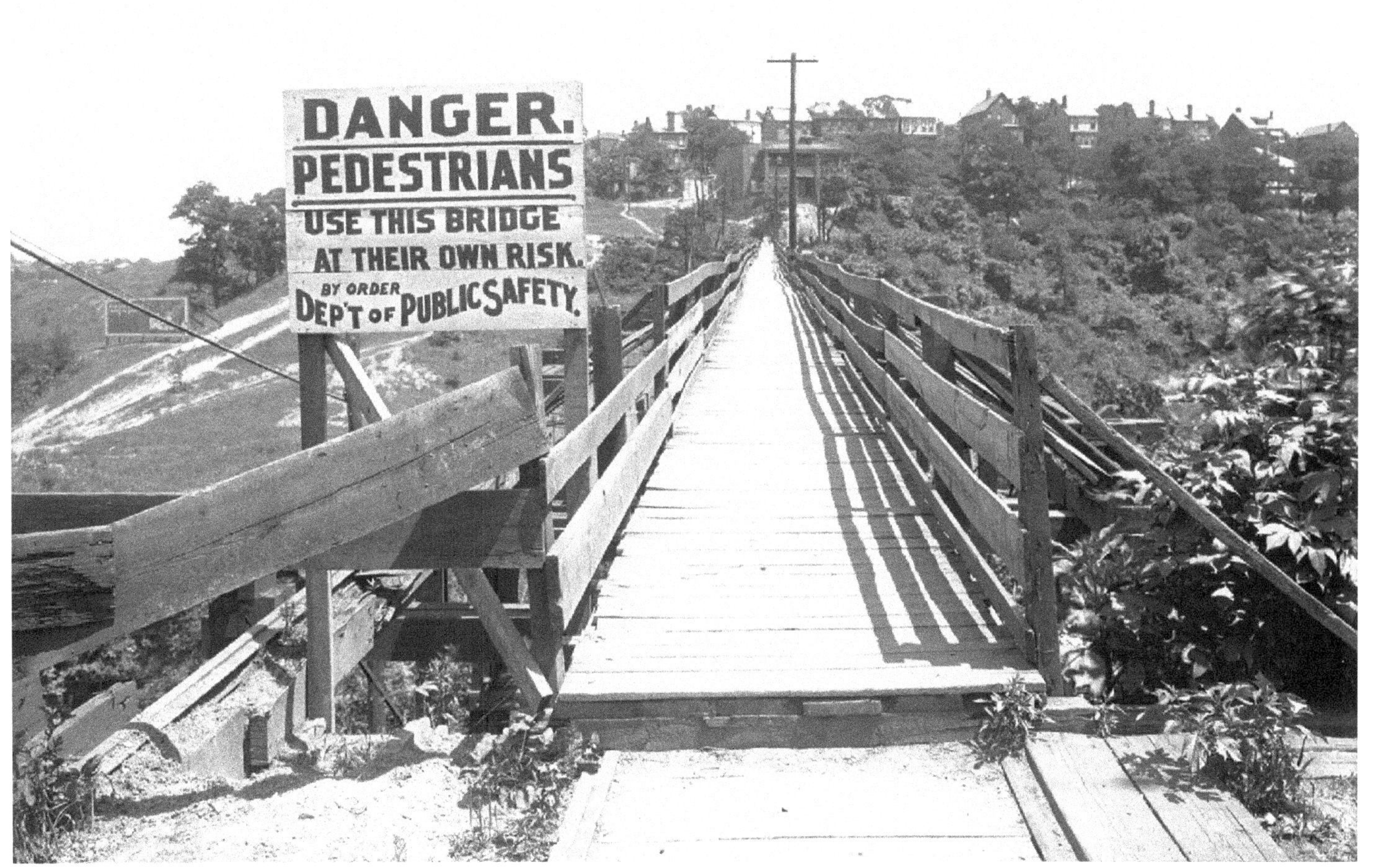

The west end of the Greenfield Avenue Bridge in 1923.

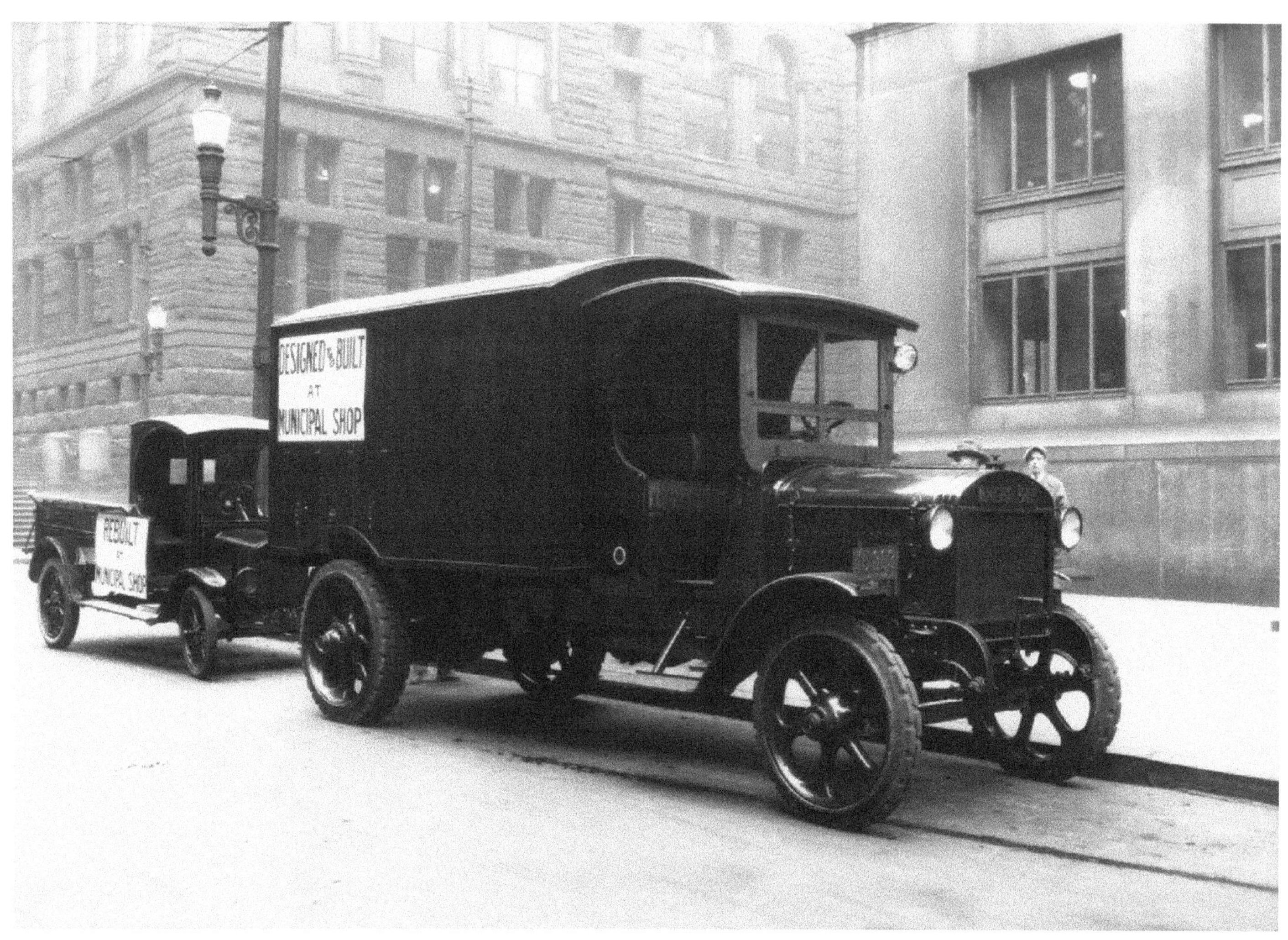

A City of Pittsburgh–built emergency repair truck parked on Grant Street near the City-County Building and the Allegheny County Courthouse.

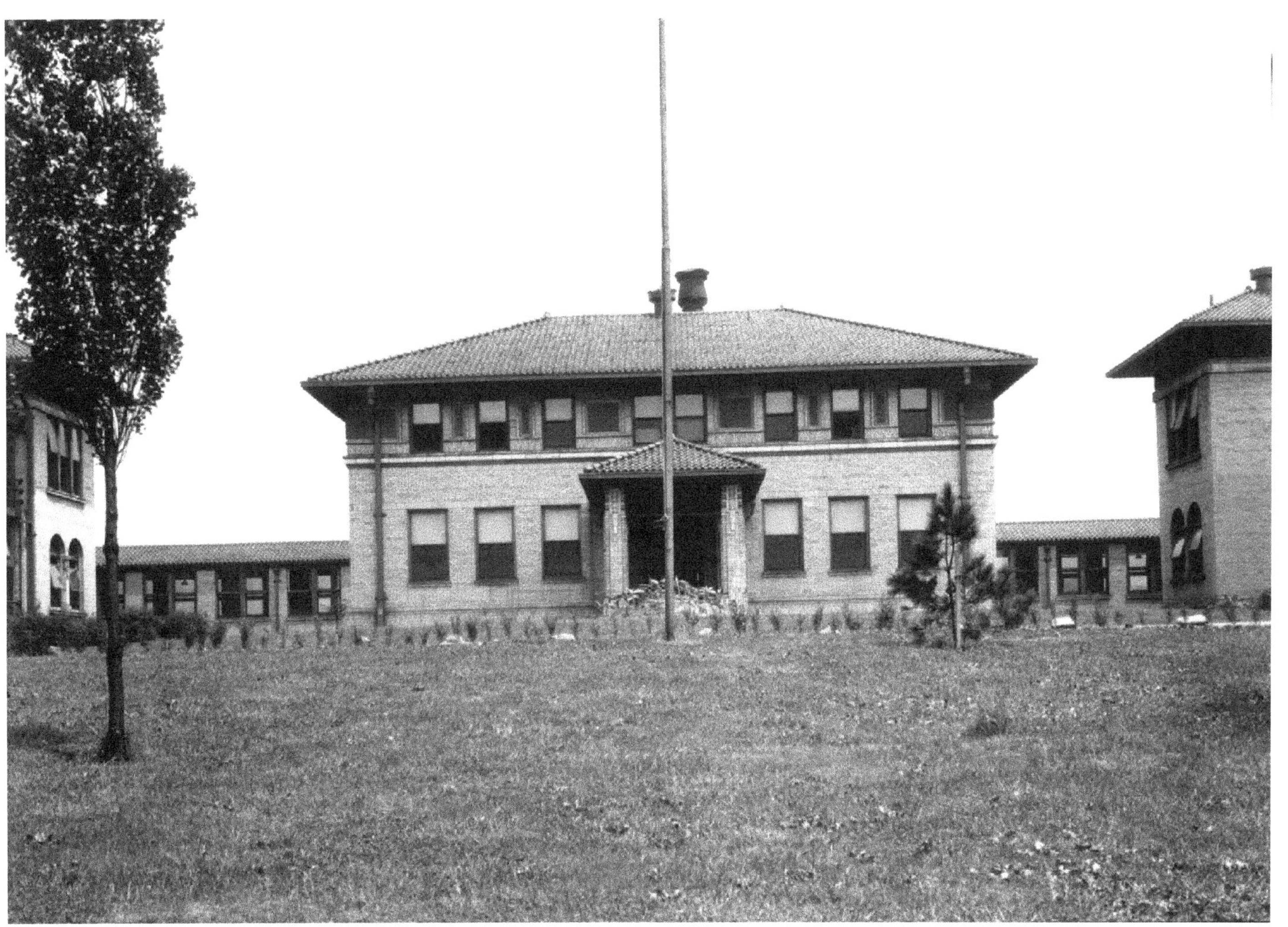

Central building of the Tuberculosis Hospital, as it appeared in 1925. Tuberculosis Hospital was built on the former Leech Farm, in the Lincoln-Lemington neighborhood, and occupied 100 acres. The hospital was supposed to be state-of-the-art and eventually included as many as 10 buildings. The first was completed in 1915 and the last buildings were completed in 1927.

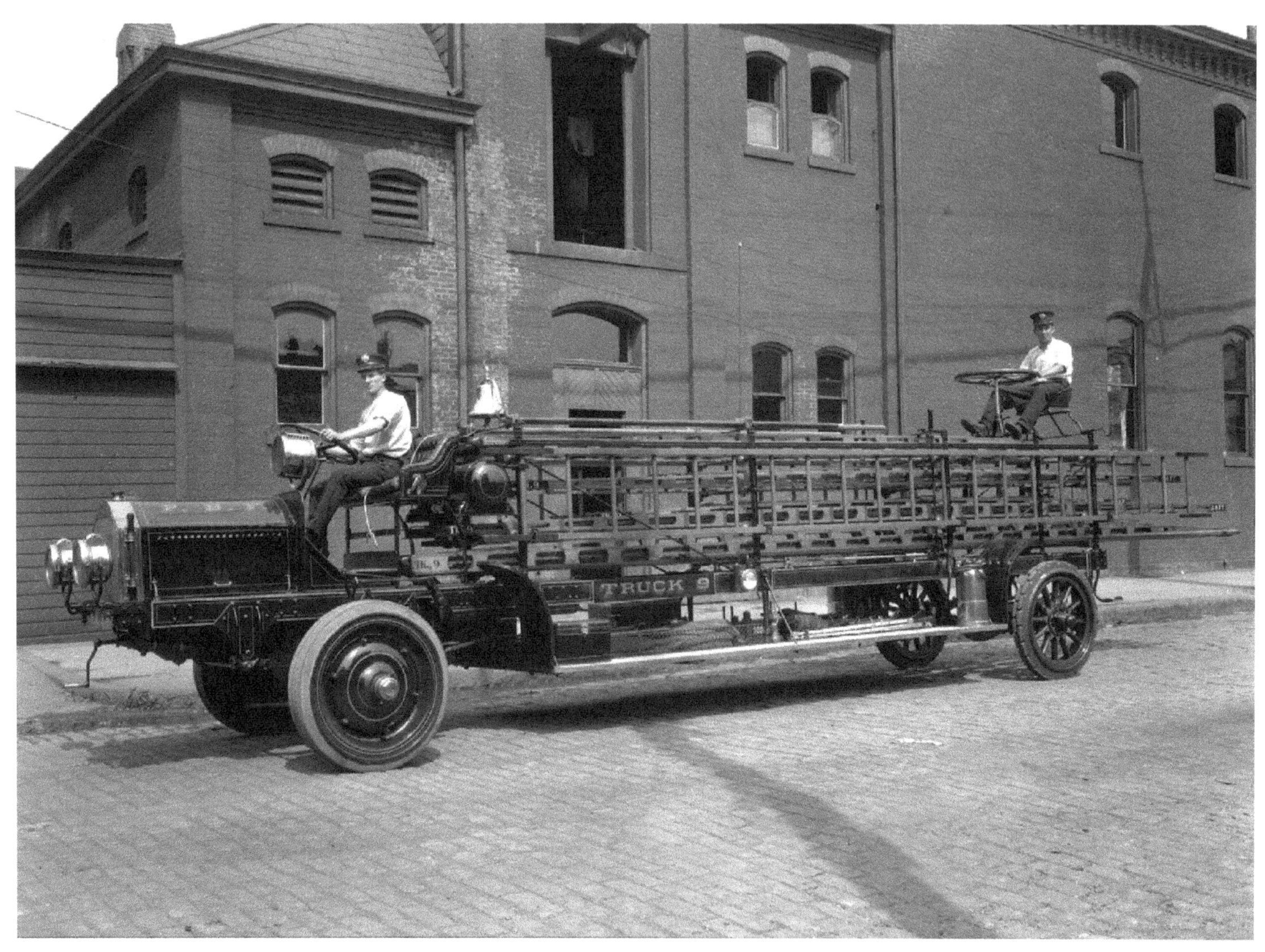

Fire fighters pose with the Pittsburgh Bureau of Fire Service ladder truck no. 9, built by the city garage.

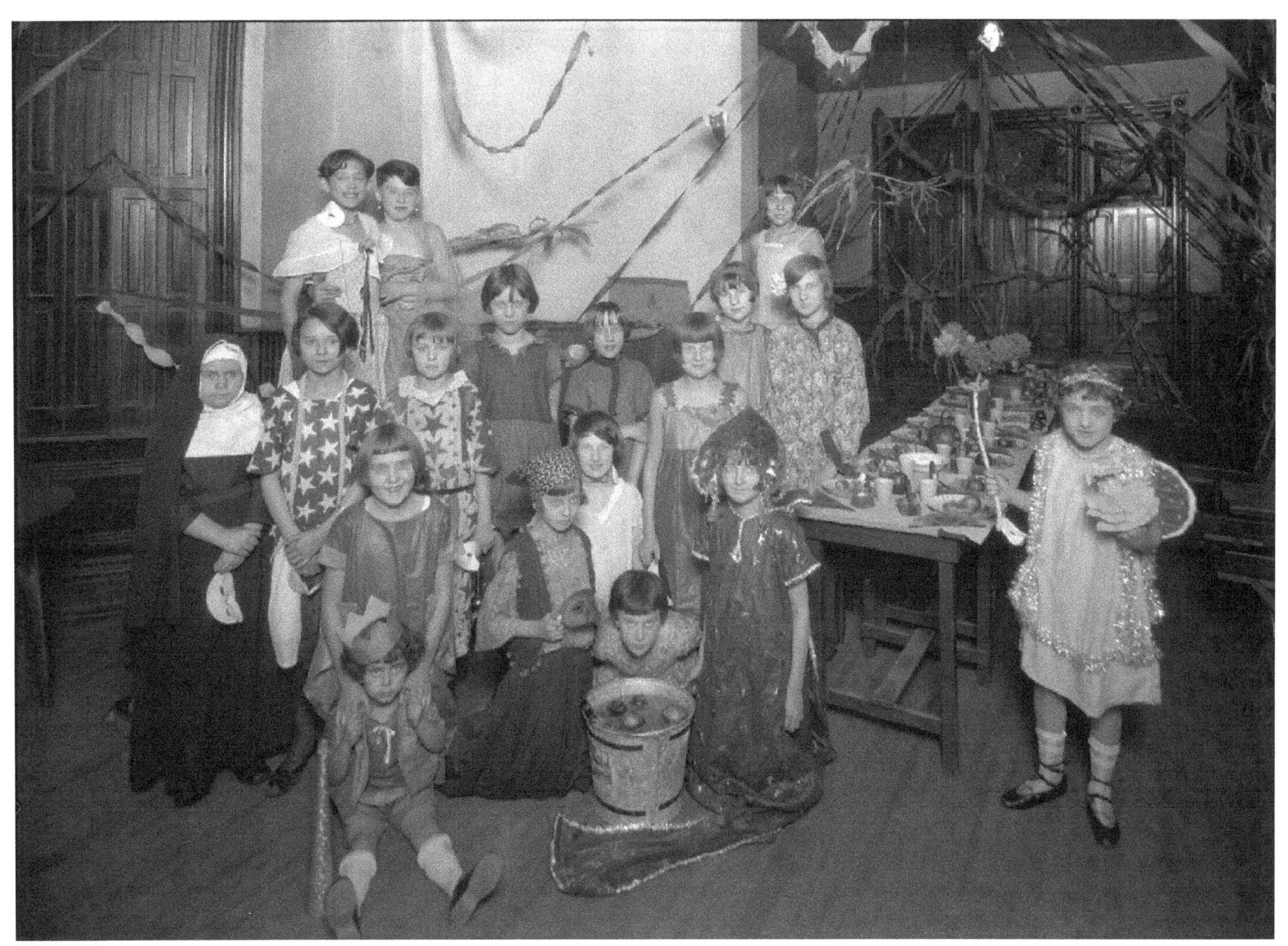

The Ormsby Park Busy Bee Club, on October 28, 1925.

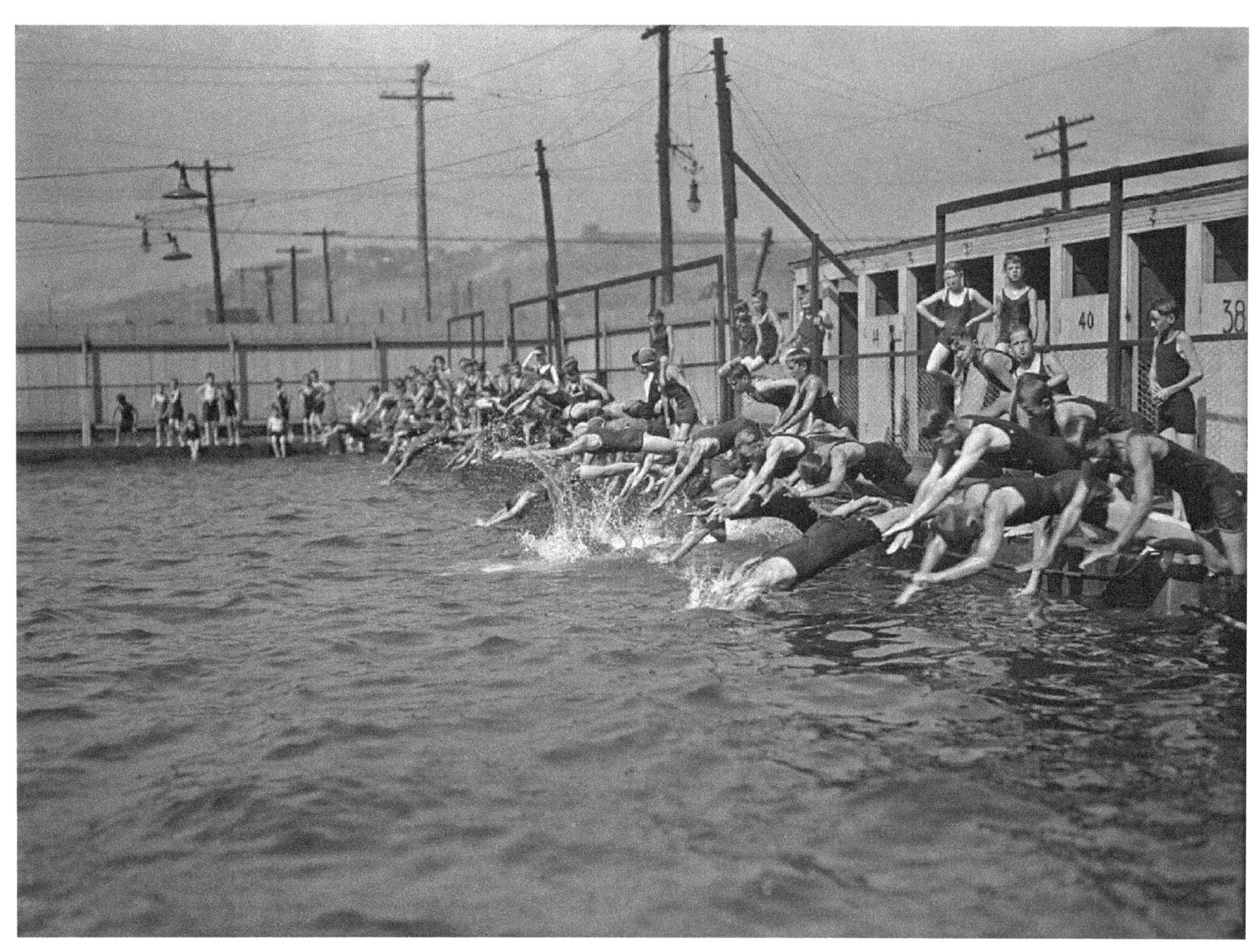

Swimming at South Side pool. When the photographer says "smile," dive!

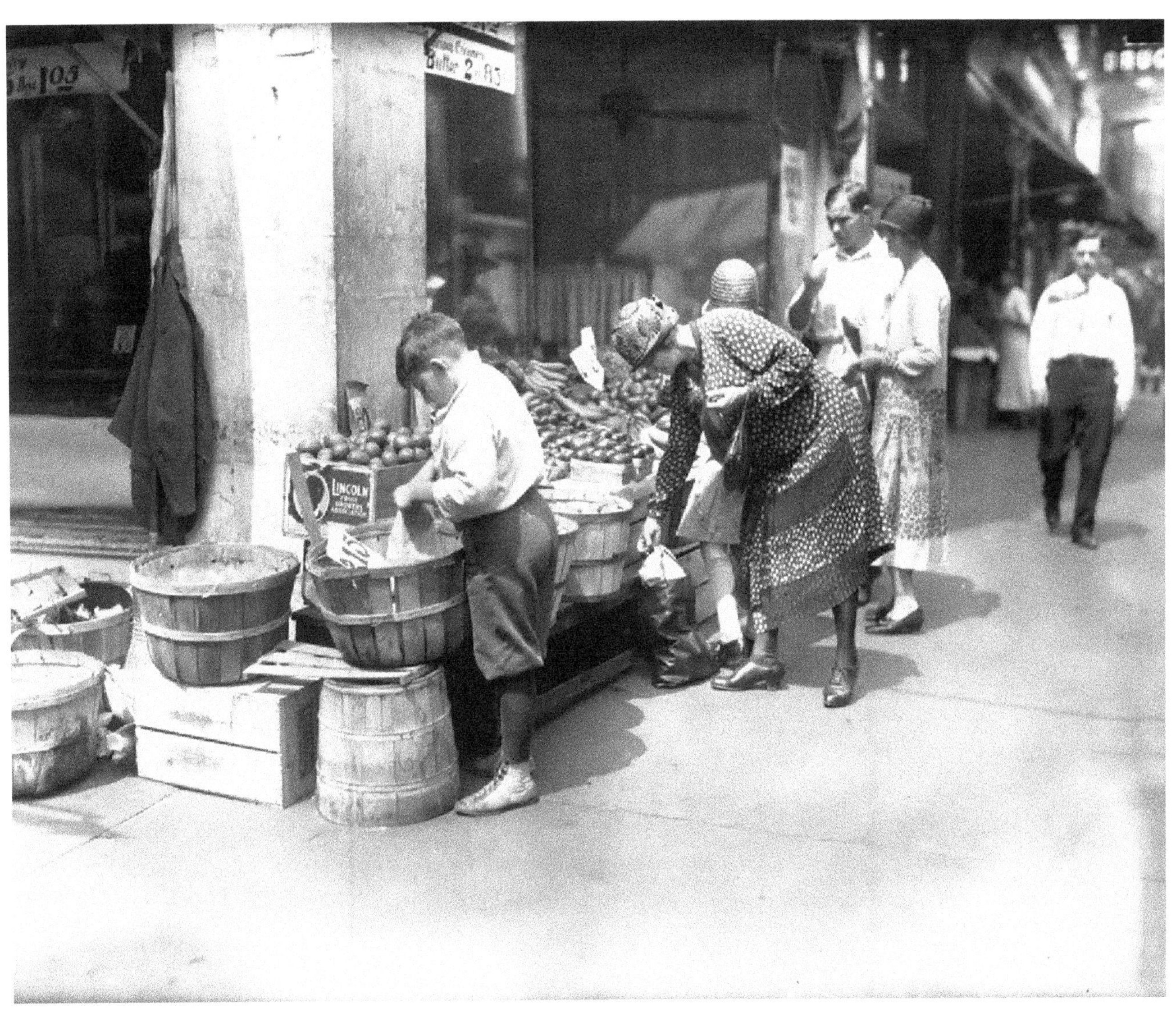

Shopping for produce at Spagnola Fruit Company, at 19 McMasters Way, downtown.

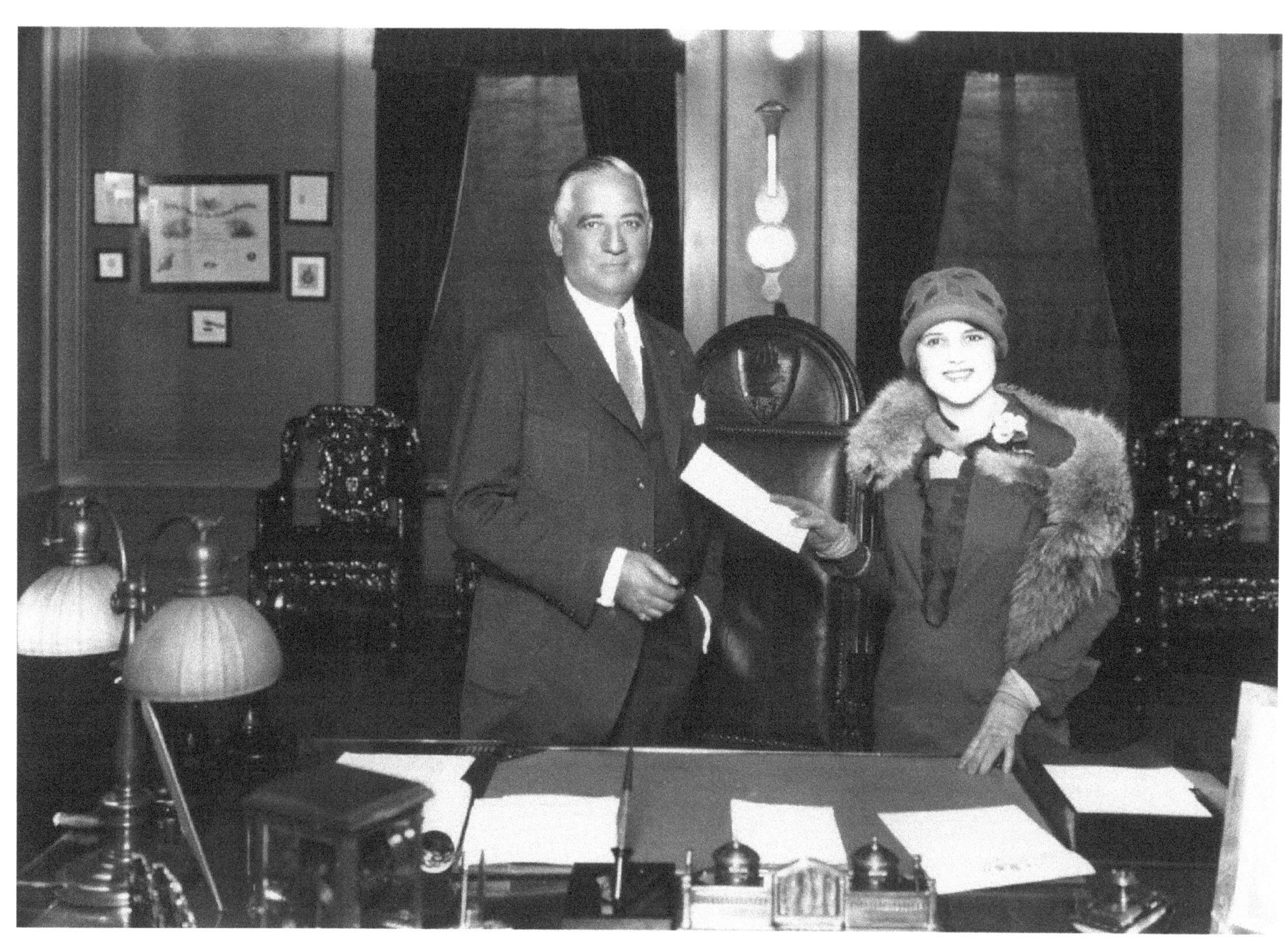

Miss Pittsburgh, also known as Miss Thelma Williams, presents a letter to Mayor Charles H. Kline upon her return from Atlantic City, September 21, 1926.

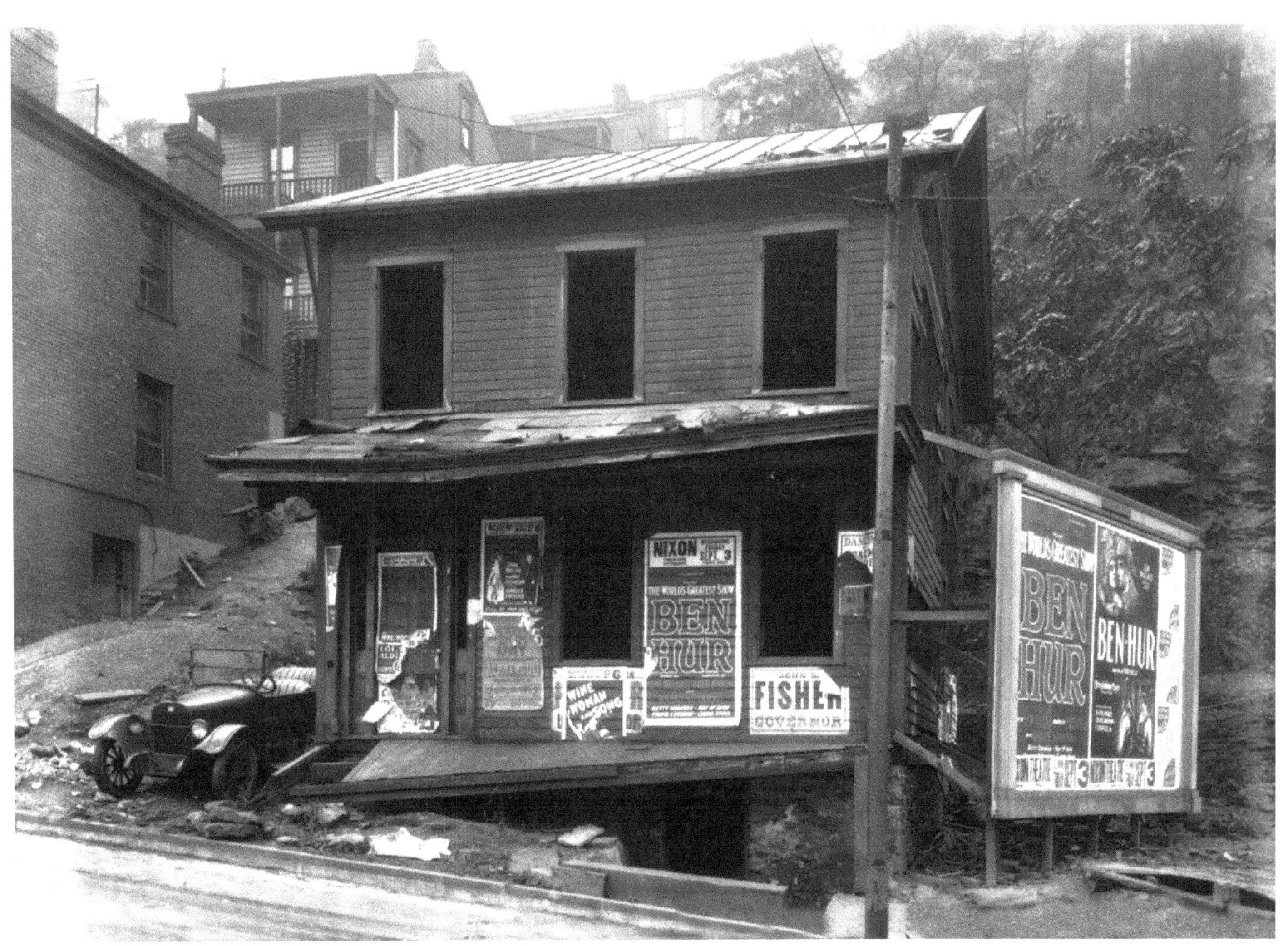

State of the house at 310-312 Brownsville Avenue.

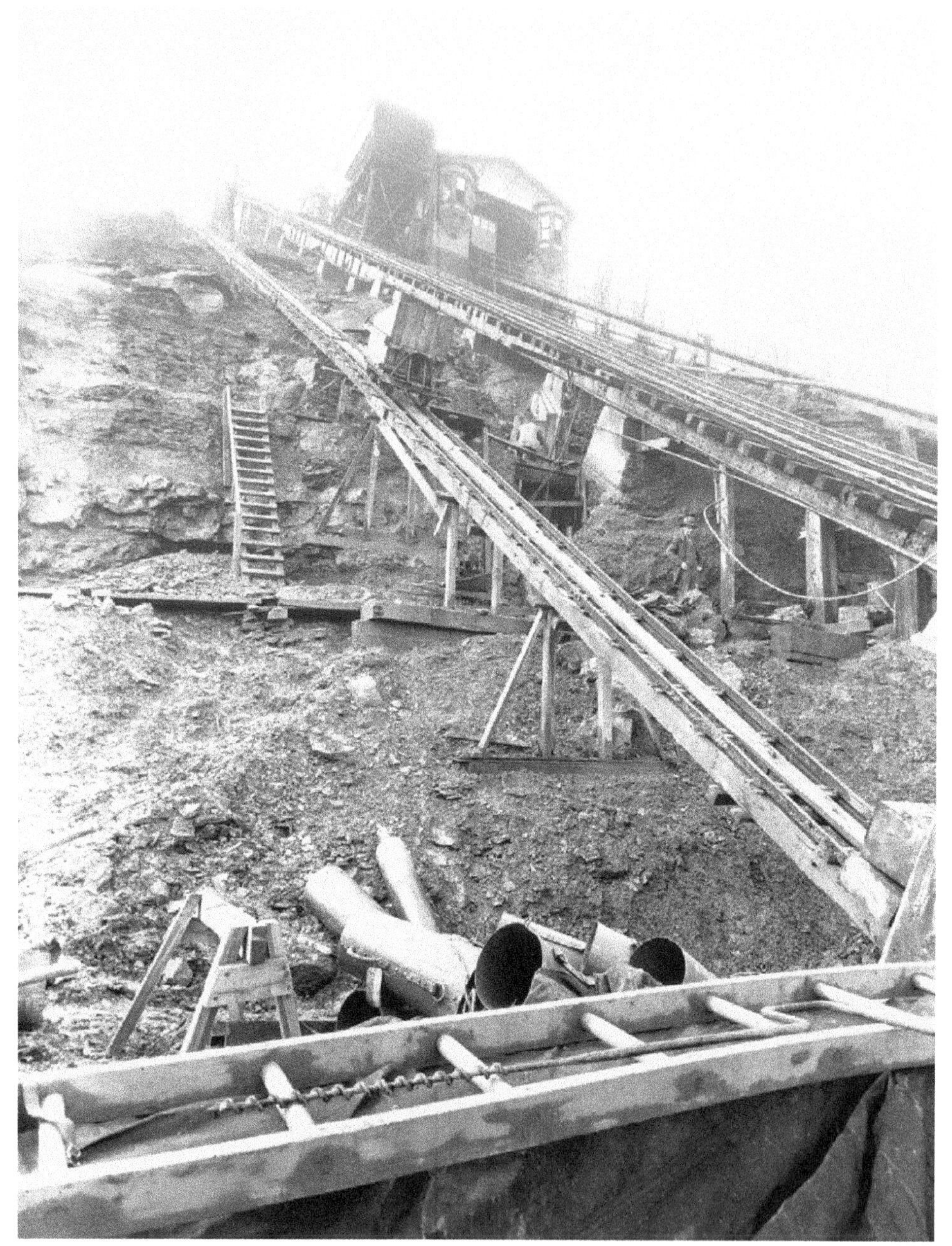

The Monongahela Incline, showing one track for people and one for carriages. The third track is for pulling items up the hill, for construction and repair.

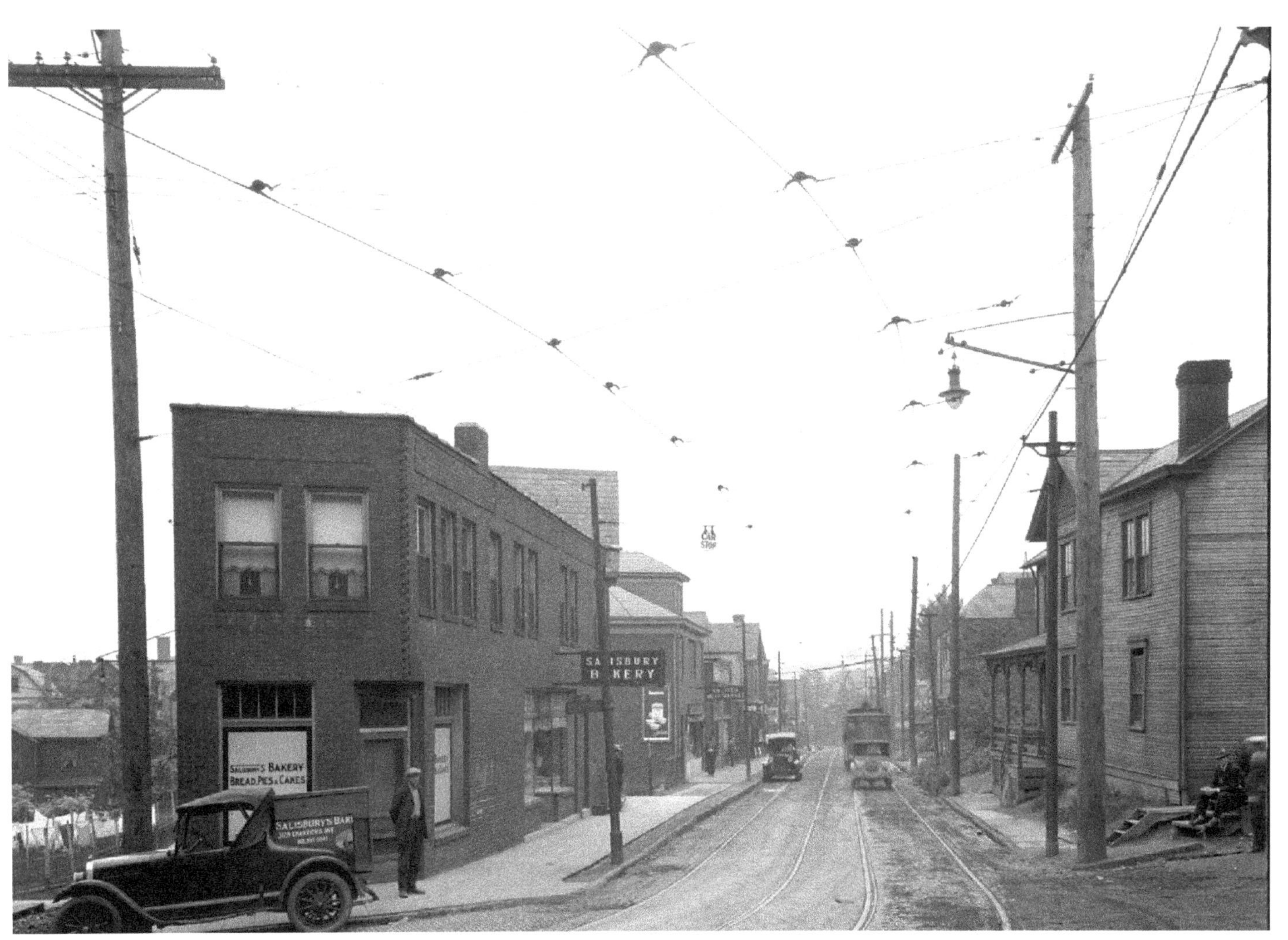

The Salisbury Bakery at 3128 Chartiers Avenue and Huxley Street.

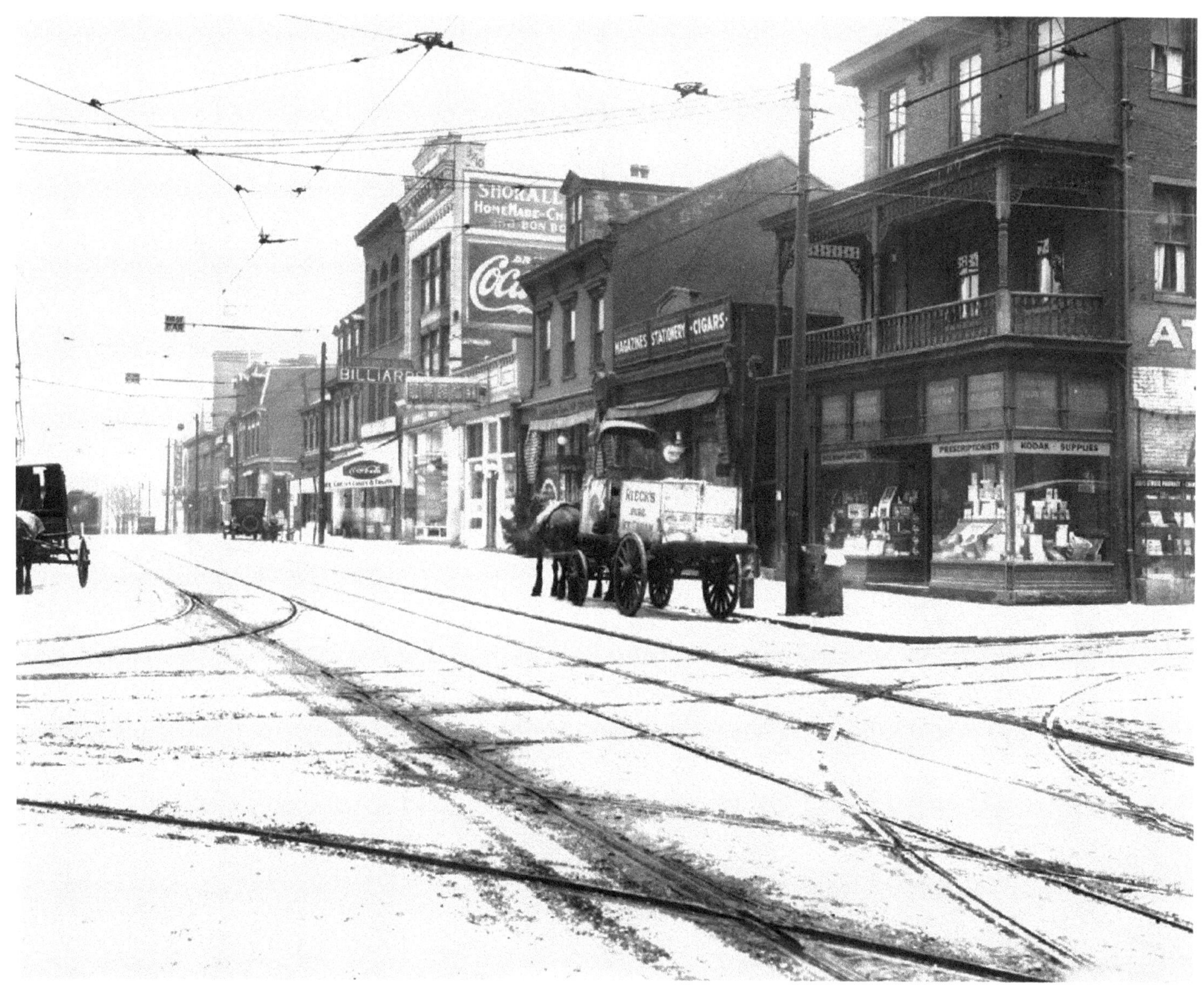

The 3700 block of Forbes Avenue at Atwood Street in Oakland features the Atwood Pharmacy, C. M. Stauft, and the Oakland 5 and 10 Cent Store.

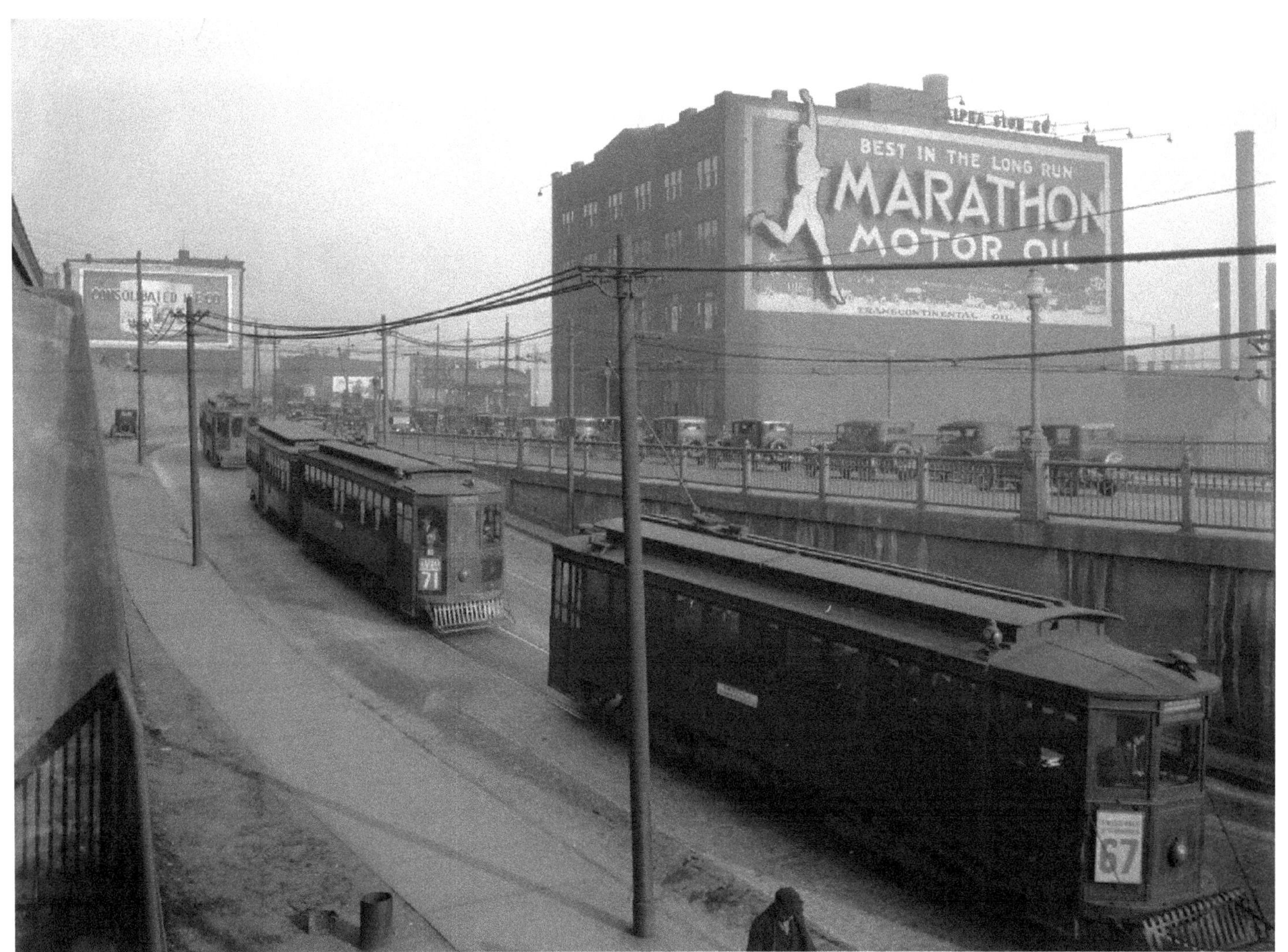

This view of Forbes Avenue at the Boulevard of the Allies shows local traffic passing in the opposite direction of the no. 71 Negley–Highland Park and the no. 67 Rankin-Swissvale-Braddock trolleys.

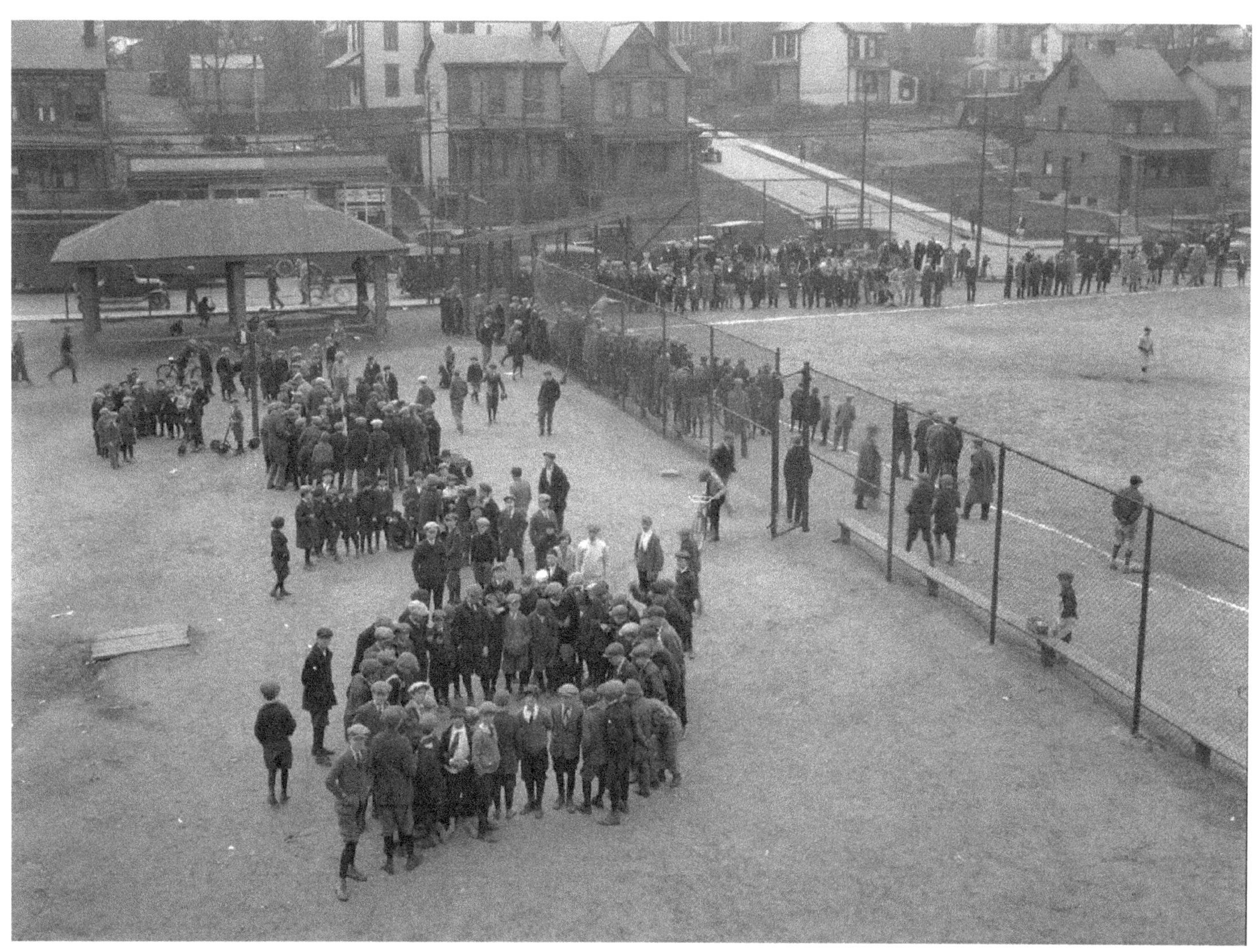

First round of the marble tournament held April 26, 1926, at Warrington Park in Beltzhoover.

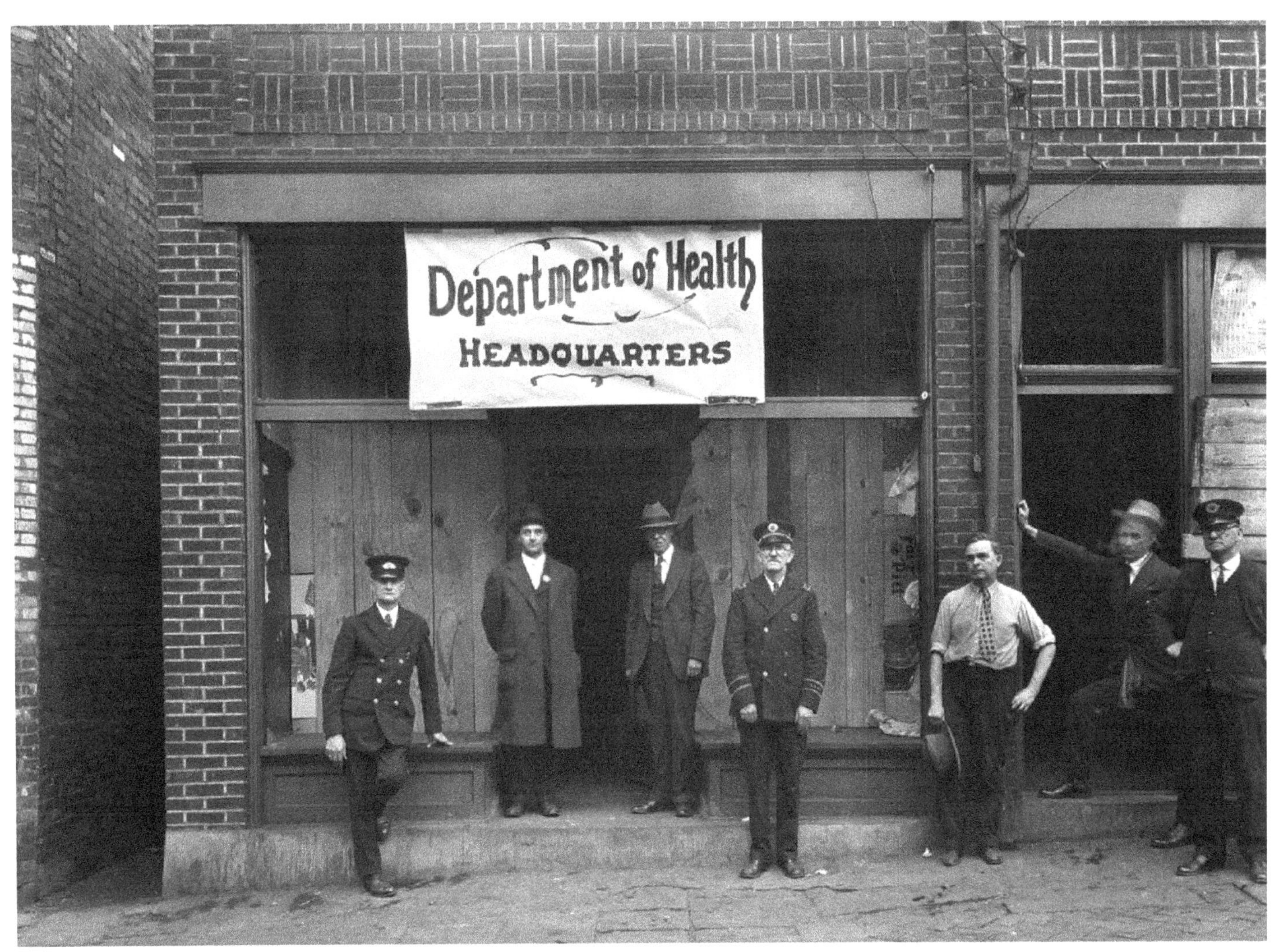

Emergency station set up by the Department of Health in a building near Reedsdale Street and Ridge Avenue after the explosion of the Equitable Gas tanks on the North Side, November 15, 1927. The explosion destroyed many homes and businesses within a 20-mile radius.

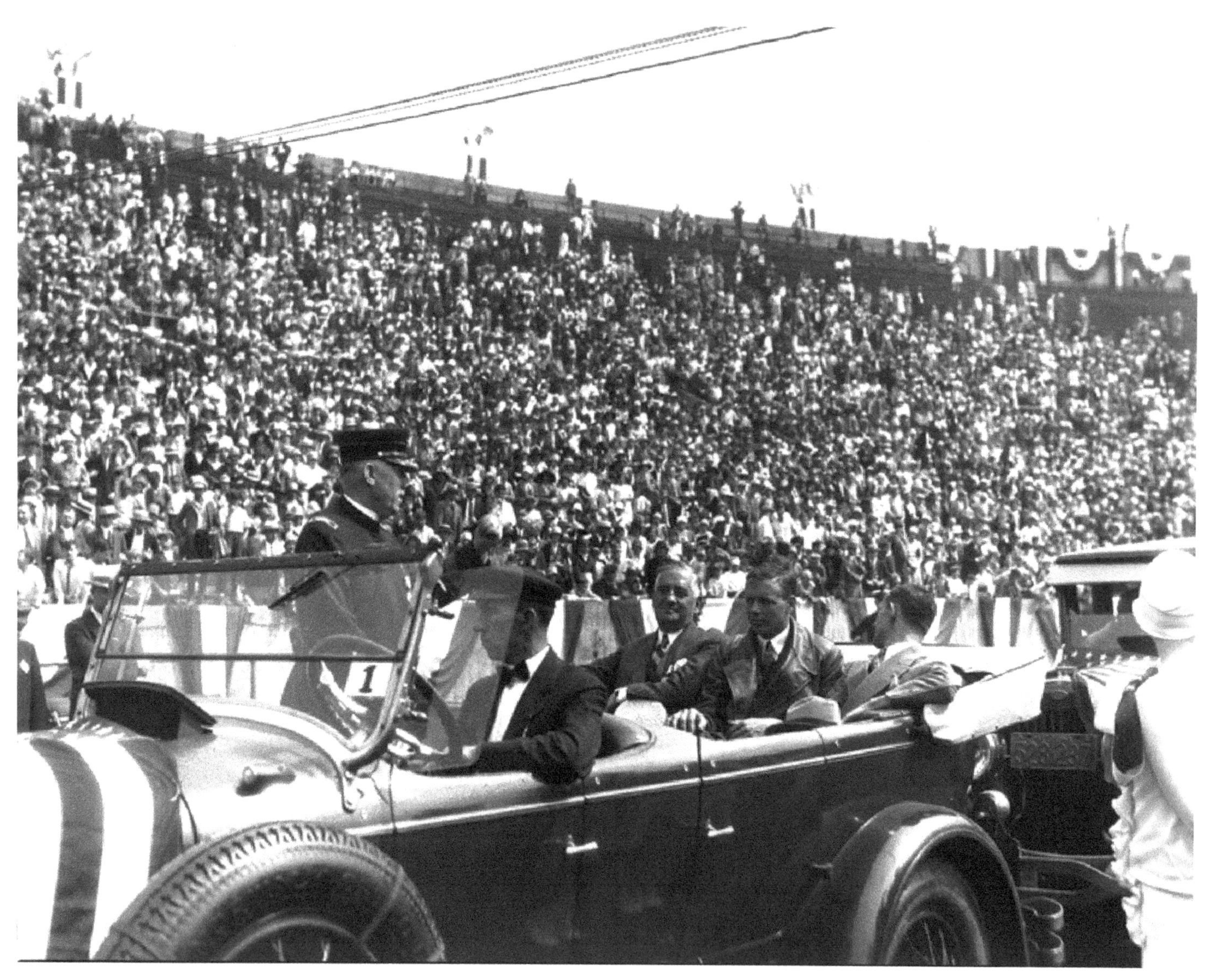

Charles Lindbergh with Pittsburgh mayor Charles H. Kline in a motorcade at Pitt Stadium, August 3, 1927. He had flown two and a half hours from Cleveland to Pittsburgh.

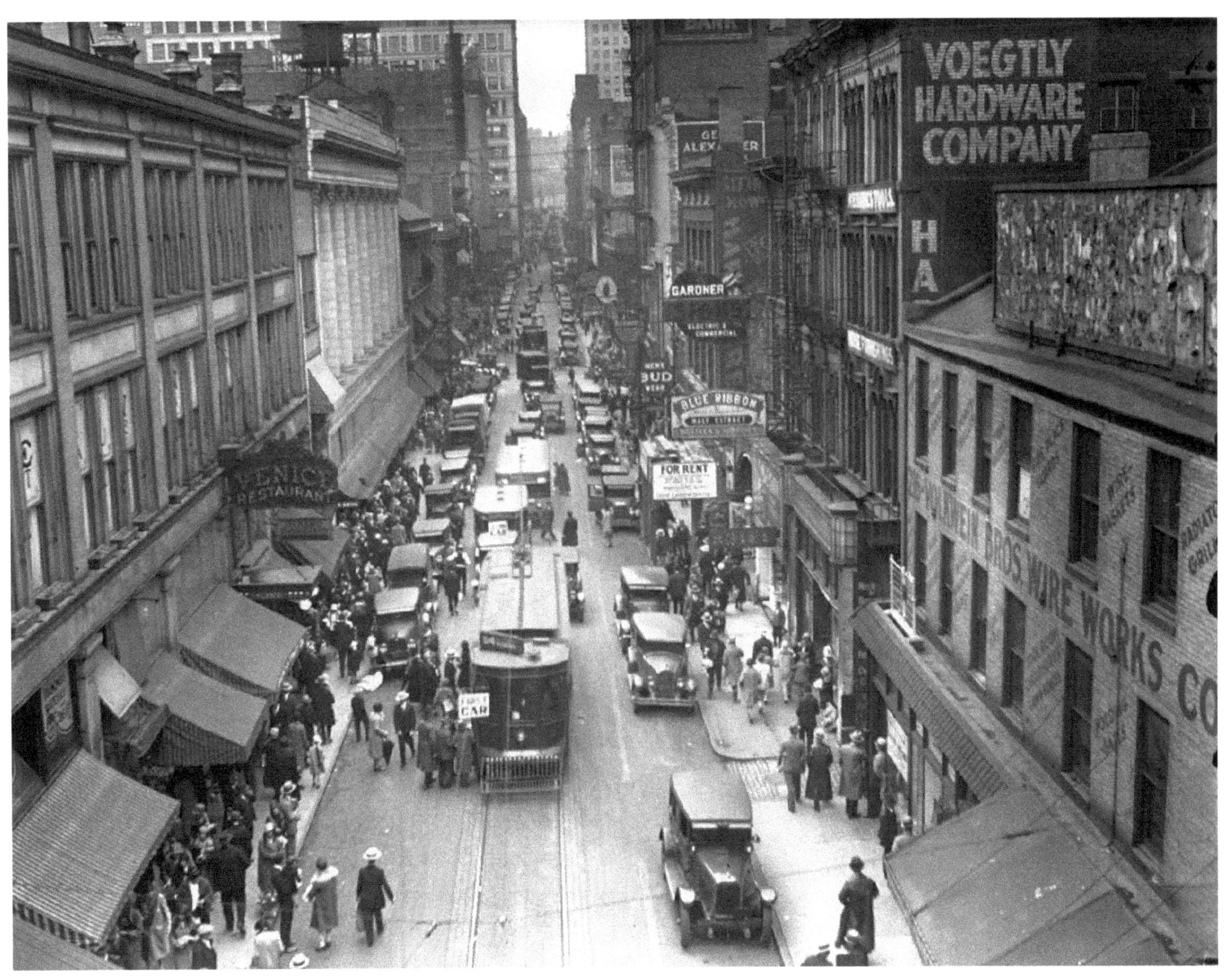

Diamond Street near the Diamond Market, as it appeared in 1928.

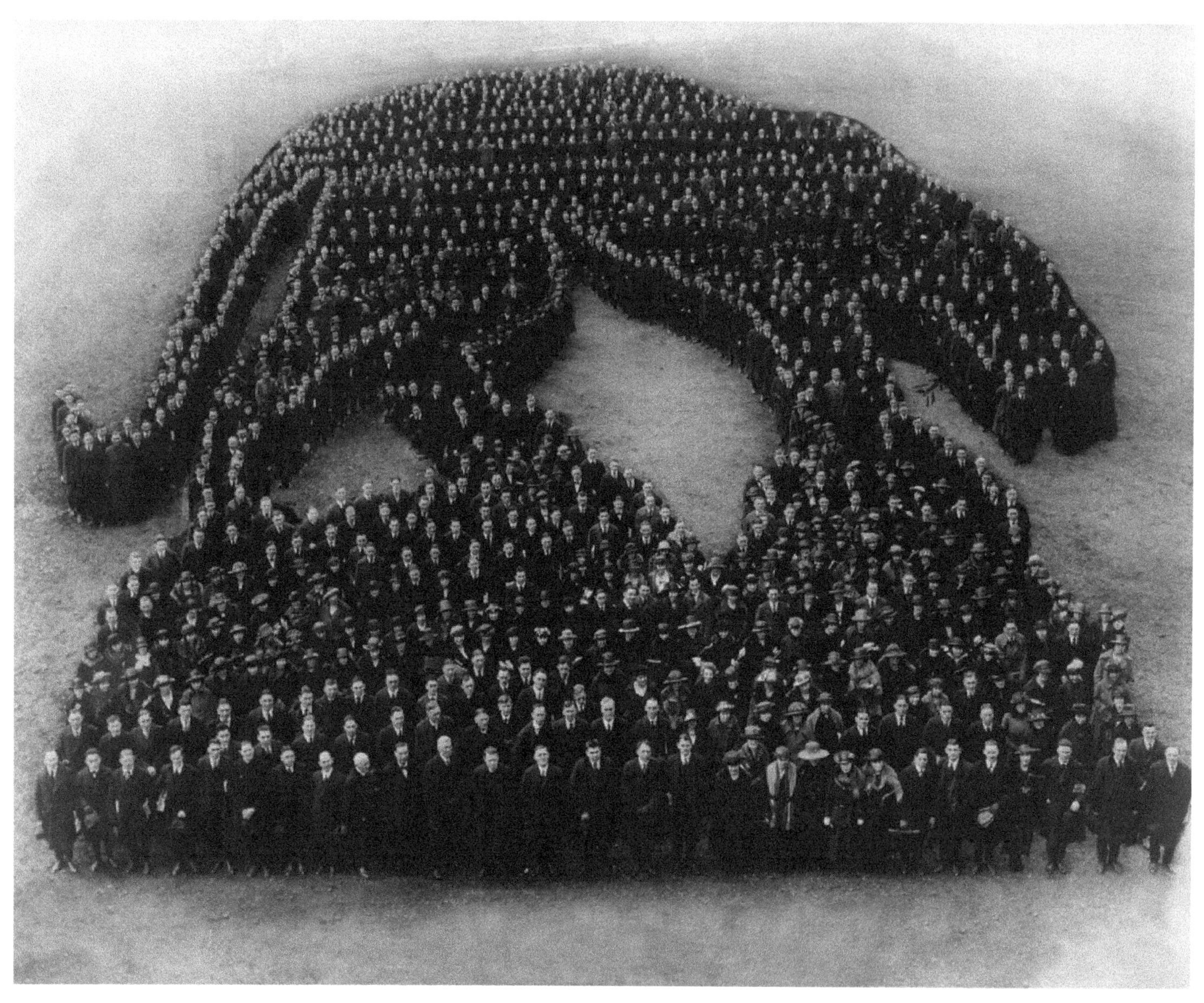

Students and faculty, filled with school spirit, gather to create the Pitt Panther. A closer look reveals a rope outline of the panther, used to make this representation possible.

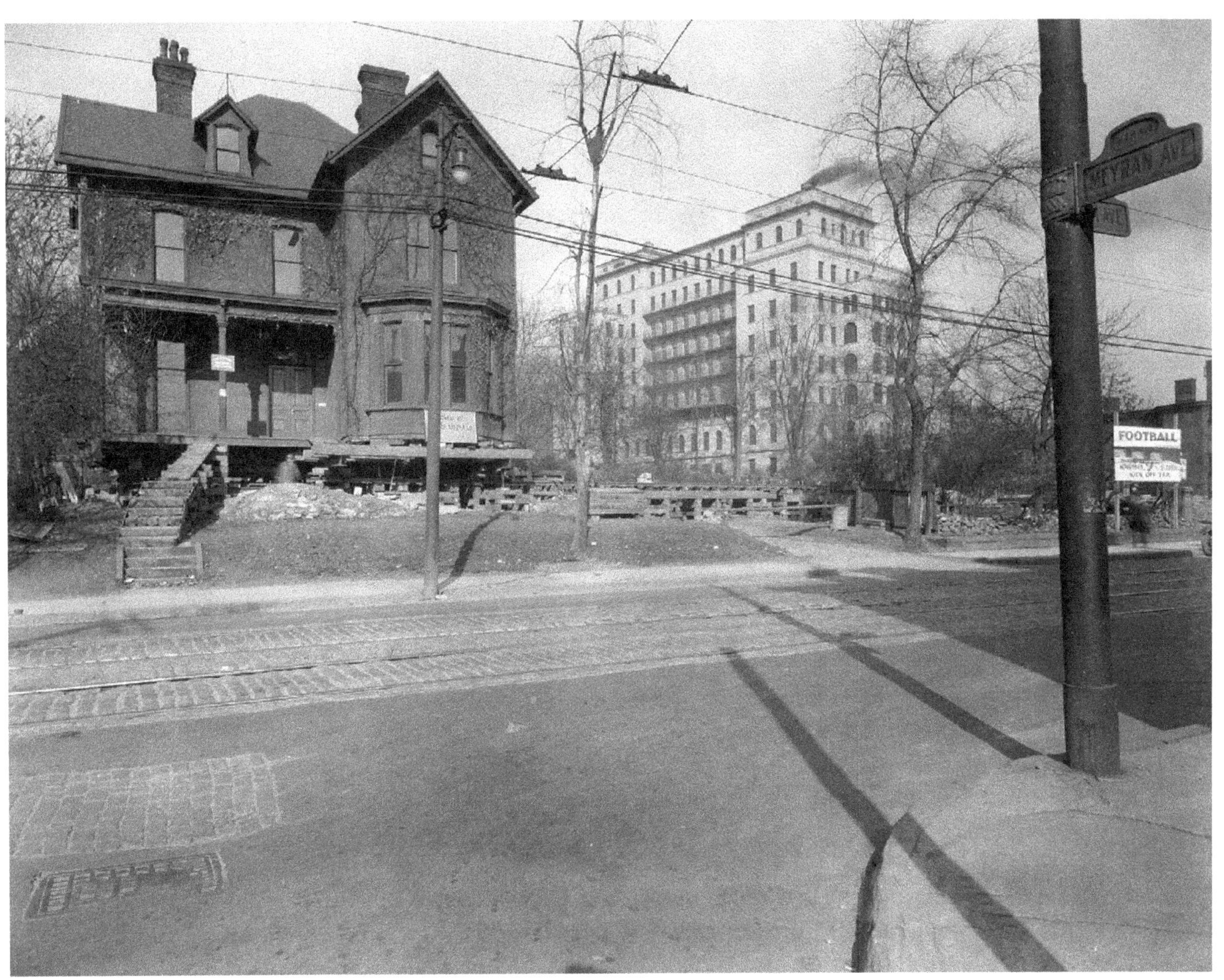

Progress at the University of Pittsburgh never stops. Shown here are preparations by the John Eichleay Jr. Company to move a house so that the new Falk Clinic can be built at Fifth and Meyran avenues.

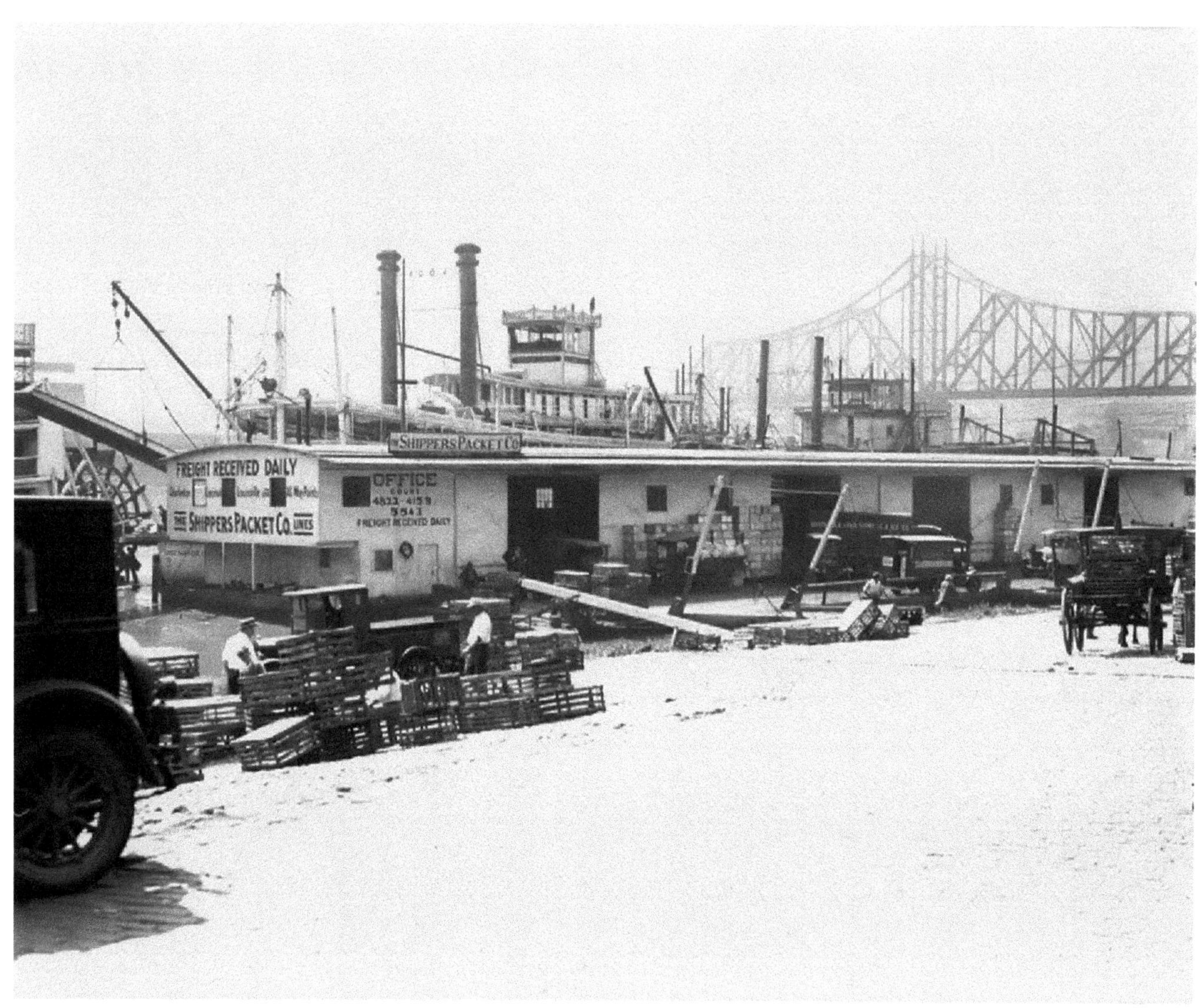

Shippers Packet Company offices on the Monongahela River wharf, 1929.

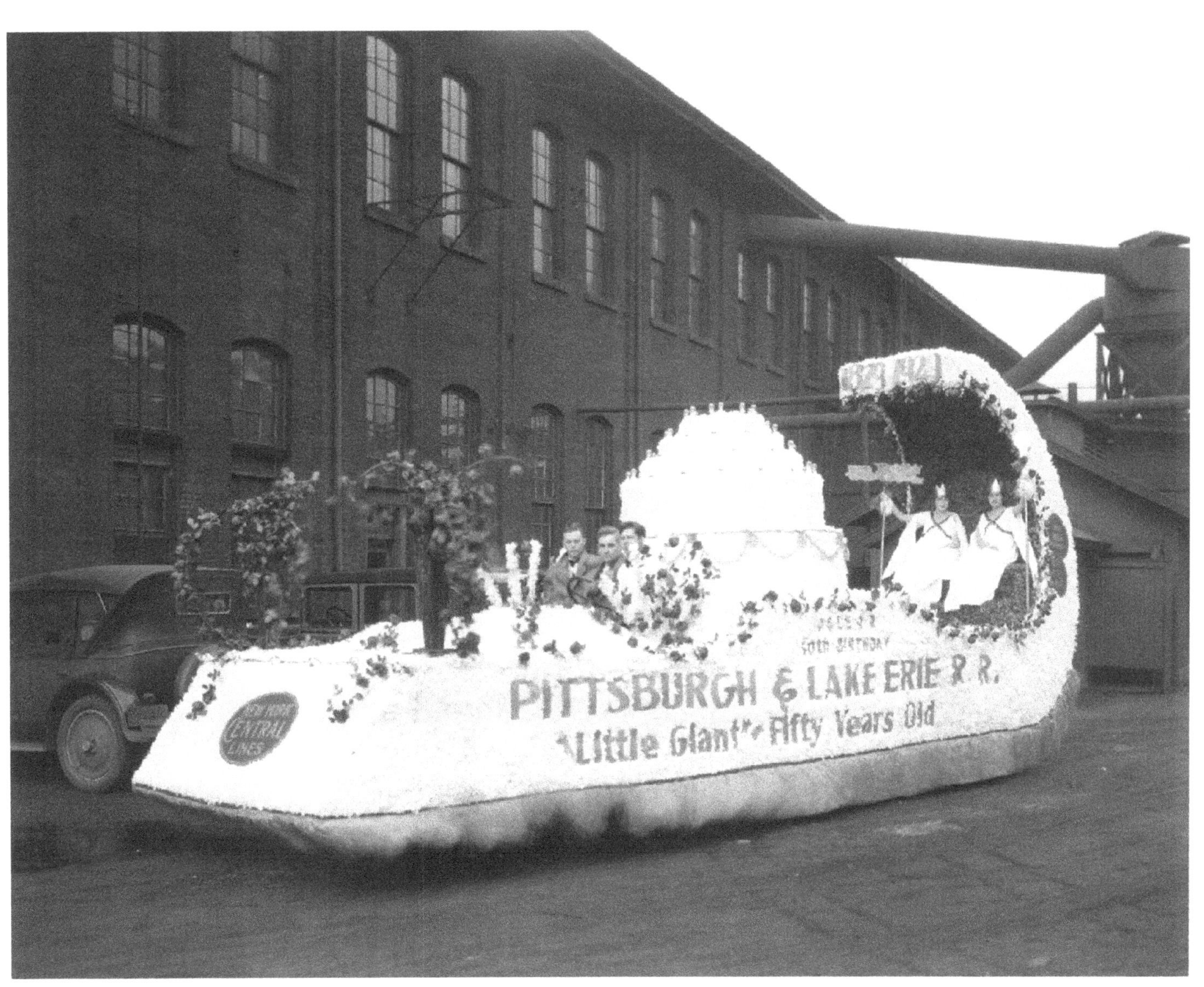

A parade float commemorates the 50th anniversary of the founding of the Pittsburgh and Lake Erie Railroad in 1879.

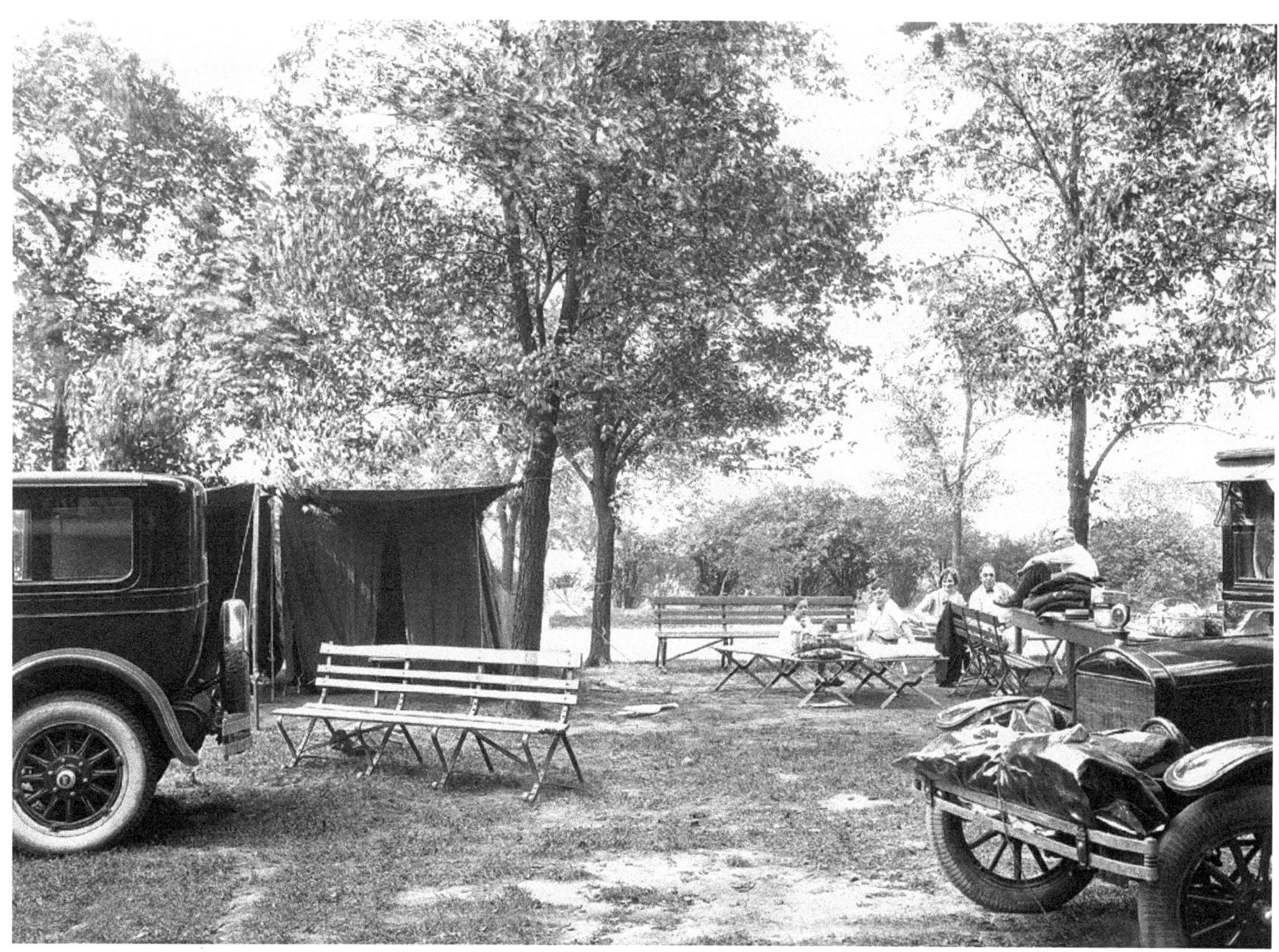

Car camping at Schenley Park.

Hard Times and Other Challenges

(1930–1939)

By the 1930s, the city's population had grown to nearly 670,000 residents. Businesses and government services were expanding. The Fifth and Bellefield area in Oakland seemed to be the busiest construction zone in the city. Mellon Institute construction began in 1930. The University of Pittsburgh completed its 42-story, Gothic-revival Cathedral of Learning, seen in nearly every aerial photograph taken of the city, in 1937. The Heinz Chapel was built mere steps away from the cathedral, and across the street from the Mellon Institute.

Flooding was nothing new to Pittsburgh. Photographs dating as far back as 1874 document the devastation caused by Pittsburgh's rivers leaving their banks. Pittsburgh had experienced flooding as high as 31.3 feet before, but nothing prepared it for March 16 and 17, 1936. That day would be remembered as the "Great St. Patrick's Day Flood," with floodwaters cresting at 46 feet. Even this would pale in comparison with what would happen the following year when the Ohio River reached nearly 80 feet. The Monongahela and Allegheny rivers rose to within 6 feet of floodstage and Pittsburgh felt the impact, but Cincinnati and Louisville, farther downriver, were devastated. Both floods brought to light the serious issue of flood control. On June 22, 1936, Congress passed the Flood-Control Act.

Even though Pittsburgh was not able to take the advice of New York Parks Commissioner Robert Moses at the time, his ideas for urban renewal, which included roads, housing, and a park at the Point, would be a portent of things to come. Aerial views of the city show why changes needed to be made. Without traveling through all of the various neighborhoods, there was really no way to reach downtown in a timely manner. The solution would not be fully realized until the 1950s.

Like most of the nation during this time, Pittsburgh was not immune to the effects of the Great Depression. Residents turned to the aid of charitable organizations, and men like James R. Cox rose to the challenge to lend a hand to a hurting community. People stood in bread lines, a shantytown with a population of 300 was built in the Strip District, and some faced even more grave situations.

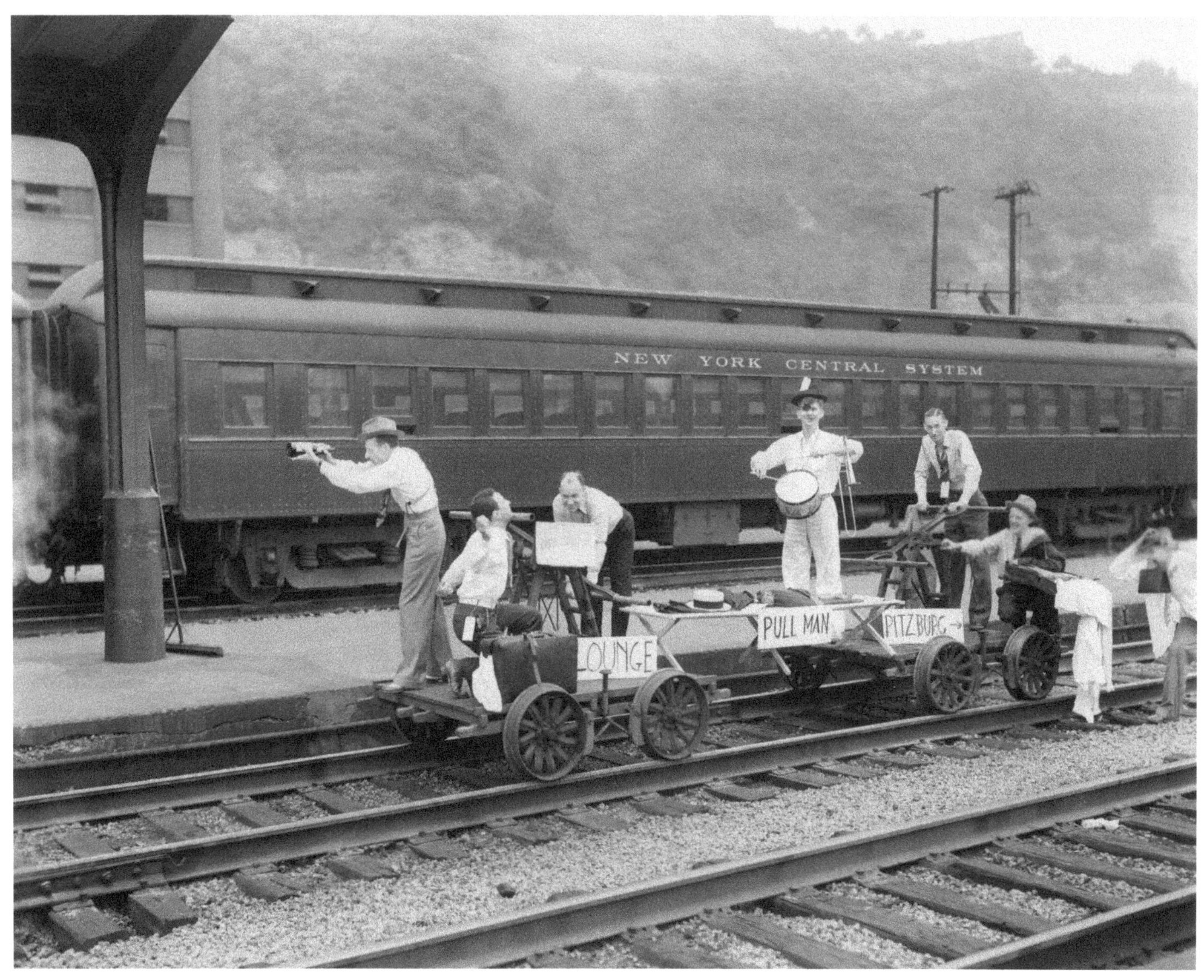

Studebaker automotive salesmen have a bit of fun at the Pennsylvania Railroad station.

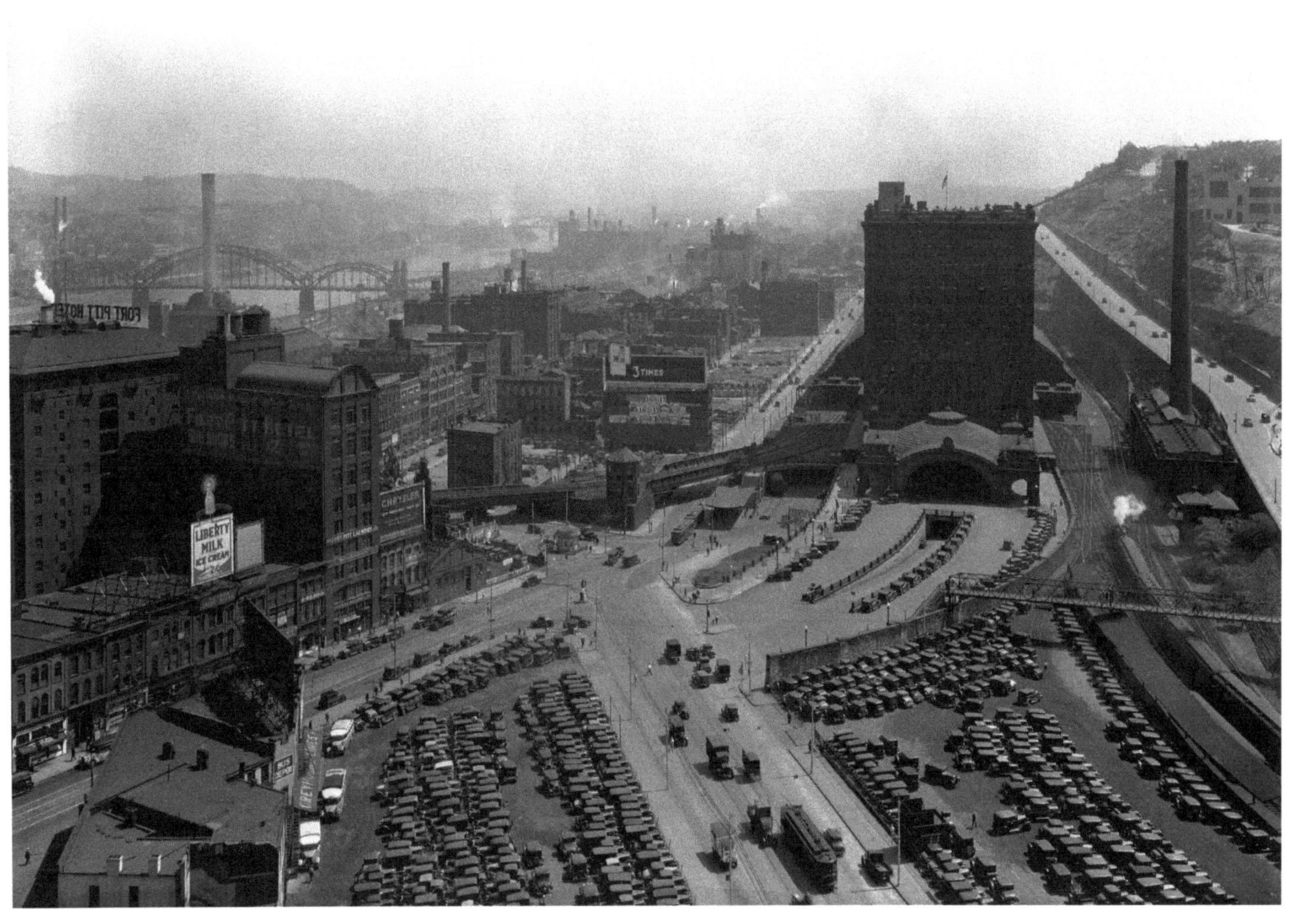

An aerial view toward the Strip District shows the Fort Pitt Laundry, Greyhound Bus Station, the Pennsylvania Railroad Station, and other landmarks as they appeared in 1930.

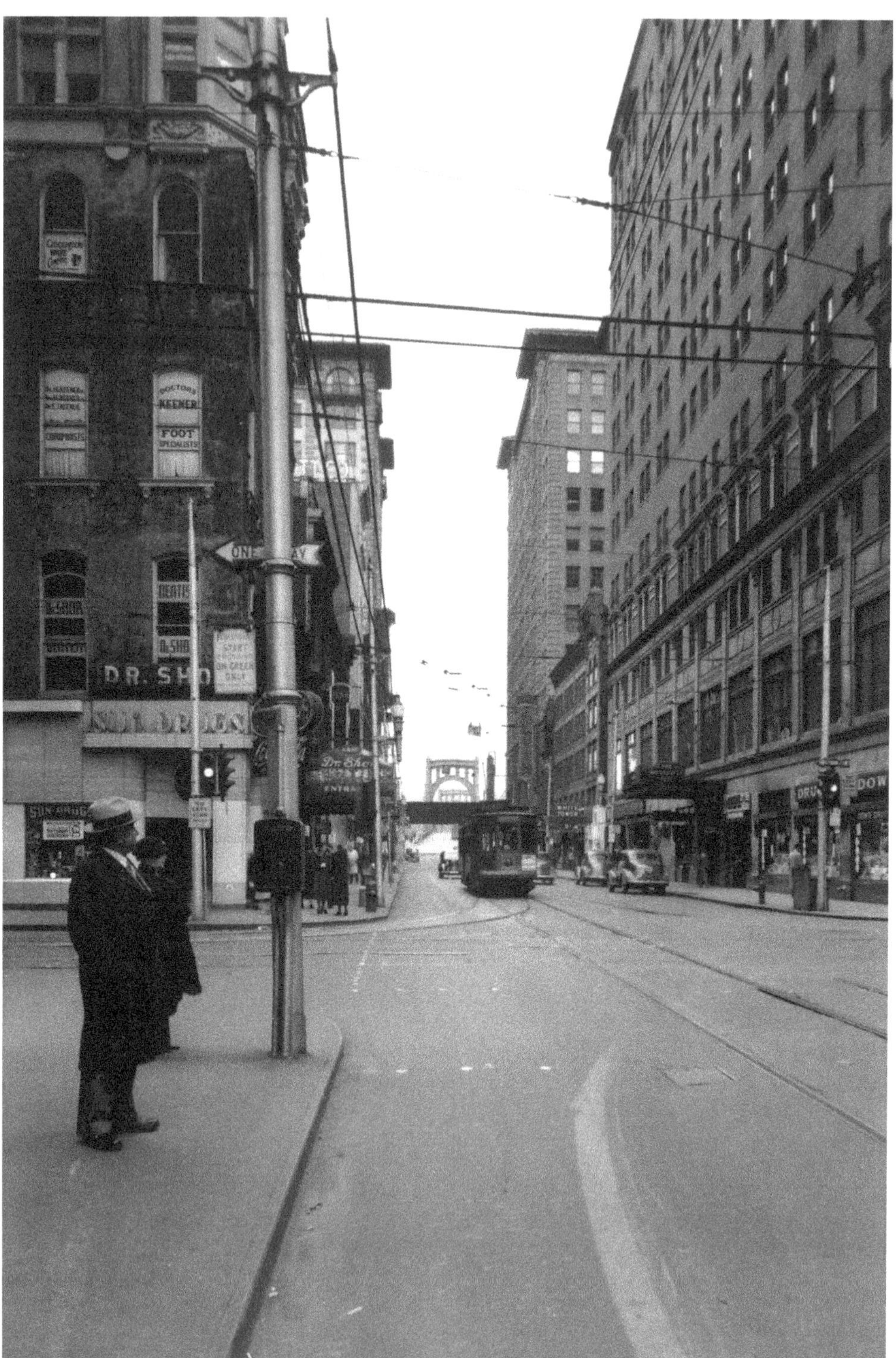

Sixth Street facing north from Penn Avenue to the Roosevelt Hotel and the Alvin Theatre. The bridge just beyond is the Sixth Street Bridge, now known as the Roberto Clemente Bridge.

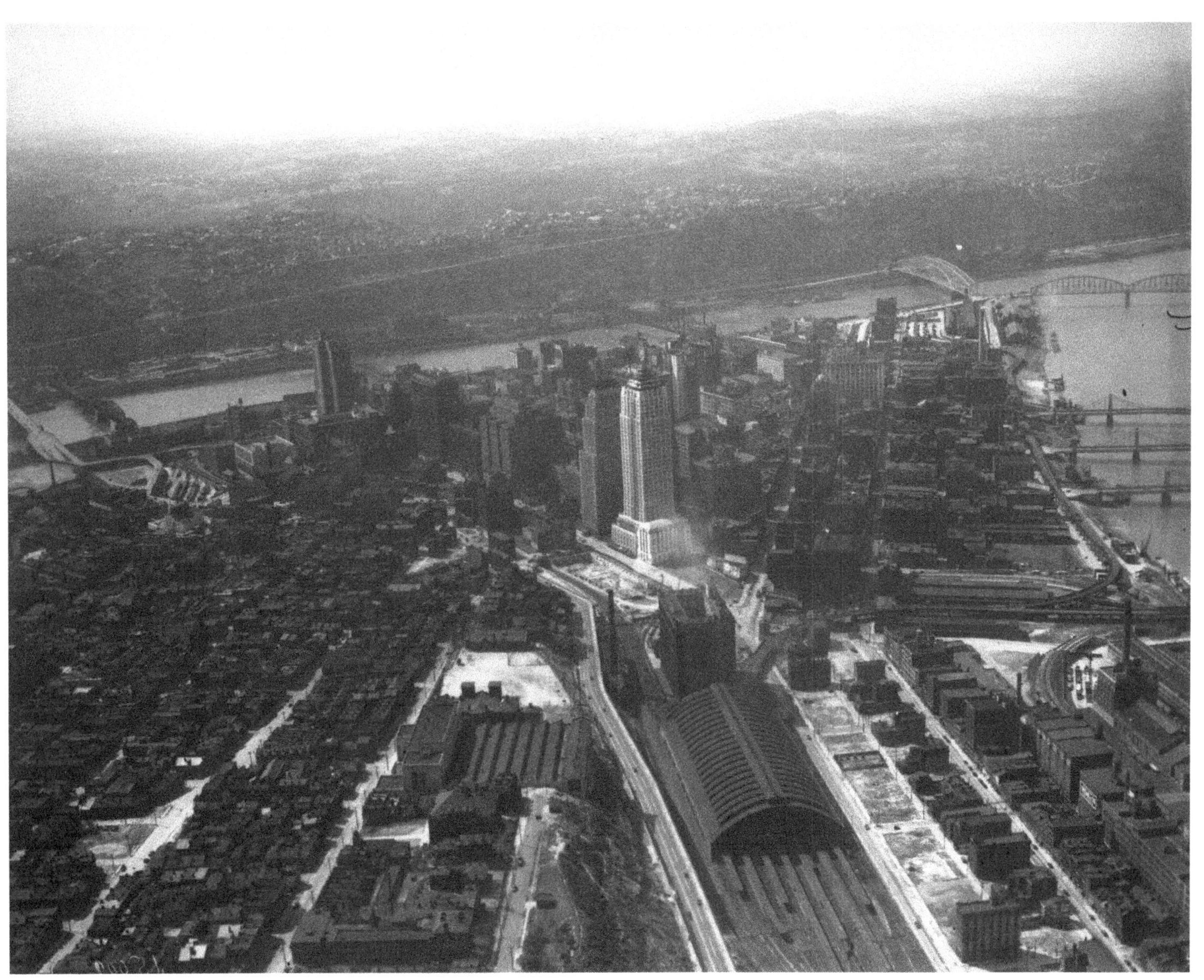

Aerial view of the Strip District, Hill District, and downtown, facing southwest toward the Point. Shown are the Pennsylvania train station, the Sixth, Seventh, and Ninth Street bridges, as well as the Point Bridge and the Manchester Bridge.

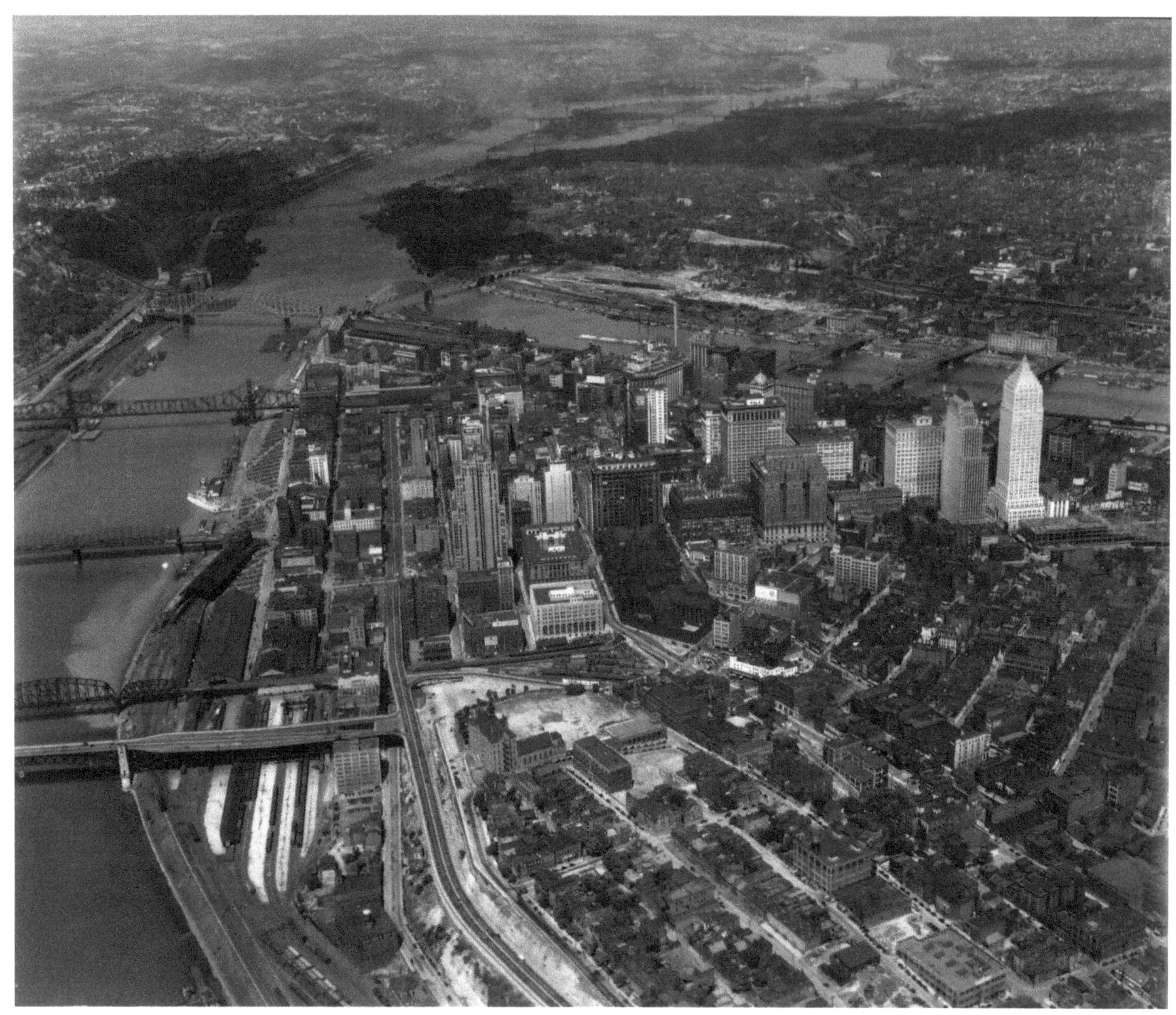

A 1932 aerial view facing west toward the Point. This image makes clear why Pittsburgh is known as the "City of Bridges." The Smithfield Street Bridge, the Wabash Bridge, the Point Bridge, the Manchester Bridge, the Sixth Street Bridge, and the Seventh Street Bridge are all visible.

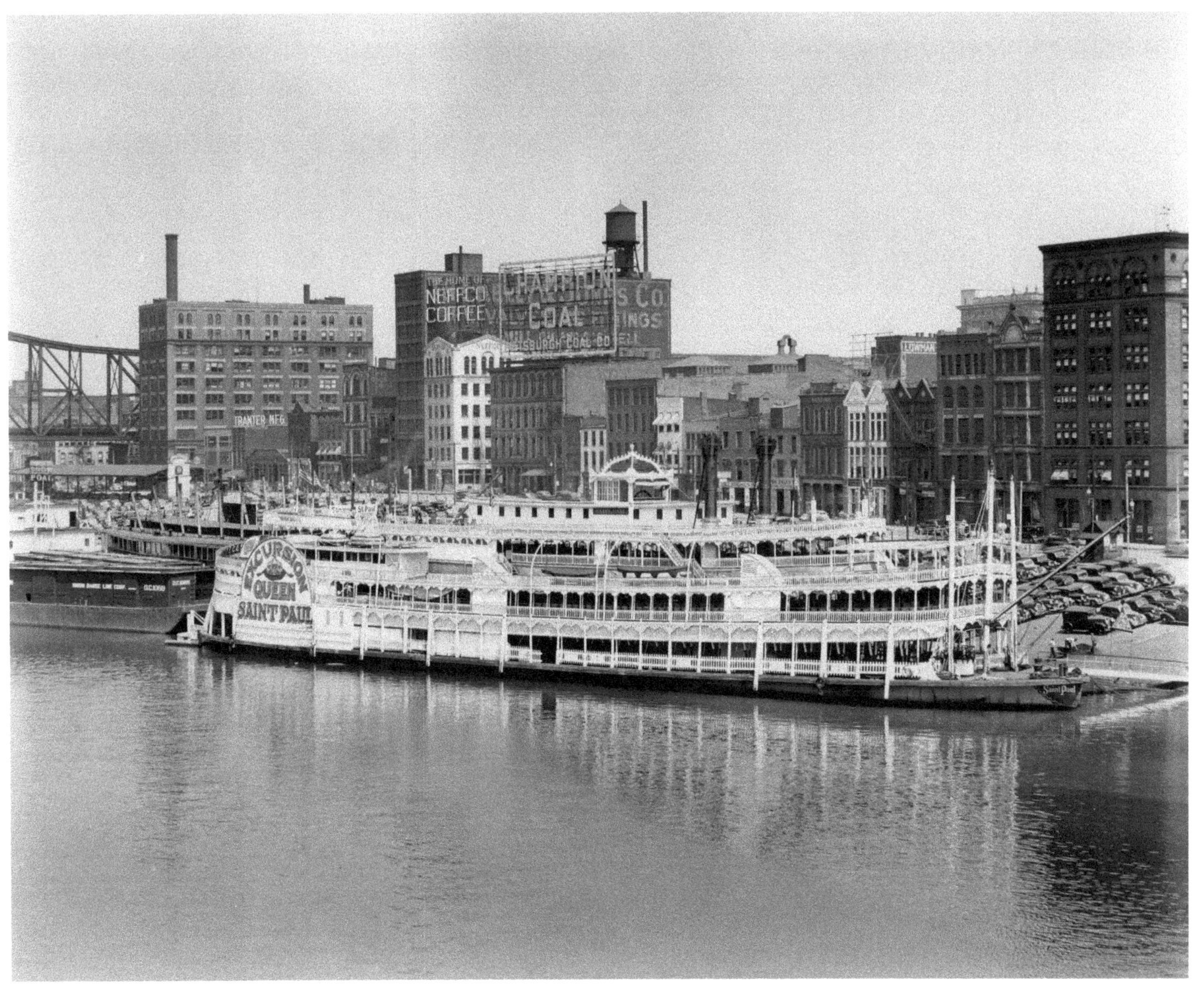

The *St. Paul Excursion Queen* is docked at the Monongahela Wharf. The wharf was one of the main commerce points for the city. Shipping, trading, shopping, and travel all originated here. Just beyond is Water Street and downtown.

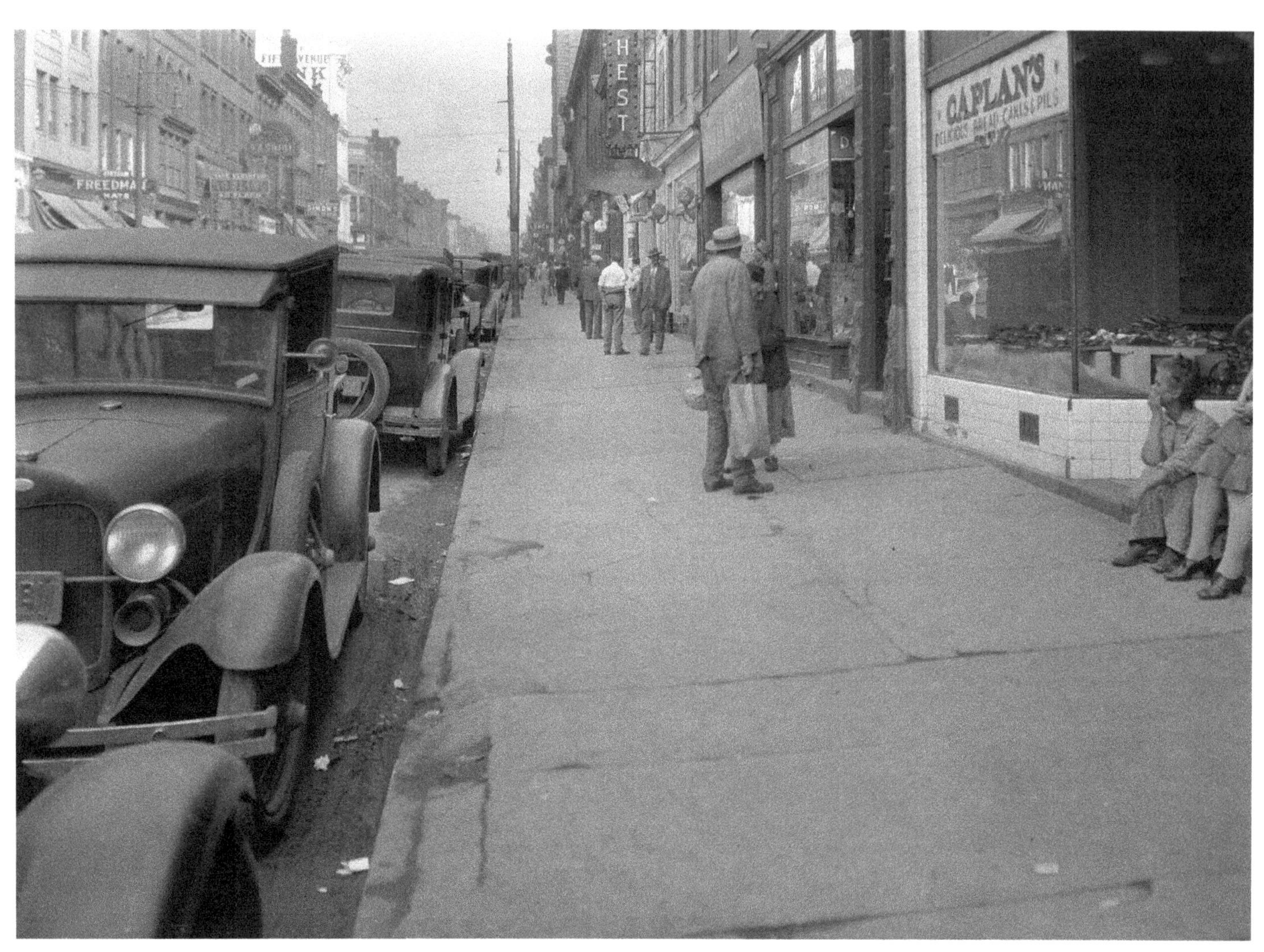

1308 Fifth Avenue, facing east.

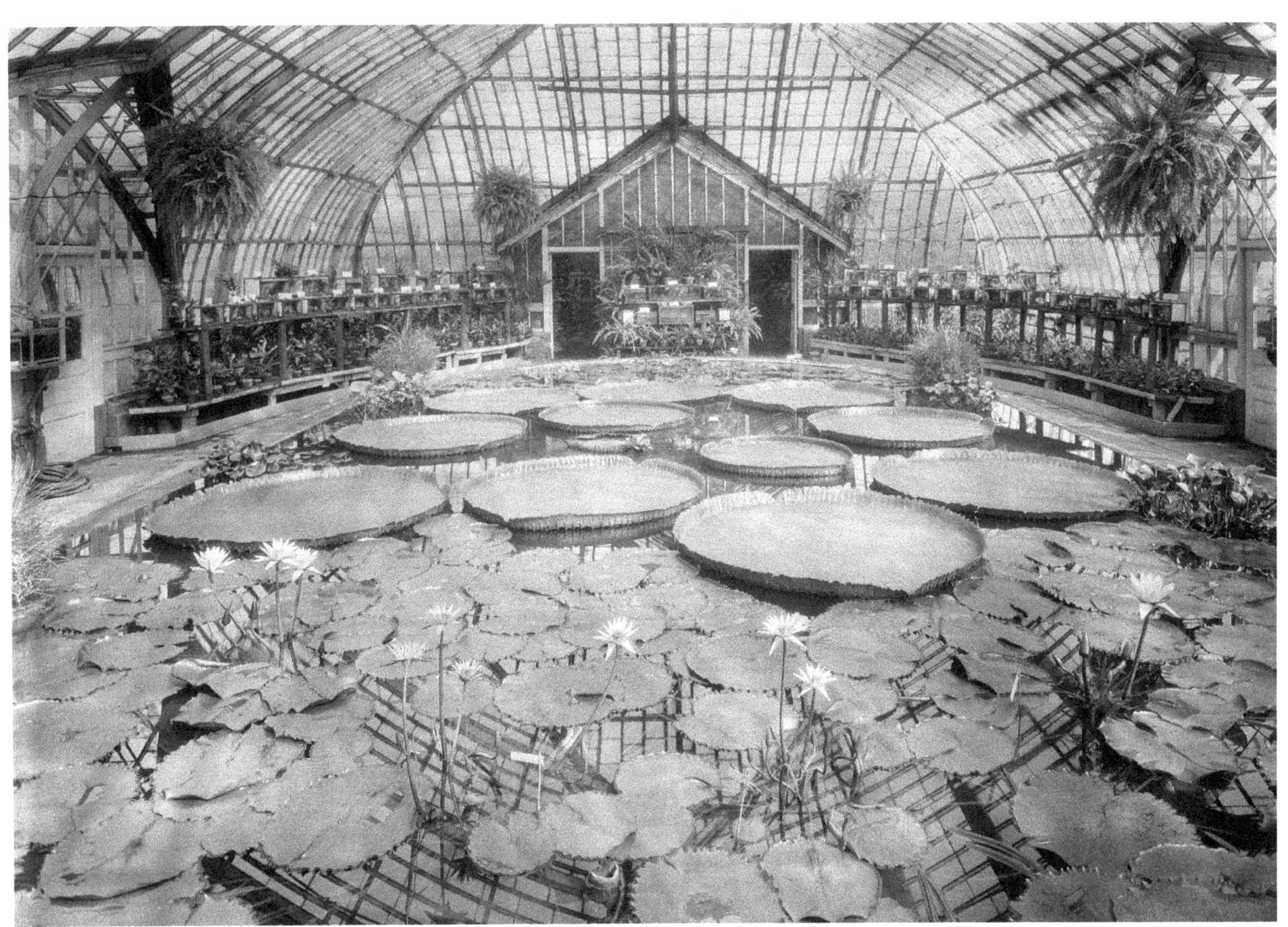

The Aquatic House at the West Park Conservatory on the North Side, as it appeared in 1933.

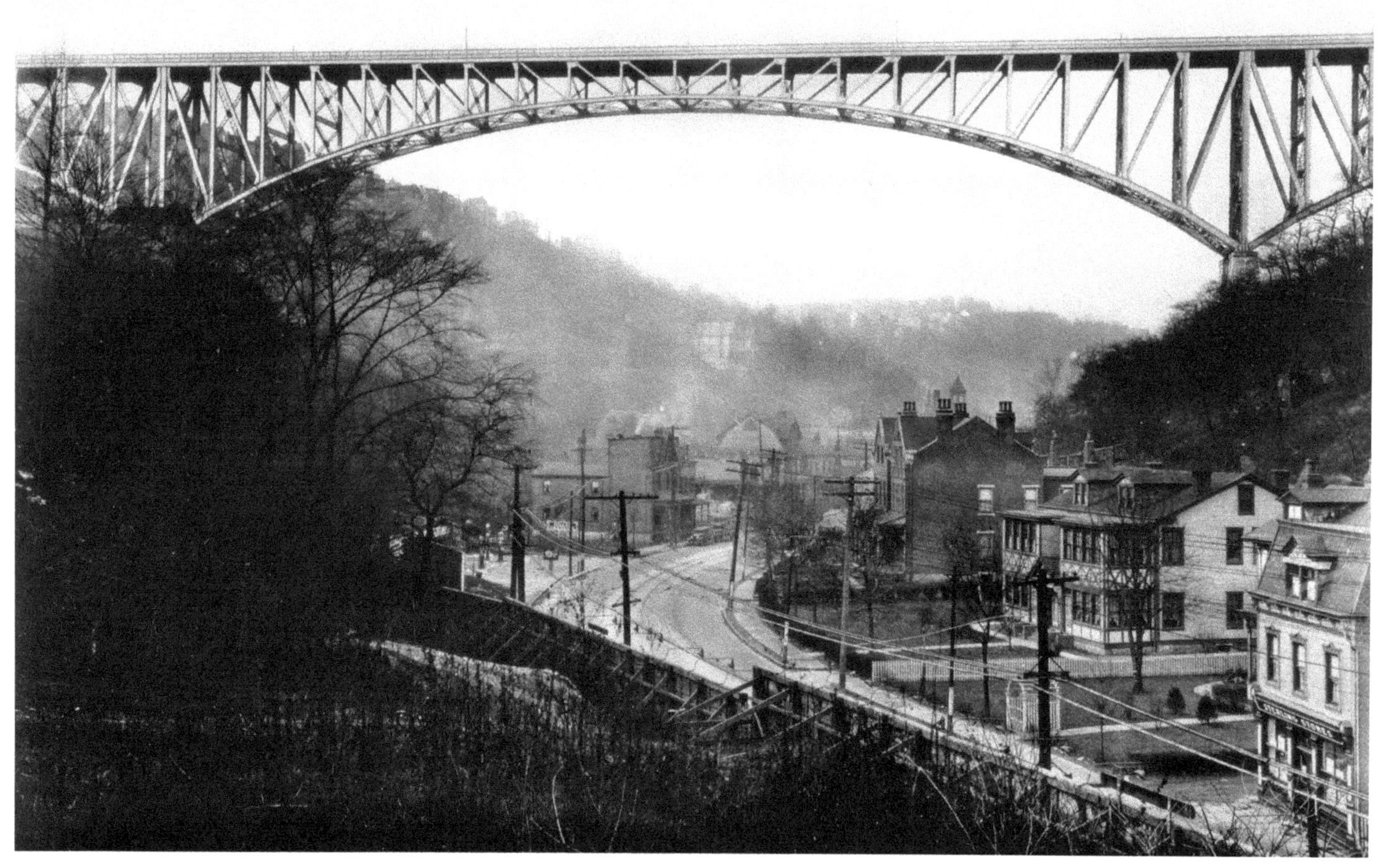

East Street Bridge spanning the East Street Valley on the North Side. The arched cantilever bridge opened in 1930.

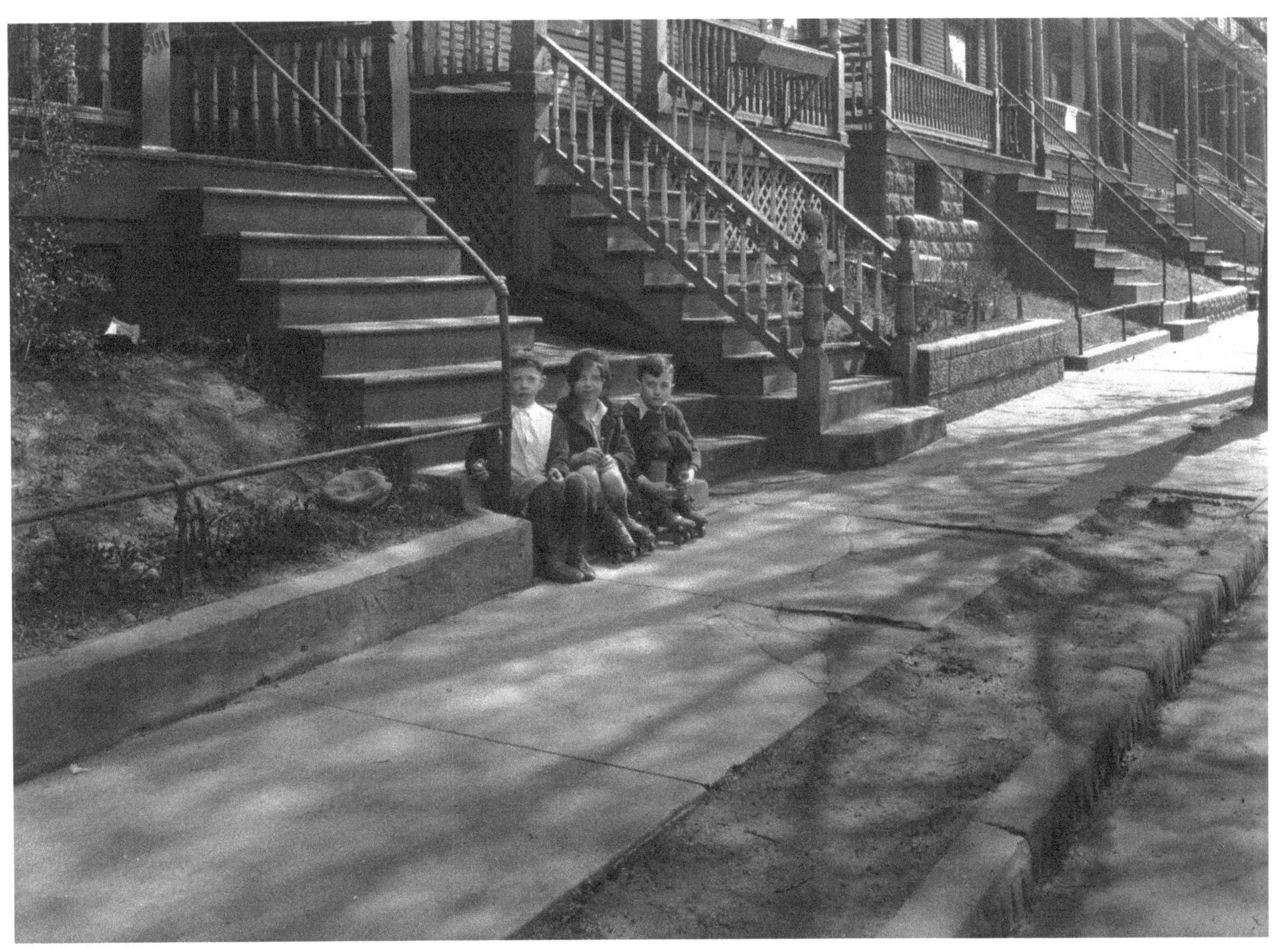

Children on roller skates pose for the photographer at 5111 Broad Street in 1931.

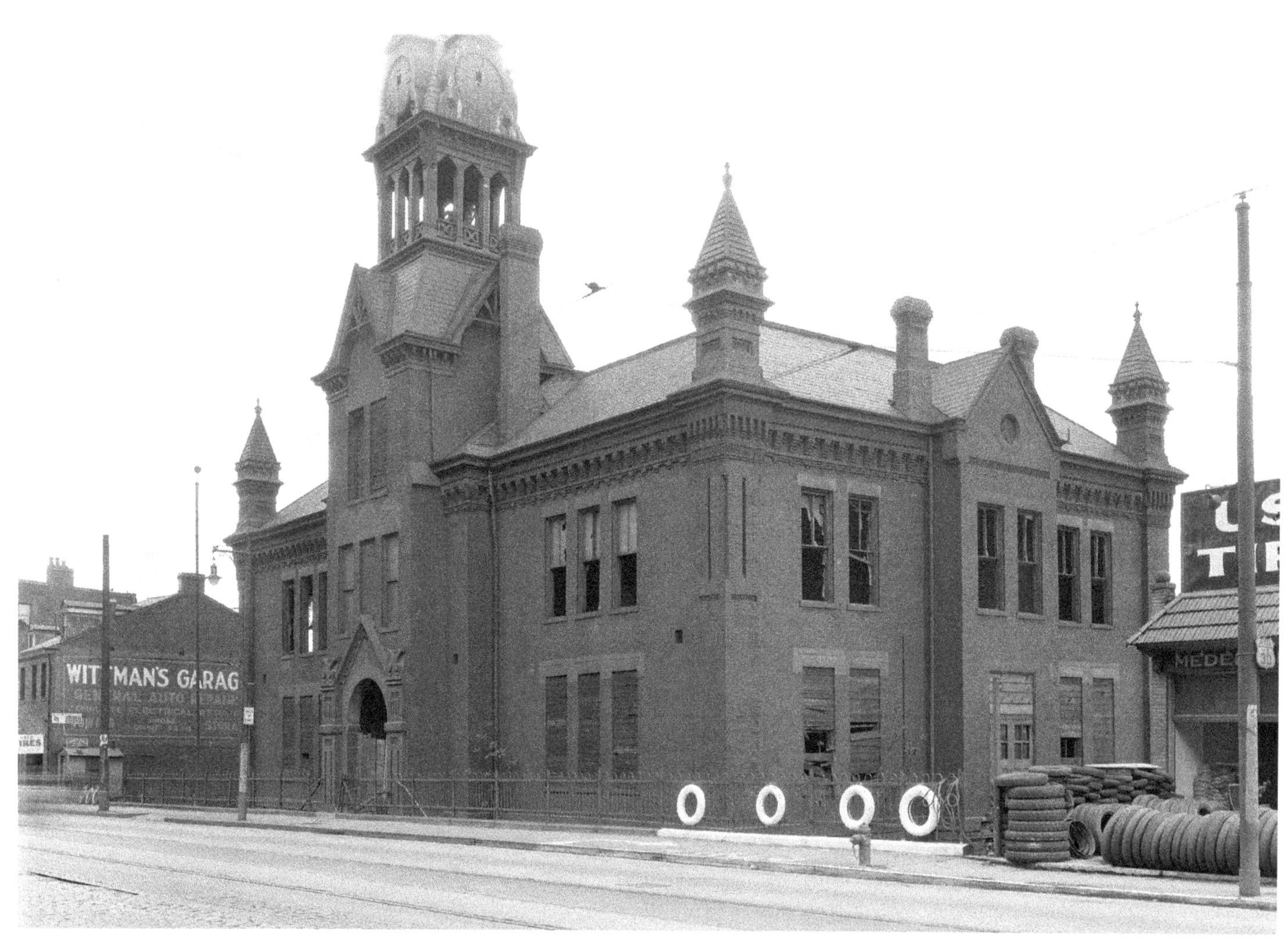

Riverside High School was built in 1882 on West Carson Street. It stands abandoned here in 1931.

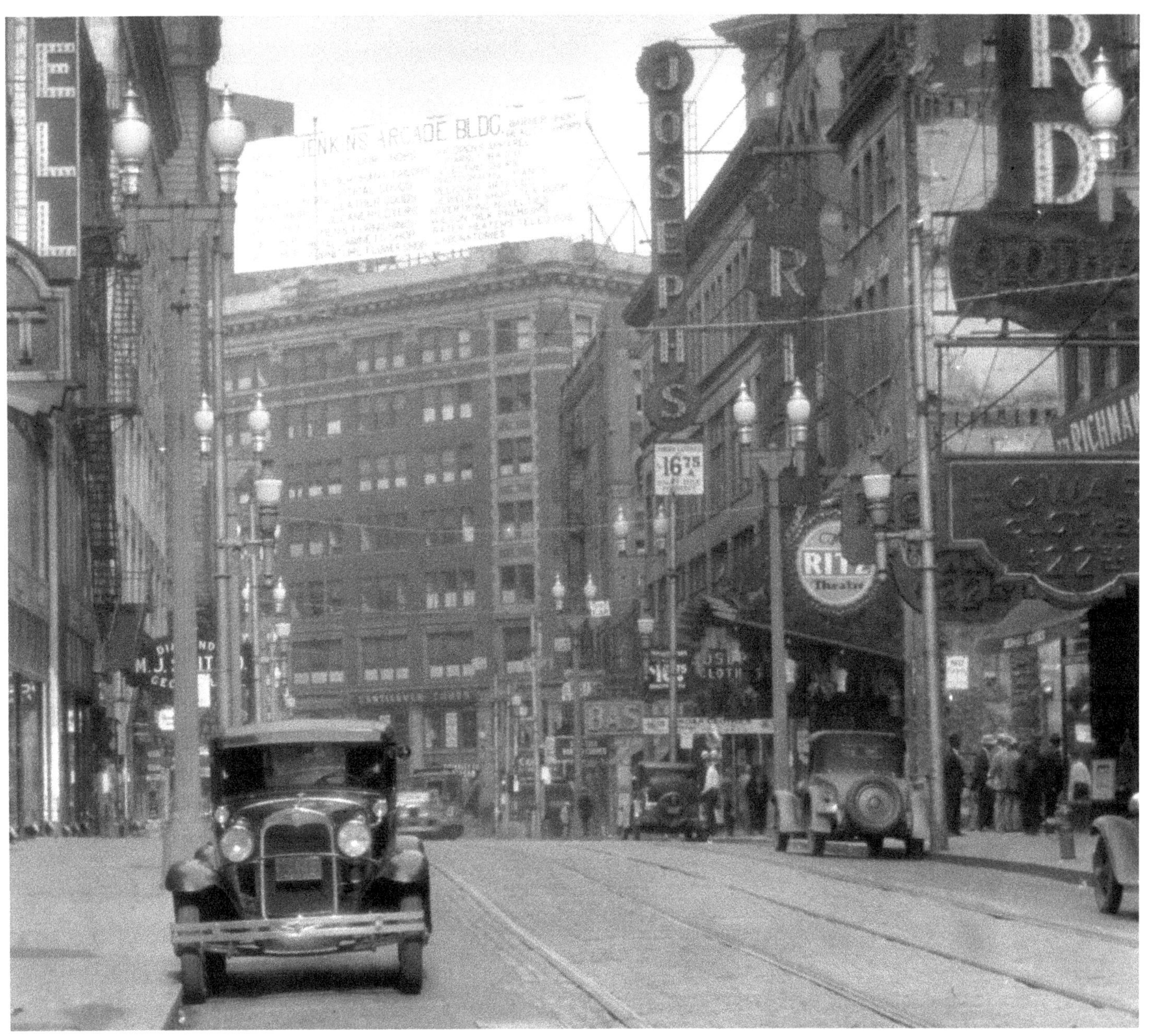

Fifth Avenue of days gone by. Nearby are the Jenkins Arcade, the Ritz Theatre, and several clothing stores.

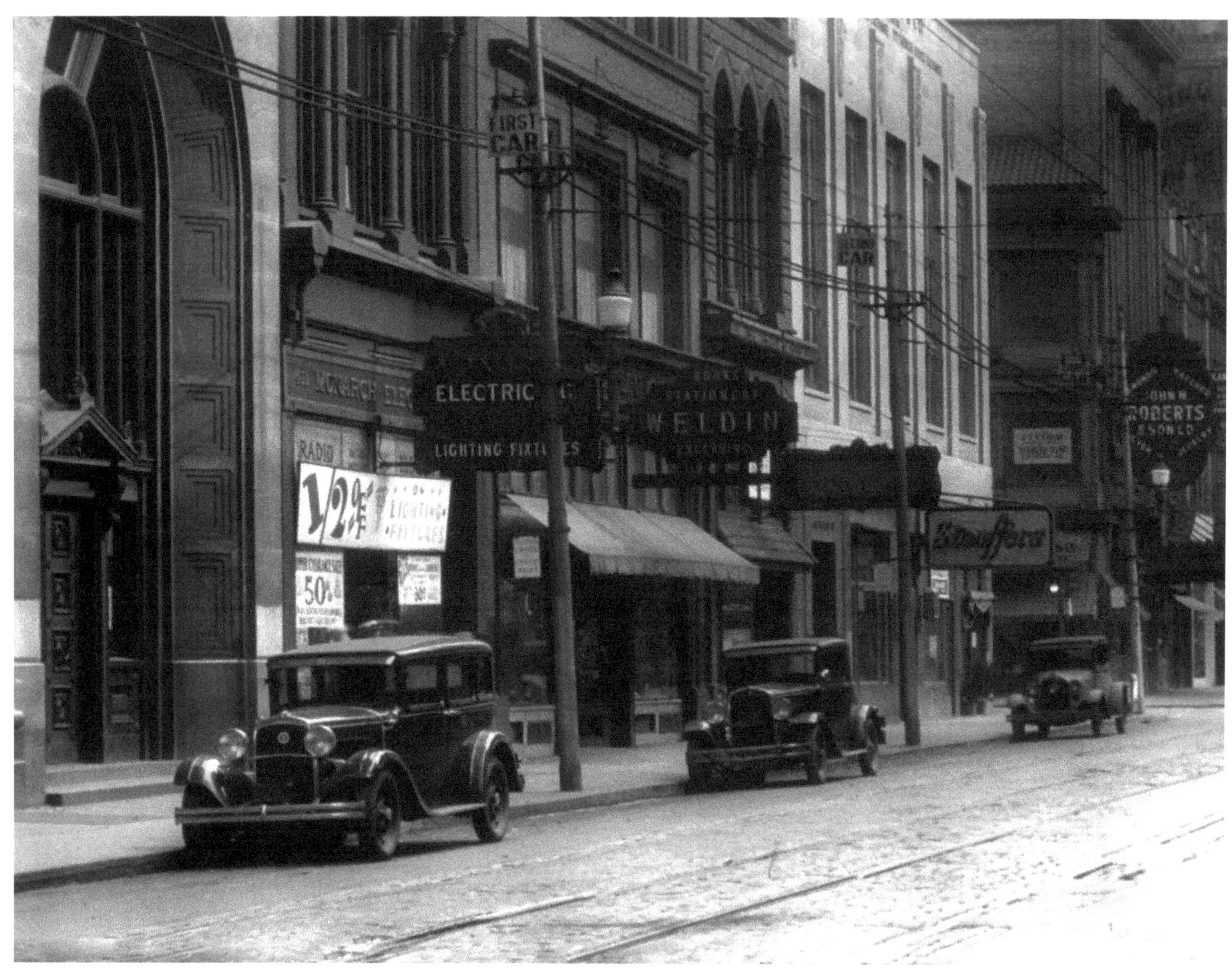

Wood Street view downtown showing the still popular Weldin's Stationery. Until 2007, the Roberts and Sons Jewelers sign was still on the building.

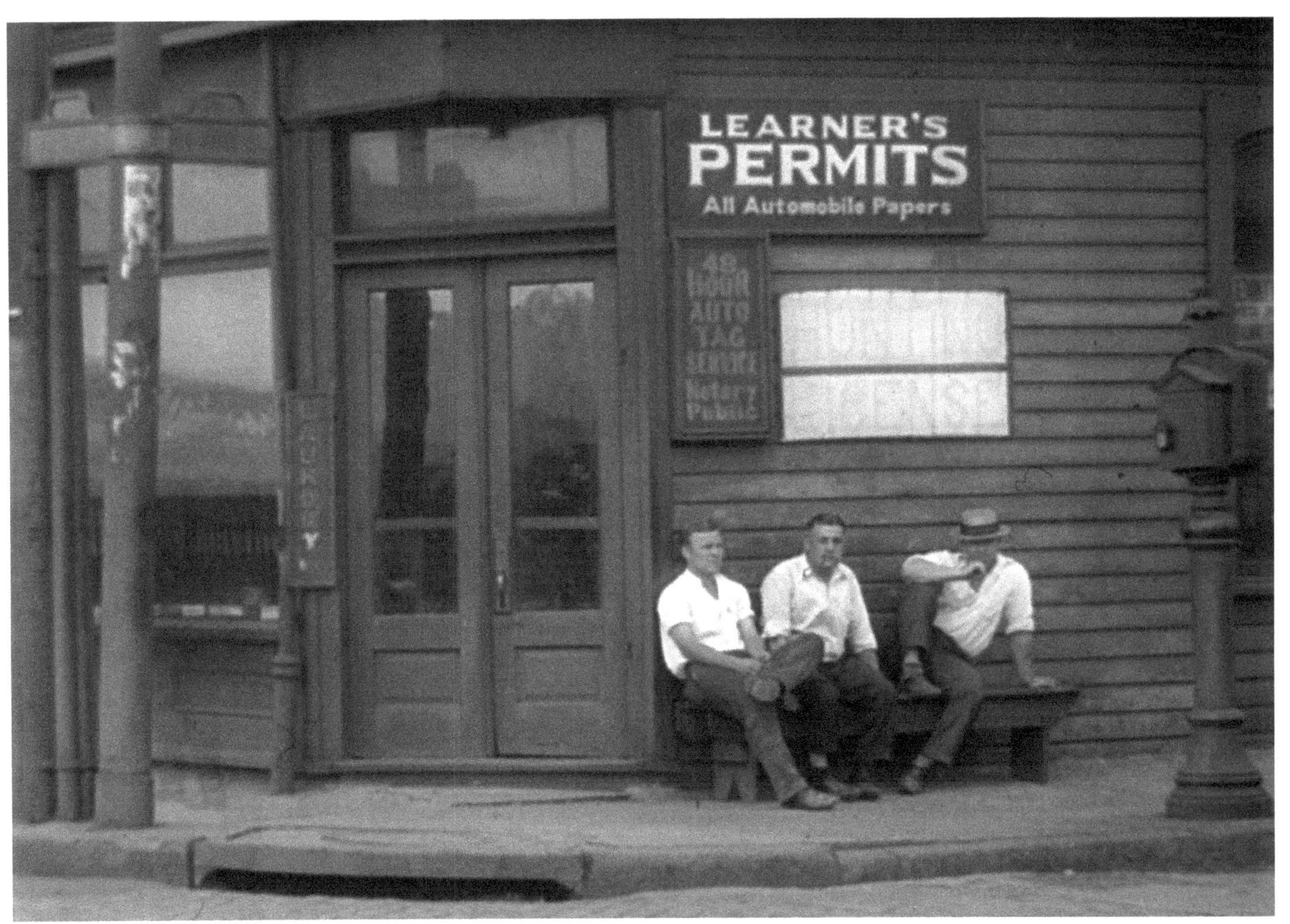

Three men sit outside a shop that seems to offer many services.

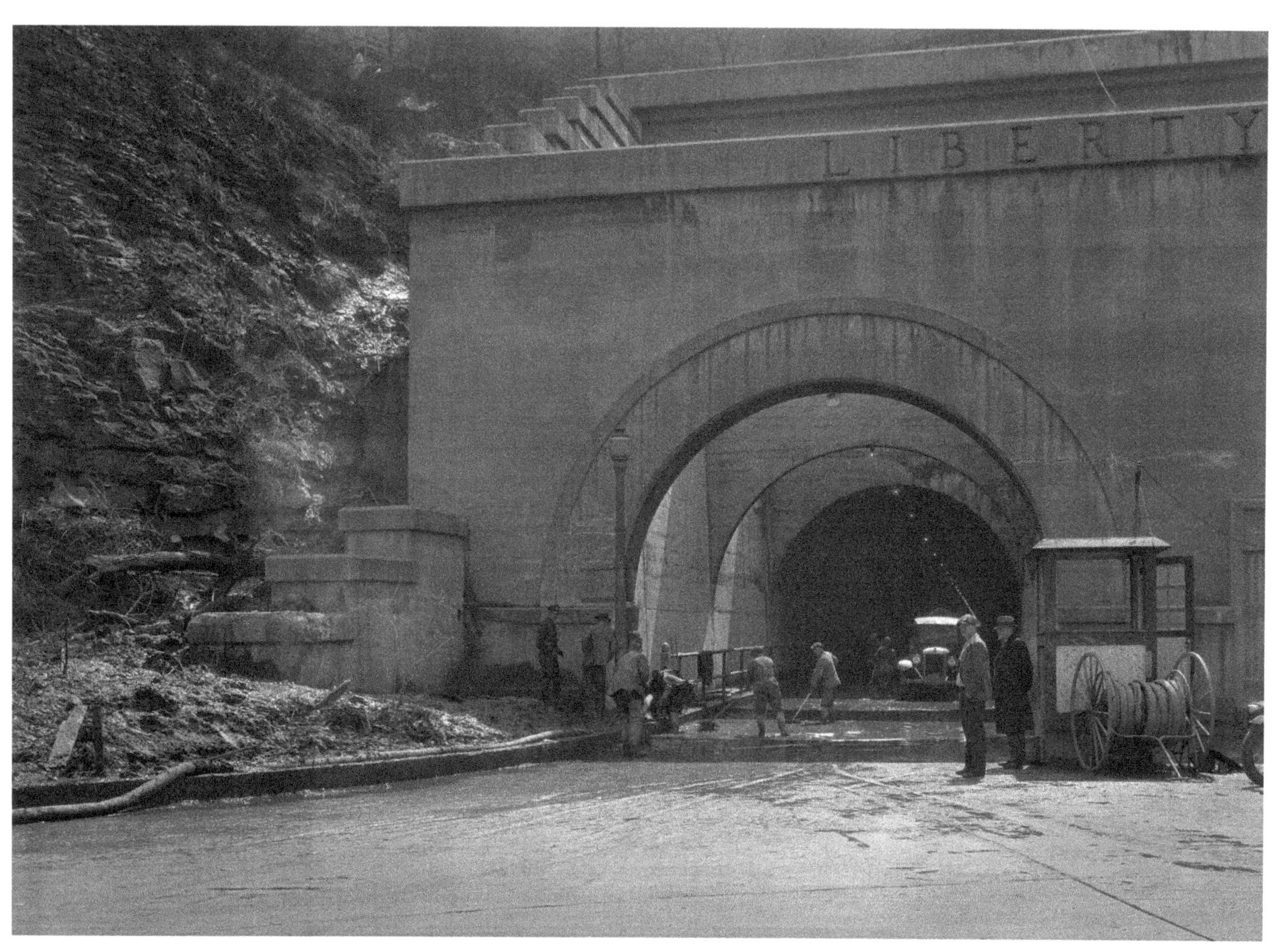

North end of the Liberty Tunnels, in 1933.

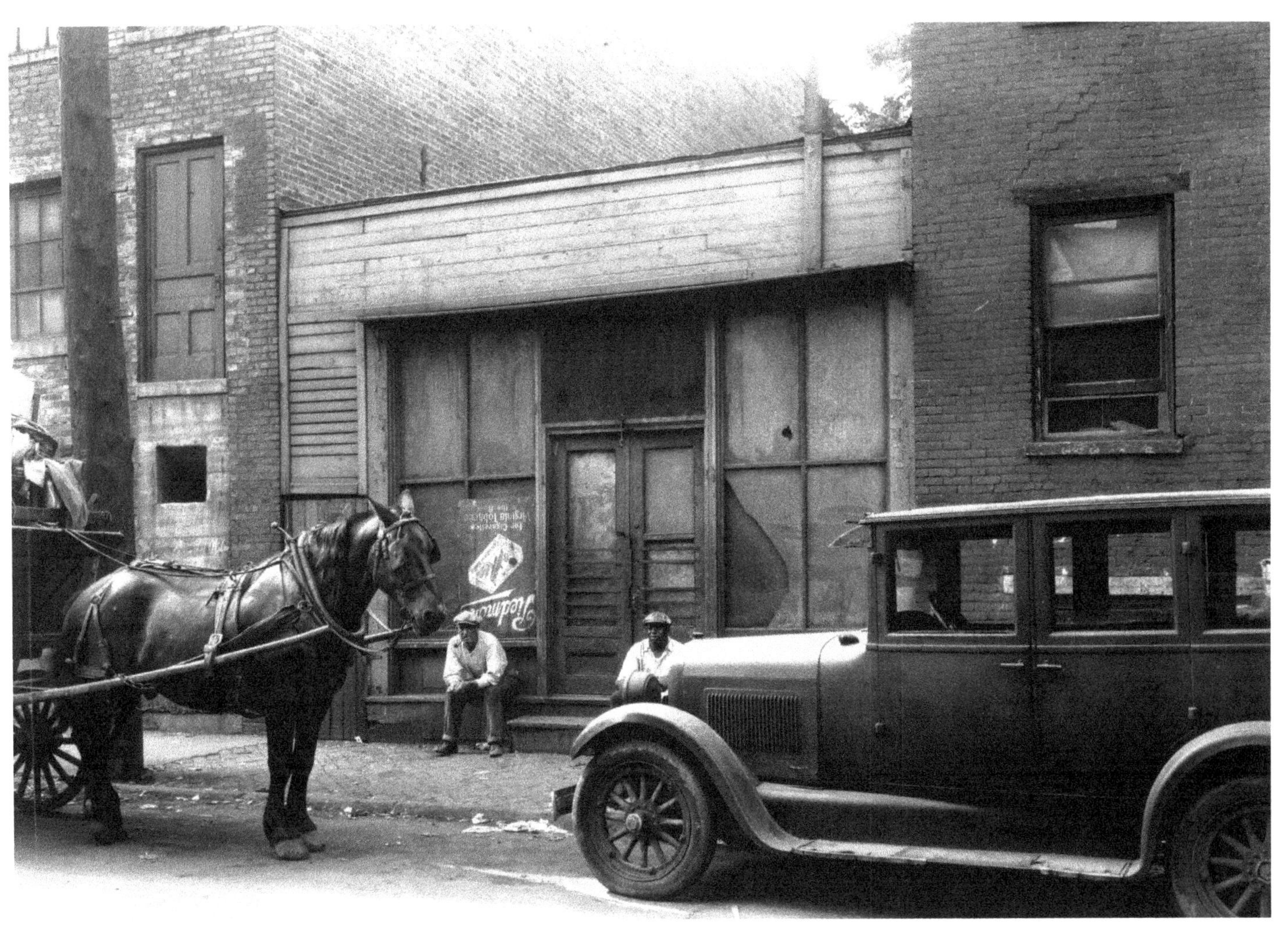

Life in the slow lane at 527 Shore Avenue on the North Shore.

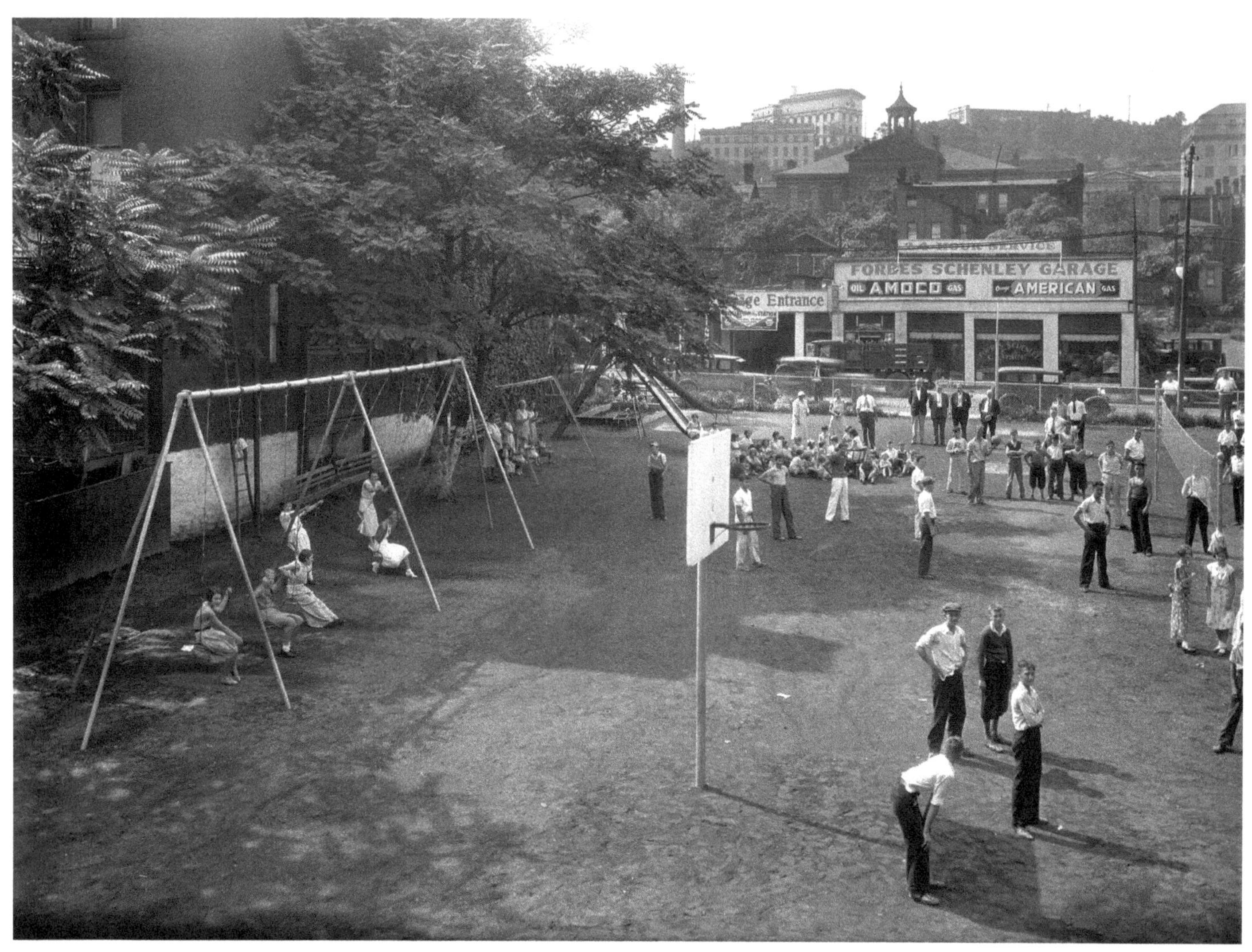

Volleyball and other activities are in progress at the playground in front of the Forbes and Schenley Garage.

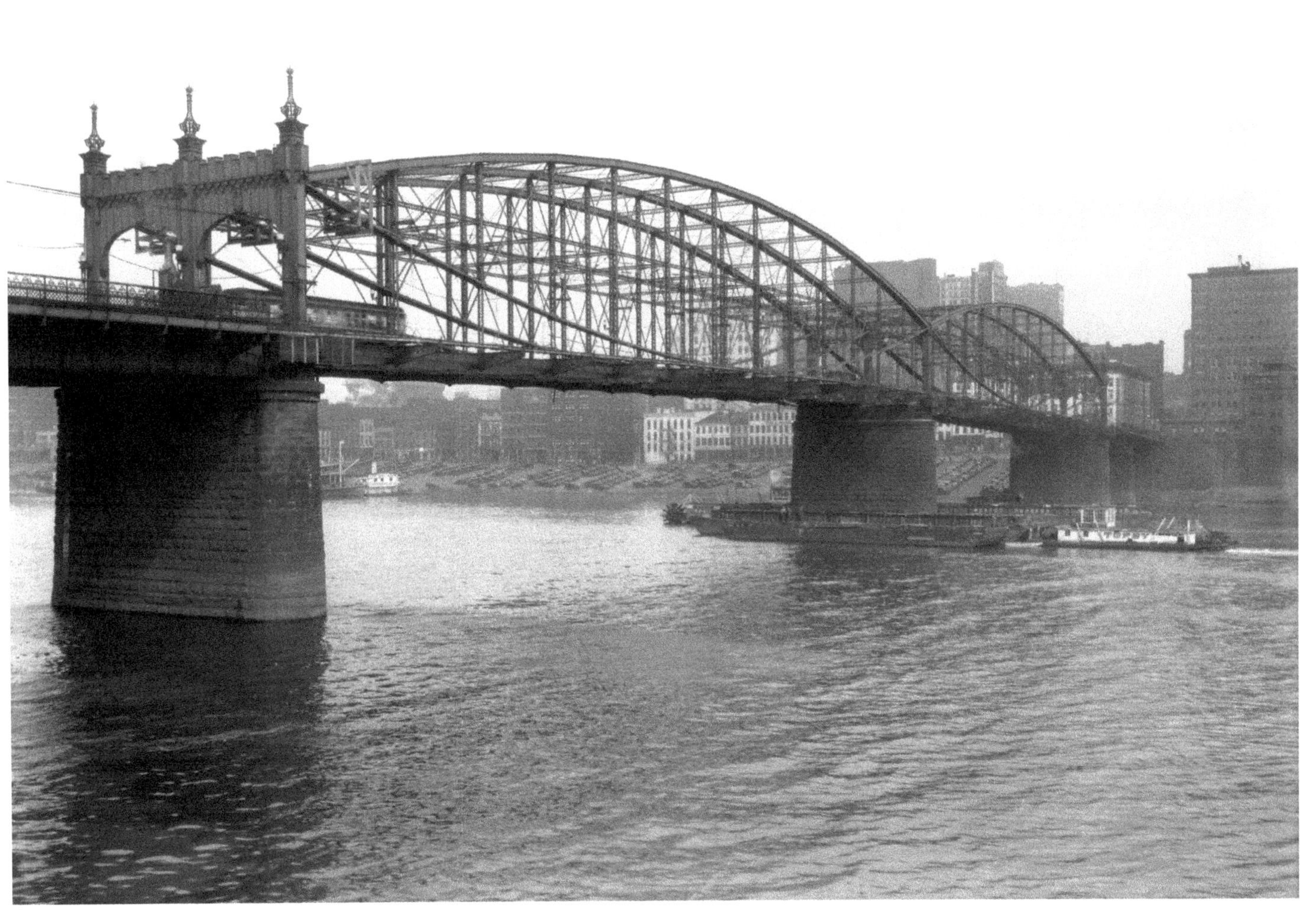

The Smithfield Street Bridge in 1933, as seen from the Monongahela River facing downtown.

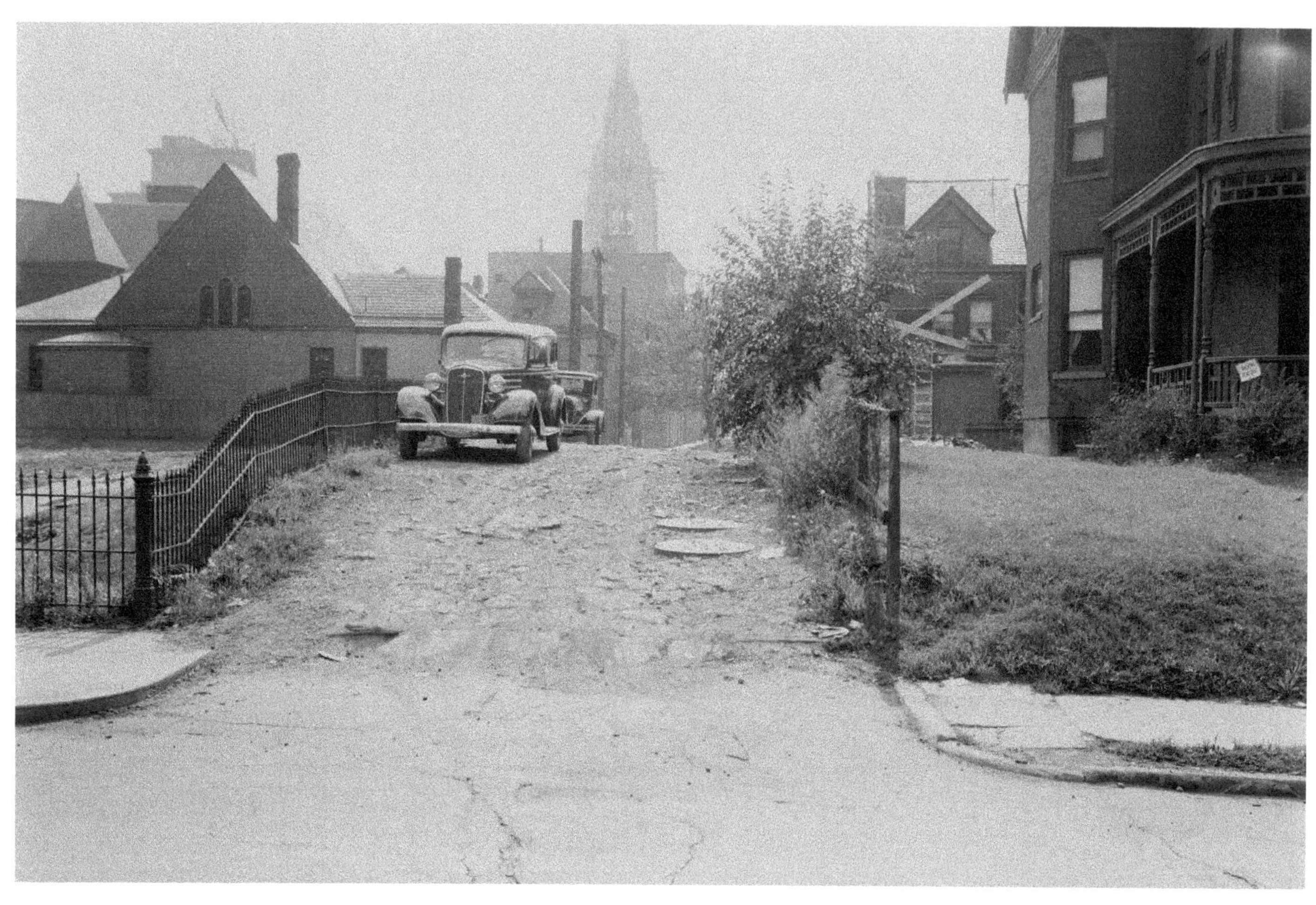

Whitfield Street from Rural Street in 1934, with the Bethany Evangelical Lutheran Church steeple visible in the background.

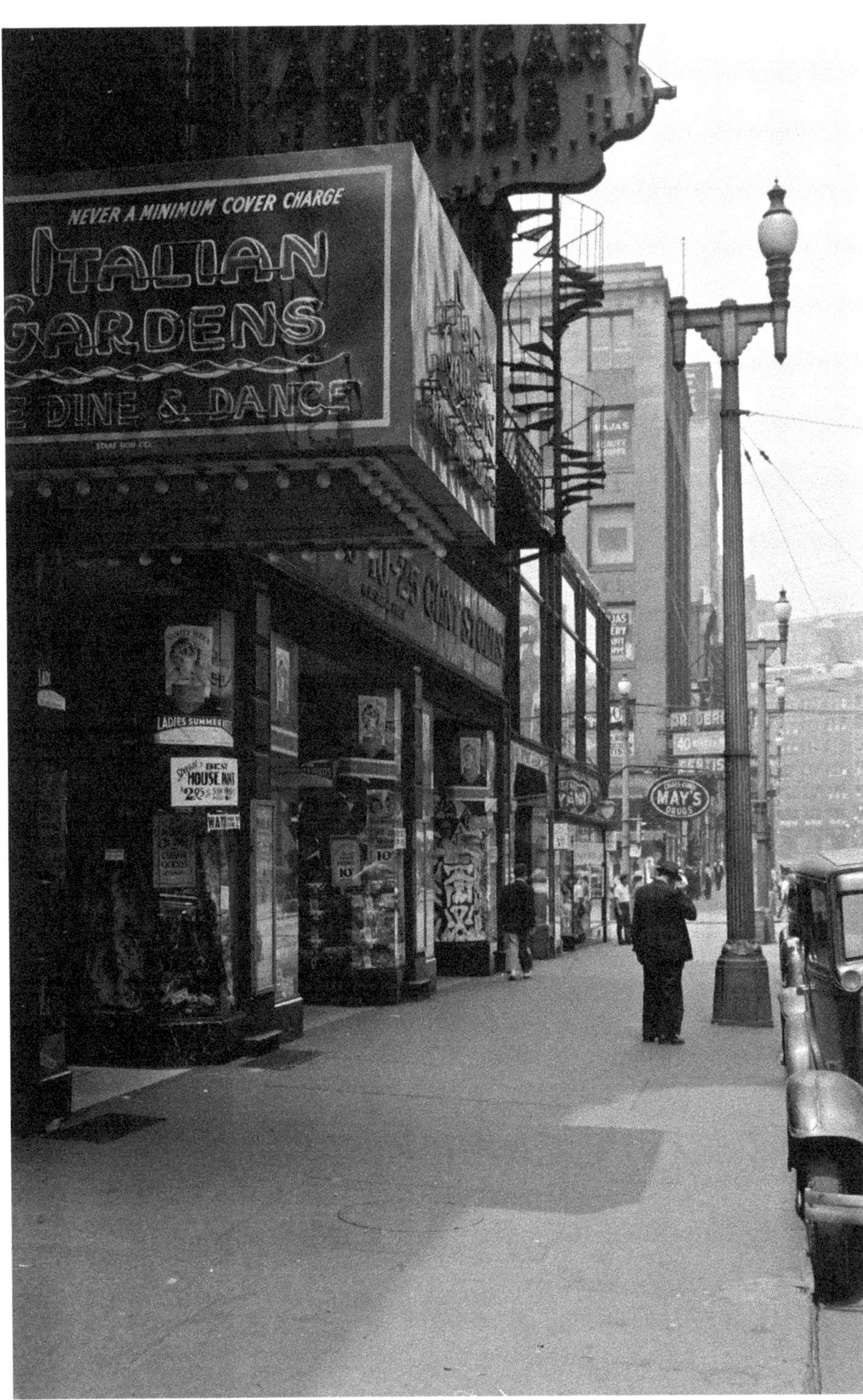

The Italian Gardens restaurant at 306 Fifth Avenue downtown. Next door, chocolate fruit fudge is available for ten cents a pound.

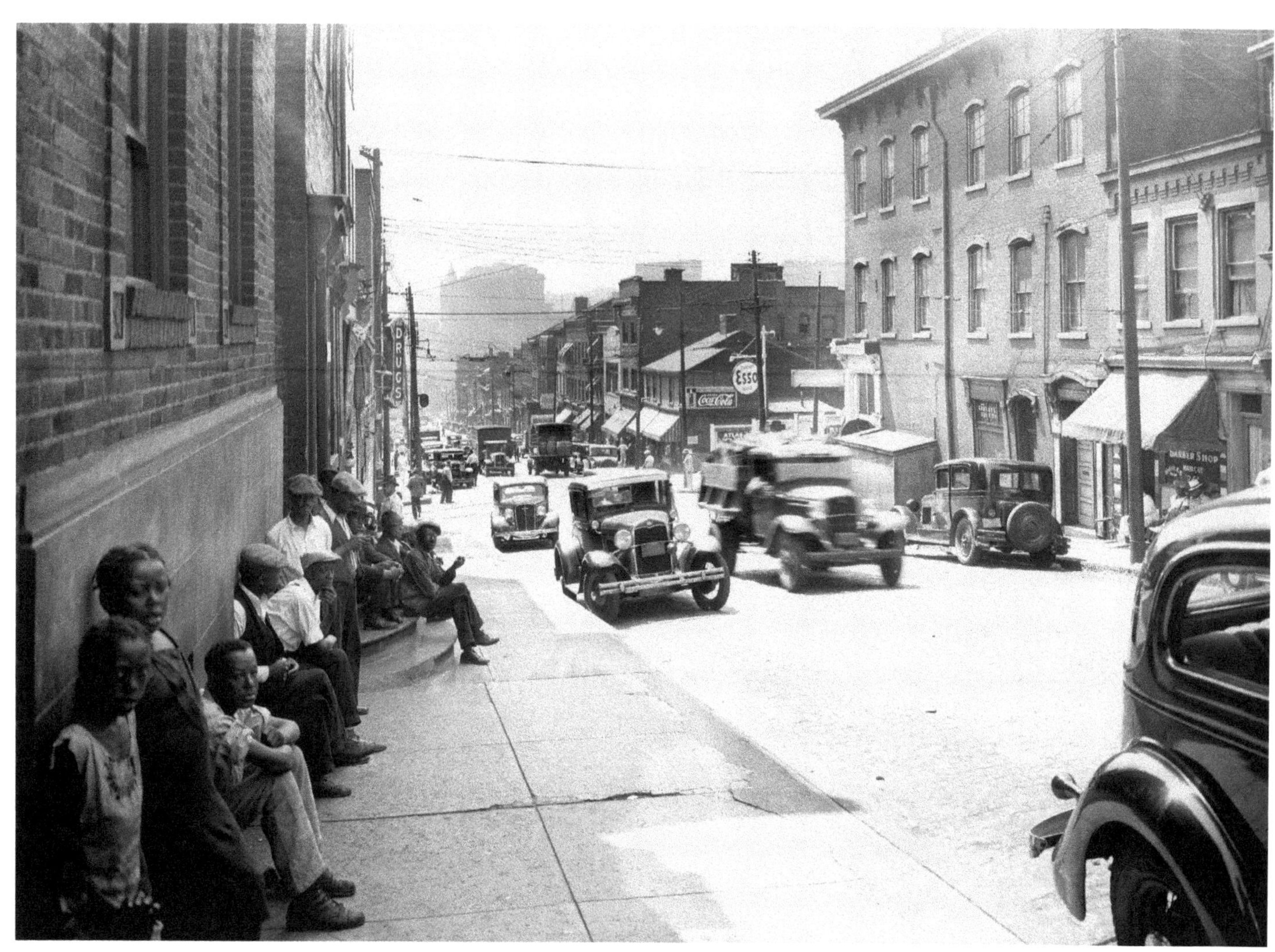

A sunny, hazy day at 1510 Wylie Avenue in the Hill District.

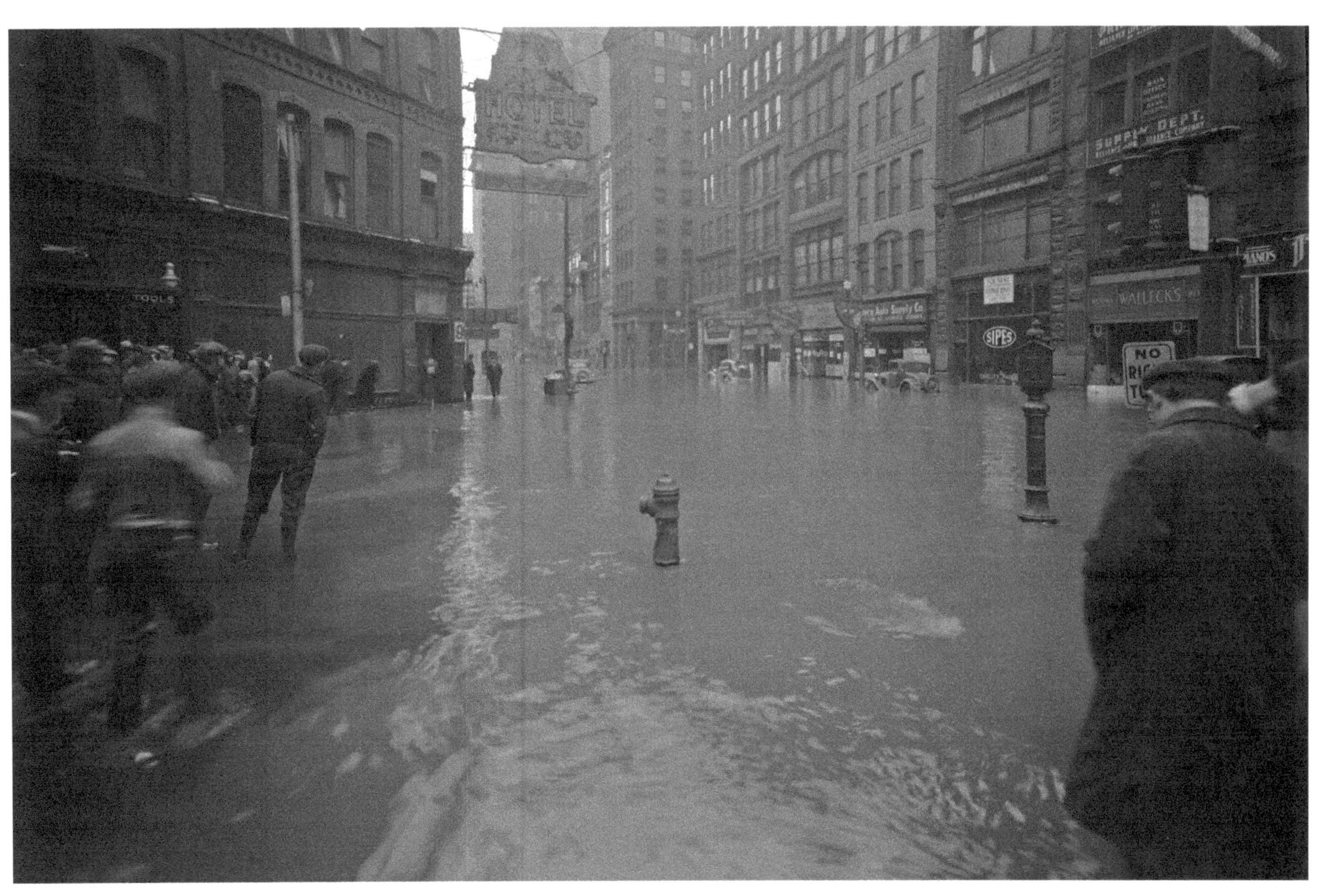

Liberty and Seventh avenues during the Great St. Patrick's Day Flood of March 1936.

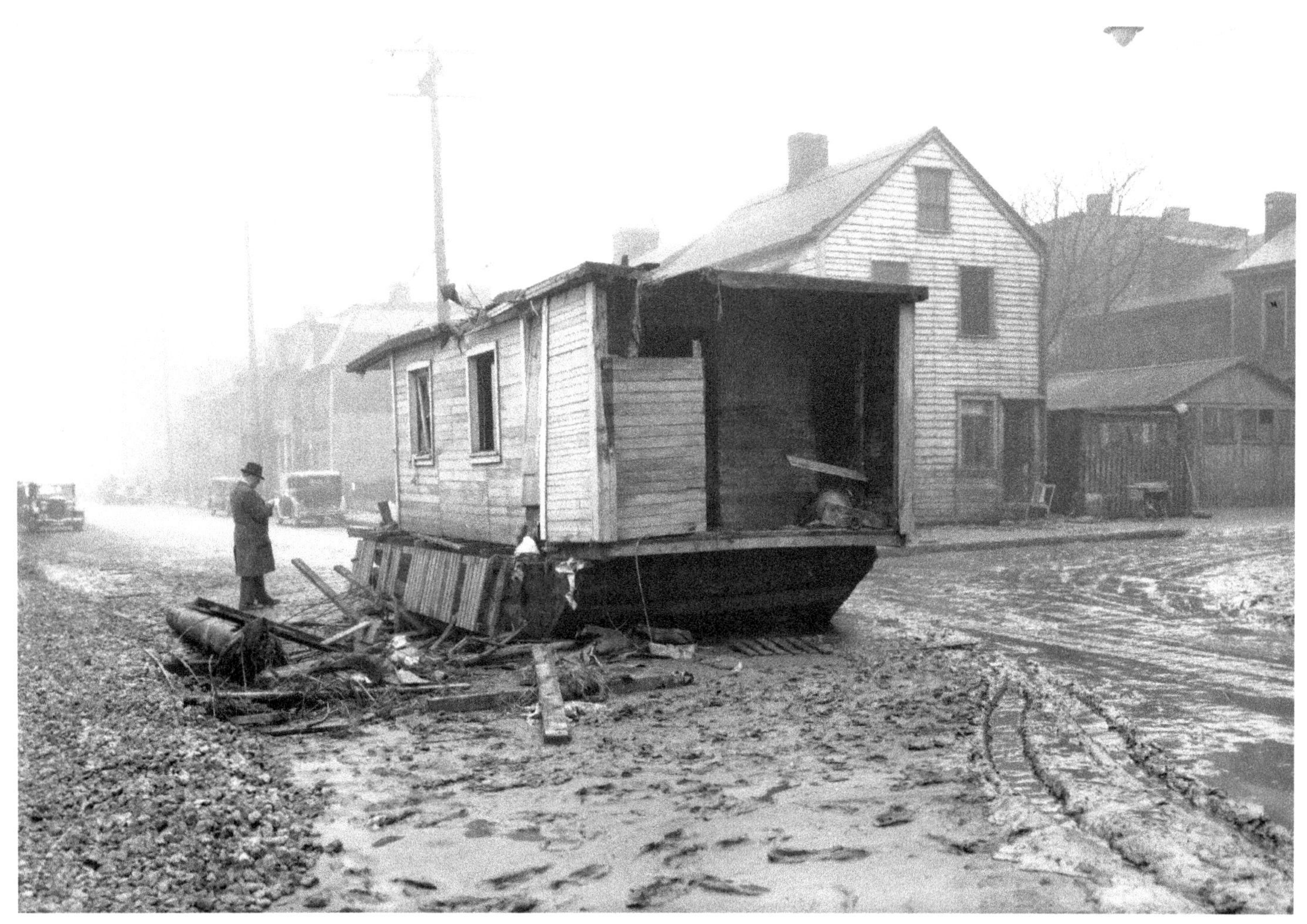

A houseboat sits at the intersection of River Avenue and Vine Street after the 1936 floodwaters have receded.

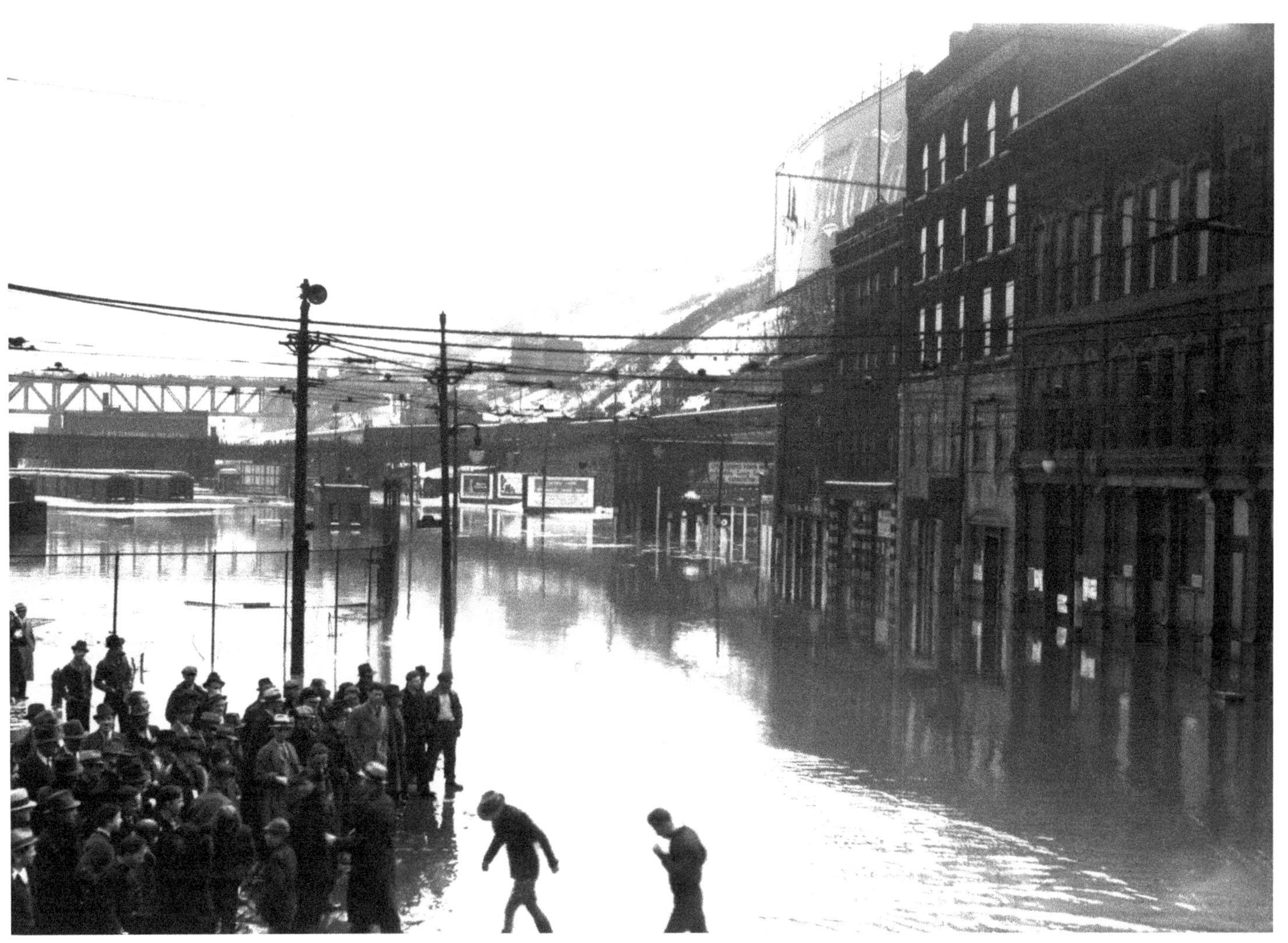

The scene on Carson Street, just beyond the Pittsburgh and Lake Erie Railroad Terminal and the Smithfield Street Bridge, during the Flood of 1936.

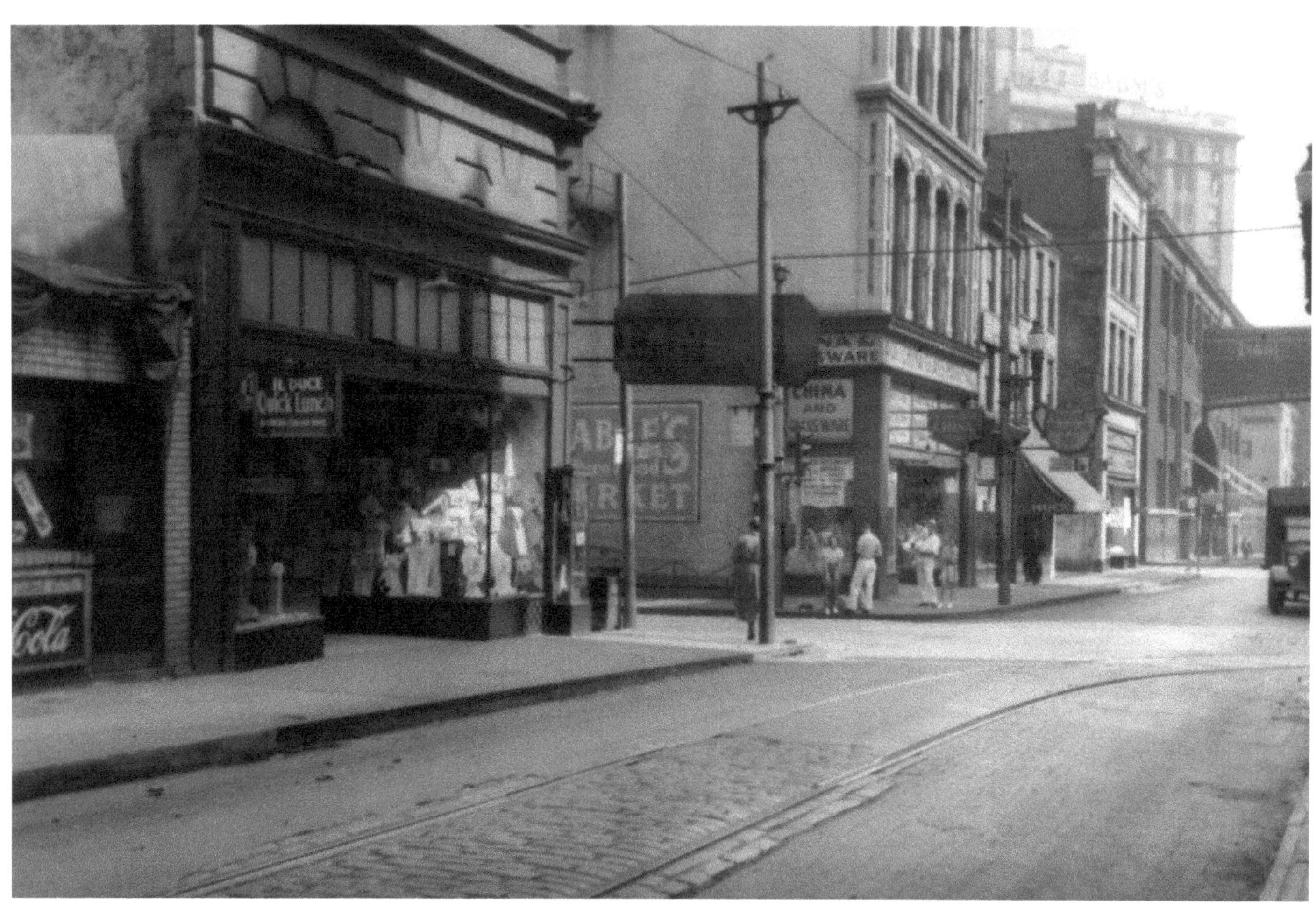

View of the Il Duce Quick Lunch with the Diamond Market House just beyond, in 1936.

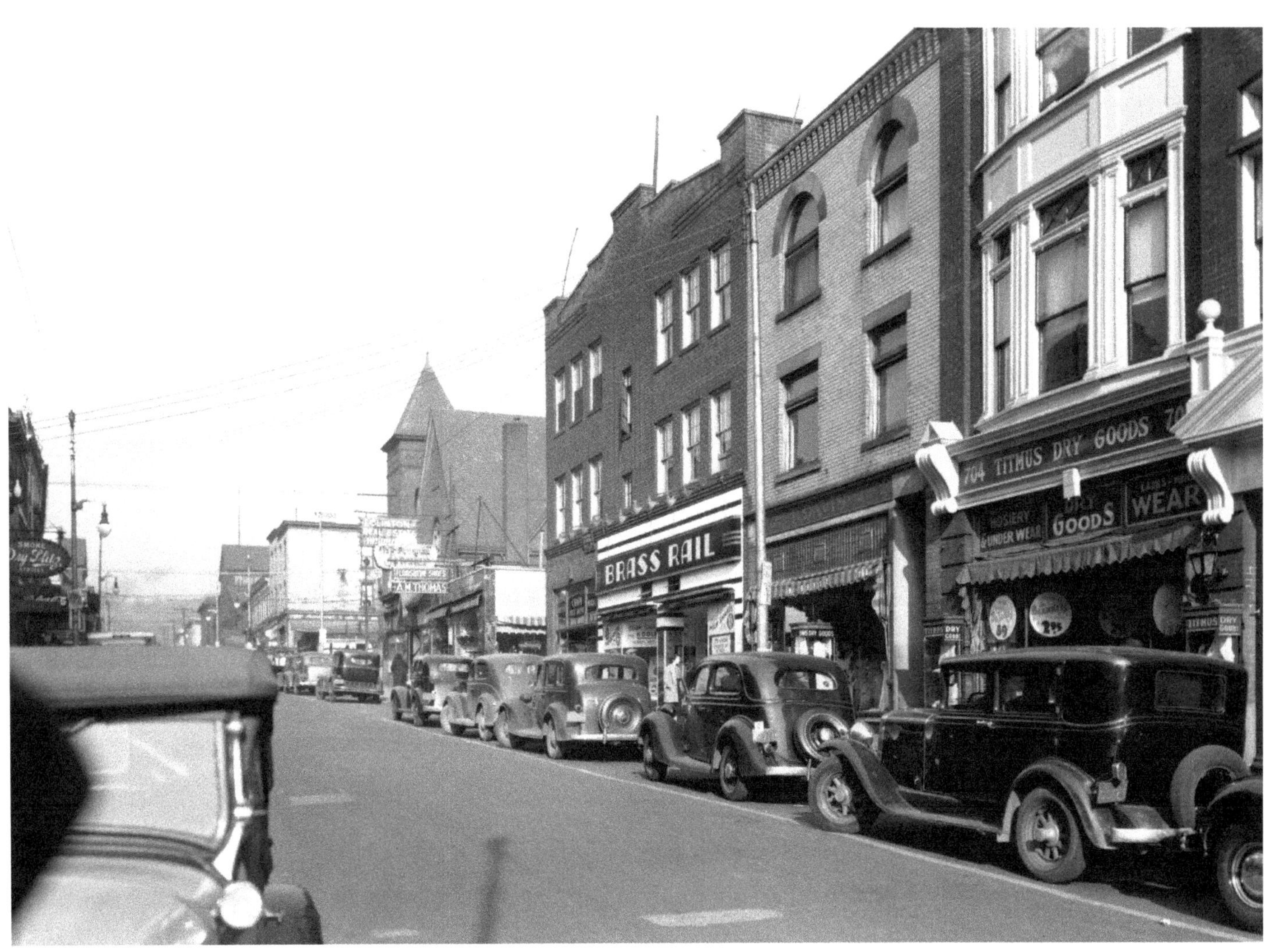

The 700 Block of Homewood Avenue, 1937.

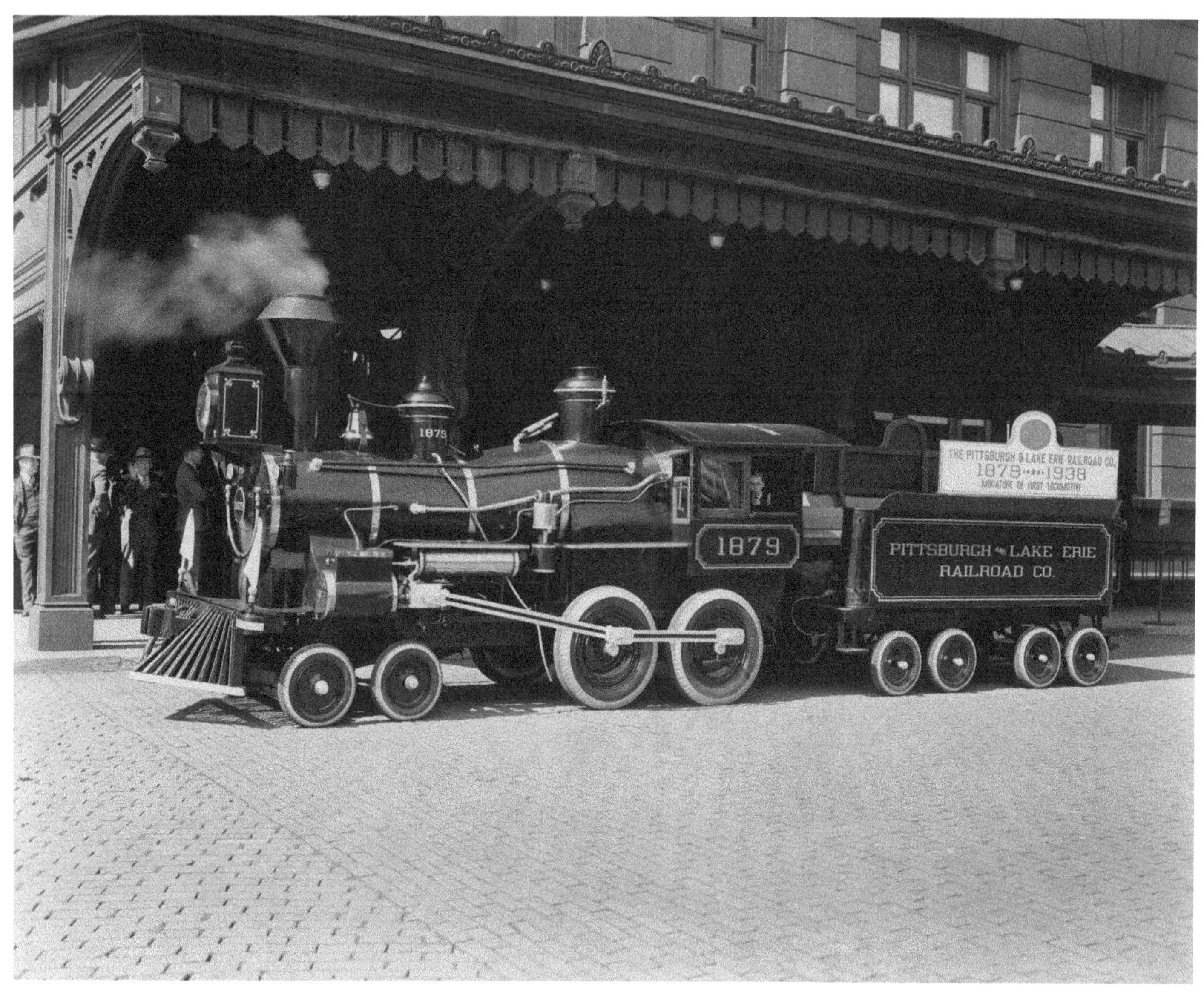

A small-scale replica of the first Pittsburgh and Lake Erie Railroad locomotive.

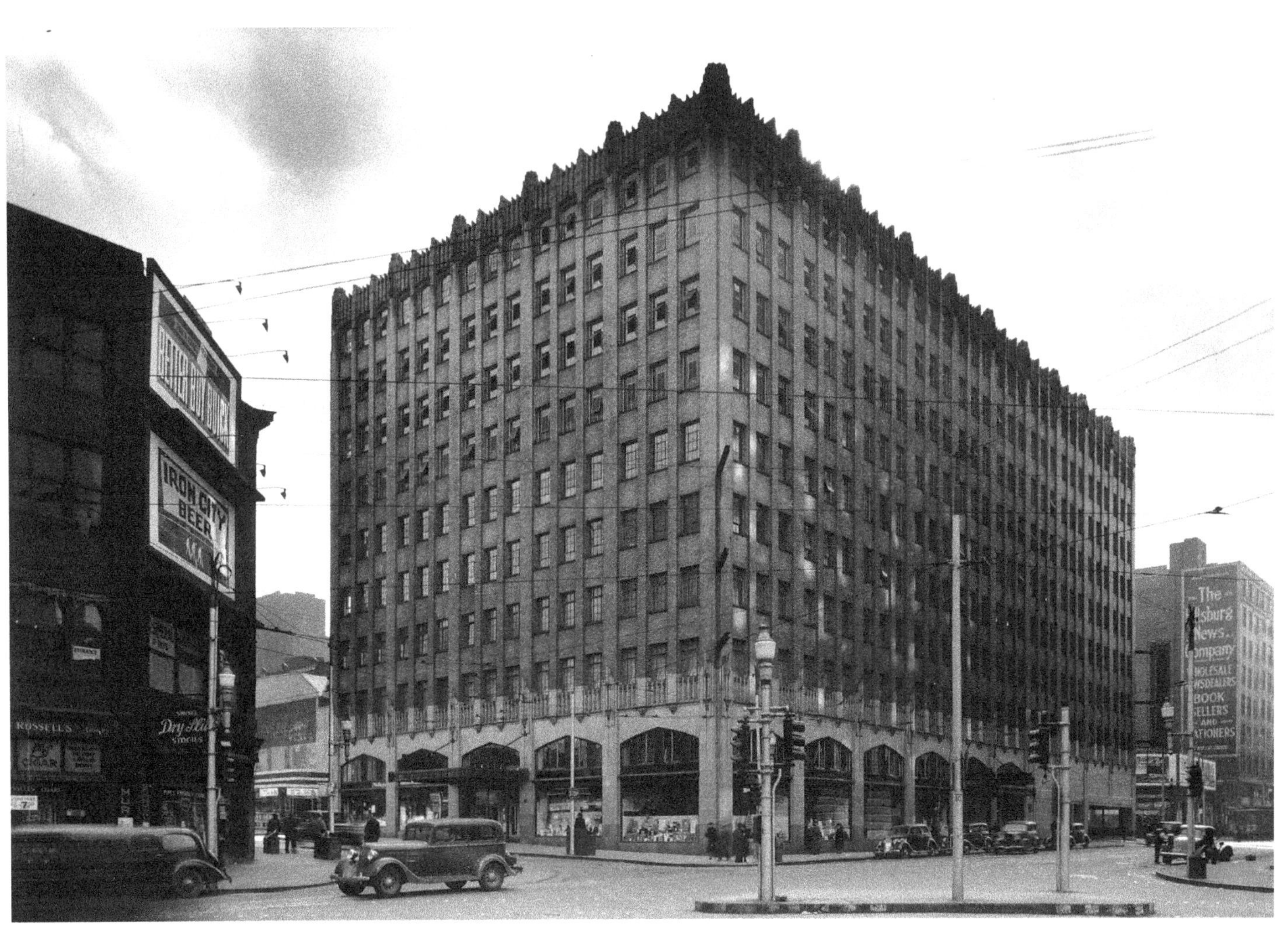

McCann & Co. at Ferry Street and Diamond Street, from Liberty Avenue. Shops occupied the lower level, but this building is for the most part a parking garage. The building's prime location placed it within a block of the Diamond Market and the Wabash Building, housing the Pittsburgh Terminal Railroad.

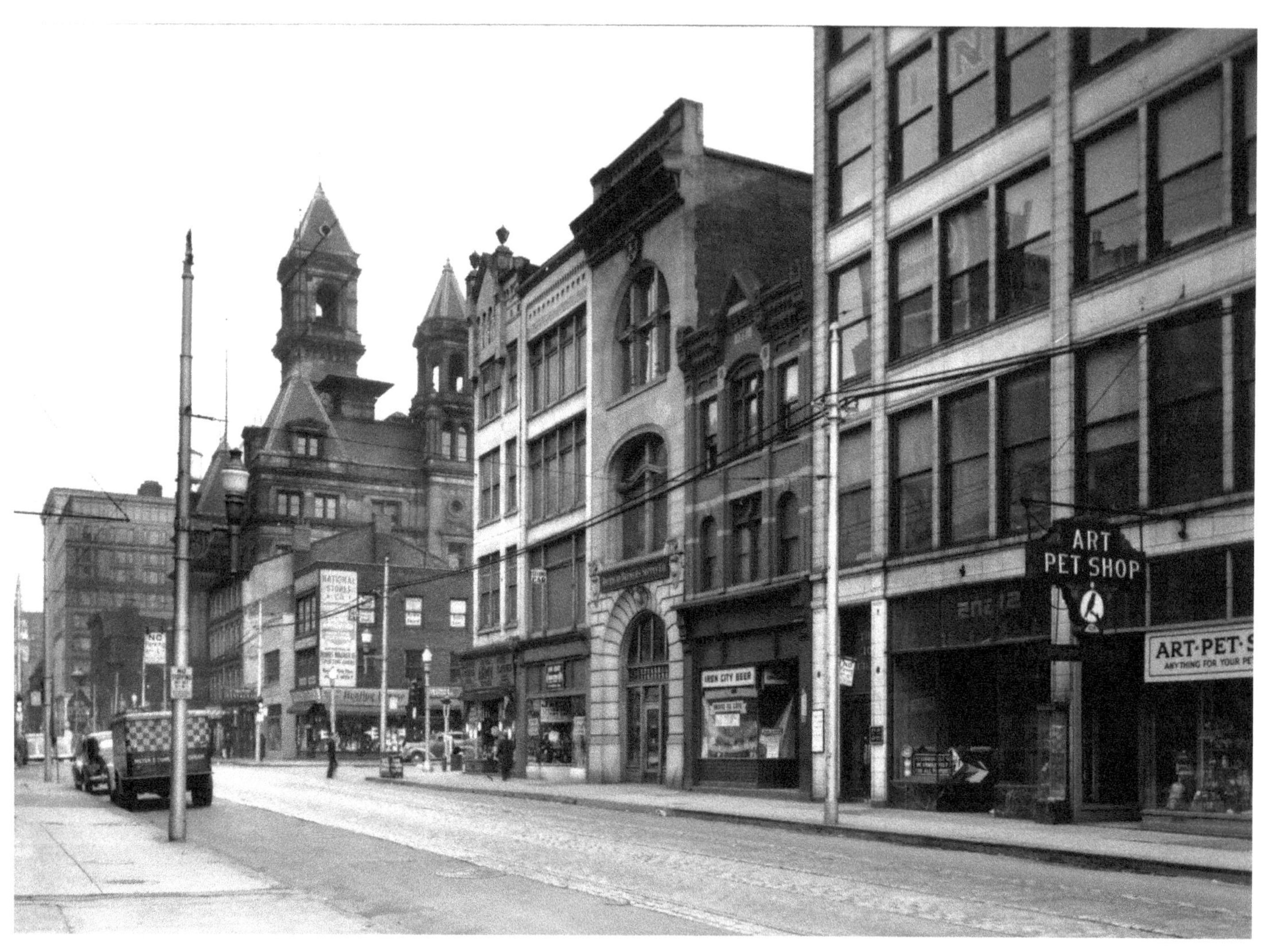

Smithfield Street near Boulevard of the Allies. The building towering above all the rest is the former Pittsburgh Post Office, erected in 1892, leveled in 1966.

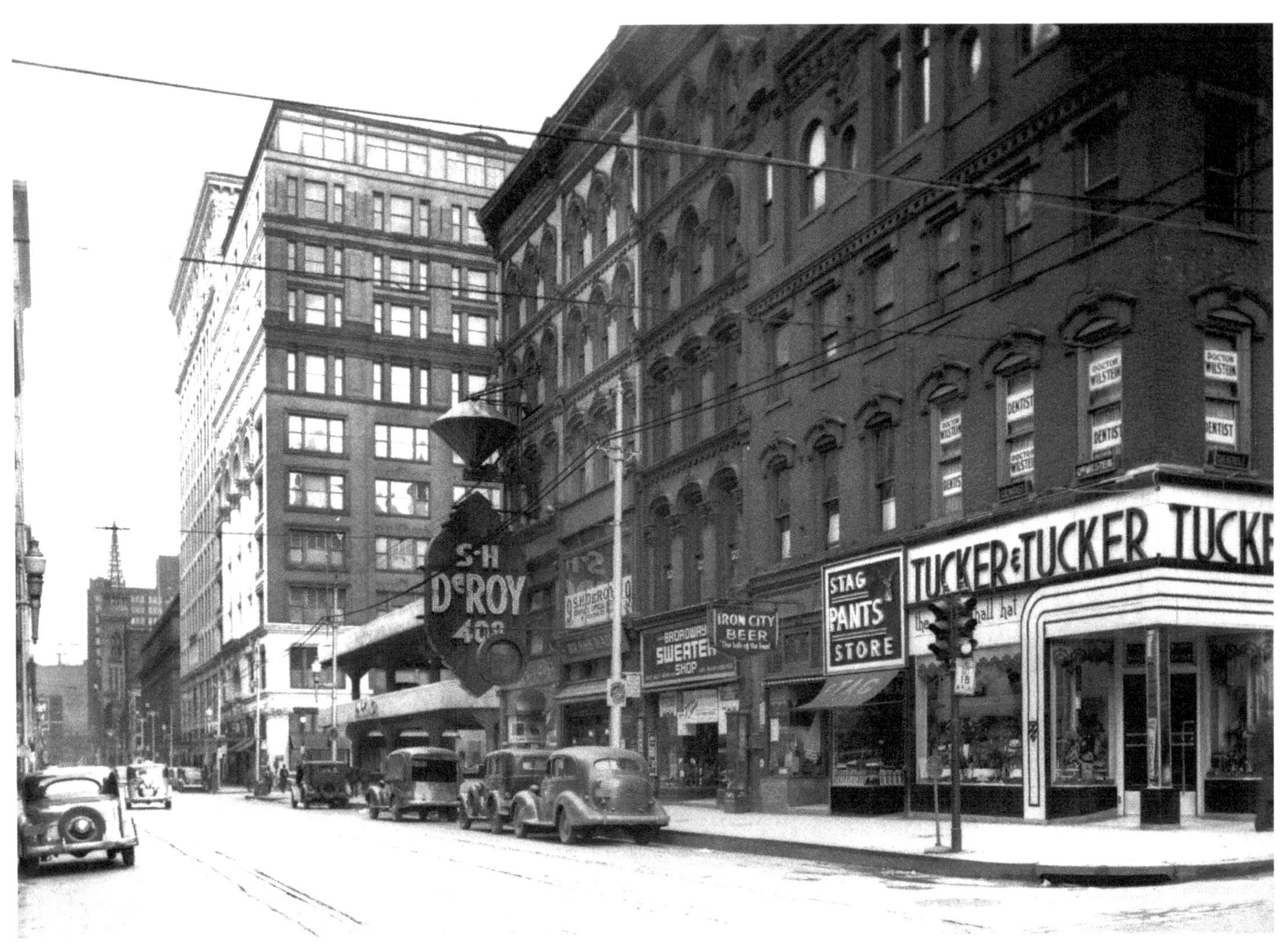

Smithfield Street businesses, including the S. H. DeRoy Jewelers and, down the street, Kaufmann's Department Store.

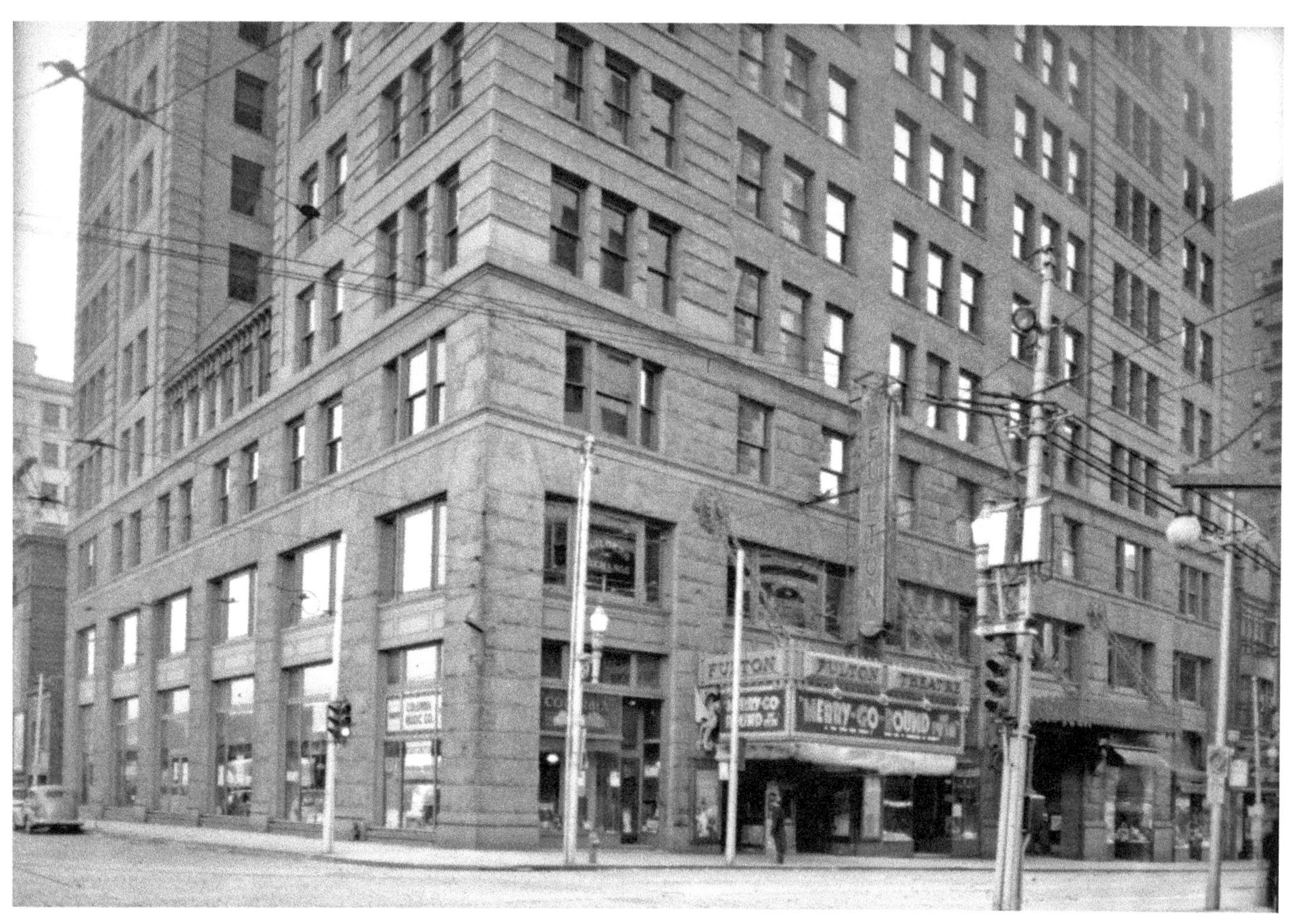

The Fulton Building and the Fulton Theatre, showing *The Merry-Go-Round of 1938,* on Sixth Street at Duquesne Way.

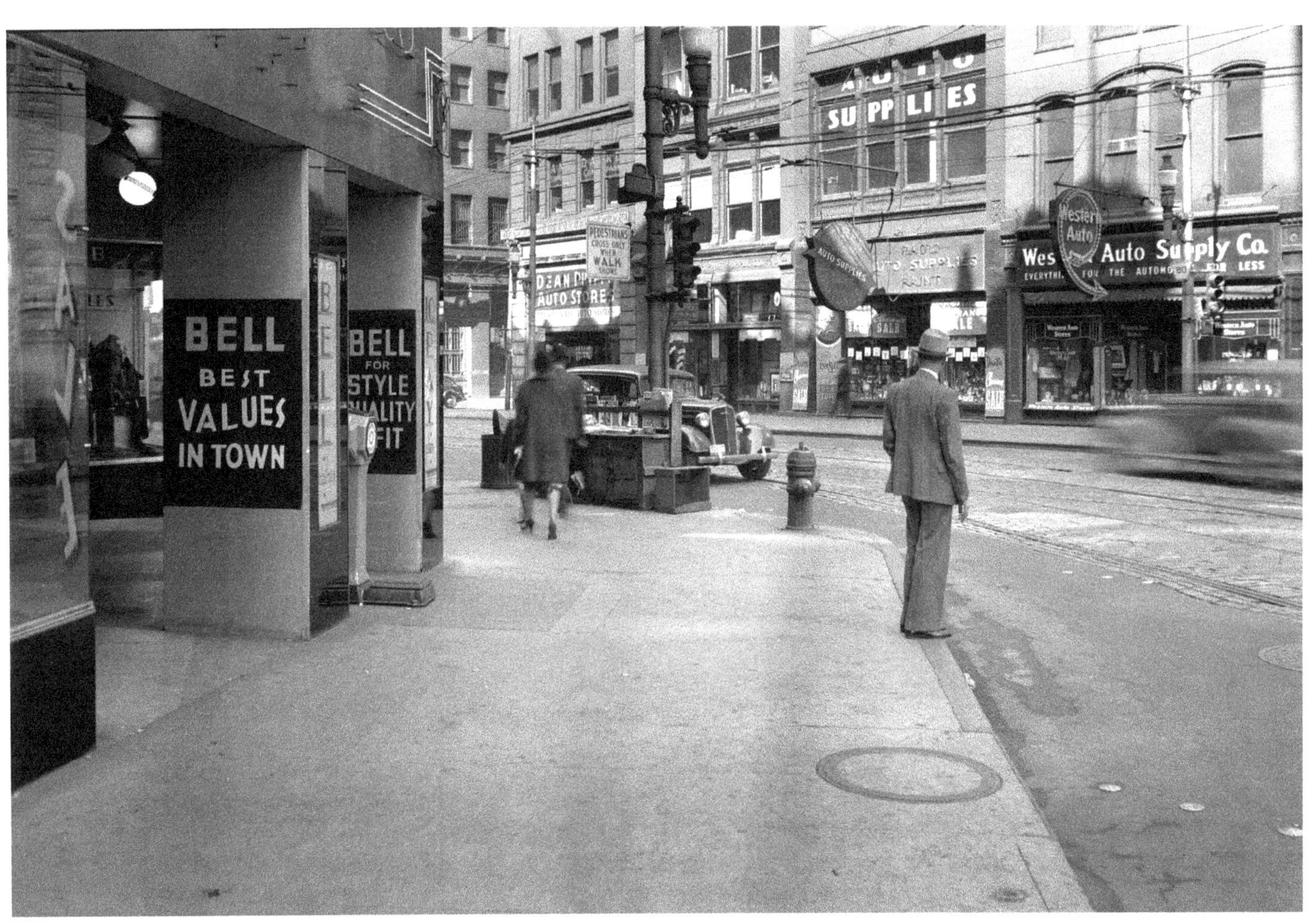

Seventh Avenue with a view to the 900 block of Liberty Avenue.

Macedonia Baptist Church on Bedford Avenue in the Hill District, as it appeared in 1939.

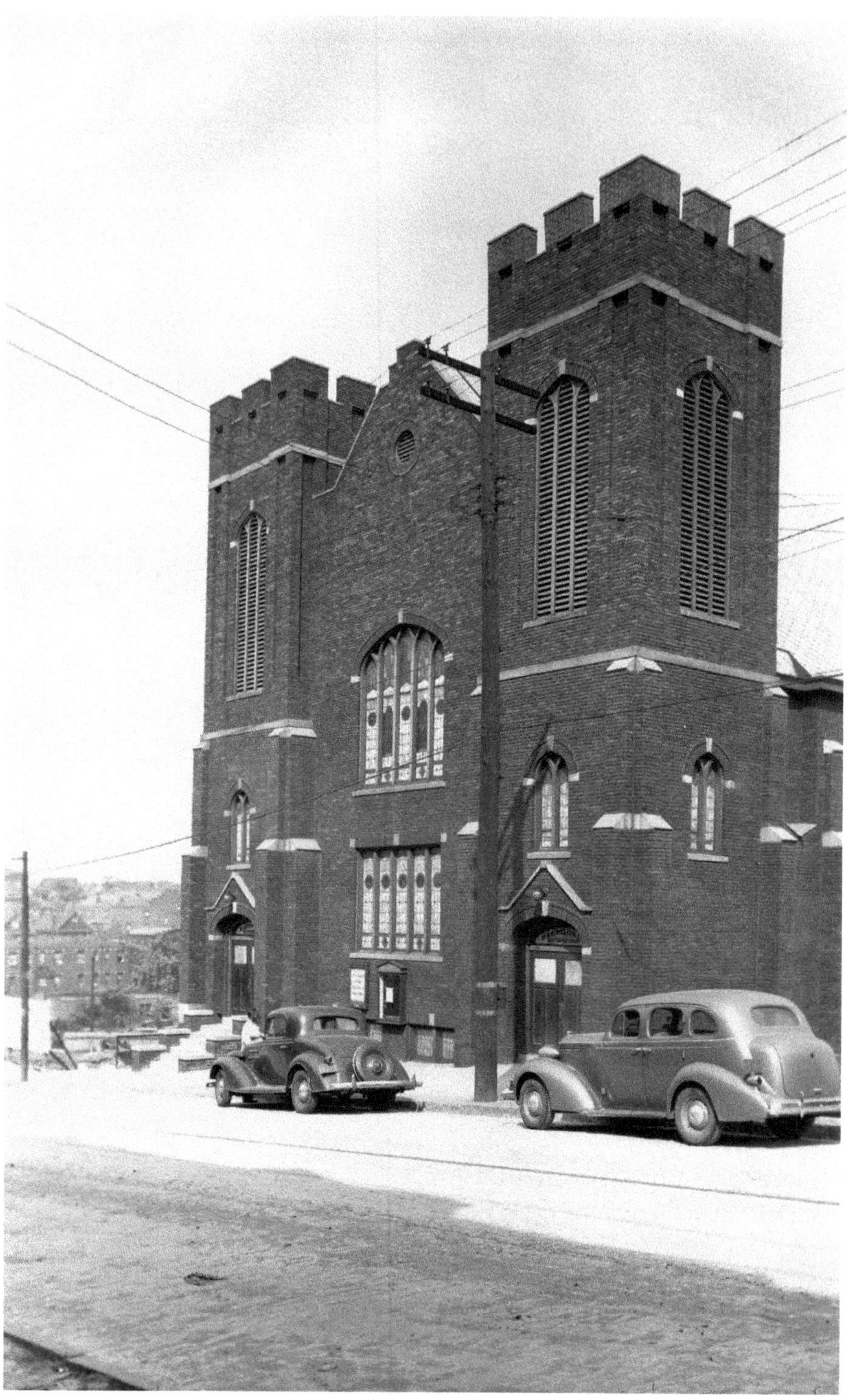

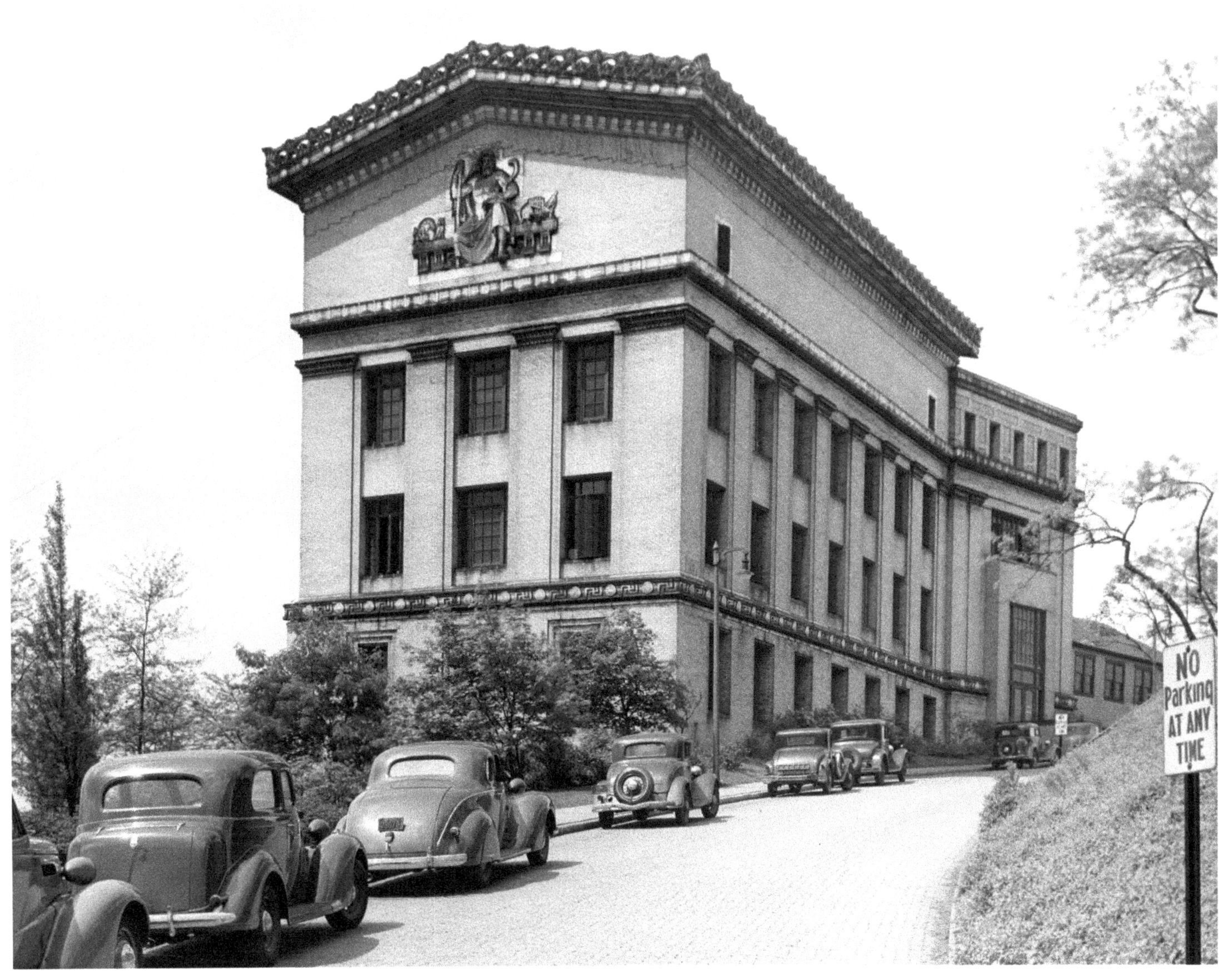

Originally part of Hornbostel's Acropolis Plan for the University, Pennsylvania Hall was completed in 1911. The building was torn down and replaced with a residence hall in 2004.

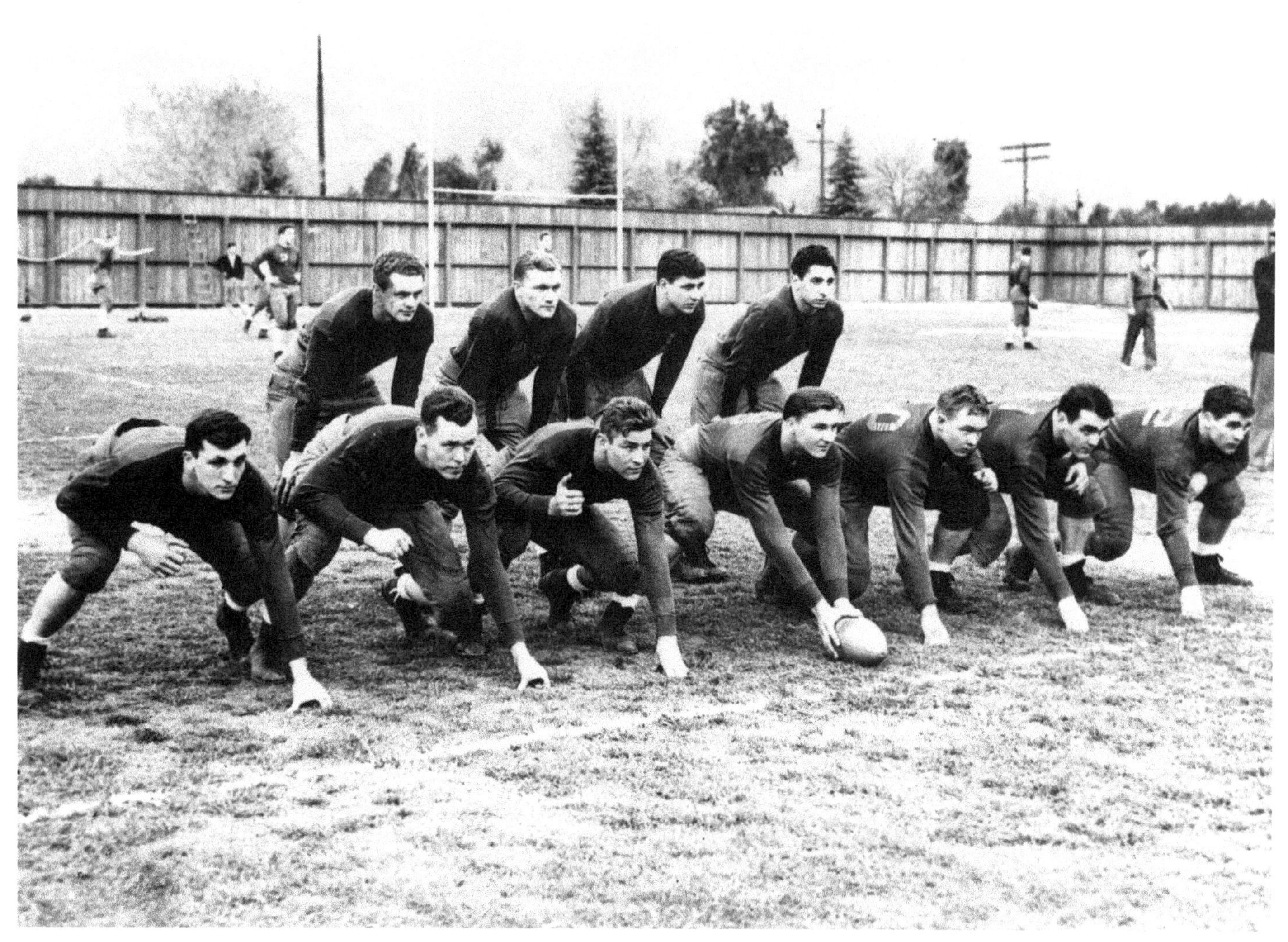

The 1936-37 Pittsburgh Panthers football team. They were to play a New Year's Day game against the University of Washington Huskies.

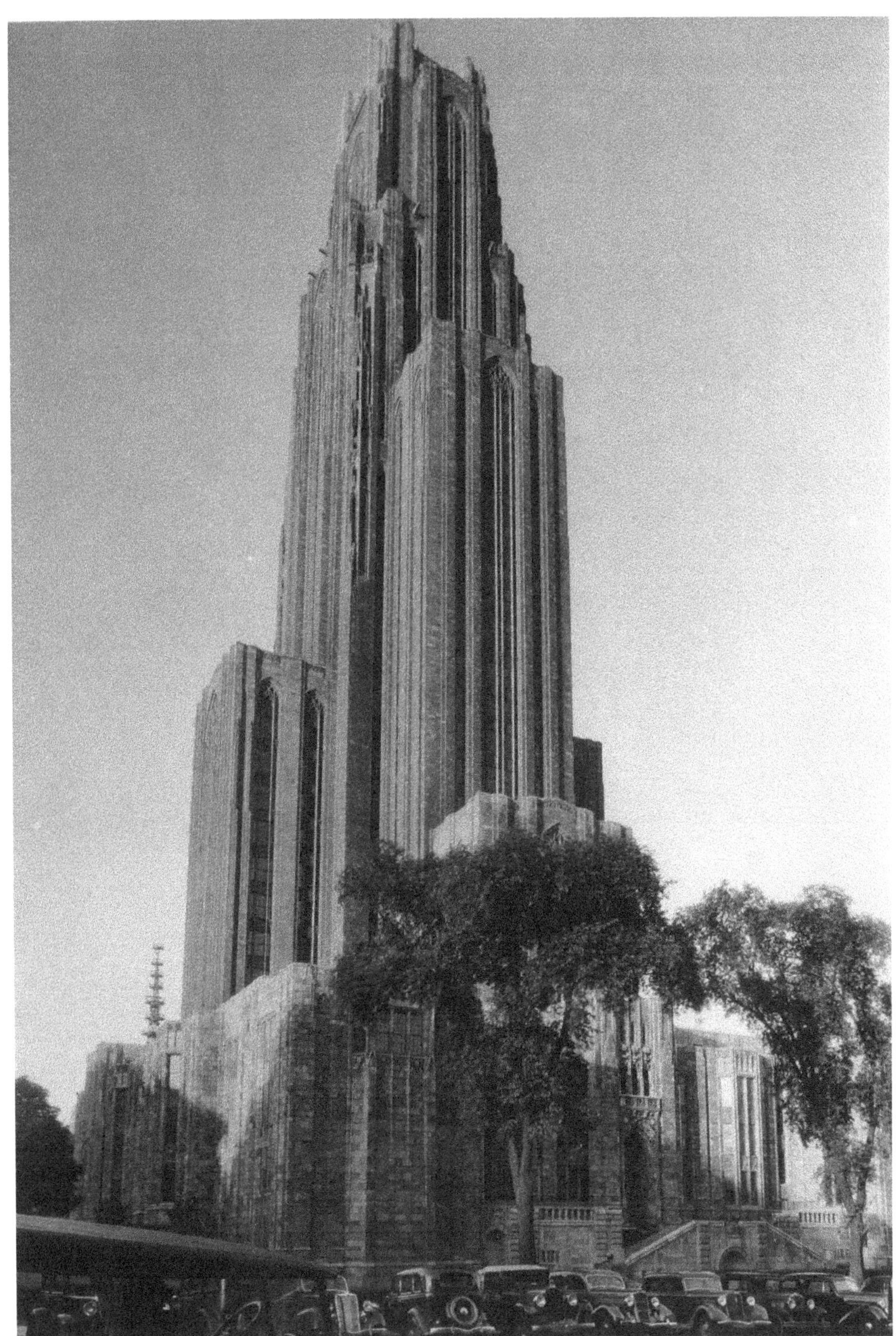

Photographed from Bigelow Boulevard, this is the University of Pittsburgh's Cathedral of Learning in 1937, shortly after construction. A close look to the left reveals the steeple of Heinz Chapel, which was still under construction that year.

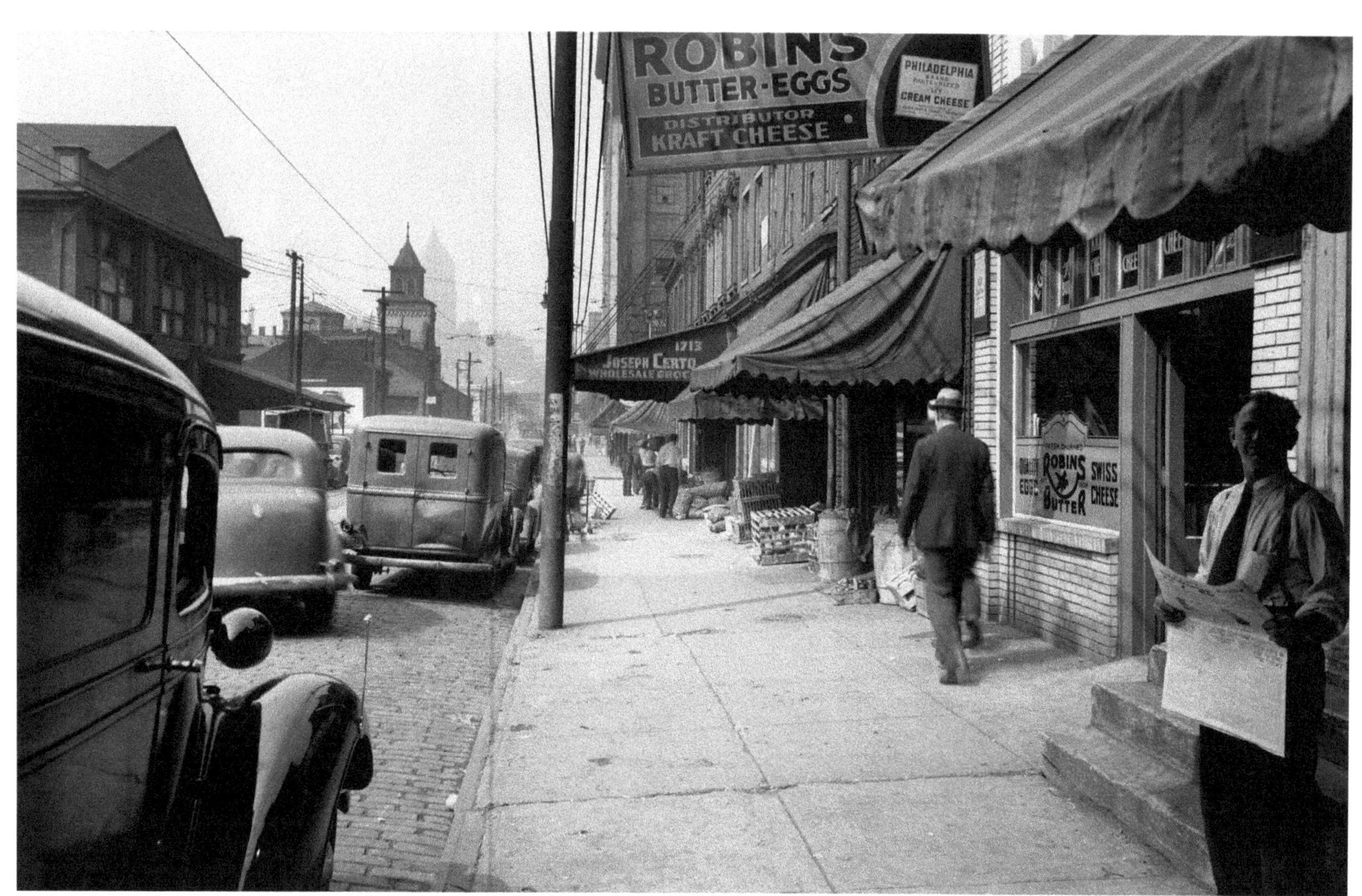

The Strip District in 1937, at 1723 Penn Avenue.

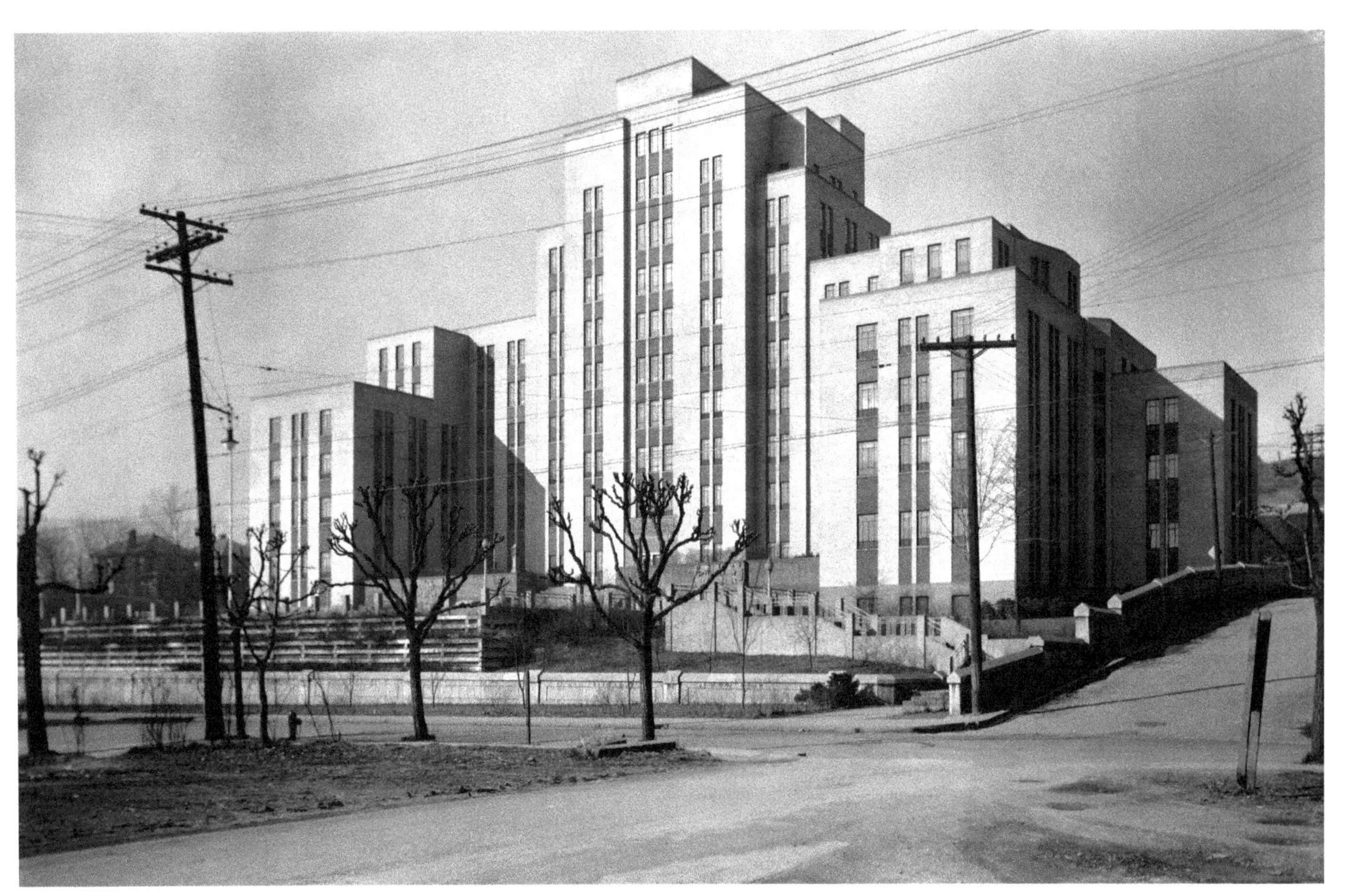

Municipal Hospital in 1939 shortly after construction.

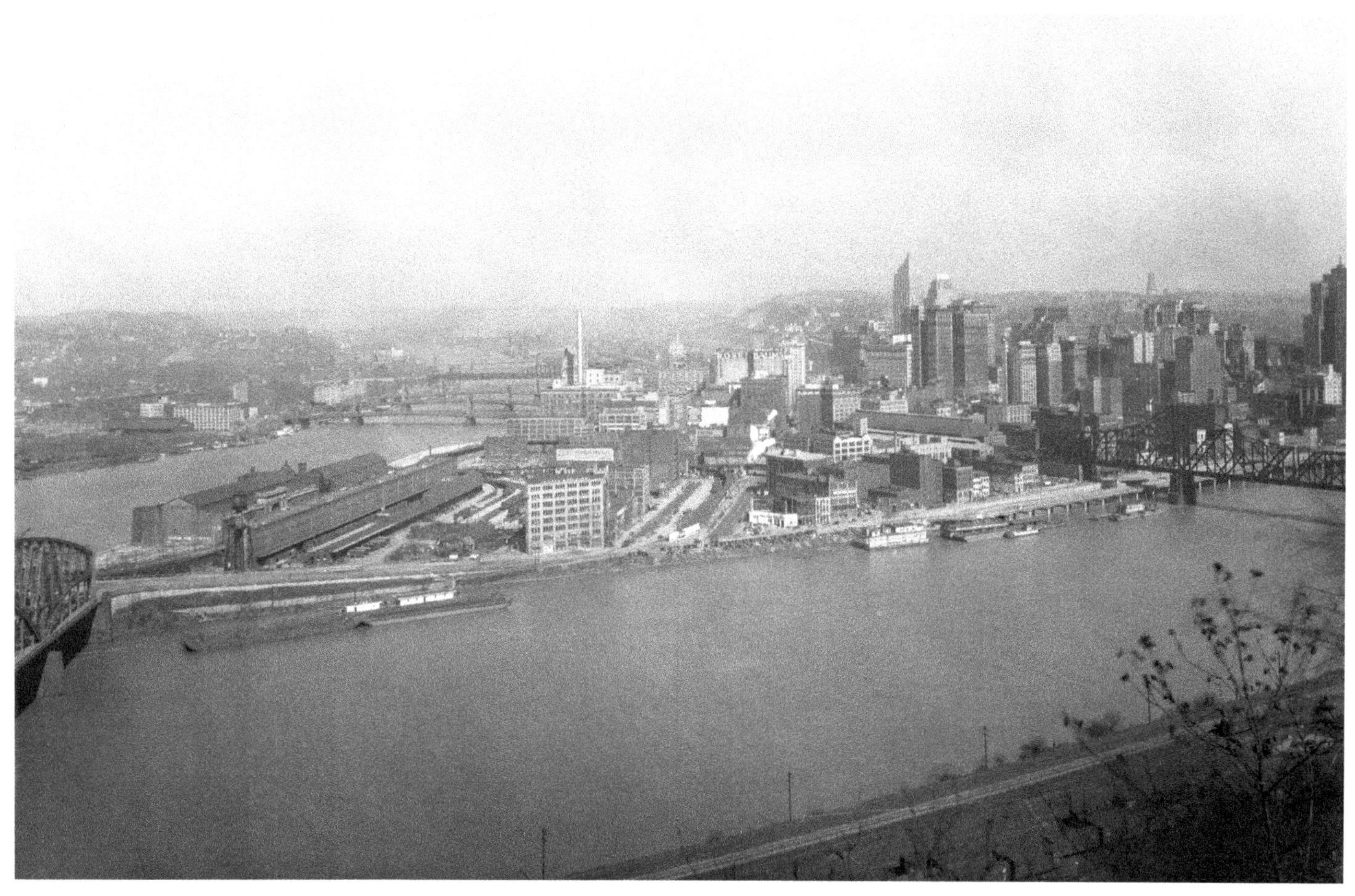

Downtown Pittsburgh, prior to the 1950s, from Duquesne Heights looking toward the Point. Landmarks visible here include the Exposition buildings, without the merry-go-round and roller coaster, the Monongahela River and wharf with its bustle of activity, the Allegheny River, and downtown businesses. A close look reveals the Fort Pitt Blockhouse between the warehouse and the Point Building.

Smoky City No More

(1940–1949)

President Roosevelt paid a visit to Pittsburgh in 1940, observing the WPA projects of the 1930s, such as flood control efforts and Terrace Village in the Hill District, the second-largest housing project in the country. He also visited the impressive steel mills, which would lend strength to the war effort.

Pittsburgh's industrial past caught up to it in the 1940s. For nearly 75 years, Pittsburgh had been a center of progress and steel capital of the world. The gloomy gray skies and streetlights lit during the day were a reminder of the need for smoke control. Taking inspiration from St. Louis and Chicago, industrial cities that had also contended with air pollution, Pittsburgh passed its own clean-air ordinance in 1941. With America's sudden entry into World War II and the effects of production for the war effort during this crucial period, these environmental ordinances did not officially take effect until October 1, 1946.

During the war years, Pittsburgh heeded the call to action. Thousands of men and women took jobs in various industries, many taking jobs in steel. Pittsburghers also pledged money through war loan drives, conserved resources, and planted Victory Gardens among other wartime activities.

In response to the challenge of Pittsburgh's topography, the Pitt Parkway project, later renamed the Penn-Lincoln Parkway, was on the drawing board. The parkway was designed to connect downtown with the eastern part of the city and to create a faster route between downtown and the Greater Pittsburgh Airport. In order to make changes in traffic, the Monongahela Wharf and Water Street underwent significant alterations and a tunnel was forged through Squirrel Hill. Former New York Parks Commissioner Robert Moses devised a plan for the parkway, the Point, and other city road connectors to the parkway. On July 25, 1946, ground was broken for the project after years of planning.

In his 1946 inaugural speech, Mayor David L. Lawrence vowed to make Pittsburgh "outstanding where it is now merely good," a promise he would keep in the next decade. The following year other seeds of renewal were sown as business leader Richard King Mellon announced plans for his "Pittsburgh Center," which included redeveloping the Lower Hill District.

For Pittsburgh, the haze was beginning to clear and a new decade of growth brought hope to the city.

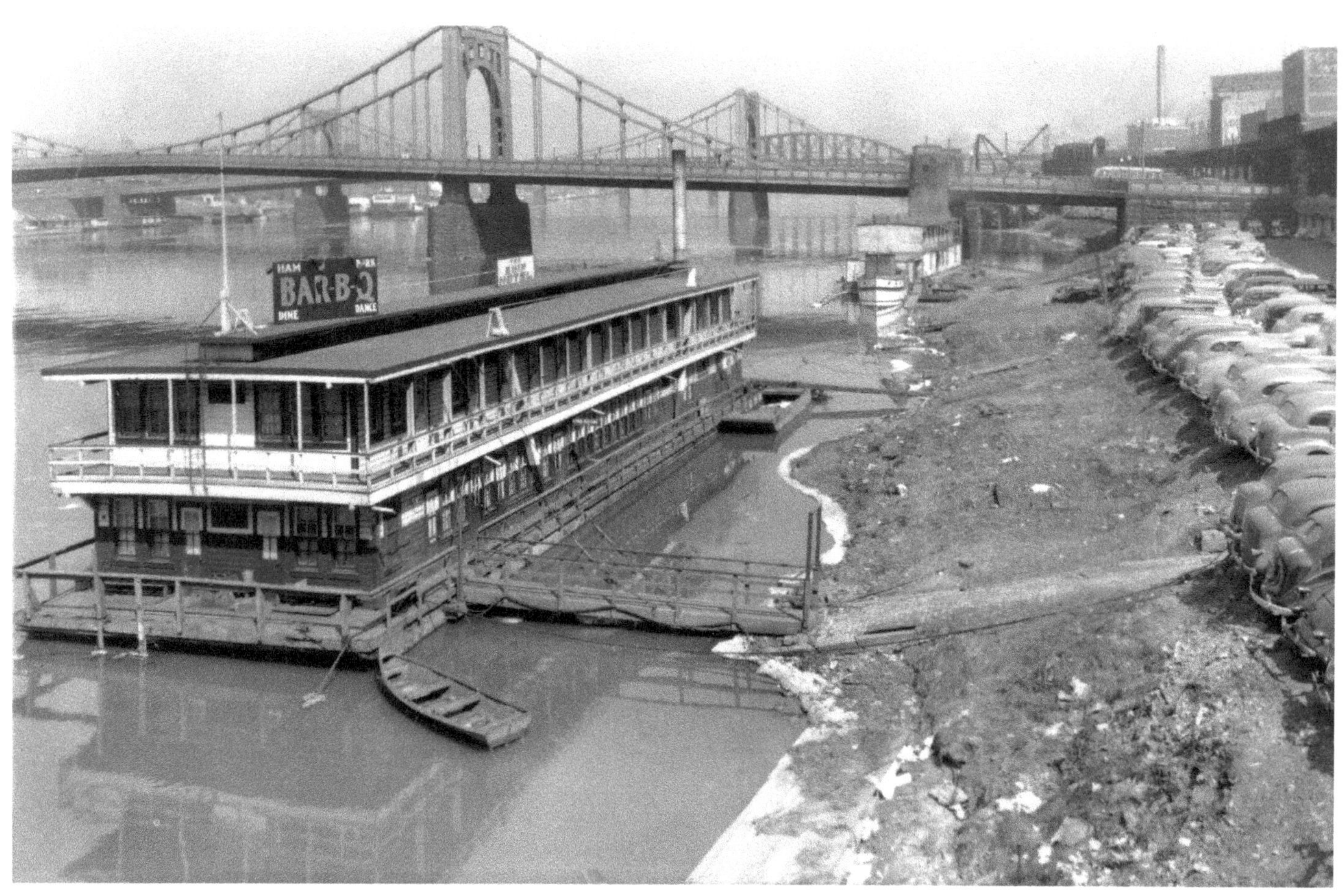

The Bar-B-Q and Ship Hotel, docked along the Duquesne Way Wharf between the Sixth and Seventh Street bridges.

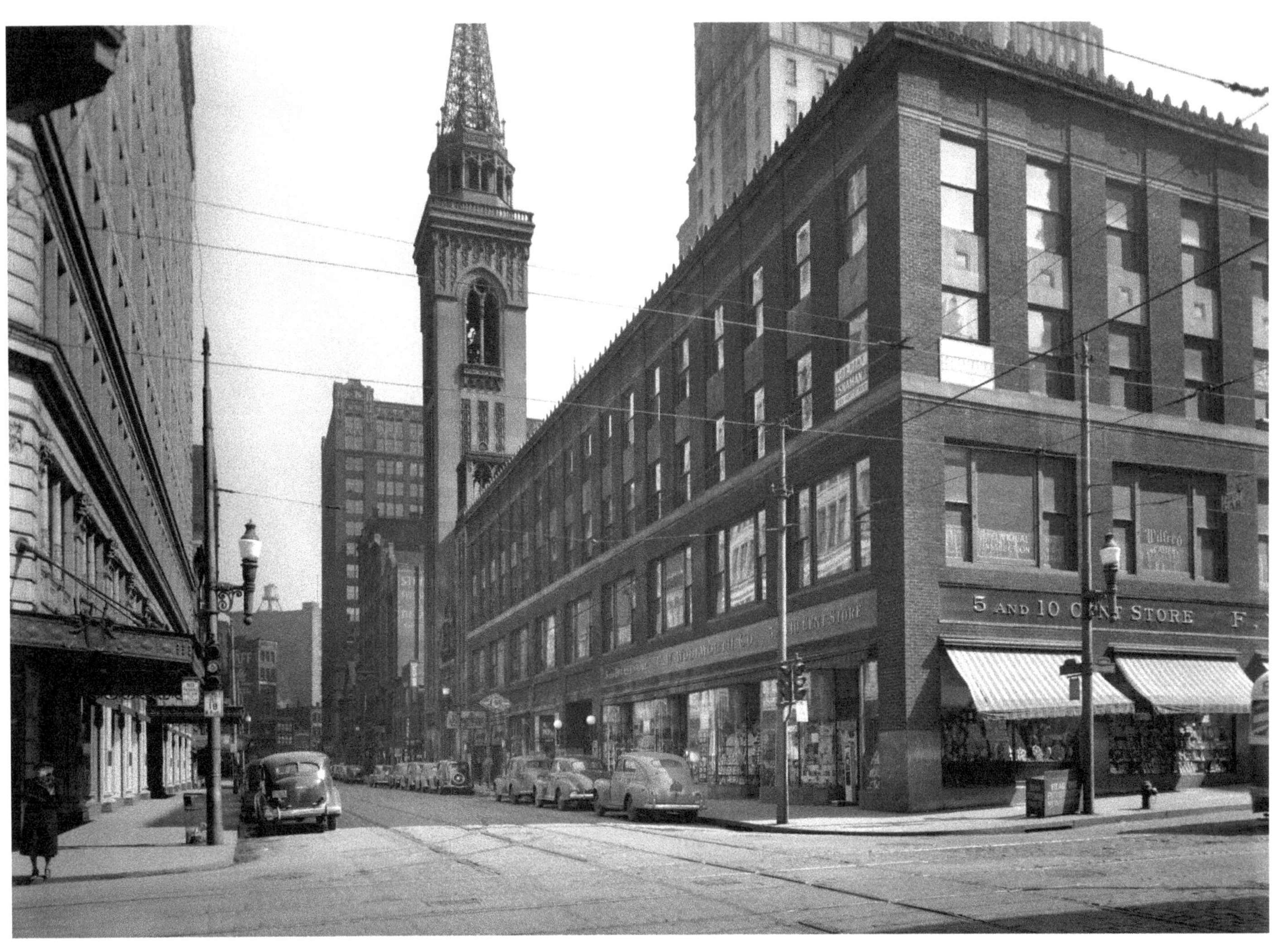

The Woolworth Company store at Sixth Avenue and Smithfield Street.

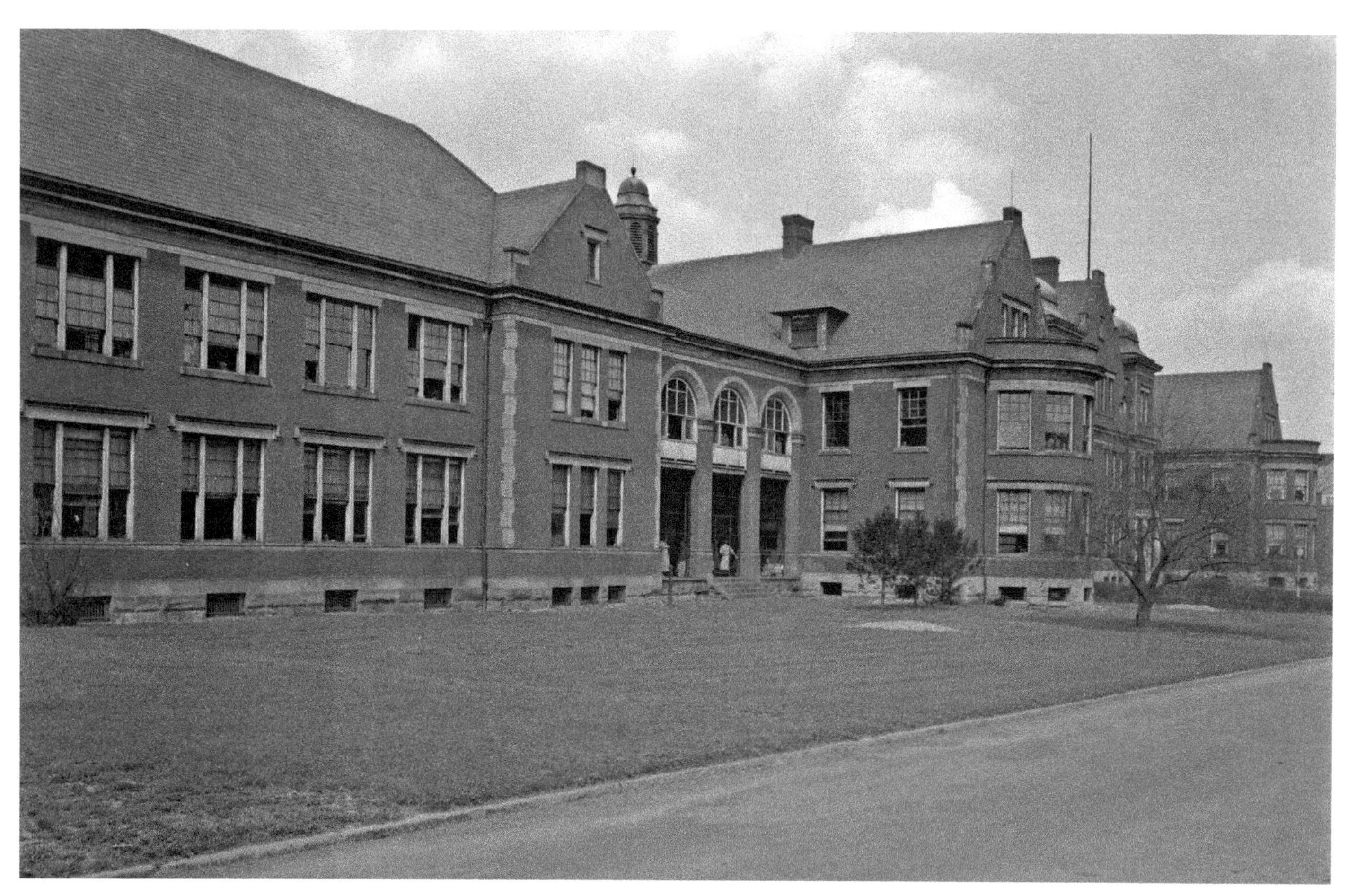

Woman's wing of the Pittsburgh City Home and Hospital for mentally ill patients.

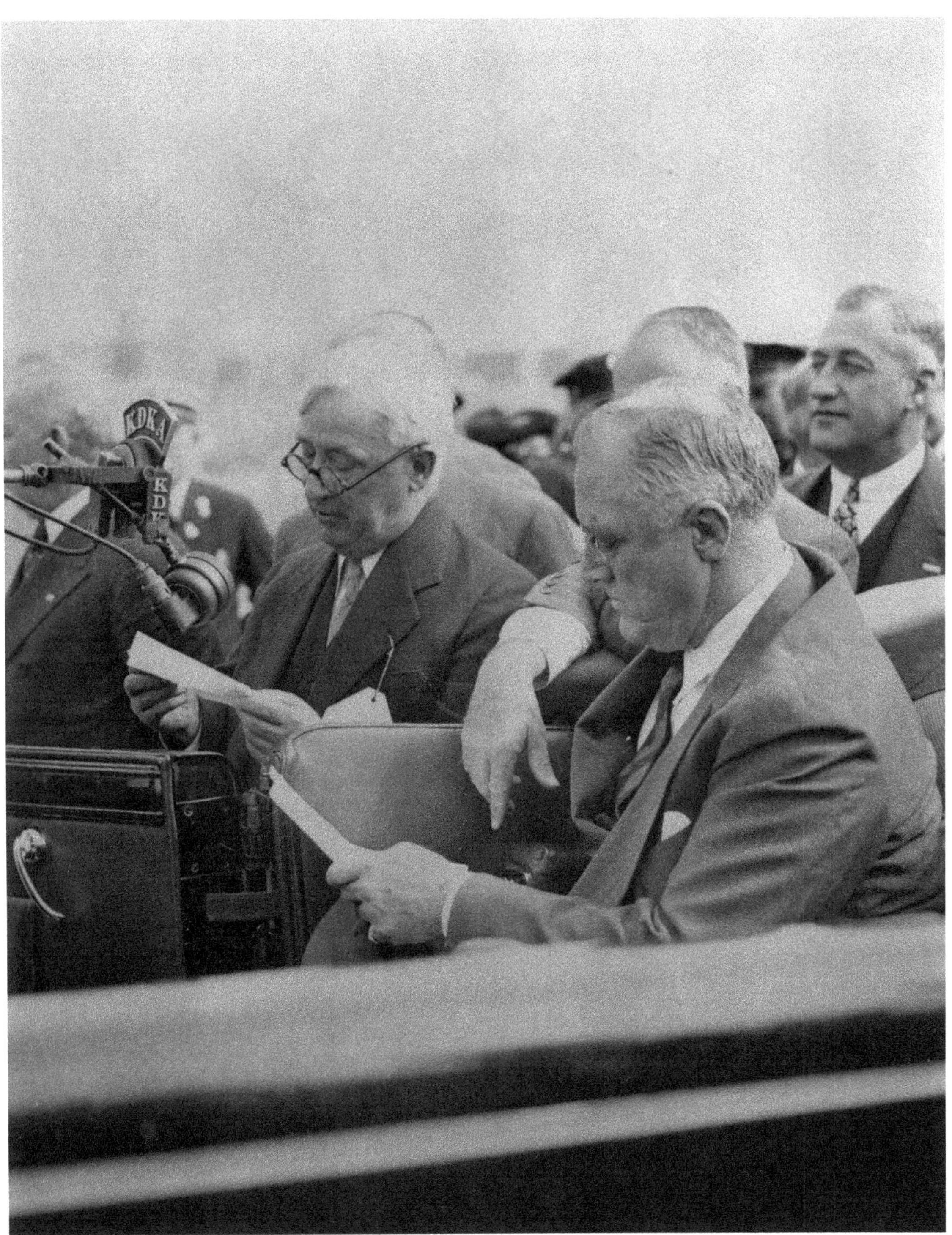

Franklin Delano Roosevelt with Pittsburgh's mayor during his visit to Pittsburgh in 1941.

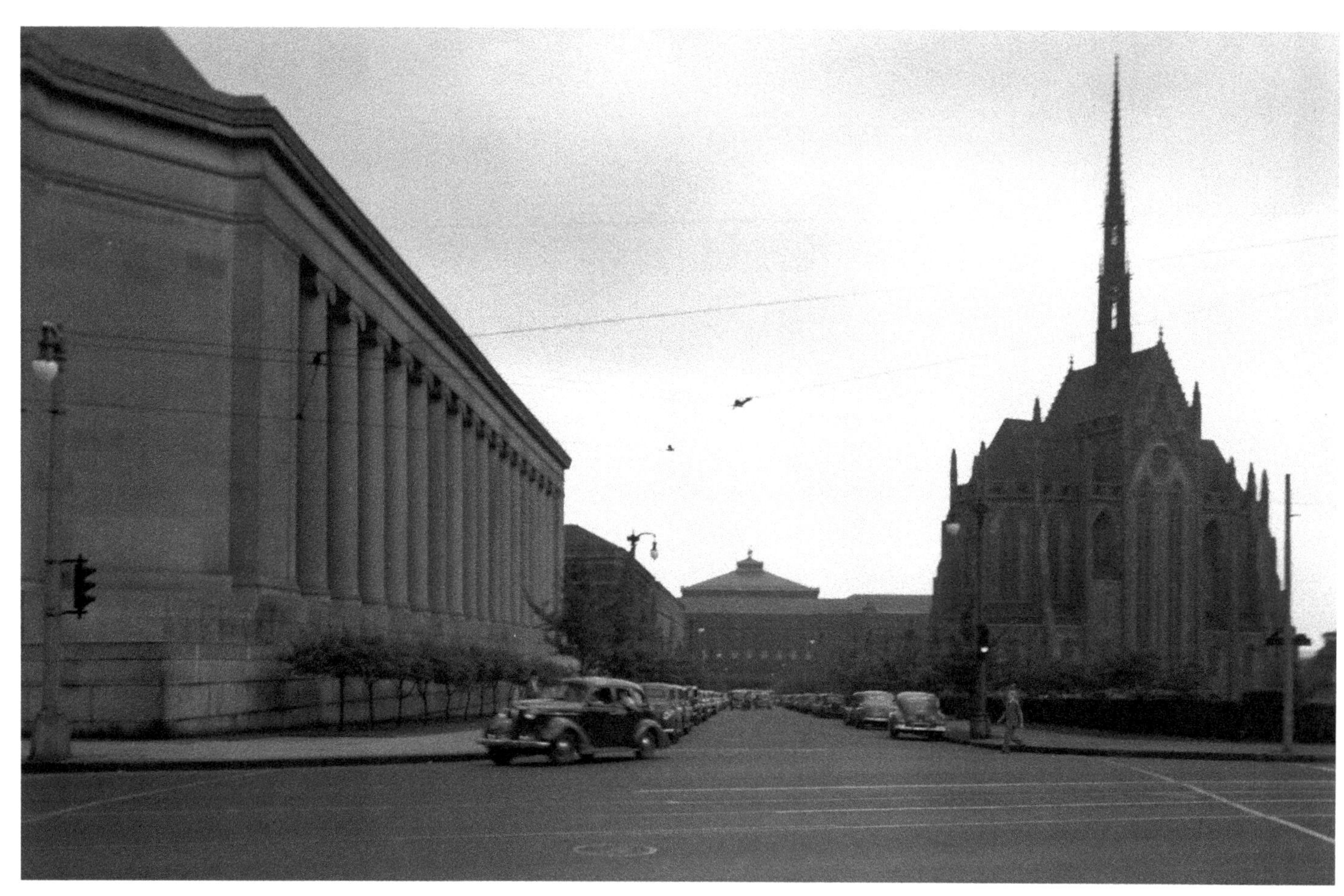

Heinz Chapel and the Mellon Institute at Fifth and Bellefield avenues, facing east toward the Carnegie Museum in 1944.

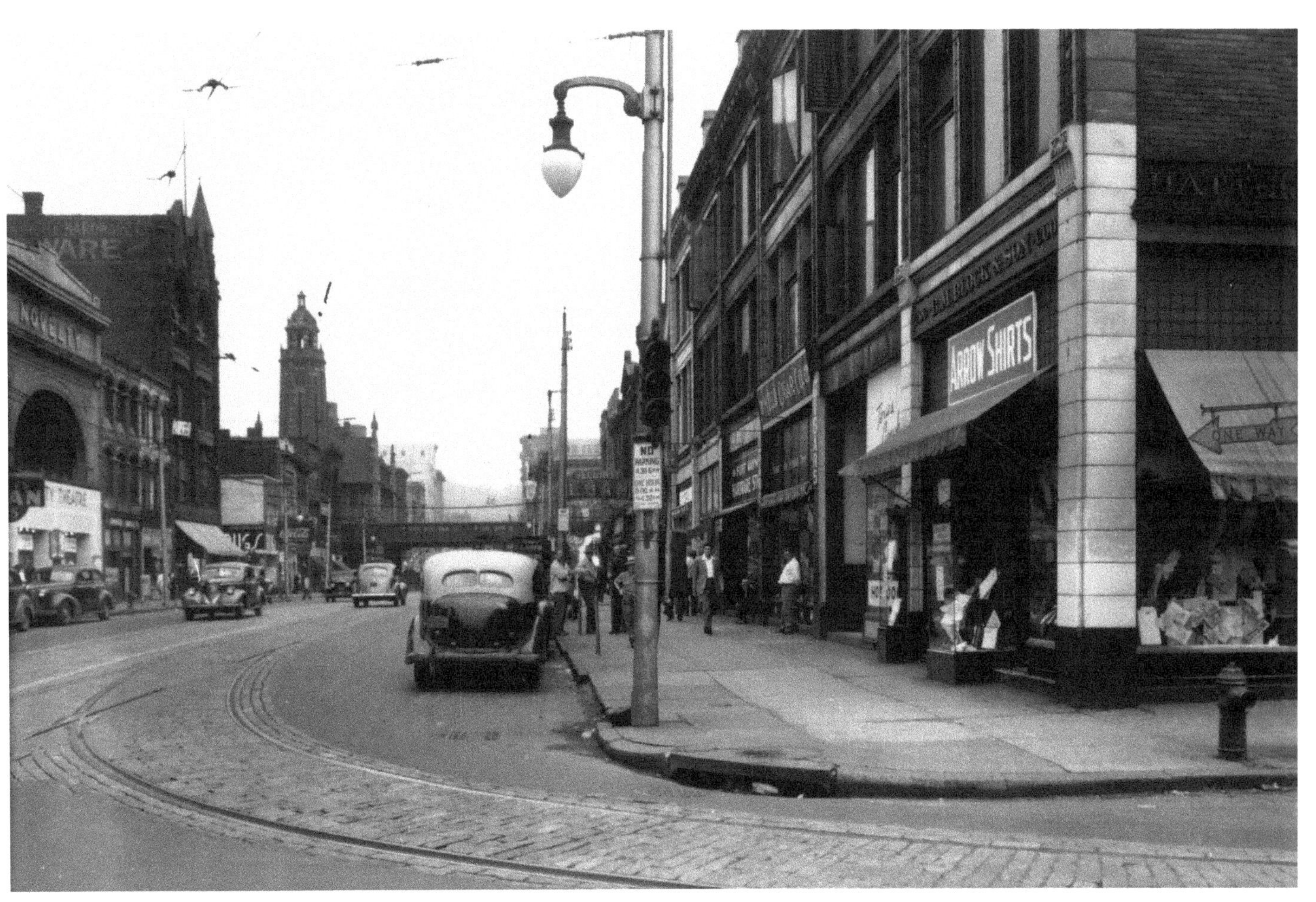

The B. M. Block & Son Arrow Shirt store, at right, and the Novelty Theatre on the left, line the 200 block of Federal Street on the North Side.

The city before the era of smoke control. This view from above street level at the corner of Liberty and Fifth avenues was recorded at 11:25 A.M. The smoke hung so thickly that neon signs and other lights were being run overtime.

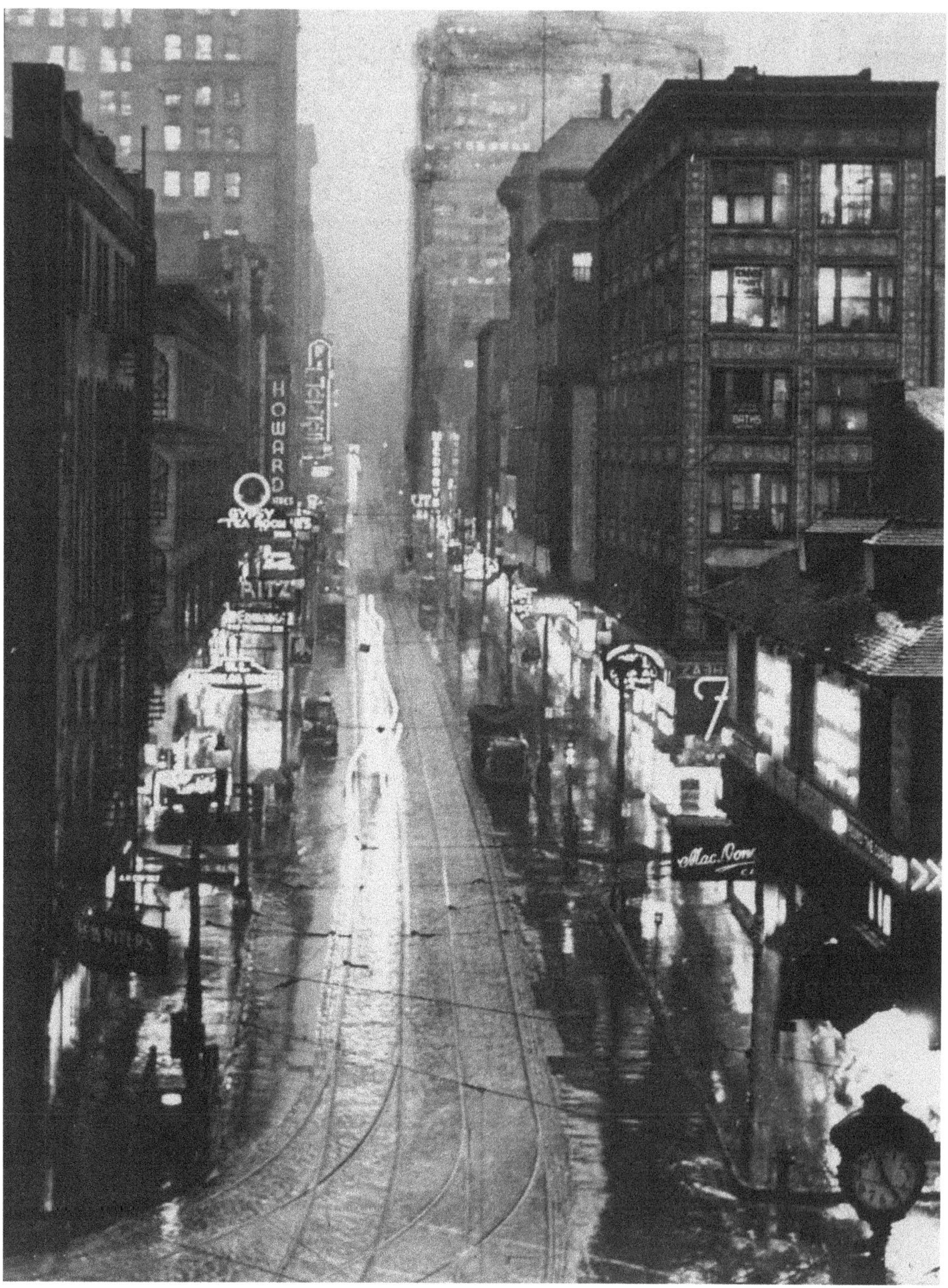

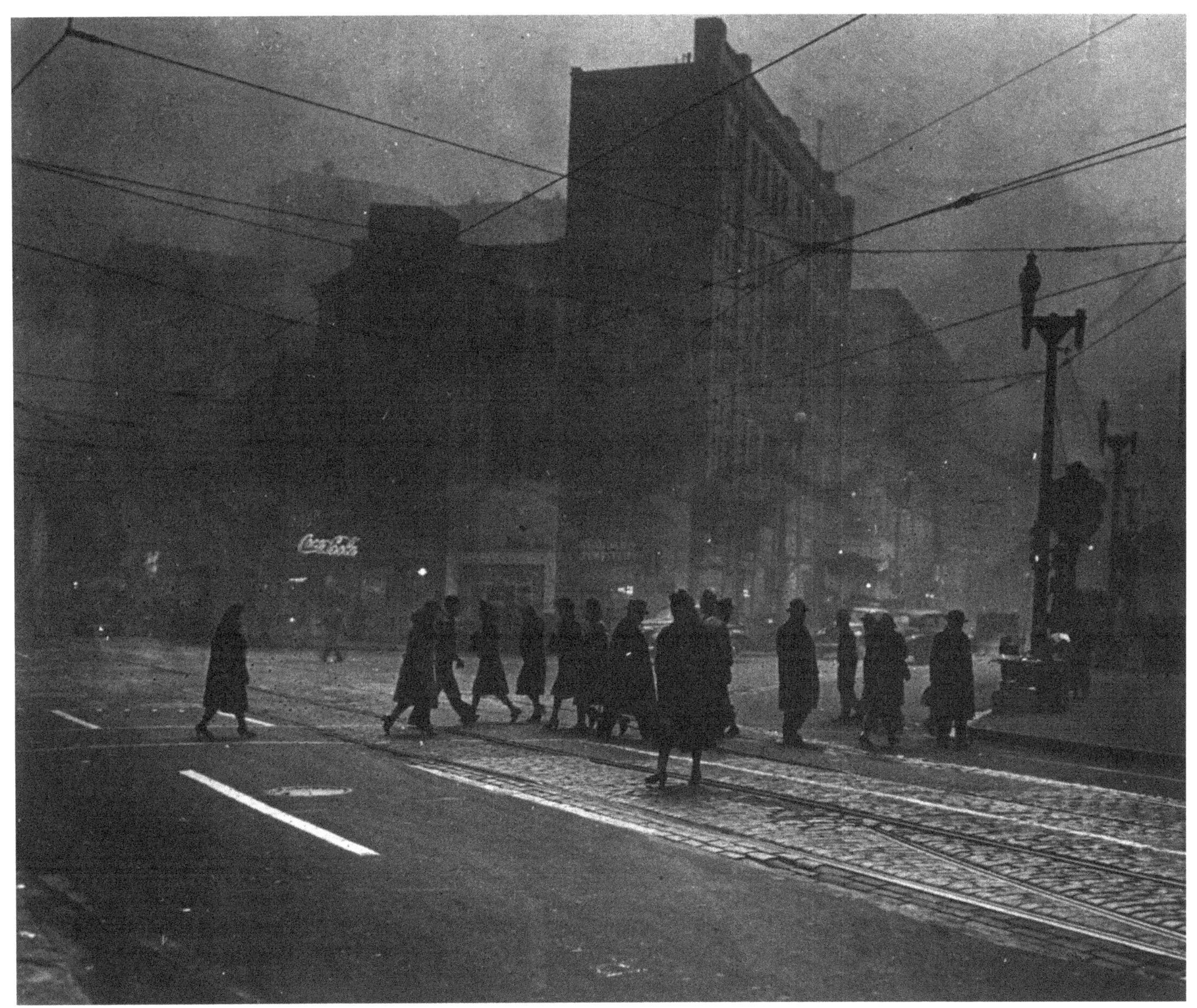

Daytime downtown before the advent of smoke control.

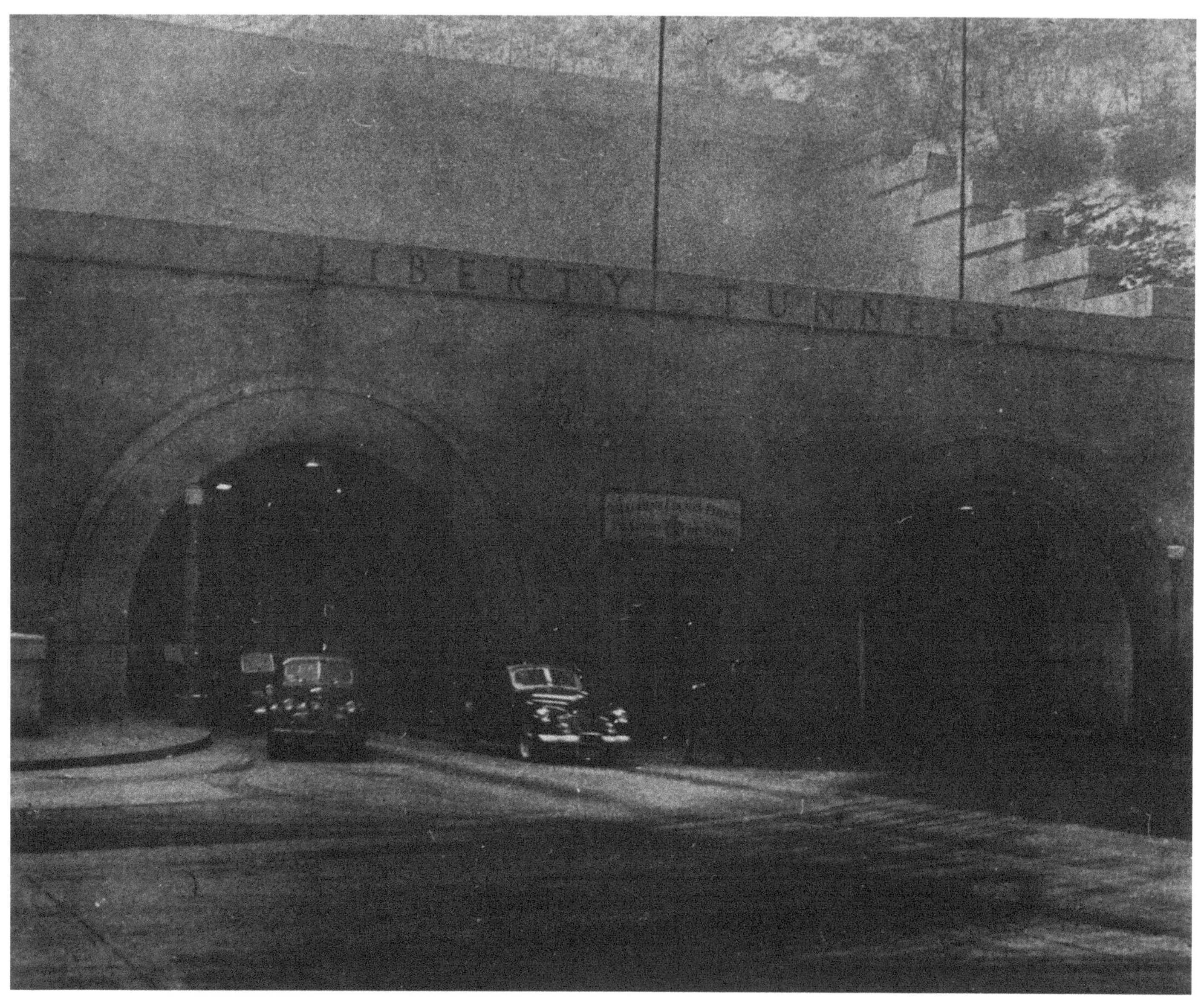

In the 1940s, before the advent of smoke control, the city side of the Liberty Tunnels appears dark and has low visibility.

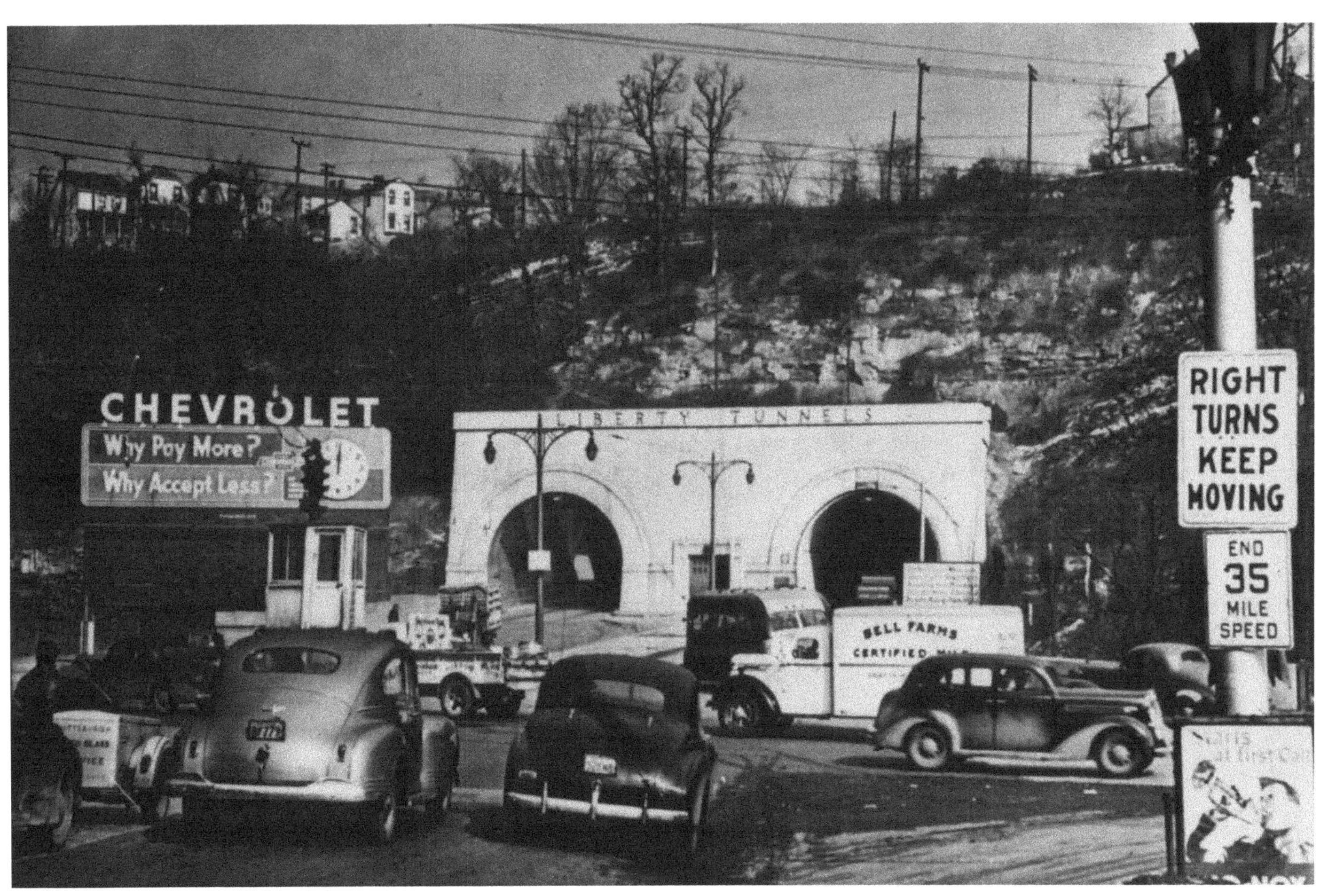

The sky at the south end of the Liberty Tunnels is clear, in contrast to that at the north end. Pittsburgh's air pollution was a problem that needed addressing.

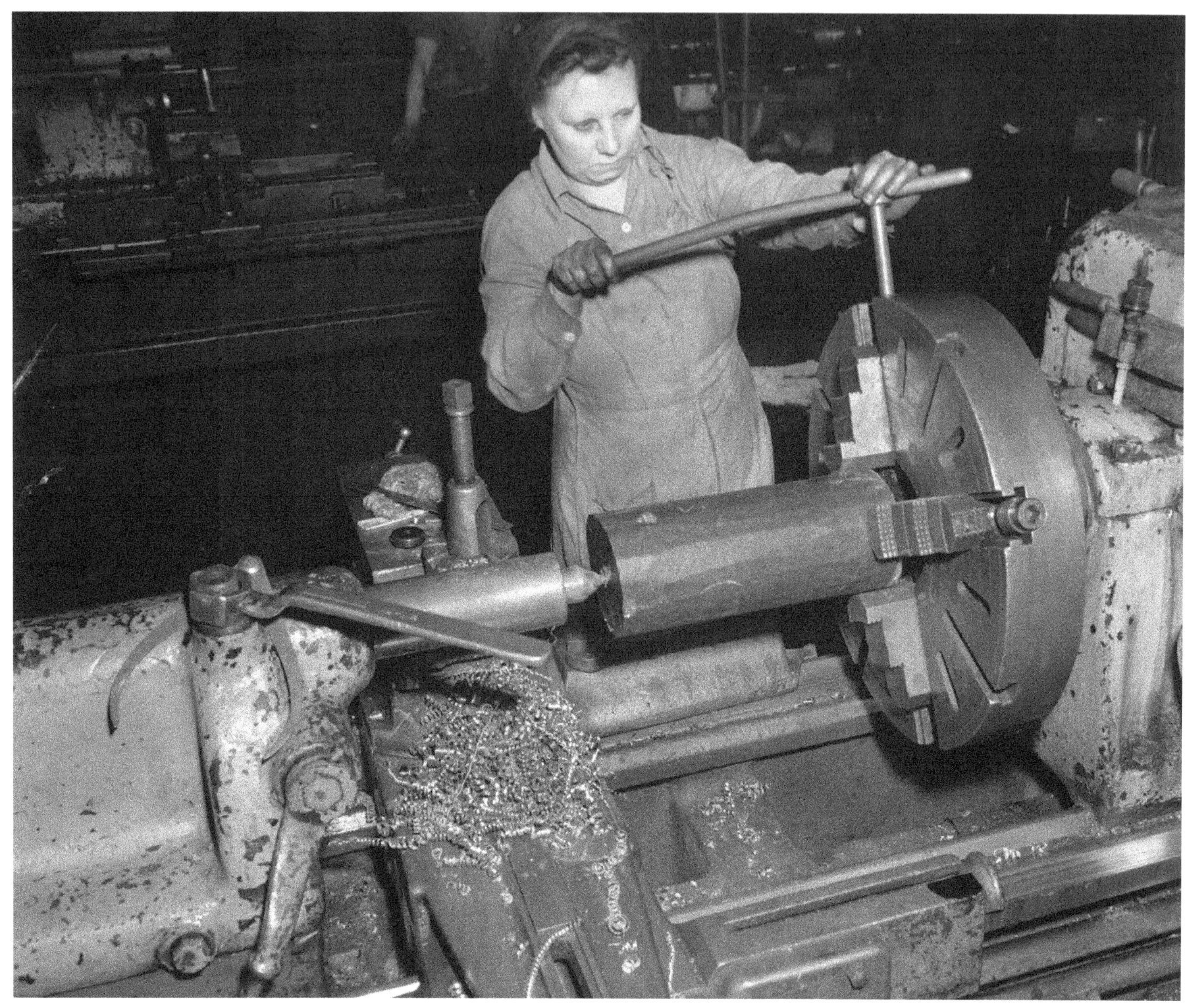

Women joined the workforce in large numbers, filling positions left vacant as men went to war. This woman is working in the machine shop at the Homestead Mill on May 8, 1945, Victory in Europe (V-E) Day.

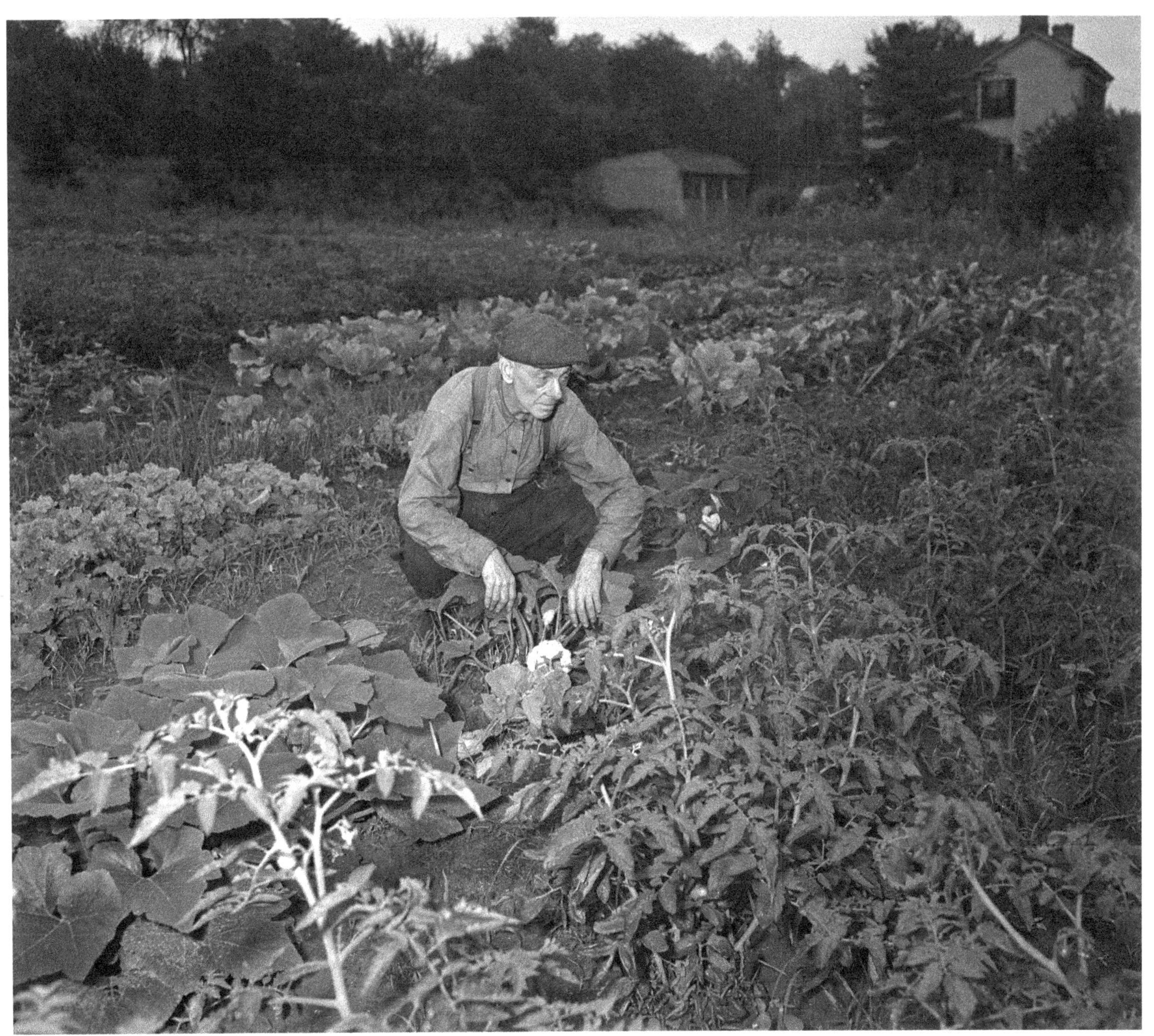

A man tends his Victory Garden in 1945.

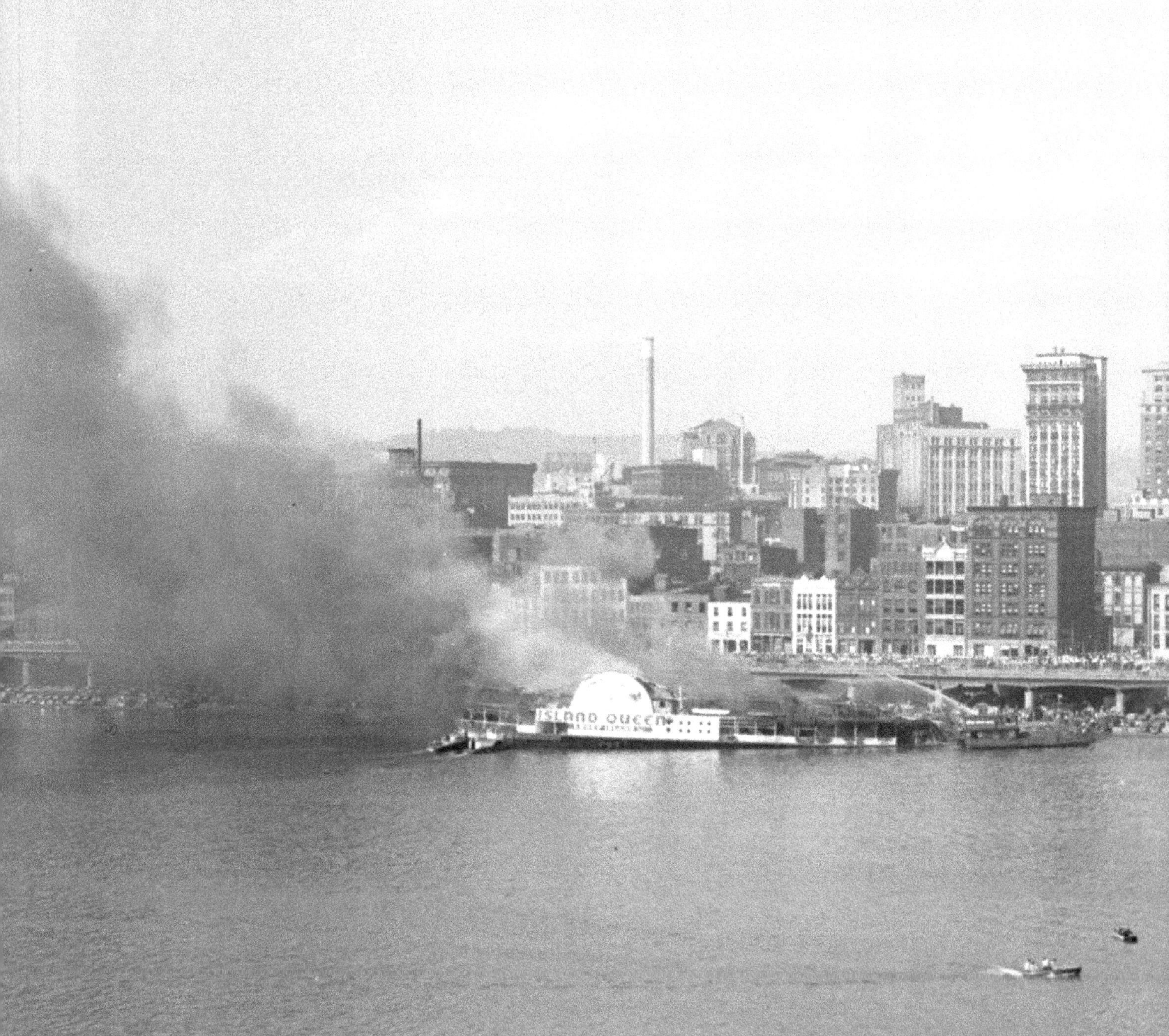
ISLAND QUEEN

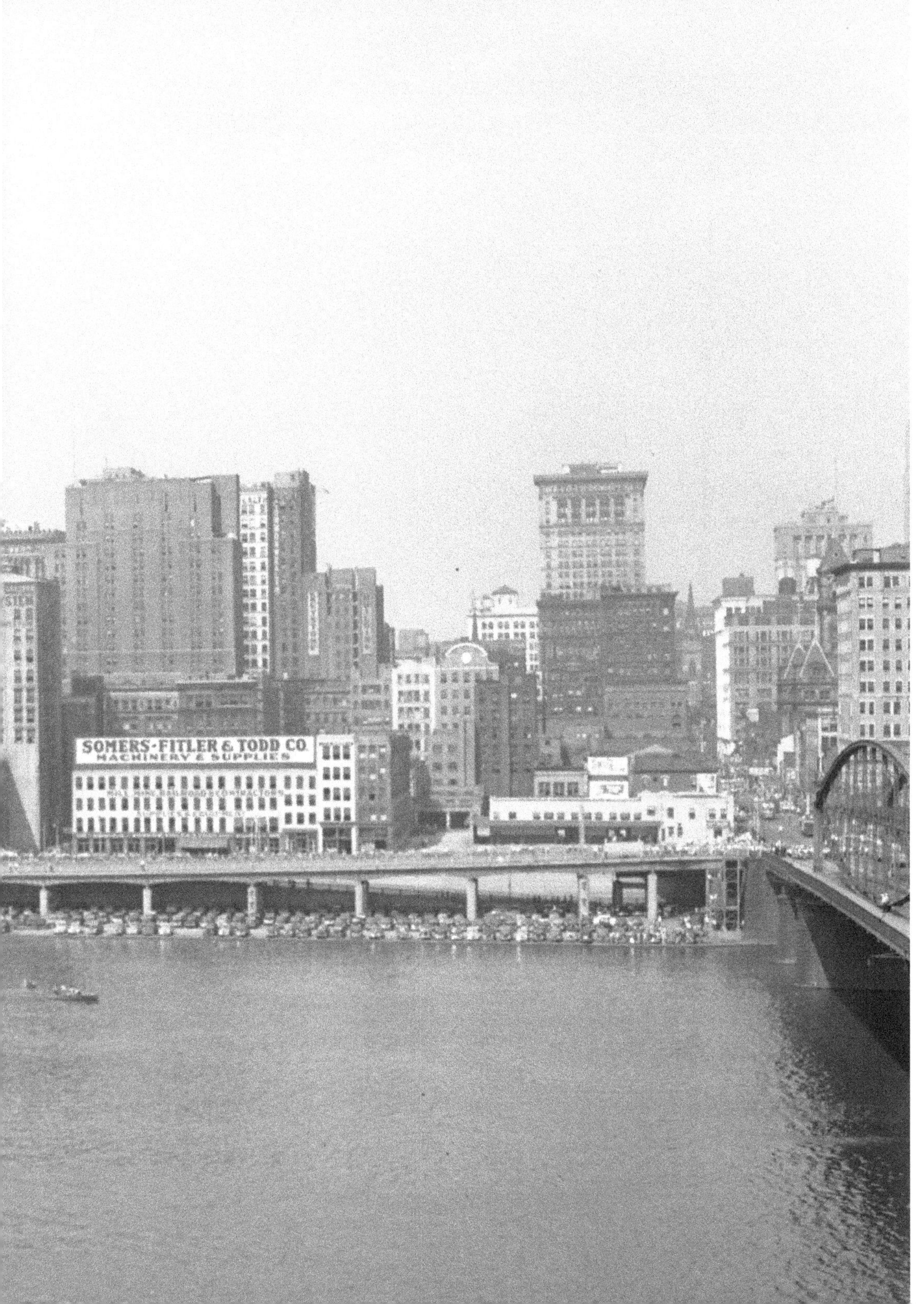

The *Island Queen* riverboat goes up in flames while docked at the Monongahela Wharf. The event was documented in this view from the Pittsburgh and Lake Erie Railroad tracks on the South Side.

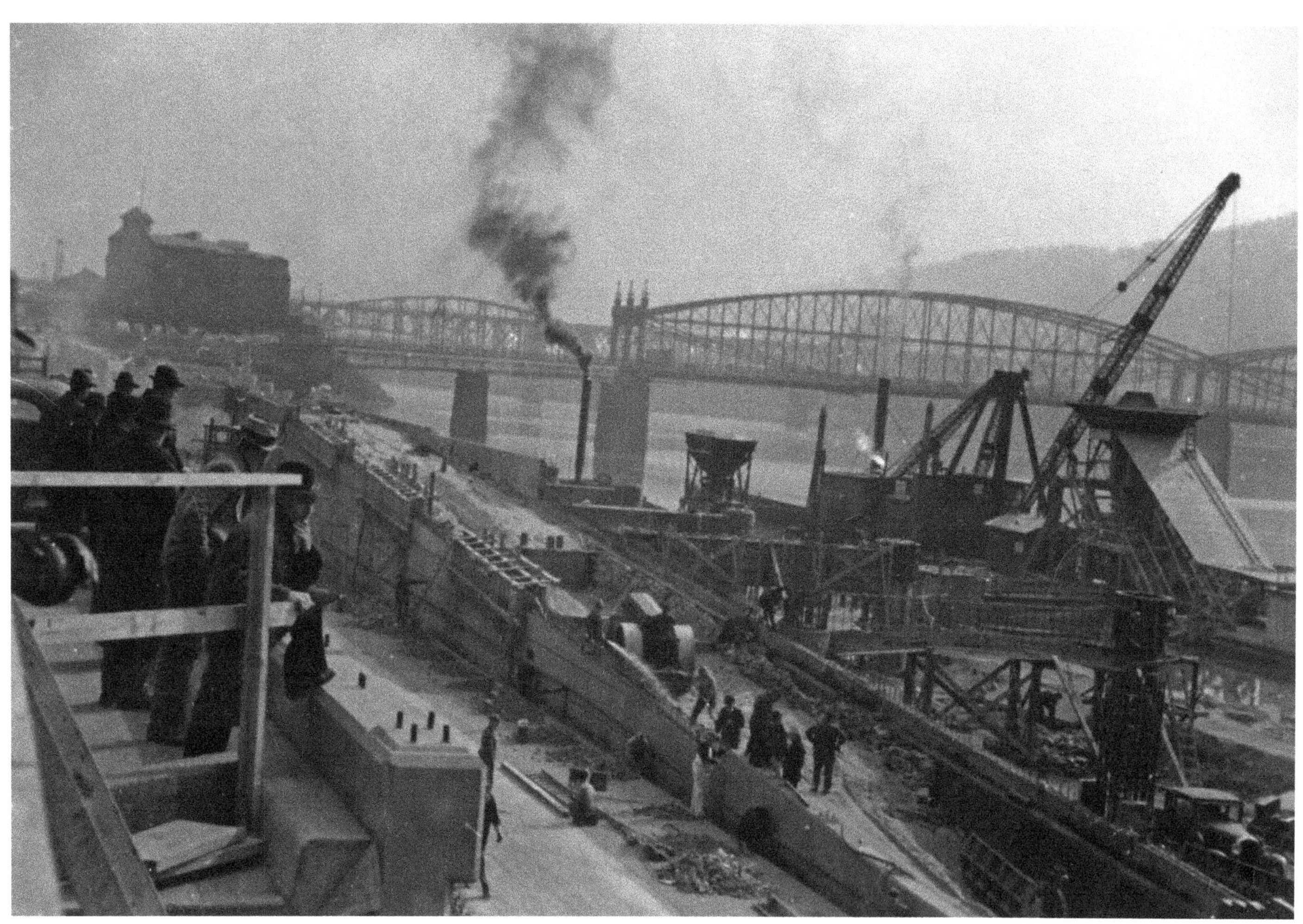

The changes to the area between the Monongahela Wharf and Water Street were extensive. What had been a two-lane street and part of the wharf area is now filled with concrete and ramps that will eventually carry thousands of vehicles around the city.

Era of Renewal
(1950–1970s)

Urban renewal marks the period between the 1950s and the early 1970s. The Penn-Lincoln Parkway project was in full swing, construction of which would connect downtown and the eastern suburbs as well as downtown and the west, including the Greater Pittsburgh Airport. A large stumbling block was the B&O Railroad station and terminal, which was directly in the path of the parkway. In 1951, the B&O agreed to move their headquarters to Smithfield and Grant so that the Parkway project could proceed.

To revive the city, Mayor David L. Lawrence created an unlikely partnership with Richard King Mellon, founder of the Allegheny Conference on Community Development. Their ideas and actions would become known as the "Pittsburgh Renaissance." Plans called for the clearing of 95 acres in the Lower Hill District, which disrupted life and businesses, having a detrimental effect on the Hill District community. People began moving to the suburbs, making the need for the Penn-Lincoln Parkway even more important. Other key projects during this period included Point State Park and the construction of Gateway Center office complex. Urban parks were planned in order to provide green space for the city. A good example is the Mellon Square Park project designed by James A. Mitchell and Dahlen K. Richey. The park incorporated a subterranean parking garage beneath a terraced garden, which is still used today.

In the 1960s and 1970s, landmarks like the Diamond Market, once a popular shopping destination for meats, produce, and other goods, were disappearing. The removal of the Diamond left a gaping hole downtown. Where Pittsburghers had once flocked to make their purchases became nothing more than four empty grassy areas. The development of the Allegheny Center Mall complex brought huge changes to the North Side, clearing 518 buildings that stood in its way. Created on what was once part of the very center of Allegheny City, the mall, a 79-acre shopping, office, and residential complex, replaced independent businesses and green space such as the Market House, Ober Park, and the Boggs and Buhl Department Store.

On the positive side, Pittsburgh still featured world-class attractions such as its universities, museums, and zoo. The construction of Three Rivers Stadium and a world premiere of art during the Pittsburgh Arts Festival were milestones as the city considered its future.

Shown here in 1957, the 42-story Gothic revival Cathedral of Learning was designed by Charles Klauder. The granite and bronze Mary Schenley Memorial Fountain was built in 1918 as a tribute to Mary Schenley, who donated the land for Schenley Park. The sculpture of a flute-playing Pan and a lyre-playing woman was designed by Victor David Brenner, and its base was designed by H. Van Magonigle. The University of Pittsburgh's Frick Fine Arts Building, built in 1965, currently stands directly behind it.

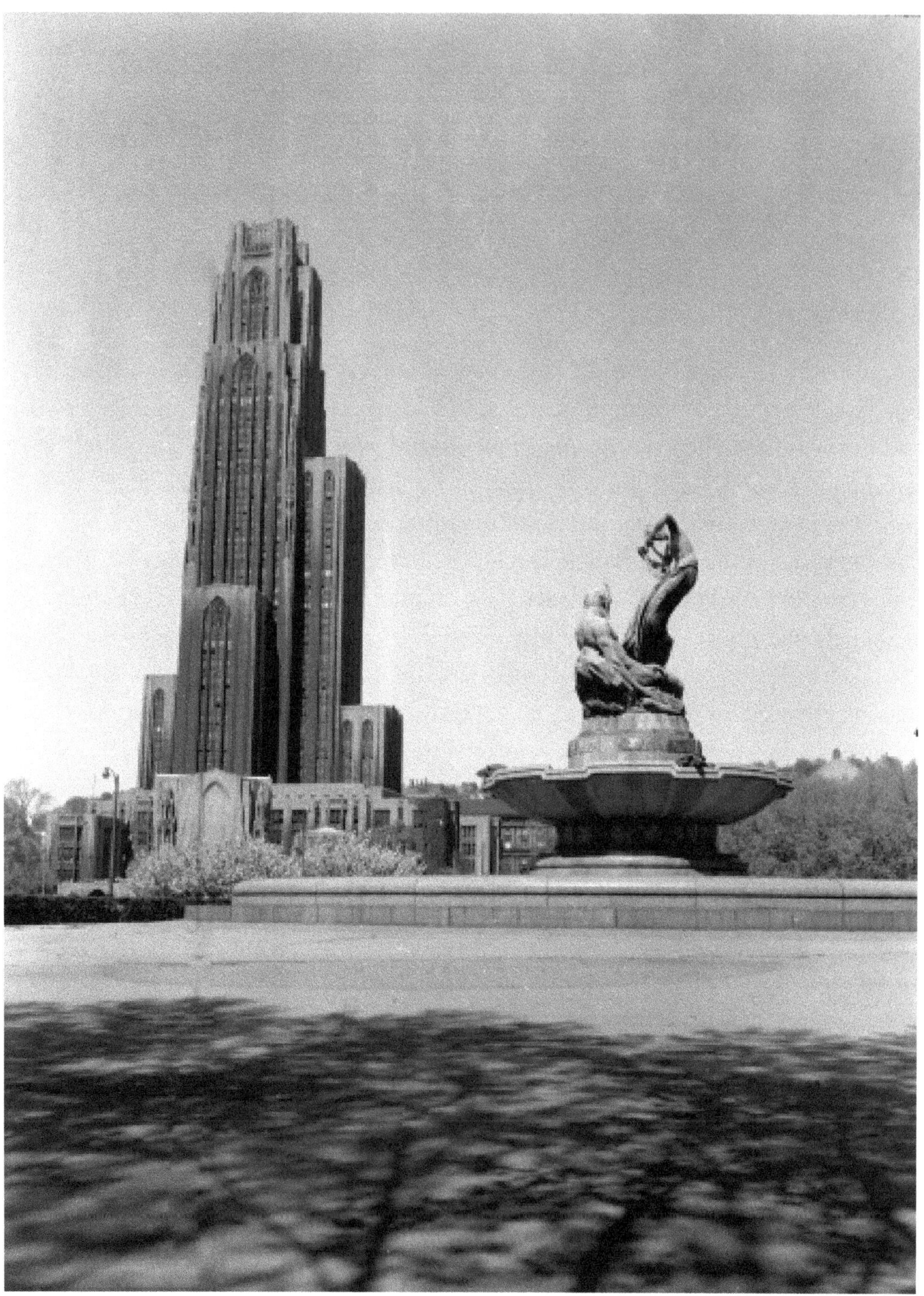

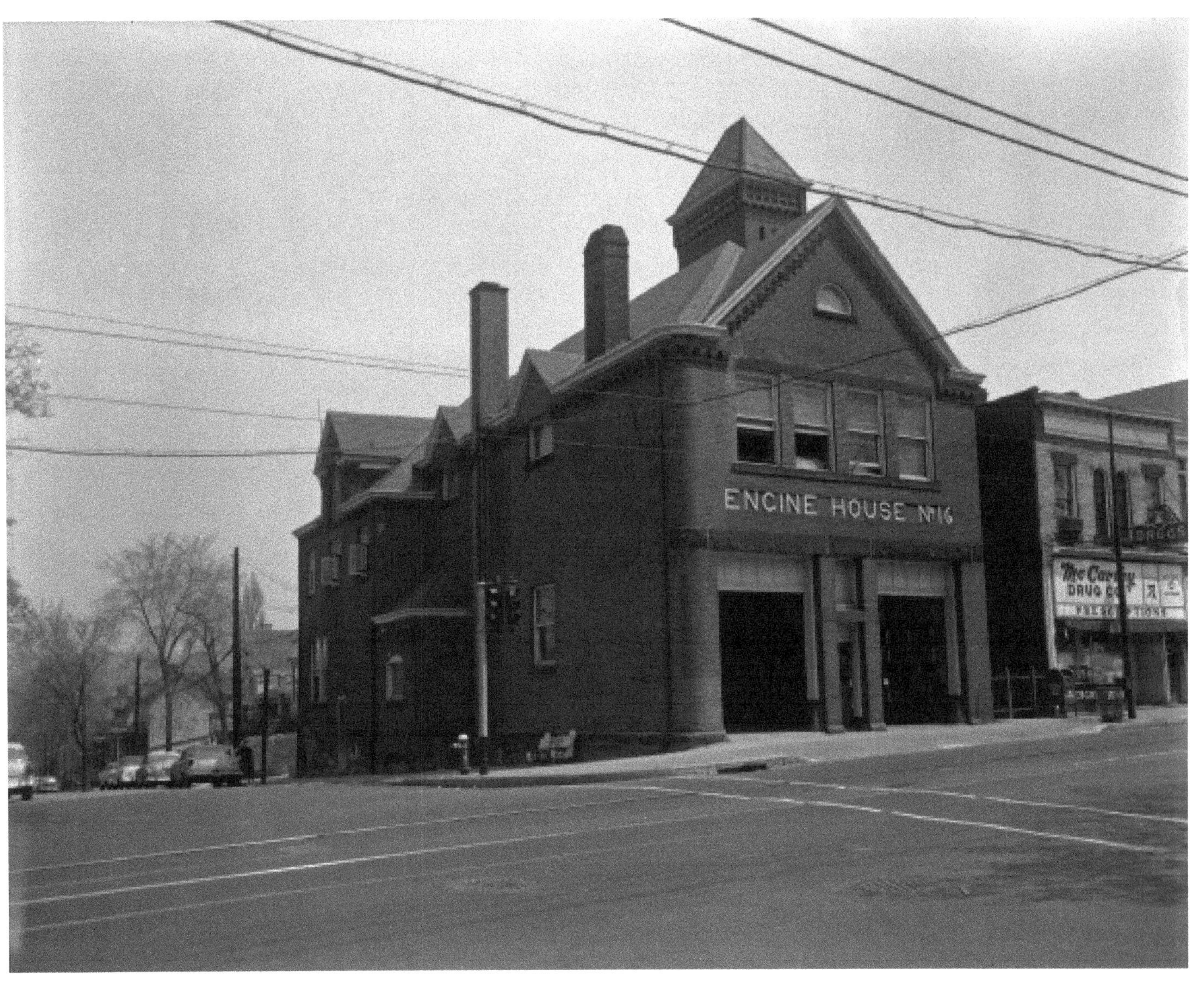

The Pittsburgh Bureau of Fire Engine Company No. 16 on Penn Avenue in Point Breeze.

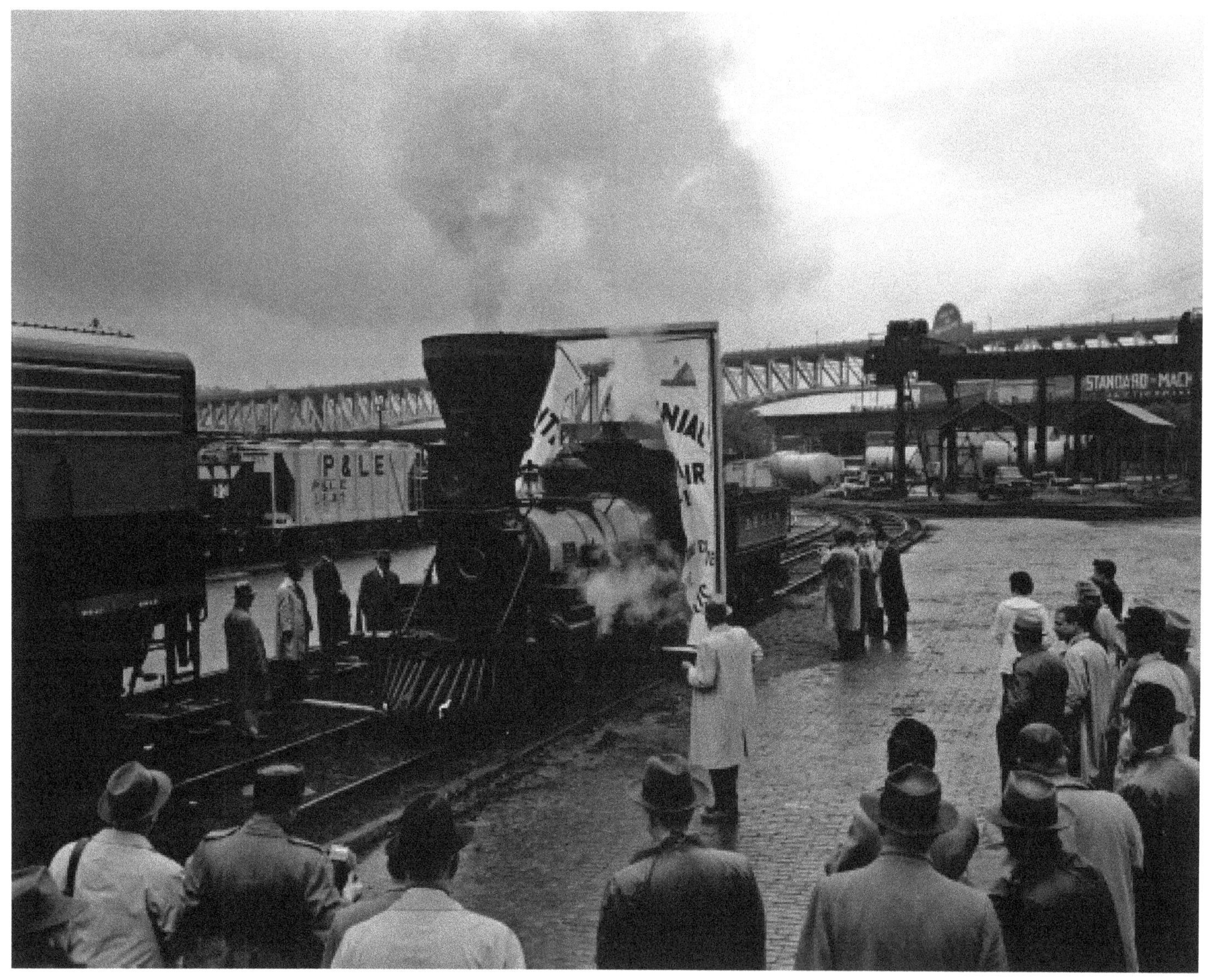

Originally built in 1856, the exhibition B&O Railroad steam locomotive #25, also known as the William Mason, officially opens the Bicentennial Railroad Fair on May 15, 1959.

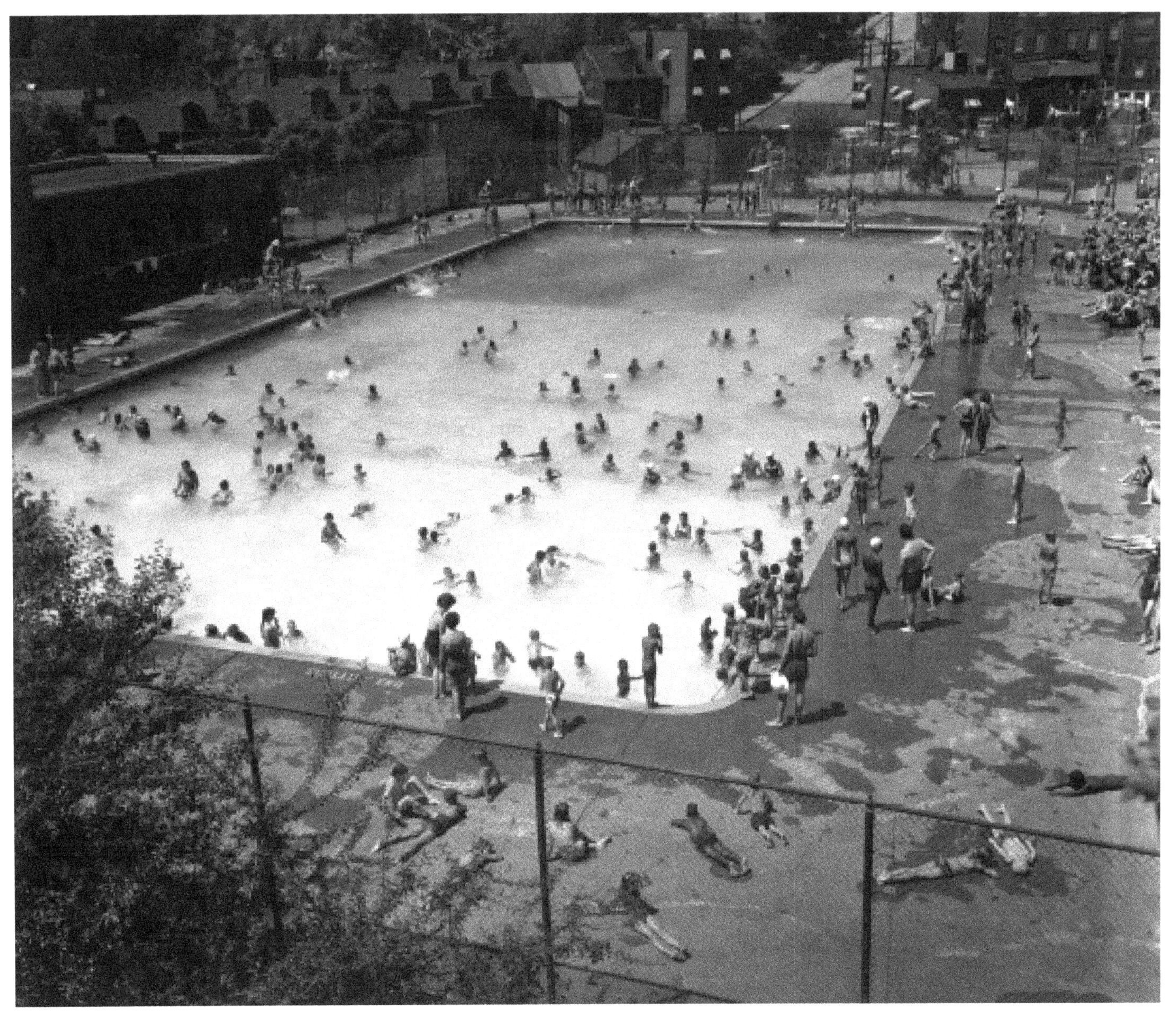

Let's swim! Swimmers cool off at Fowler Pool on the North Side in 1962.

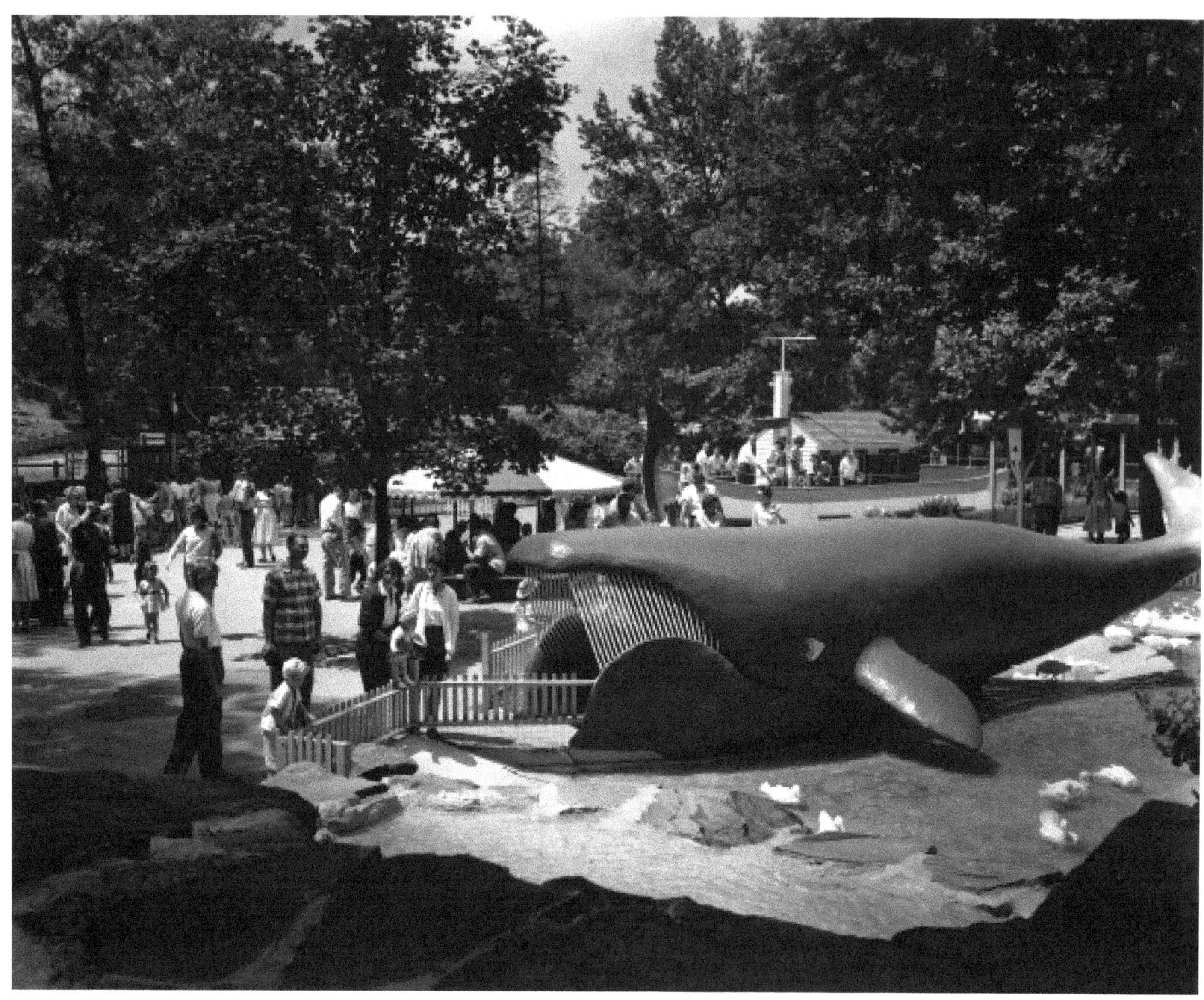

Children could walk inside the whale and jump on his spongy tongue at the Pittsburgh Zoo's children's zoo in Highland Park. Attractions like this one, aimed for children, were added in 1949. Several changes were made throughout the years, but by 1995 the entire area would be renovated, restructured, and renamed "Kids Kingdom."

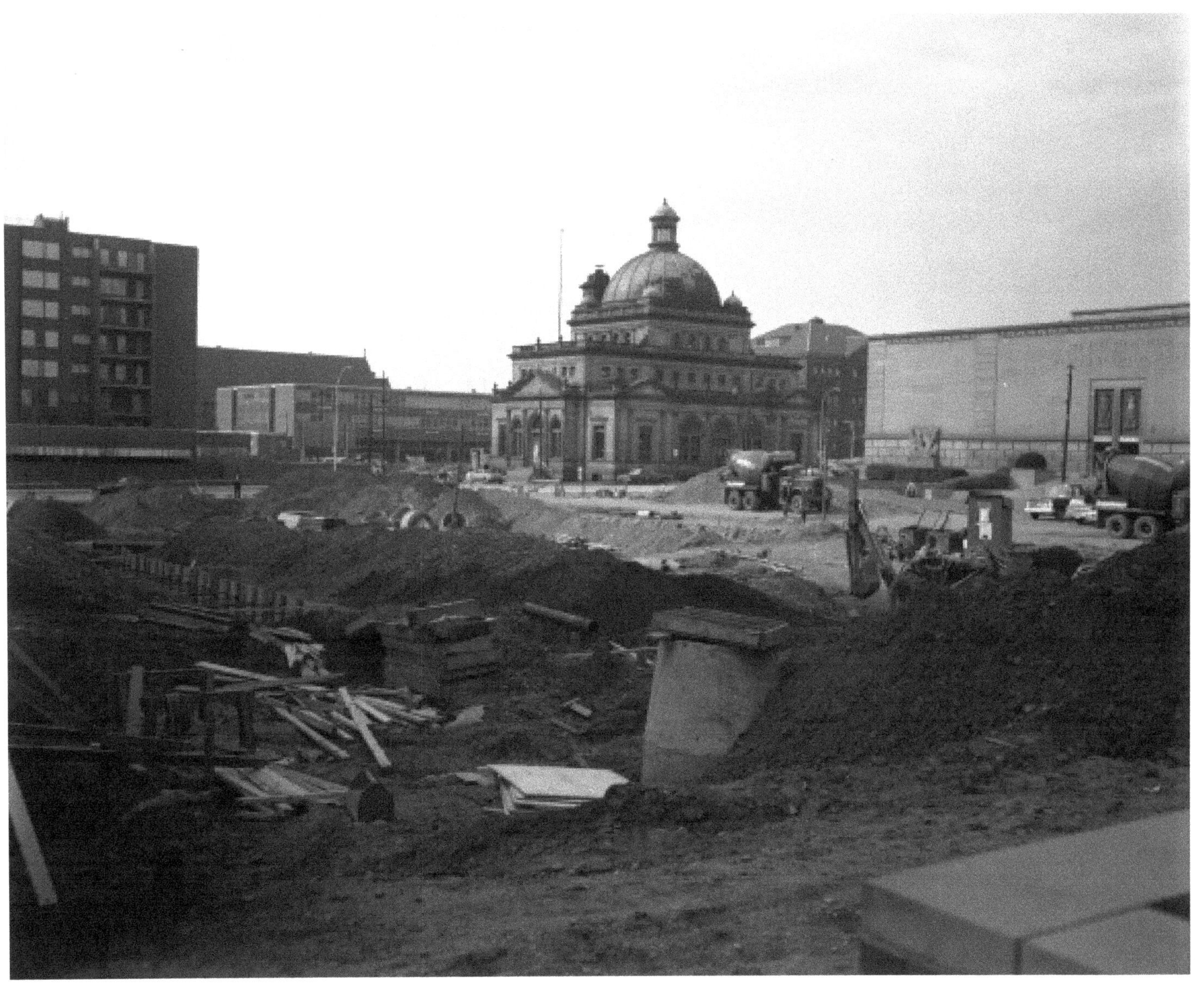

Ground is being cleared for the construction of the Allegheny Center Mall, in front of the former Allegheny Post Office and the Buhl Planetarium. Allegheny Center was designed by architects Detter & Ritchey at a cost of $65 million. In order to make way for this new shopping, residential, and office complex, the North Side lost more than 500 buildings, Ober Park, the market house, and its traditional grid of streets.

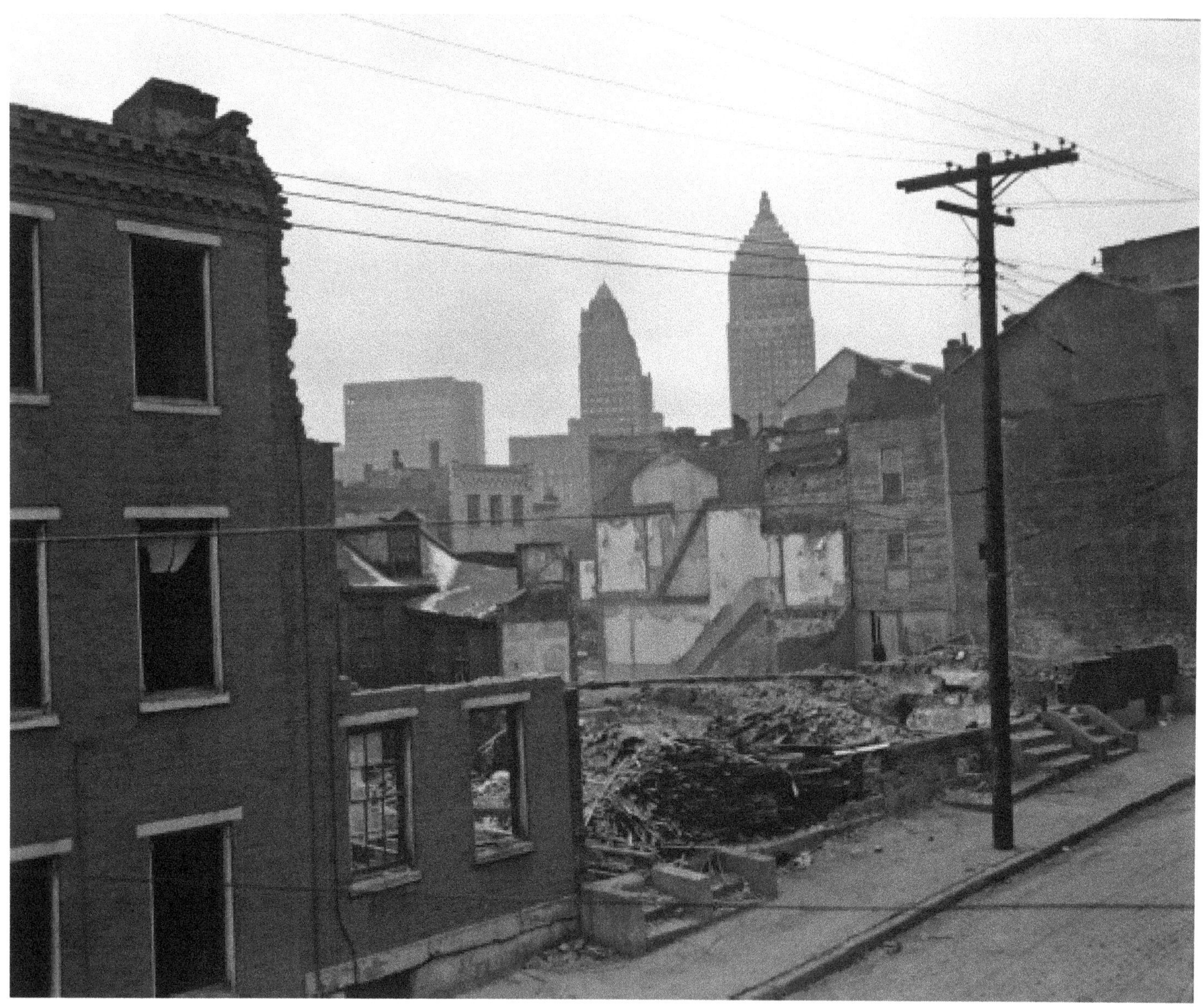

Beginning in 1956, the city began clearing slums to redevelop the Lower Hill District. To the residents of this neighborhood, urban renewal meant demolition. The Hill would be the first of several neighborhoods to undergo a renewal.

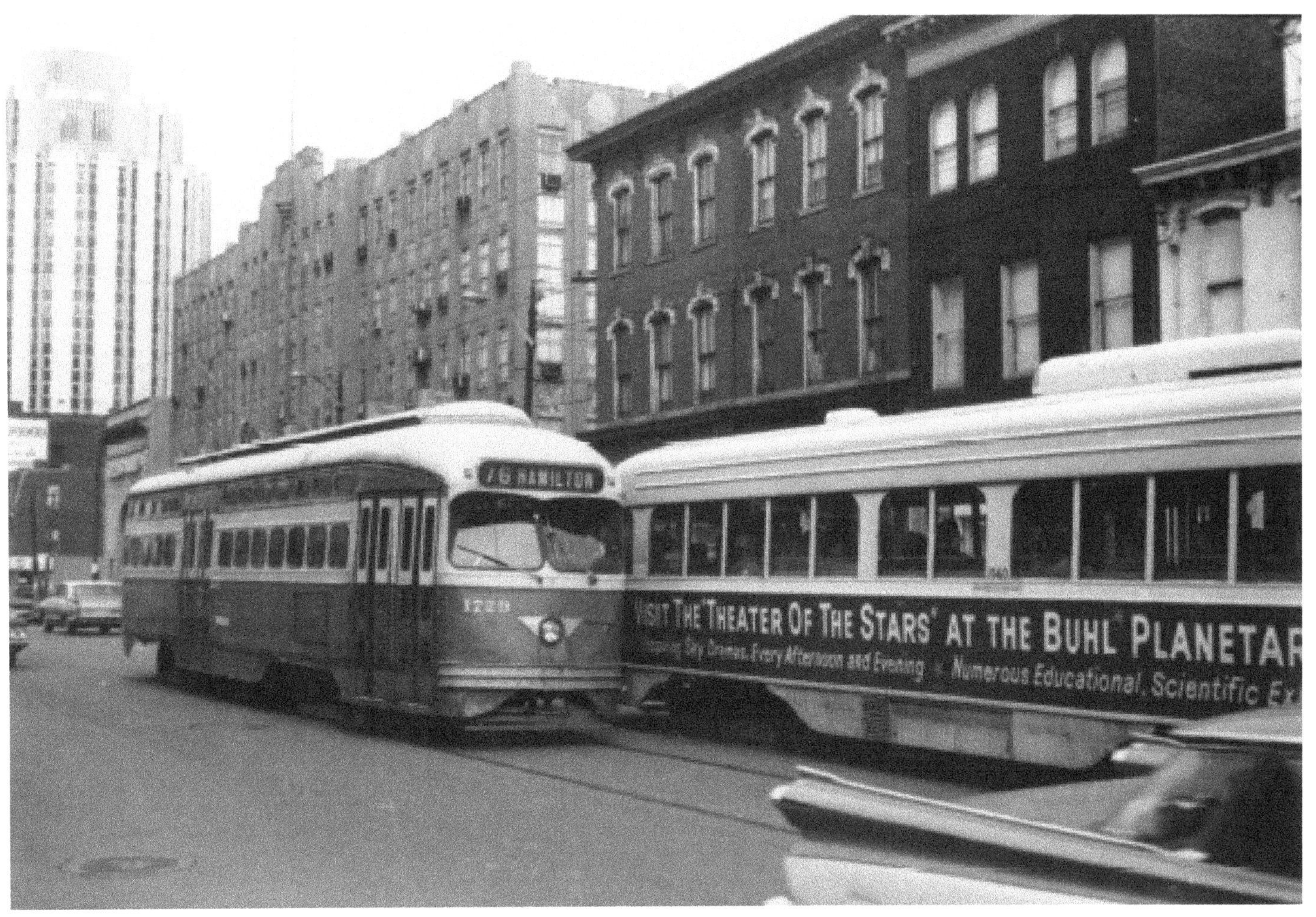

These streetcars operating on Fifth Avenue in Oakland in 1966 were atypical in American cities of the day, which had long since favored buses for public transport.

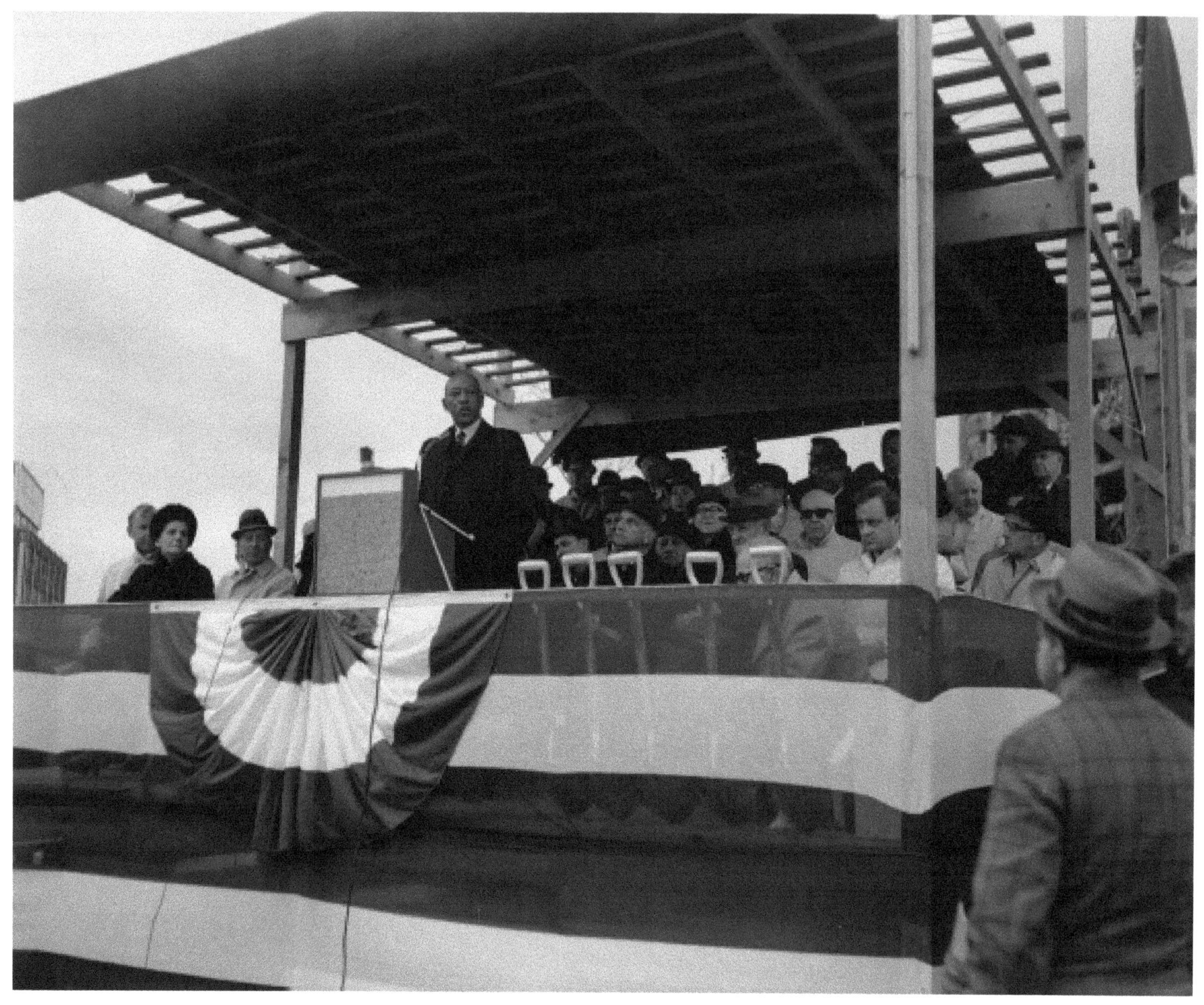

Olympic medalist Jesse Owens speaks at the groundbreaking for Three Rivers Stadium on April 25, 1968.

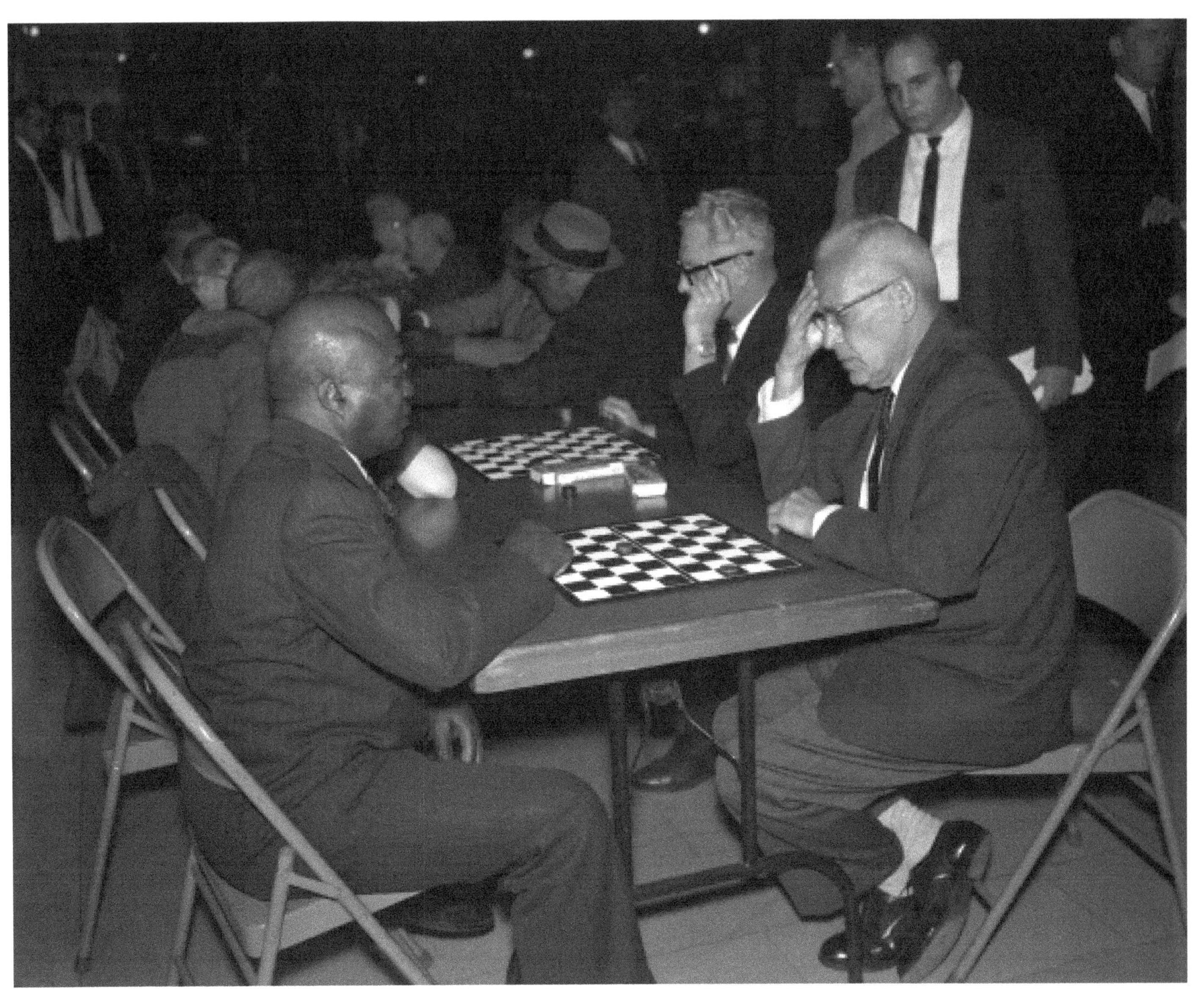

Senior Checkers Tournament, 1966.

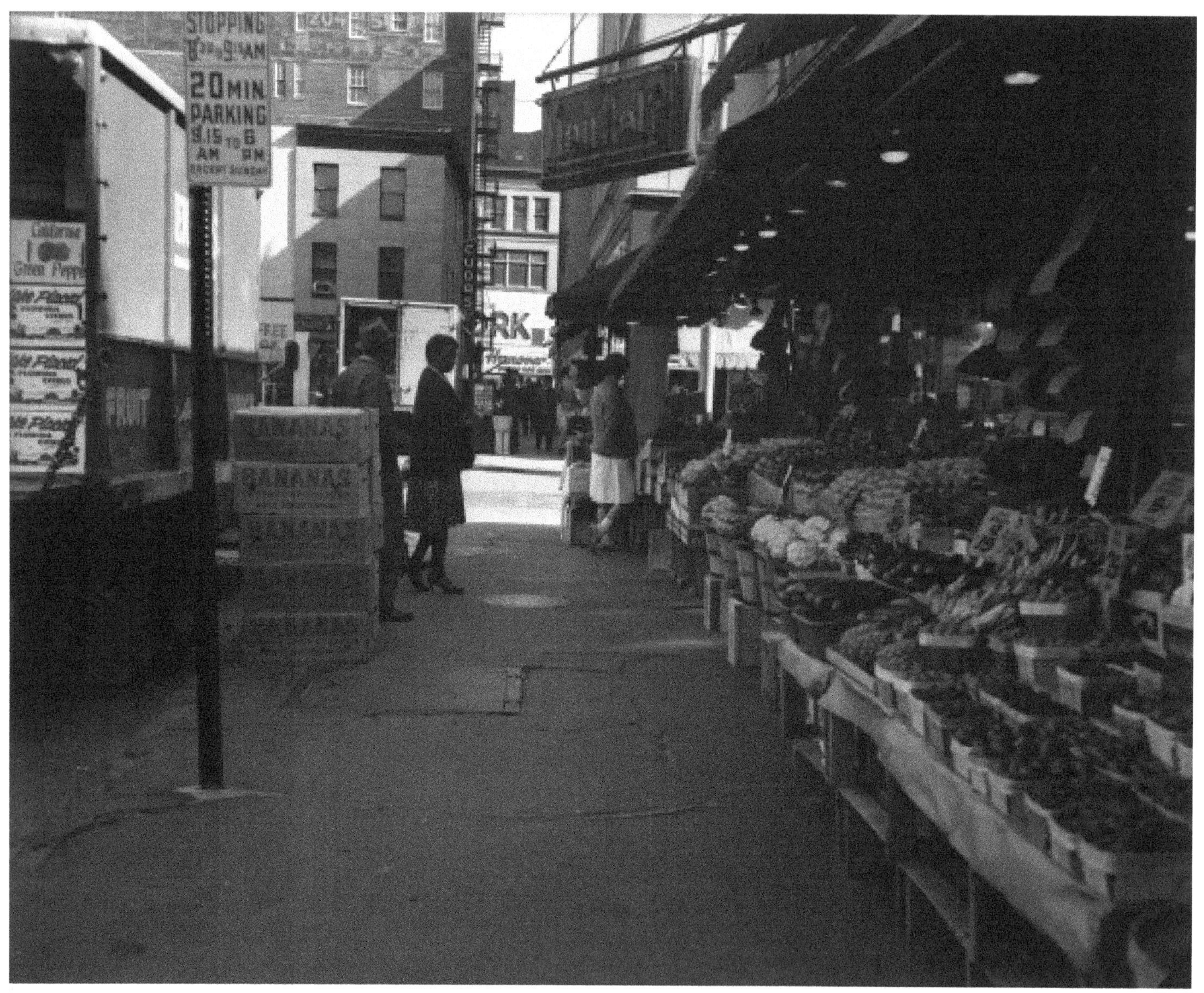

Hendel's Fruit Market near Market Square.

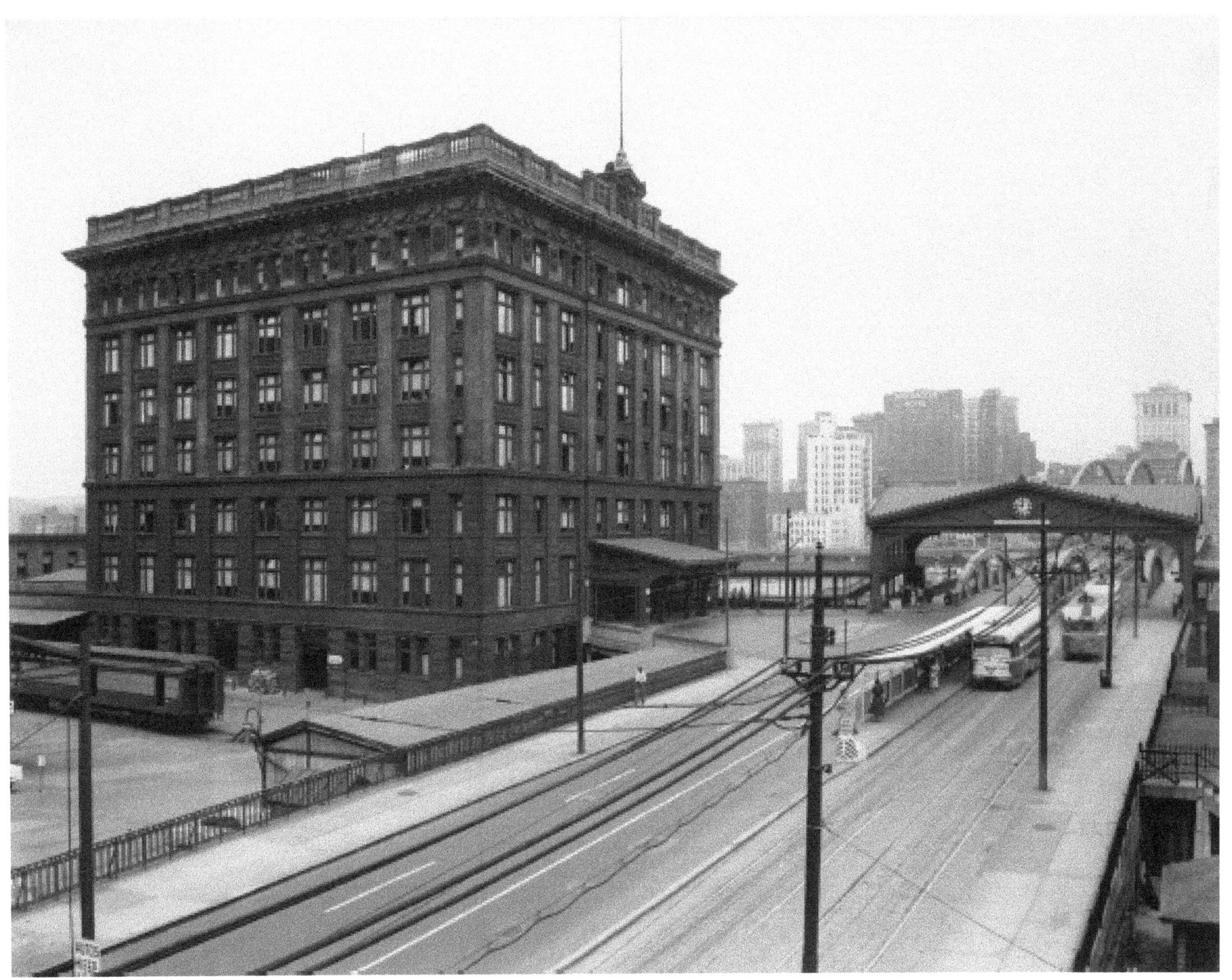

The Pittsburgh and Lake Erie Railroad Terminal Station and the South Side end of the Smithfield Street Bridge.

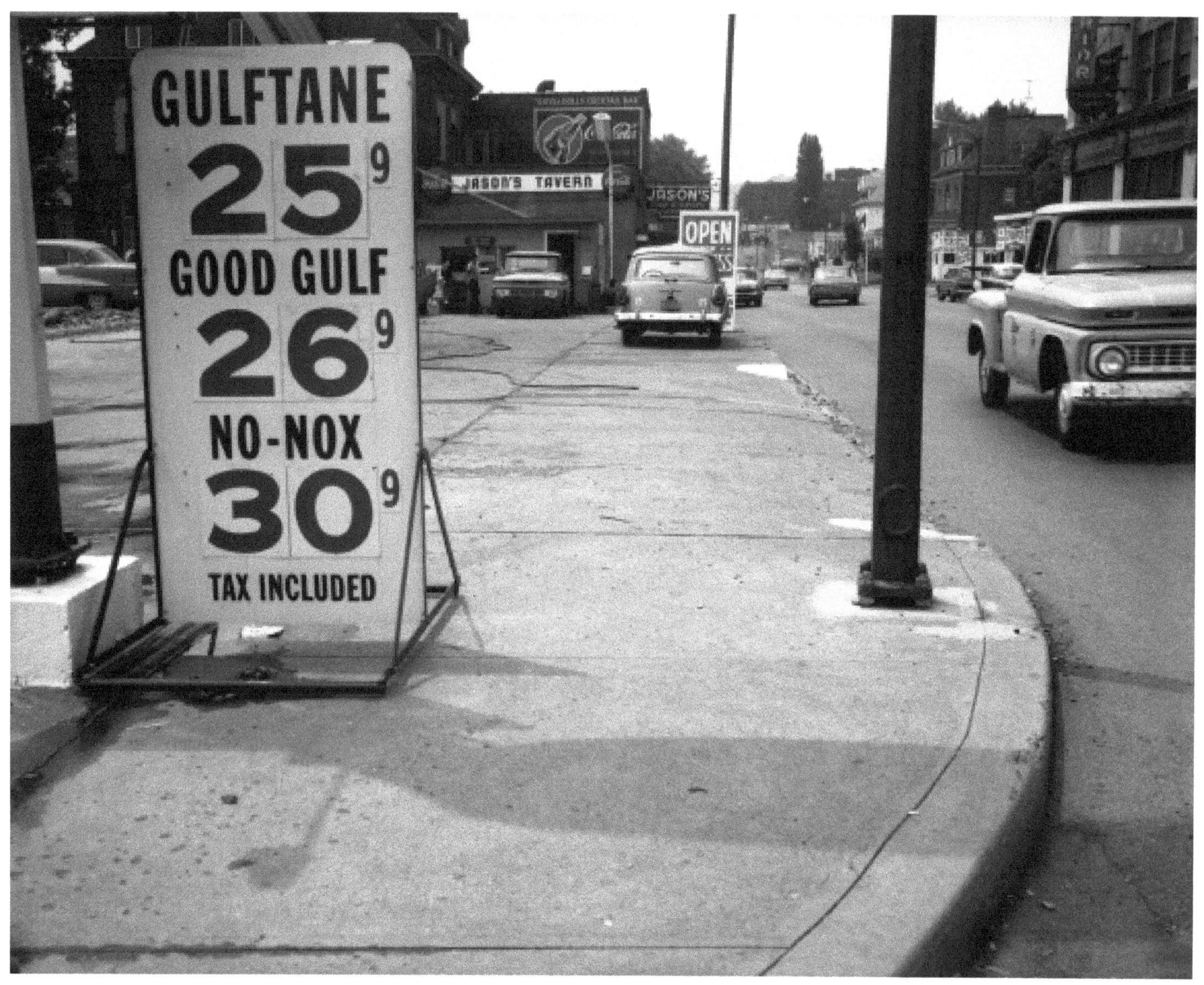

At the Baum Boulevard Gulf station in Oakland in this view south from Morewood Avenue, the price of gasoline seems to be a bargain in July 1964.

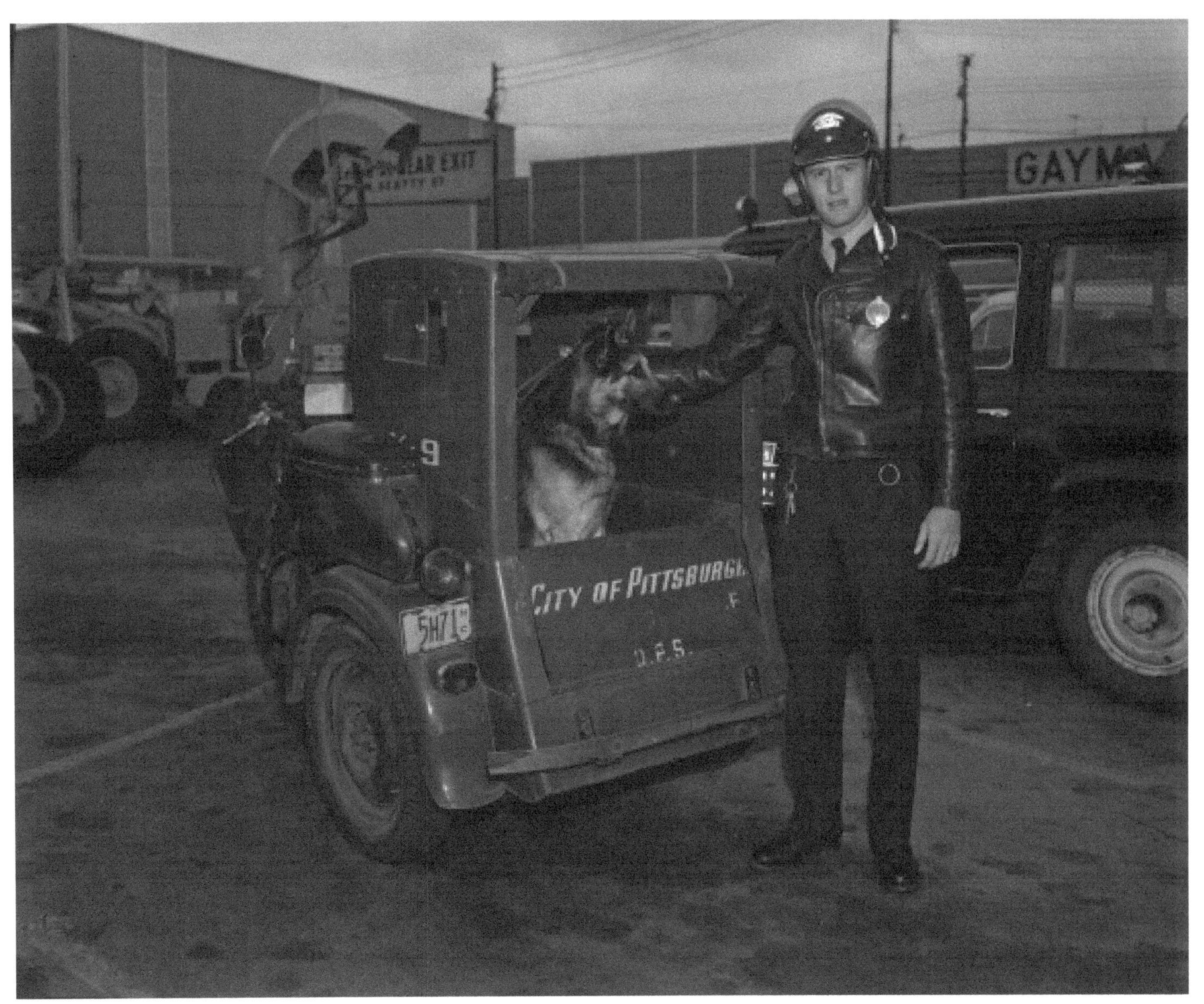

A City of Pittsburgh Police K-9 officer with his dog.

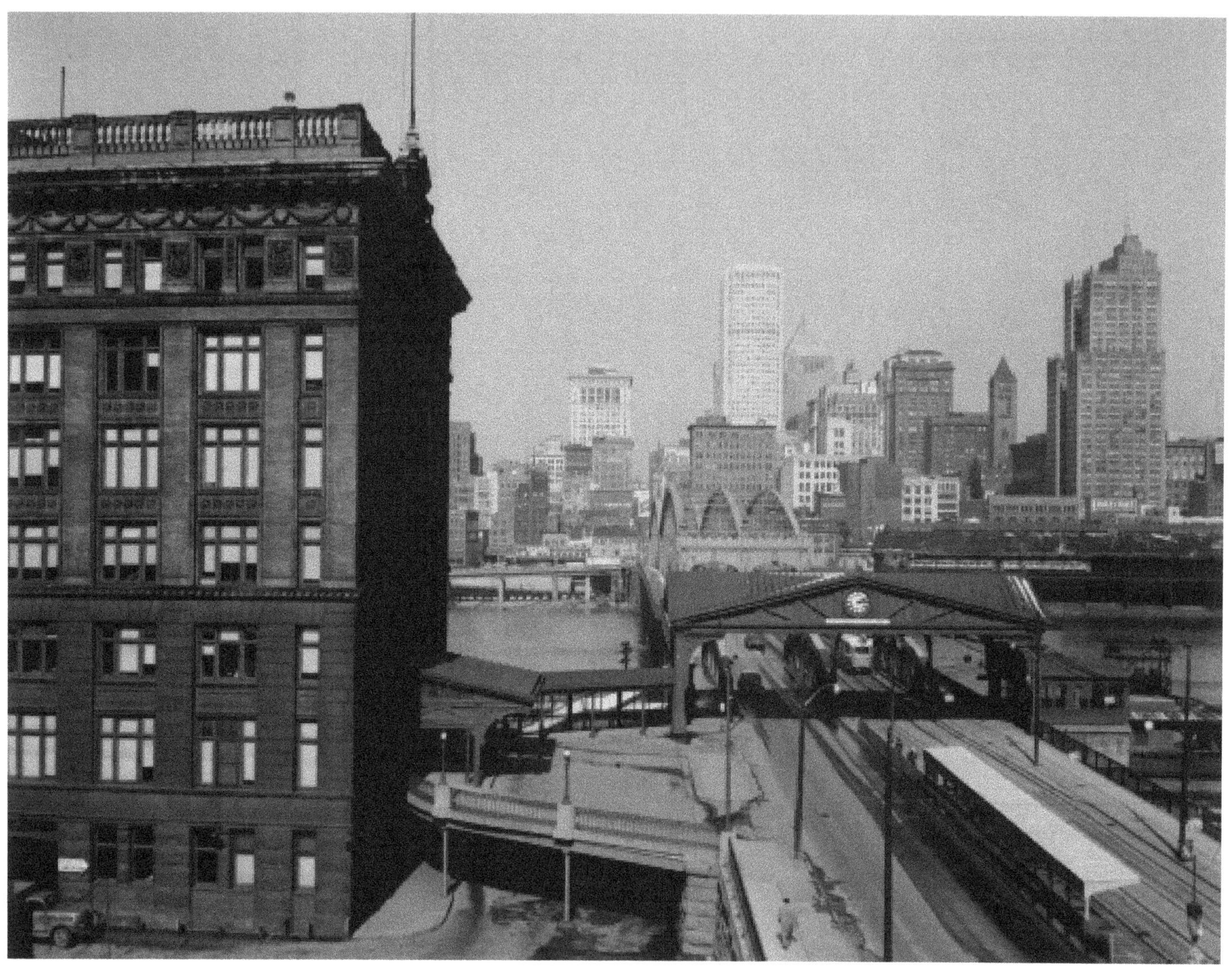

The Pittsburgh and Lake Erie Railroad Terminal Station and the South Side end of the Smithfield Street Bridge.

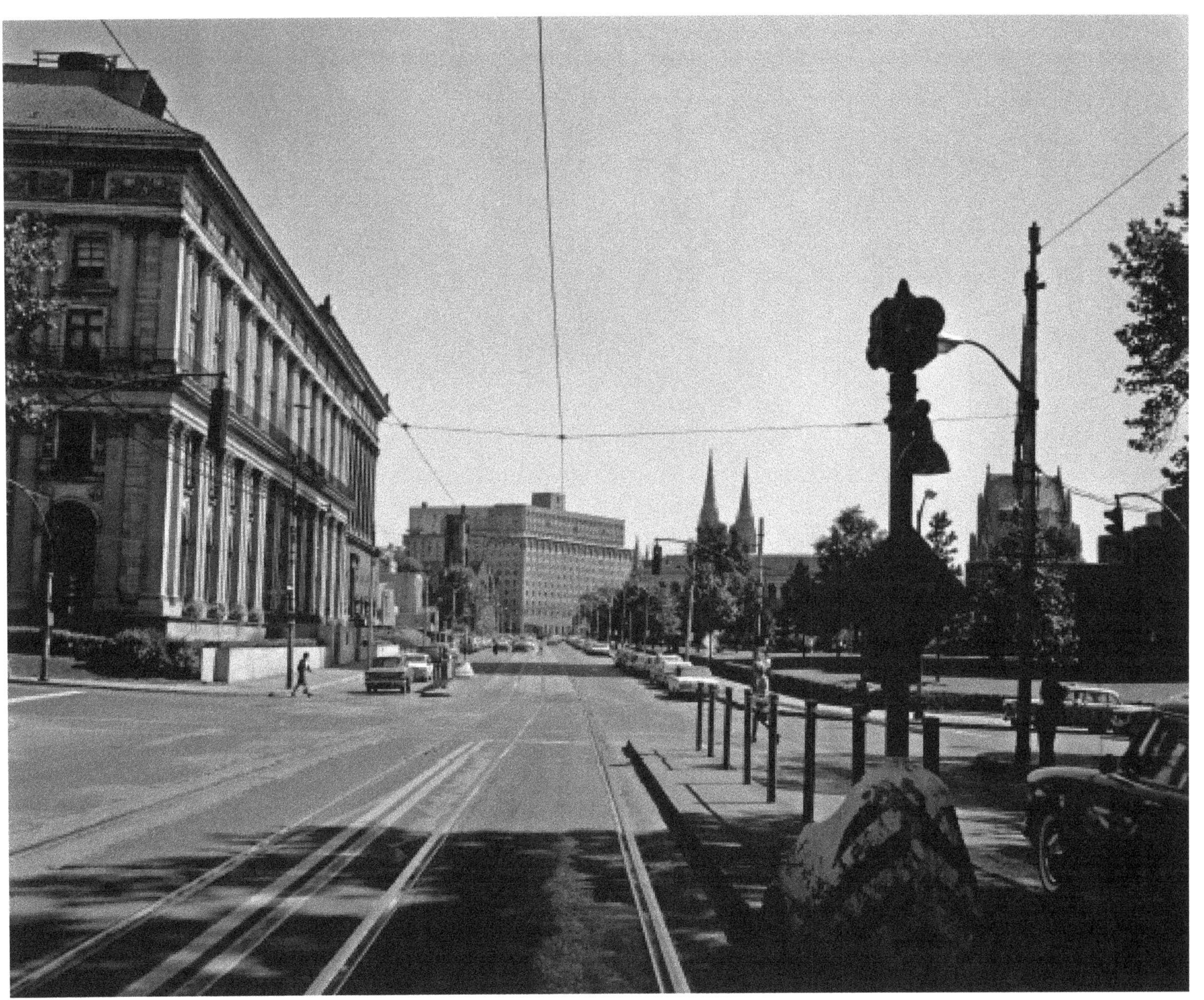

Fifth Avenue at Bigelow Boulevard, facing north with a view of the Pittsburgh Athletic Association.

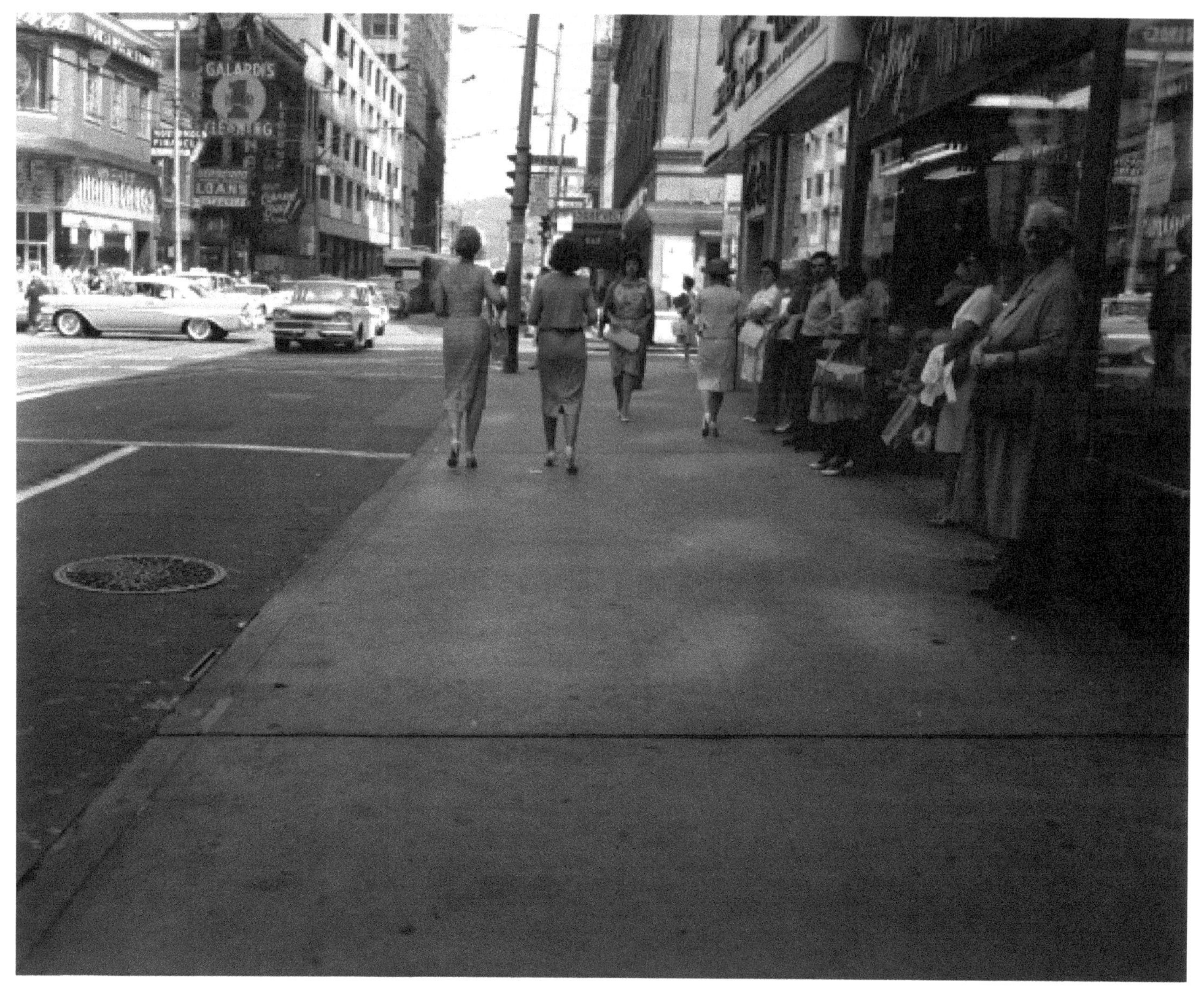

Pedestrians at Sixth Street and Penn Avenue.

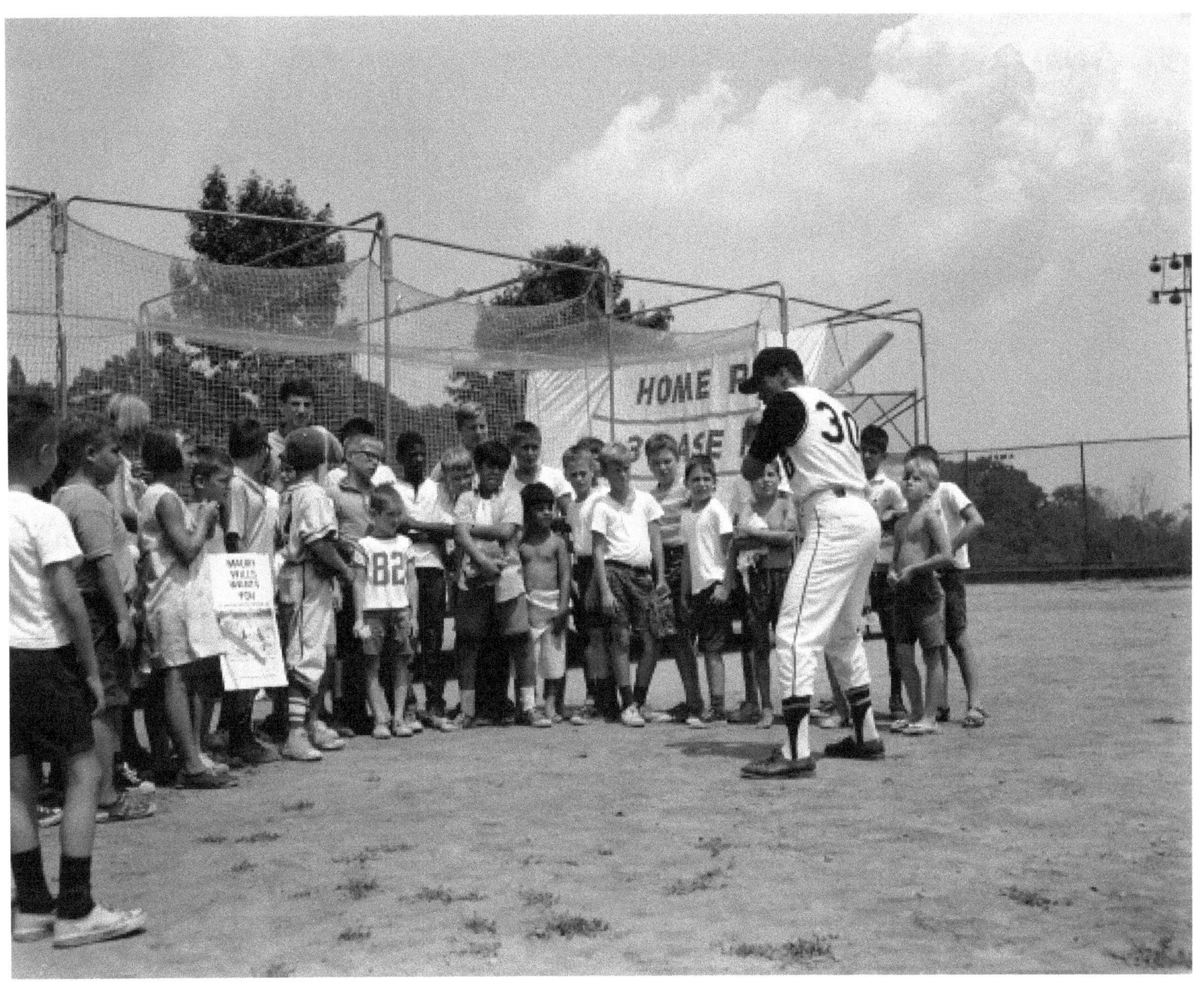

Baseball clinic with Pittsburgh Pirate Maury Wills, at Moore Field in 1968.

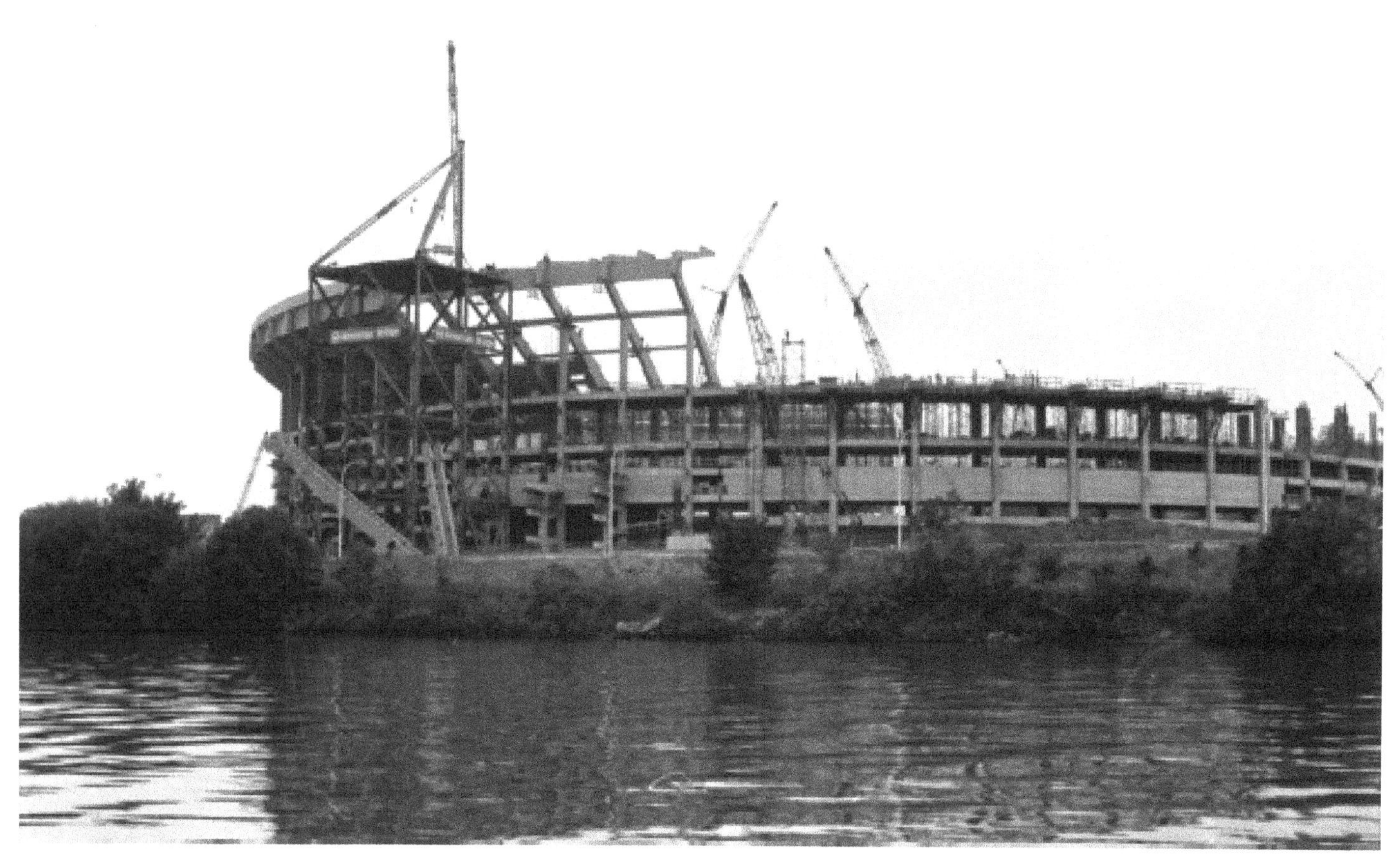

Three Rivers Stadium construction is in progress in 1969.

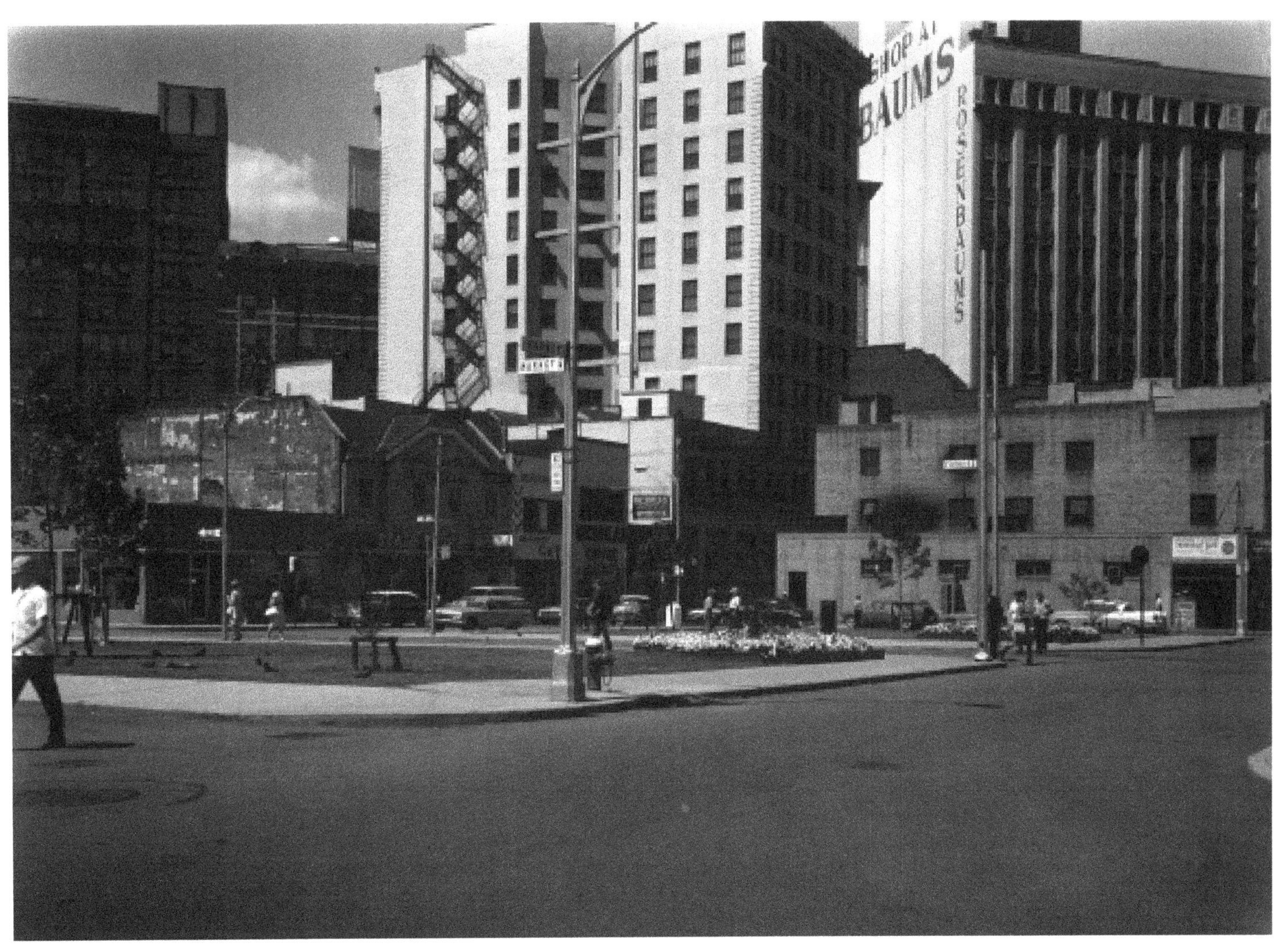

Market Square Commons, 1962.

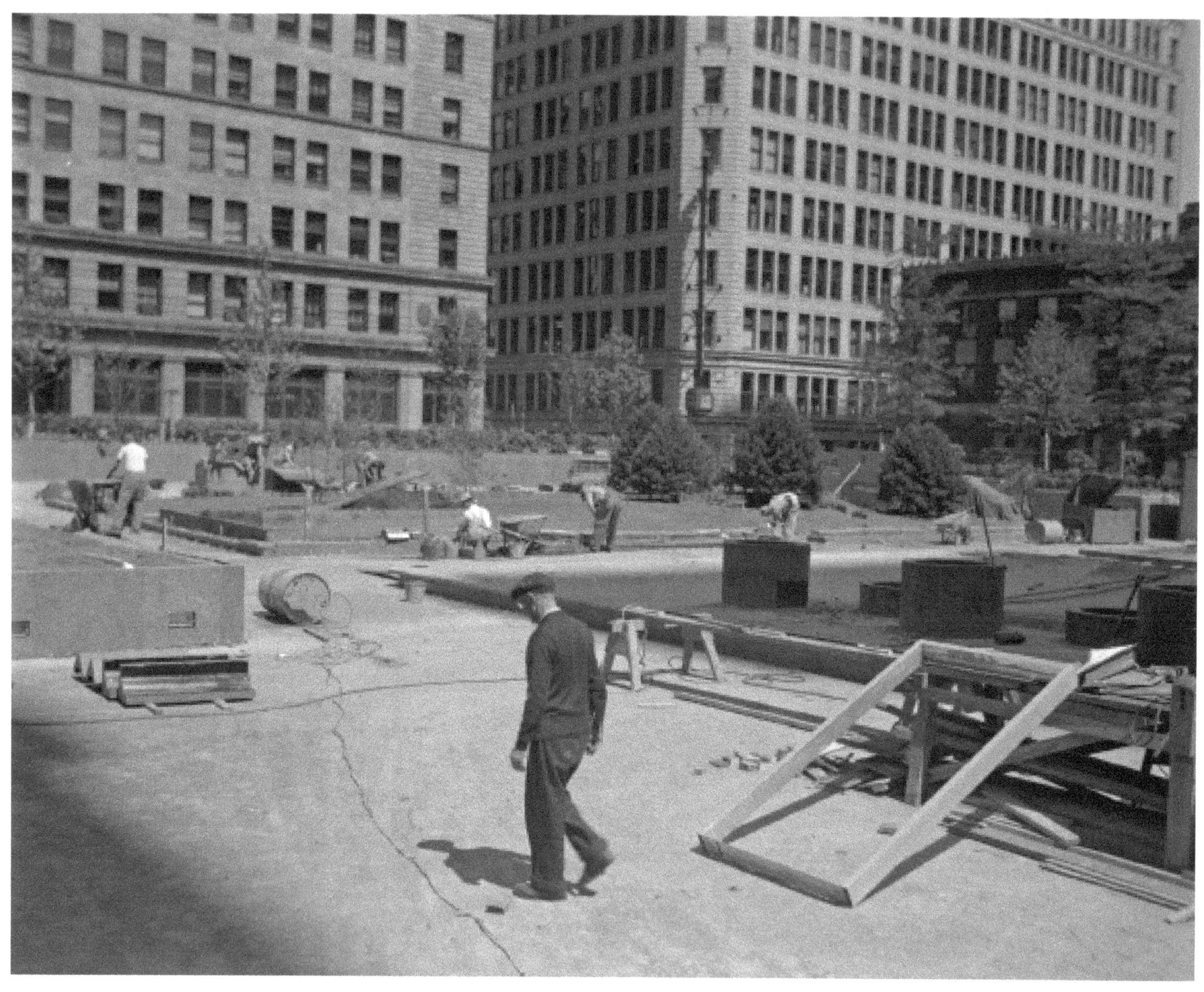

Construction of Mellon Square. This urban garden was designed by Mitchell and Ritchey with landscape design by Simonds and Simonds.

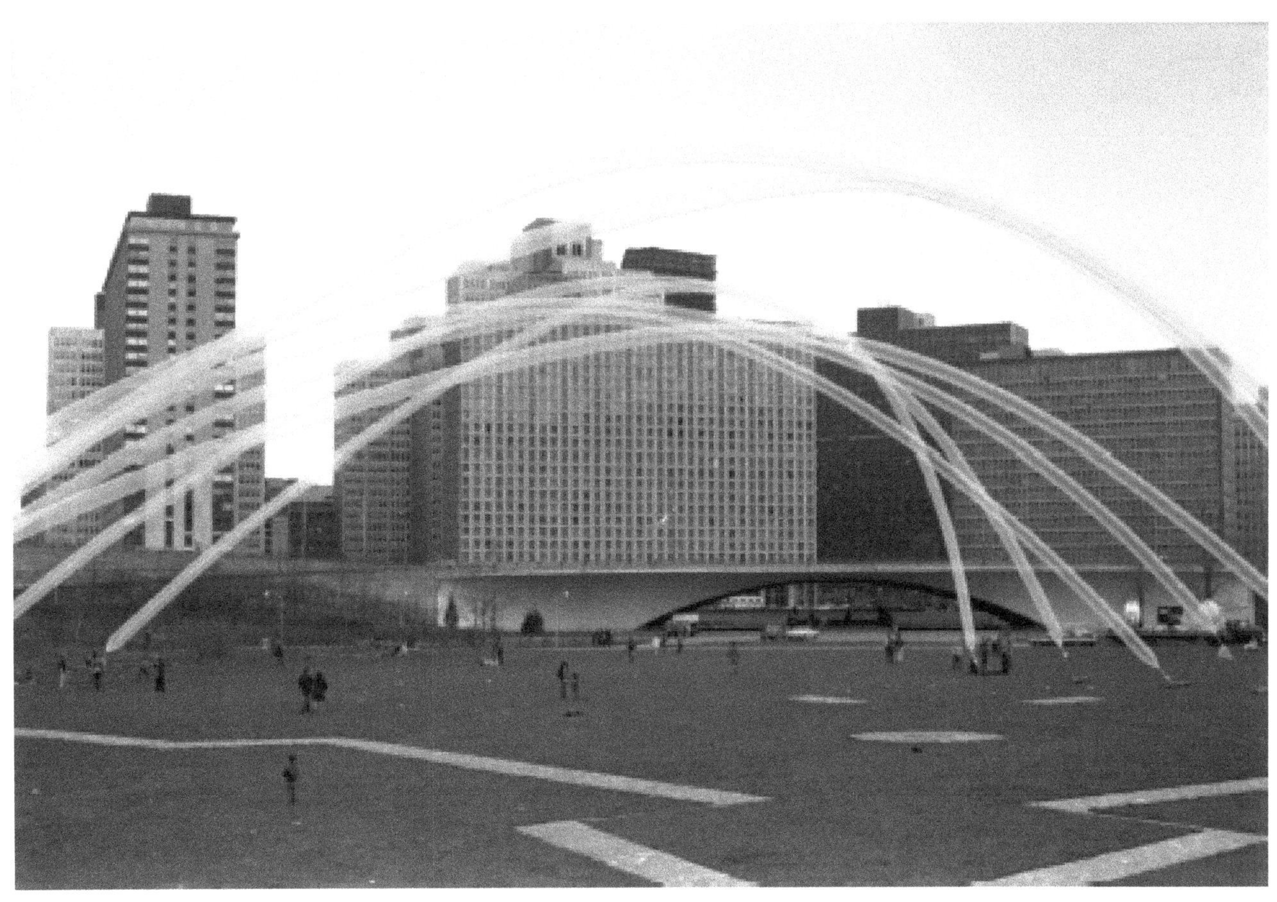

Artist Otto Piene's "Sky Ballet," created in Point State Park in 1970.

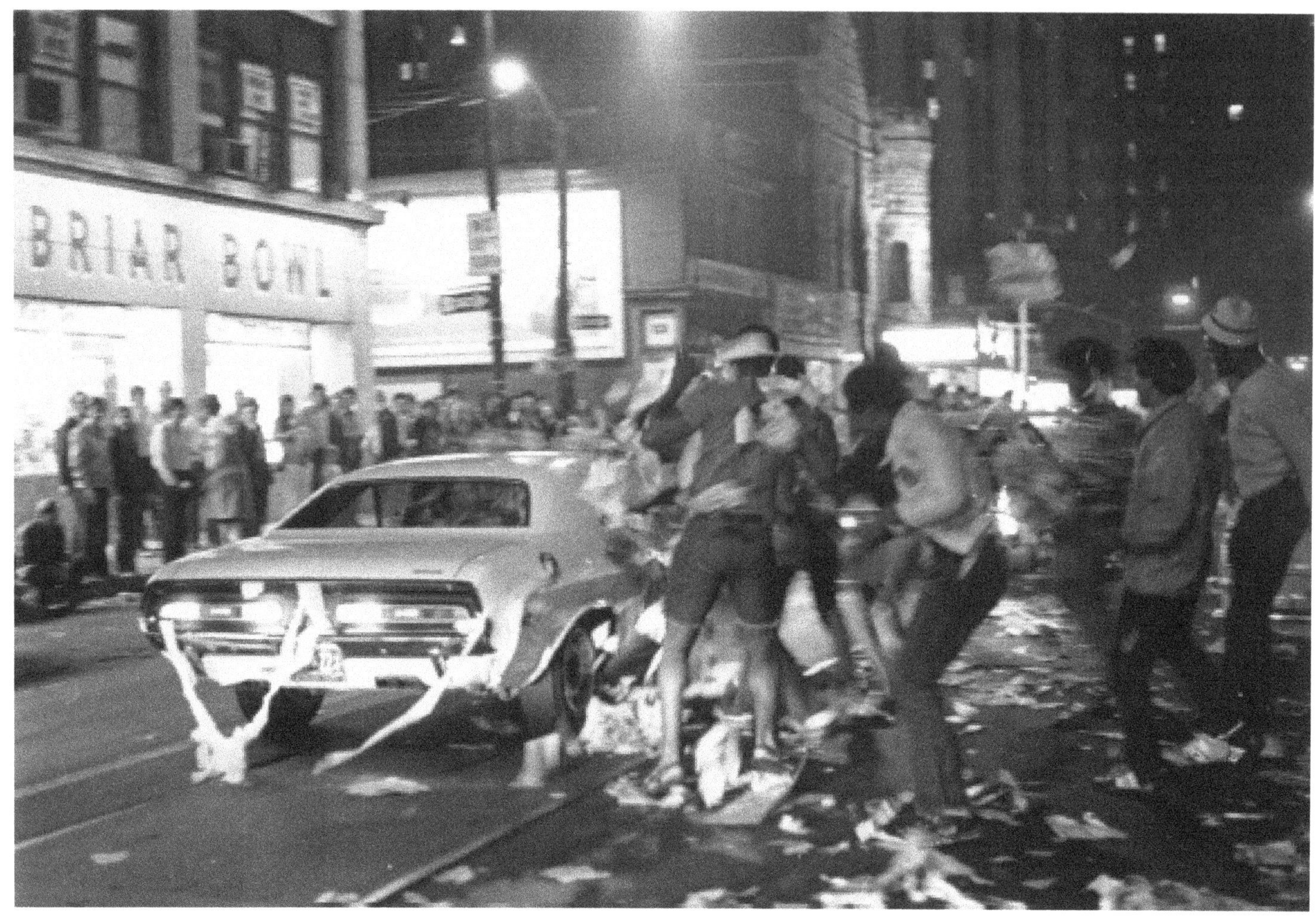

Pirates Win! University of Pittsburgh students celebrate the Pittsburgh Pirates' World Series victory against the Baltimore Orioles on October 17, 1971. The Pirates beat the Orioles 2-1 in game seven, finishing the year with a 97-65 record.

Notes on the Photographs

These notes, listed by page number, attempt to include all aspects known of the photographs. Each of the photographs is identified by the page number, photograph's title or description, photographer and collection, archive, and call or box number when applicable. Although every attempt was made to collect all available data, in some cases complete data was unavailable due to the age and condition of some of the photographs and records.

II **Workers on a Boat**
Archives Service Center
University of Pittsburgh
06874CP

VI **Rail Repair**
Archives Service Center
University of Pittsburgh
101649CP

X **Sixth Avenue and Webster Avenue**
Archives Service Center
University of Pittsburgh
08706CP

2 **Pittsburgh Amateur Photographers' Society**
Archives Service Center
University of Pittsburgh
4.23.DA

3 **Landscape Near Fair Haven**
Archives Service Center
University of Pittsburgh
5.22.DA

4 **The Browne House**
Archives Service Center
University of Pittsburgh
Brown01 UA

5 **Guyasuta Train Platform**
Archives Service Center
University of Pittsburgh
5.22.DA

6 **The Swisshelm House**
Archives Service Center
University of Pittsburgh
5.23.DA

7 **Rooftops and Garden**
Archives Service Center
University of Pittsburgh
907.167A.SF

8 **Milking a Cow**
Archives Service Center
University of Pittsburgh
907.191A.SF

9 **Electric Streetcar**
Archives Service Center
University of Pittsburgh
7429.0001.PR

10 **Electric Rail Cars**
Archives Service Center
University of Pittsburgh
7429.0002.PR

11 **Football Team**
Archives Service Center
University of Pittsburgh
FTBL02UA

12 **The Junction Hollow Bridge**
Archives Service Center
University of Pittsburgh
Magee Family Papers,
Darlington Memorial Library
0002MA

13 **Office Staff**
Archives Service Center
University of Pittsburgh
3160RR

14 **Railroad Employees**
Archives Service Center
University of Pittsburgh
6280RR

15 **Allegheny Observatory**
Archives Service Center
University of Pittsburgh
6422.15.AO

16 **Horse-drawn Trolley**
Archives Service Center
University of Pittsburgh
7429.0003.PR

17 **Citizens Passenger Rail Car**
Archives Service Center
University of Pittsburgh
7429.0003.PR

18 **Monongahela River**
Archives Service Center
University of Pittsburgh
69807.CP

20 **Class Photo**
Archives Service Center
University of Pittsburgh

21 **Basketball Team**
Archives Service Center
University of Pittsburgh
BKBL07UA

22 **Engineering Classroom**
Archives Service Center
University of Pittsburgh
WUP02.UA

23 **The Spencer Children**
Archives Service Center
University of Pittsburgh
907.2129A.SF

24 Charles and Elizabeth Spencer
Archives Service Center
University of Pittsburgh
907.2160C.SF

25 Springbank
Archives Service Center
University of Pittsburgh
Magee Family Papers,
Darlington Memorial Library
0004MA

26 Workers at Steel Company
Archives Service Center
University of Pittsburgh
00026GN

27 Steel Workers 2
Archives Service Center
University of Pittsburgh
00023GN

28 Highland Park
Archives Service Center
University of Pittsburgh
John Gates Collection
91221GT

30 Western Pennsylvania Exposition Building
Archives Service Center
University of Pittsburgh
91222GT

31 River Barge
Archives Service Center
University of Pittsburgh
011499.CP

32 Penn Avenue
Archives Service Center
University of Pittsburgh
0069074

33 Grandview Avenue
Archives Service Center
University of Pittsburgh
07396CP

34 Federal Street
Archives Service Center
University of Pittsburgh
08895CP

35 Sagamore Street
Archives Service Center
University of Pittsburgh
101550CP

36 Lemon Alley
Archives Service Center
University of Pittsburgh
111158CP

37 Federal and Isabella Streets
Archives Service Center
University of Pittsburgh
112250

38 The Pittsburgh Dispatch Building
Archives Service Center
University of Pittsburgh
112080CP

39 Sixth Street and Wylie Avenue
Archives Service Center
University of Pittsburgh
12BCP

40 Mayor William A. Magee
Archives Service Center
University of Pittsburgh
121000CP

41 Man and Carriage
Archives Service Center
University of Pittsburgh
05530CP

42 Construction of the Sheraden
Archives Service Center
University of Pittsburgh
08925CP

43 Sheraden Bridge
Archives Service Center
University of Pittsburgh
08924CP

44 Business District
Archives Service Center
University of Pittsburgh
08975CP

45 Chaucer Street
Archives Service Center
University of Pittsburgh
08955CP

46 Eichley's Hill Top Milk Depot
Archives Service Center
University of Pittsburgh
11205CP

47 Pittock Street
Archives Service Center
University of Pittsburgh
091042CP

48 Cobblestone Paving
Archives Service Center
University of Pittsburgh
091355CP

49 Excelsior and Eureka Streets
Archives Service Center
University of Pittsburgh
091309 CP

50 Steam Power Roller
Archives Service Center
University of Pittsburgh
081077CP

51 Simpson's Cafe
Archives Service Center
University of Pittsburgh
091406CP

52 Wrights Alley
Archives Service Center
University of Pittsburgh
091429CP

53 Sandusky and General Robinson Street
Archives Service Center
University of Pittsburgh
091954CP

54 South Side of Brownsville Avenue
Archives Service Center
University of Pittsburgh
092103CP

55 Craig Street
Archives Service Center
University of Pittsburgh
101565CP

56 Fifth Avenue
Archives Service Center
University of Pittsburgh
122078CP

57 Alex Williamson
Archives Service Center
University of Pittsburgh
122603CP

58 Hot Waffles
Archives Service Center
University of Pittsburgh
122069CP

59 Lyceum Theatre
Archives Service Center
University of Pittsburgh
133097CP

60 Syria Mosque
Archives Service Center
University of Pittsburgh
Edward J. Shourek Collection
9119BXXIV3SH

61 The "Hump" at Grant's Hill
Archives Service Center
University of Pittsburgh
121161CP

62 **Forbes Field**
Archives Service Center
University of Pittsburgh
John Gates Collection
156AGT

63 **Fifth Avenue "Hump" Project**
Archives Service Center
University of Pittsburgh
131272CP

64 **Lincoln Ice Company Delivery Wagon**
Archives Service Center
University of Pittsburgh
14100CP

65 **Neiman's Department Store**
Archives Service Center
University of Pittsburgh
112082CP

66 **Department of Public Works**
Archives Service Center
University of Pittsburgh
148738CP

67 **Carrick Street**
Archives Service Center
University of Pittsburgh
162652CCP

68 **Diamond Market**
Archives Service Center
University of Pittsburgh
143815CP

69 **Laundry Facilities**
Archives Service Center
University of Pittsburgh
143941CP

70 **Telephone Company Building**
Archives Service Center
University of Pittsburgh
188318CP

71 **Fifth and Sixth Avenue**
Archives Service Center
University of Pittsburgh
168815CP

72 **Pittsburgh Food Division**
Archives Service Center
University of Pittsburgh
148826CP

73 **Department of Public Works**
Archives Service Center
University of Pittsburgh
128092CP

74 **Western Pennsylvania Exposition Building 2**
Archives Service Center
University of Pittsburgh
154637CP

75 **Allegheny County Courthouse**
Archives Service Center
University of Pittsburgh
168807CP

76 **Ice-skaters**
Archives Service Center
University of Pittsburgh
178928CP

77 **W. P. Bailey Offices**
Archives Service Center
University of Pittsburgh
111958CP

78 **The First Bridge**
Archives Service Center
University of Pittsburgh
4369065

79 **Straub Brewing Company**
Archives Service Center
University of Pittsburgh
133347CP

80 **The Strip District**
Archives Service Center
University of Pittsburgh
L120CP

81 **Monongahela River 2**
Archives Service Center
University of Pittsburgh
7429.0097.PR

82 **Union Arcade**
Archives Service Center
University of Pittsburgh
022UT

83 **William Penn Hotel**
Archives Service Center
University of Pittsburgh
William Penn Hotel Photographs
20080128WP

84 **Rosenbaum Company**
Archives Service Center
University of Pittsburgh
17964A

85 **Municipal Band**
Archives Service Center
University of Pittsburgh
189121CP

86 **Pennsylvania Reserve Militia**
Archives Service Center
University of Pittsburgh
189116CP

87 **Volleyball**
Archives Service Center
University of Pittsburgh
189104CP

88 **Oregon Street Footbridge**
Archives Service Center
University of Pittsburgh
195679CP

89 **City-County Building Gathering**
Archives Service Center
University of Pittsburgh
199201CP

90 **11:00 a.m. View**
Archives Service Center
University of Pittsburgh
19CP

92 **Public Health Nurse**
Archives Service Center
University of Pittsburgh
Oliver M. Kaufmann Collection of the Irene Kaufmann Settlement
152IKS

93 **Fifth Avenue 2**
Archives Service Center
University of Pittsburgh
192495CP

94 **Atlantic Refining Company**
Archives Service Center
University of Pittsburgh
2182CP

95 **Sixth Street**
Archives Service Center
University of Pittsburgh
211494CP

96 **Cooling Down**
Archives Service Center
University of Pittsburgh
212359CP

97 **Track and Field Meet**
Archives Service Center
University of Pittsburgh
219277CP

98 **Toddlers' Check-up**
Archives Service Center
University of Pittsburgh
221897CP

99 **Greenfield Avenue Bridge**
Archives Service Center
University of Pittsburgh
236962CP

100 **Emergency Repair Truck**
Archives Service Center
University of Pittsburgh
251013CP

101 **Tuberculosis Hospital**
Archives Service Center
University of Pittsburgh
25511CP

102 **Ladder Truck No. 9**
Archives Service Center
University of Pittsburgh
25616CP

103 **Busy Bee Club**
Archives Service Center
University of Pittsburgh
25945CP

104 **South Side Pool**
Archives Service Center
University of Pittsburgh
259450CP

105 **Spagnola Fruit Company**
Archives Service Center
University of Pittsburgh
261832ACP

106 **Miss Pittsburgh**
Archives Service Center
University of Pittsburgh
262128CP

107 **Brownsville Avenue**
Archives Service Center
University of Pittsburgh
262020CP

108 **Monongahela Incline**
Archives Service Center
University of Pittsburgh
262673CP

109 **Salisbury Bakery**
Archives Service Center
University of Pittsburgh
273994CP

110 **Forbes Avenue at Atwood Street**
Archives Service Center
University of Pittsburgh
5152082A

111 **Forbes Avenue**
Archives Service Center
University of Pittsburgh
261259CP

112 **Marble Tournament**
Archives Service Center
University of Pittsburgh
261266CP

113 **Emergency Station**
Archives Service Center
University of Pittsburgh
275535CP

114 **Charles Lindbergh**
Archives Service Center
University of Pittsburgh
274623CP

115 **Diamond Street**
Archives Service Center
University of Pittsburgh
286932CP

116 **Pitt Panther**
Archives Service Center
University of Pittsburgh
PANT01UA

117 **Moving a House**
Archives Service Center
University of Pittsburgh
FLK1393UA

118 **Shippers Packet Company Offices**
Archives Service Center
University of Pittsburgh
294805CP

119 **Parade Float**
Archives Service Center
University of Pittsburgh
Pittsburgh and Lake Erie
Railroad Collection
8223366ARR

120 **Car Camping**
Archives Service Center
University of Pittsburgh
26198CP

122 **Studebaker Automotive Salesmen**
Archives Service Center
University of Pittsburgh
Pittsburgh and Lake Erie
Railroad Collection
6256RR

123 **Fort Pitt Laundry**
Archives Service Center
University of Pittsburgh
3011875C

124 **Sixth Street 2**
Archives Service Center
University of Pittsburgh
3736498CP

125 **Strip District**
Archives Service Center
University of Pittsburgh
15002AP

126 **The Point**
Archives Service Center
University of Pittsburgh
Aerial Photographs of
Pittsburgh
15689AP

127 **St. Paul Excursion Queen**
Archives Service Center
University of Pittsburgh
386670CP

128 **Fifth Avenue 3**
Archives Service Center
University of Pittsburgh
3012326CP

129 **Aquatic House**
Archives Service Center
University of Pittsburgh
3012334CP

130 **East Street Bridge**
Archives Service Center
University of Pittsburgh
311306CP

131 **Broad Street**
Archives Service Center
University of Pittsburgh
3113844CP

132 **Riverside High**
Archives Service Center
University of Pittsburgh
3113965CP

133 **Fifth Avenue**
Archives Service Center
University of Pittsburgh
3115069CP

134 **Wood Street**
Archives Service Center
University of Pittsburgh
3115073CP

135 **Three Men Sitting**
Archives Service Center
University of Pittsburgh
3216799CP

136 **Liberty Tunnels**
Archives Service Center
University of Pittsburgh
3318235CP

137 **Shore Avenue**
Archives Service Center
University of Pittsburgh
3118580CP

138 **Playground**
Archives Service Center
University of Pittsburgh
3118860CP

139 Smithfield Street Bridge
Archives Service Center
University of Pittsburgh
3319270CP

140 Whitfield Street
Archives Service Center
University of Pittsburgh
3421622CP

141 The Italian Gardens
Archives Service Center
University of Pittsburgh
3525209CP

142 Wylie Avenue
Archives Service Center
University of Pittsburgh
3525209CP

143 The Flood
Archives Service Center
University of Pittsburgh
3627441CP

144 The Flood 2
Archives Service Center
University of Pittsburgh
3627600CP

145 The Flood 3
Archives Service Center
University of Pittsburgh
Pittsburgh and Lake Erie
Railroad Collection
5800RR

146 Il Duce Quick Lunch
Archives Service Center
University of Pittsburgh
3629389CP

147 Homewood Avenue
Archives Service Center
University of Pittsburgh
3736364CP

148 Small Scale Replica
Archives Service Center
University of Pittsburgh
Pittsburgh and Lake Erie
Railroad Collection
6715RR

149 McCann and Co.
Archives Service Center
University of Pittsburgh
3736514CP

150 Smithfield Street
Archives Service Center
University of Pittsburgh
3736551CP

151 Smithfield Street Businesses
Archives Service Center
University of Pittsburgh
3736557CP

152 The Fulton Building
Archives Service Center
University of Pittsburgh
3736591CP

153 Seventh Avenue
Archives Service Center
University of Pittsburgh
3841818CP

154 Macedonia Baptist Church
Archives Service Center
University of Pittsburgh
3949919CP

155 Pennsylvania Hall
Archives Service Center
University of Pittsburgh
University Archives,
University of Pittsburgh
PAHL01UA

156 Pittsburgh Panther Football Team
Archives Service Center
University of Pittsburgh
University Archives,
University of Pittsburgh
FTBL11UA

157 University of Pittsburgh Cathedral
Archives Service Center
University of Pittsburgh
CTL037AUA

158 Penn Avenue
Archives Service Center
University of Pittsburgh
3734722

159 Municipal Hospital
Archives Service Center
University of Pittsburgh
00100CP

160 Downtown Pittsburgh
Archives Service Center
University of Pittsburgh
000101

162 Bar-B-Q and Ship Hotel
Archives Service Center
University of Pittsburgh
4054609

163 Woolworth Company
Archives Service Center
University of Pittsburgh
4160579C

164 Women's Wing
Archives Service Center
University of Pittsburgh
4160936CP

165 Franklin Delano Roosevelt
Archives Service Center
University of Pittsburgh
4161711C

166 Heinz Chapel
Archives Service Center
University of Pittsburgh
44070702C

167 B. M. Block & Son Arrow Shirt Store
Archives Service Center
University of Pittsburgh
4776767CP

168 11:25 a.m. Smoke
Archives Service Center
University of Pittsburgh
Smoke Control Lantern Slide
Collection
SCLS002

169 Downtown
Archives Service Center
University of Pittsburgh
Smoke Control Lantern Slide
Collection
SCLS007

170 Liberty Tunnel 2
Archives Service Center
University of Pittsburgh
Smoke Control Lantern Slide
Collection
SCLS019

171 Liberty Tunnel 3
Archives Service Center
University of Pittsburgh
Smoke Control Lantern Slide
Collection
SCLS020

172 Homestead Mill
Archives Service Center
University of Pittsburgh
William J. Gaughan
Collection
54588GN

173 Victory Garden
Archives Service Center
University of Pittsburgh
William J. Gaughan
Collection
84504GN

174 Island Queen Fire
Archives Service Center
University of Pittsburgh
Pittsburgh and Lake Erie
Railroad Collection
563RR

176 Monongahela Wharf
Archives Service Center
University of Pittsburgh
Harry Walter Photograph Collection
90180002

178 Gothic Revival Cathedral
Archives Service Center
University of Pittsburgh
57100041

179 Fire Engine Company No. 16
Archives Service Center
University of Pittsburgh
111833_10CP

180 Locomotive No. 25
Archives Service Center
University of Pittsburgh
6310RR

181 Fowler Pool
Archives Service Center
University of Pittsburgh
112003_3CP

182 Children's Zoo
Archives Service Center
University of Pittsburgh
60109663_5

183 Allegheny Center Mall
Archives Service Center
University of Pittsburgh
67120321_5cp

184 Ground Clearing
Archives Service Center
University of Pittsburgh
57990889

185 Streetcars
Archives Service Center
University of Pittsburgh
74290023

186 Jesse Owens
Archives Service Center
University of Pittsburgh
68120610

187 Checkers Tournament
Archives Service Center
University of Pittsburgh
119681_8CP

188 Hendel's Fruit Market
Archives Service Center
University of Pittsburgh
114065_9CP

189 Railroad Terminal Station
Archives Service Center
University of Pittsburgh
Pittsburgh and Lake Erie Railroad Collection
3423crr

190 Baum Boulevard Gulf Station
Archives Service Center
University of Pittsburgh
113042_3CP

191 Police K-9
Archives Service Center
University of Pittsburgh
119107_2CP

192 Pittsburgh and Lake Erie Terminal Station
Archives Service Center
University of Pittsburgh
Pittsburgh and Lake Erie Railroad Collection
3771RR

193 Fifth Avenue 4
Archives Service Center
University of Pittsburgh
113073_2CP

194 Sixth Street and Penn Avenue
Archives Service Center
University of Pittsburgh
111946_7CP

195 Baseball Clinic
Archives Service Center
University of Pittsburgh
68120727

196 Three Rivers Stadium
Archives Service Center
University of Pittsburgh
69121580

197 Market Square
Archives Service Center
University of Pittsburgh
62111986_10

198 Mellon Square
Archives Service Center
University of Pittsburgh
5594545_11CP

199 Sky Ballet
Archives Service Center
University of Pittsburgh
70121948

200 Pirates Win!
Archives Service Center
University of Pittsburgh
CAMP03UA

HISTORIC PHOTOS OF PITTSBURGH

As an important port at the confluence of the Monongahela and Allegheny rivers, home to a leading university, and once the producer of nearly half the nation's steel, Pittsburgh traces its history deep into the nation's past.

The images collected in *Historic Photos of Pittsburgh* combine to form a remarkable portrait of this "City of Bridges." Included here are vignettes and early views of trolley cars, the Allegheny Conservatory, Diamond Market, the Western Pennsylvania Exposition buildings, Straub Brewing, the Strip District, the grading of Grant's Hill, Forbes Field, the Point, the Flood of 1936, construction of the Cathedral of Learning at the University of Pittsburgh, and countless other subjects.

In stunning black-and-white photography, this handsome coffee-table book details the historical growth of Pittsburgh from its early days up to recent times. Spanning two centuries and nearly 200 images, the book follows the growth of this history-rich city, offering a compelling look into the past for any longtime resident and every history buff of Pittsburgh.

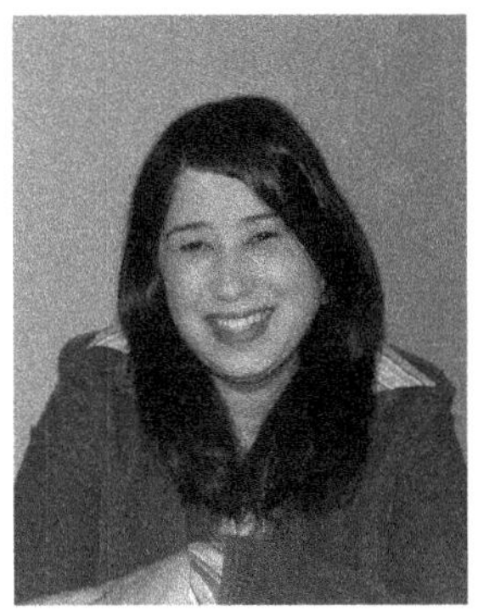

Miriam Meislik is the Media Curator for the Archives Service Center at the University of Pittsburgh and Adjunct Faculty in the School of Information Science, University of Pittsburgh.

She is an active member of the Society of American Archivists where she has served as chair of the Visual Materials Section and the Visual Materials Cataloging and Access Roundtable.

WWW.TURNERPUBLISHING.COM

www.ingramcontent.com/pod-product-compliance
Lightning Source LLC
LaVergne TN
LVHW060612110826
845154LV00003B/76

* 9 7 8 1 6 8 3 3 6 9 4 4 8 *